To Chuck

Sincerely,
Ron Bailey
Matt 6:33

ISBN: 978-0-9859384-9-9

Printed in USA

Seek ye first the kingdom of God and His righteousness, and all these things will be added unto you. Matthew 6:33

RON BAILEY

A GLIMPSE BEHIND HEAVEN'S VEIL

One man's journey into the Supernatural!

There is nothing more riveting than the truth.

Dedication

First to Jesus Christ my Lord and Savior, who through the power of the Holy Spirit totally changed my life.

My thanks to my friend Don Black, Founder of Finishing Strong Ministries, for his help and guidance while writing this story and producing my book.

Thanks to Mike Dunkin for help with editing what I wrote.

Special recognition to Pastor David C. Crabtree who is now with the Lord, but was instrumental in helping me understand who Jesus was and helped me to grasp what the Holy Spirit was doing supernaturally in my life.

Special recognition to Dawn Crabtree who challenged me to trust God and totally surrender my life to Jesus, which meant turning my business over to Him and joining the choir, at a time when I was spending seven days a week working hard to build it.

Shout out to my kids; Kim Bailey Lee and Todd Roland Bailey and their families for allowing me the opportunity to share some of their stories, along with my grandchildren; Lauren Lee Hungate, Kyle Bai Lee, Blake Roland Bailey and Abby Elizabeth Bailey, who have made grand-parenting fun, exciting and memorable.

Last but not least to Joanne Meggers Bailey, the girl who still is the love of my life and has been on this wild and crazy journey with me for the last 53 years.

Table of Contents

Introduction

On this day my life changed from living in the natural, to experiencing the supernatural — God showed up!

It was Tuesday morning. I needed to create an itinerary for the annual manager's meeting scheduled for Friday. I discussed everything with my secretary she needed to work on. I went into my private office, locked the door, obtained some legal pads and began organizing my thoughts.

Suddenly, a rush of love settled over me and I was swept up into a heavenly-like state of mind; feeling warm and tingly all over!

I closed my eyes and fully embraced the love I was receiving. It was like I was floating, or having an out of body experience.

I opened my eyes again momentarily and saw I was grounded with my legs propped up on the desk next to the empty legal pads. I then closed them to continued the wonderful euphoria I was experiencing.

What I was experiencing, was like being on a special type of love drug — enhanced by the atmosphere in my office and energized with the presence of God. It was unbelievable! It was intoxicating and I was high on the love of Jesus! I just wanted to pray and bask in His goodness. I didn't want it to end! Then, all of a sudden while captured in His love; God appeared and His light shone upon me!

I didn't see His face. His appearance was the most beautiful radiance of glory, manifested into the purest, brightest, whitest, most blinding light I had ever beheld.

The light from His countenance emerged from above in my office and like a shot fired from a high-powered ray-gun, it penetrated my forehead!

The energy from the light was warm, similar to an electrical current and traveled from my forehead, down the right side of my neck, across my shoulder, then down my arm until it reached my hand.

Upon reaching my right hand, both my hand and arm began shaking uncontrollably. I wondered what was happening and began to get concerned! My first thought was; I had pushed the limits of my body too far.

You see; four days earlier, I had prayed for and received the baptism of the Holy Spirit and had been on a spiritual high ever since then, without the need to neither eat nor sleep. Unconsciously, I guess I was on a three-day fast.

I began wondering if my lack of sleep and food was affecting me mentally, or if I was developing a neurological problem? Neither being a good option to choose from!

My body felt radioactive all over, and mentally; well I was in a state of shock! What just happened? I walked back to my desk and sat down.

With my hand still shaking, instinct, intuition, or something else, led me to put a pen in my hand and grab a legal pad. As I put the pen near the legal pad, all of a sudden my hand began to write something; but it wasn't me! God, Jesus, the Holy Spirit, something other than me, took control of my hand and began to write. It was as if I was using an old IBM typewriter; except it wasn't a typewriter – it was my hand doing the writing. I was absolutely awestruck!

The writing started on the right side of the legal pad and wrote to the left side of the page. Then, while still in motion, the pen dropped down a line and proceeded writing from the left back over to the right, before repeating itself, dropping down one more time, to write from the right to the left.

The writings had the look of being Arabic or some other Middle Eastern language; likening itself to a form of hieroglyphics. It was definitely not anything I could have written on my own.

I continued writing in this trance-like state of mind without any control of my hand for over an hour. In that time all I could do was watch; while my hand was being used supernaturally to write something on those legal pads.

What was going on? What did all of this mean? Was there something significant to what had been written?

I found out Jesus had a special assignment for me and once accepted; living supernaturally and experiencing miracles would become my new way of life!

The first 15 Chapters are written as a family legacy story; illustrating my life growing up and showing how God positioned me later on to have the desires of my heart, while fulfilling a part of His purpose for my life.

In Chapter 16 – Jesus shows up and then supernatural events begin to happen.

Follow my story and see what the Holy Spirit revealed, when He gave me; A Glimpse Behind Heaven's Veil.

Forward

"The Lord your God is in your midst, a mighty one who will save; he will rejoice over you with gladness; he will quiet you by his love; he will exult over you with loud singing." - Zephaniah 3:17

As a young pastor I remember meeting Ron and his family at First Assembly In Des Moines, Iowa where I was head of Adult Ministries. Ron was very musical and he and his wife Joanne, opened their home to our church family over the years for different social events. Both Ron and Joanne seemed to have the gift of hospitality and were active in the church.

I remember the meeting I had with Ron in my office when he indicated he had received the baptism of the Holy Spirit. His situation was different as he seemed to have received a double portion with sort of a "Damascus Road Experience" followed by additional signs and wonders.

In the book of Acts, we read this experience was the empowerment Jesus instructed His disciples to receive before they set out to reach the world with the message (Good News) of Jesus Christ. Ron had received the same blessing and empowerment of the Holy Spirit accompanied with speaking in tongues as proclaimed in the book of Acts.

This manifestation of the Holy Spirit was given to help Christ Followers in the proclamation of the Good News of Jesus Christ. This was a blessing First Assembly encouraged Christians to seek after as part of their pilgrimage in being a Christ Follower. Ron had pursued this experience and when he did, he received a Holy boldness to encourage others in their journey with Christ. Since this was a new experience for Ron, he had questions about how to use this gift to glorify God.

Ron then shared a new manifestation I had never heard of, much less experienced. He showed me several legal pads filled with strange writings.

I asked him if he could replicate what he experienced and in a very relaxed manner Ron closed his eyes and we began to worship. While we were praying his hand began to move over the paper rapidly but with ease of motion. The hand writing was in an unknown language but appeared very legible. Ron mentioned while writing in this supernatural manifestation he felt a love and closeness to God that was beyond belief and he wondered what it all meant?

I really couldn't tell him what it meant except, it seemed like God wanted his attention, maybe to prepare his heart, gifts and abilities for a special calling. It was certainly a new form of spirit communication to me and in all my years in the ministry I have never seen anything, before or since, that even resembles the experience Ron shared with me in my office, back in November of 1980.

Pastor Roger Lane

Pastor David Crabtree, former pastor of First Assembly of God Church in Des Moines, Iowa used to say, "There is nothing more powerful to stir the hearts of men's souls, than the Holy Spirit's anointing on music and preaching during a church service."

First Assembly was a church led by the Spirit and during my time from 1977 to 1985 my family and I saw many signs, wonders and miracles take place. Those were extraordinary years of discipleship, worship, music-making, pageantry and answered prayers.

I was the Assistant Director of Music and my normal place for ministry was at the piano, following the direction of Dawn Crabtree, the pastor's wife and Director of Music. It was in the choir where I met Ron Bailey. He had an exceptional voice with kind of a pop/rock/folk style. Ron had a winning smile, a great personality and could handle everything musically we gave him. He was someone I wanted to use in a musical I had just written, if he was available.

Ron was an insurance man and had a very busy schedule to work around when he started singing in the choir. His involvement in the church started out with him attending choir rehearsals on Wednesday nights and singing at the Sunday morning and evening services.

One Sunday, Mrs. Crabtree decided to expand the choir's ministry to other small churches in the area who didn't have a choir and recruited a number of singers to sing in this special program. Ron was one of the singers asked to sing in this. The group went by the name of "Reflections" and they started their rehearsals after choir practice was over on Wednesday night. With so much to be done by Easter and to keep from rehearsing late into the night, "Reflections" rehearsal time was later changed to another night. It was about the same time I approached Dawn about using the singers in "Reflection" to sing in my new musical, called, "Canticle of the Wind." It was a musical about "Acts 2" and the coming of the Holy Spirit to the early church. This was going to be a large undertaking consisting of acting, singing, set design, and a full orchestra. There would be a lot of memorization with about six months to prepare for everything.

I asked Ron if he could be a part of the program and he said yes and will try to rearrange his time schedule, to make everything work.

Ron was a new Christian and he wanted to be a faithful servant. He said God asked him to sing and he wanted to be obedient to his calling. When Ron poured himself into the work of the Lord, he found his business grew almost exponentially. What was most amazing, his business grew the most when he was the busiest in his service to the Lord and he was living the message I was presenting in my musical.

The "Canticle of the Wind" was presented to the congregation in October of 1981 with a call for us to all walk closer to the Lord through the person of the Holy Spirit.

I witnessed how Ron's experience with the Holy Spirit was filled with signs and wonders from trusting in the Lord and to that "I say, to God be the glory."

Pastor Philip Pfaltzgraff

Preface

"You Lord are forgiving and good, abounding in love to all who call upon your name." Psalm 86:5

A Glimpse Behind Heaven's Veil is a true story about my journey to find God, lessons learned along the way and what was experienced when I found Him.

This story spans several decades and highlights memories stored up from a lifetime of living.

The memories chosen were reflective of different time periods in my life: some good, some bad and some even supernatural. But all proving one thing: God was always in control.

Initially, my journey references growing up in the Unitarian Church and working through unanswered questions like: Who or what was God, and does this God I'm searching for know me personally?

As a Unitarian, I studied how my ancestors left England in 1620 to come to America on the Mayflower, to live freely and worship in the manner of choosing without fear of persecution. They were the Pilgrims who befriended the Indians and established the Colony of Massachusetts.

Initially, it was trusting in the family's legacy that led me to believe in a higher power. That is; in a god of one form or another.

Unitarianism was, and still is, an all-inclusive religion; embracing many different religious beliefs; giving members a lot of choices to believe in. Consequently, what you believed was largely influenced by the leaders in the church — and at times it was even confusing to them.

Unitarianism was considered Protestant by design, but as I later discovered — not Christian. They recognized Jesus as a great teacher, maybe even a prophet, but being saved by God's grace was never discussed in church; because they didn't recognize Him as God — and since we never talked about it, I didn't know any difference.

Starting this journey I didn't know what I was looking for. I just had questions about who God was; so I decided to try and find an answer by studying different religions.

Most of the religions I studied were also Protestant, but they believed in the concept of heaven and hell. That led me to learning more about Jesus and forgiveness of sin.

As a Unitarian, we never talked about sin — we had the freedom to believe what we wanted — without feeling the guilt of being a sinner.

Fundamentally, I believed in following the Ten Commandments, with the emphasis on being a good person. I thought that covered everything. But the more I learned about sin, the more questions I had about heaven? Could heaven be a real place and if so, would I go there when I died? How could I know for sure? Thus my journey starts!

Another part of my journey is about the love I had for music and the special role it played in my life.

From the time of discovery, to when I started using the gifts God gave me, music was like a fine thread woven throughout the fabric of my life. It was always there in some form; opening up amazing doors for me.

Music was the object of my love, my mistress and my drug of choice. It was my life! Music fueled my fantasies, put me in the spotlight and allowed me to play; night clubs, fairs, ballrooms, colleges, as well as venues throughout

Europe and the Mid-West. It was through music, where I fulfilled my dream of recording a record and performing live on TV. Music was everything to me! But one day I had to push music to the side, when a new love came into my life. A love of a girl by the the name of Joanne.

Joanne was special and I knew holding on to both her and music was going to be a challenge. Music and I then started going through a period of separation. It was tough at first. Putting music on the back burner of my life meant I was giving up on a childhood dream. Fame in the music industry was everything I had ever wanted. I had reached a fork in the road and changes had to be made. I knew it wasn't going to be easy, but having Joanne meant I had a partner with me on my journey.

We were happy traveling the road together and found some success along the way. Soon, children started joining us on our journey and then God brought music back into my life to open up some amazing doors.

At birth I believe God gives us a moral compass to lead us on life's pathway of right and wrong. It was my parents who guided me when I was young, but as I got older I had to learn to think for myself. I had questions, and through different studies; I discovered we are born with a void in our lives, that can only be filled by the creator of the universe; the one true God.

I spent most of my young life trying to find this one true God and at age 36 I was introduced to Jesus: His miraculous birth, His life, death and resurrection. I learned how and why He died for my sins. I found; through no fault of my own, I was born into sin. It was in my DNA and I needed a savior to cleanse me from all of my sins. I learned God hated sin and I needed my sins forgiven to be in perfect communion with Him.

I was relentless in my pursuit, and after searching for this one true God all of my life, I believe it was the spiritual connection I had with music that finally prepared me to receive the truth of God's word. Music opened my heart to receive what God was trying to tell me: I just needed faith to accept this Jesus as my Savior and receive the gift of eternal life. My search was over. I knew I had found the true God of the Bible and was going to heaven when I died.

He then gave me more — A hunger to have a special intimacy with Him.

I started reading the Bible to know more about Jesus and the gifts of the Spirit. This caused my love for the Lord to continually grow. Then one day — while praying and pursuing His love, I was baptized and filled with the Holy Spirit...Oh the joy that filled my soul!

Half of this book centers on my life and journey to find who, or what was God. The other half is about living in the supernatural — the special calling I received from Him and how it changed my life forever!

As you share this journey with me, I hope you see the supernatural gifts spoken about in the Bible are available to anyone still today and if you're not already doing so; make an effort to experience a special intimacy with Jesus.

One thing for sure — when you experience Him like I did — time will be irrelevant and the peace that passes all understanding, will flood your soul in such a way that you won't even be able to explain it.

Yes, God is alive! He wants to make himself known to all of us. So, follow my story and see how everything changed even more when I surrendered my life completely to Him and used the principal of; "Let go and let God."

Chapter 1

" God is love: Whoever lives in love lives in God, and God in them." 1 John 4:16

Before I Was Born

My mom and dad grew up during the Great Depression and went to school in Leominster, Massachusetts. Leominster was a town once considered the plastic city of the world – where money was made in plastics; during and prior to the Great Depression of 1929. This was true, especially at Foster & Grants – a company known internationally for plastic hair products and sun glasses.

Mom grew up in a middle-class family. Her dad, (my grandfather) Malcolm H. Foster was an architect and designed some of the homes in and around Leominster. In fact, the home we lived in on Orchard Street was a home he helped design. Grandpa was also a 32nd Degree Mason in the Scottish Rite, which was next to the highest degree you could hold in the Masonic Lodge; an international fraternal organization. In addition, he was an avid outdoorsman and spent a lot of his free time fishing and hunting. His passion though was collecting rare stamps, coins and watches.

Prior to the Great Depression my grandfather was a successful architect and lived in a big home in Leominster with his wife and their six children; Elenor, Happy, Clair, Ruthie, Connie and Charles.

When the Depression hit, he had to make changes to support his family, so he found work as a freelance carpenter. Those were tough times and with the exception of his stamp collection, he exhausted most of his wealth.

Following the Great Depression came WWII and he was hired as a design engineer for a wood mill near Lowell, MA. Then another set back came when his daughter Clare died from complications of diabetes.

By around 1949, Elenor, Happy and Ruthie were all married and living on their own, so Malcolm moved the remainder of his family into a large spacious home in Lowell, closer to his work. With his economic situation improving, he again continued to build his collection of rare stamps, watches and coins.

One of my fondest memories of Grandpa Foster was sitting in his lap viewing pages of rare stamps meticulously placed in albums and getting a history lesson on each one. In addition to his regular stamps, he had albums of uncirculated stamps. These were some of the very first postal stamps ever issued in the United States. Grandpa had been collecting stamps since he was a young man and his collection was worth thousands of dollars back in the 1950's.

It was around 1952 when Grandpa started me and my cousins collecting stamps. He gave each of us some of his stamps in starter stamp albums along with catalogues to look up the history and values of the stamps we were collecting.

Grandpa and Grandma Foster

Two years later Grandpa started having serious health problems and it was his stamp collection that ended up paying for a lot of the medical bills not covered by insurance.

In 1955 Grandpa passed away from a massive heart attack and left my grandmother a widow at the age of 59.

My grandmother, Henrietta Allen Jefferson grew up in West Newton, a wealthy area outside of Boston, and as a young girl spent a lot of time along the shores of Maine.

Grandma Foster was very prim and proper, appearing to be sort of a disciplinarian: Stern one moment and cordial the next, with a softer side for her grandchildren.

I was only 11 years old when my grandfather died. During that time, my grandmother donated many of the family heirlooms to the Boston Museum of Science and the Smithsonian Museum in Washington, D.C.

Most of the items donated were from the time of the Pilgrims and Revolutionary War. Grandma knew she couldn't keep them after moving from her home into a small apartment, so she made a decision to share them with the world.

To stay busy, Grandma Foster was active in the Eastern Star, Daughters of the American Revolution and Daughters of the Mayflower Society. She held offices, both local and national in each organization. She was also a house mother for the women students at Boston University.

Once employed there, Grandma moved out of her apartment and lived in the corner of the large home for the women students, owned by the University in Boston. She lived there for a number of years, before fully retiring.

After retirement she moved a few more times, but always stayed within 30 miles of where we all lived. She died, at the age of 94.

My other grandmother, Sadie Hildreth Bailey was only 40 years old when her husband, William Bailey died. She was a beautiful and resilient woman. She had to be, especially in the circumstances she found herself in when her husband unexpectedly passed away from a heart attack. She was from a prominent family and also grew up in the Boston area. Her family tree roots went all the way back to Myles Standish, Captain of the Mayflower Compact in 1620. She was very nurturing and had to be both the mother and father to her five children; Beatrice, William (Red), Roland, Phyllis and Thelma, during those tough years.

Grandma Bailey

It was not uncommon during the years following the depression, for my father to have stood in long lines waiting on food rations for people in need made available by the government. This was especially true for government cheese and other staples being rationed at the time.

Looking back, my dad grew up under pretty tough circumstances, but the one thing he never lacked was love. His mother gave him, and all her children, the special love and attention they all desired.

As a grandmother she was the best. She was fun to be with and often allowed Donnie and me to stay up late to watch TV or play cards with her when she baby sat us. She loved playing cards and taught us how to play her favorite card games. It was a win-win situation for all of us. We provided her with card playing partners and she provided us with the stay up late pass to play cards with her.

Grandma Bailey was also pretty independent. She lived alone for most of her life, with the exception of living with our family for a couple of years when she had some health problems. My dad adored her and made sure she was well taken care of. She died from colon cancer at 82 years old.

My dad was only 14 years old when his father, William Bailey died. This left his mother alone to raise 5 young children, during one of the most economically depressed times in the history of the United States.

During this time many families lost everything they had worked for their entire lives. Entire family legacies were wiped clean, almost over-night. My dad however, felt he lost even more – his father.

William Bailey was only 42 years old when he unexpectedly passed away due to heart failure. Up until the time he died, William (my grandfather) had various jobs, with his last job being the personal chauffeur for one of Leominster's wealthiest families. It was for one of the families who owned Foster & Grant; the large International Company known for sun-glasses.

I never knew much about my grandfather, but at some point in his life he made a guitar out of old cigar boxes.

One day, when I was a teenager, I found that old guitar in our basement, among other old relics and eventually learned how to play it.

In fact – it was that very guitar that fueled my love for music and later, my desire to perform.

Chapter 2

"I knew you before I formed you in your mother's womb; before you were born I set you apart."
Jeremiah 1:15

My Story Begins

It was a cold day in New England when I was born. The year was 1944. Dad was in the Navy and Mom was pregnant with me. During this time, she was living with her sister and brother-in-law, Elli and Vernon Wiles.

On the day before Thanksgiving, God decided it was nearly time for me to make my appearance.

I created quite a disturbance stretching and moving around the way I did, alerting Mom and everyone else that my coming out party was just a few hours away.

Dr. Wheeler, our family doctor was notified and Dad was brought up to date on what was happening. They told him they were going to take Mom to the hospital and he was about to become a father.

Dad & Me at 1 week old

At the time, Dad was in the Navy stationed over 100 milcs away at the Naval Submarine School in New London, Connecticut. Upon receiving the call from Mom, he got permission from his commanding officer to take an emergency medical leave to be with us. He didn't have much money and didn't own a car, so the fastest way for him to get to Leominster was to hitch hike. He then set out on his 100 mile plus trip, dressed in his Navy uniform with his thumb to the traffic, hoping he would make it in time for my arrival.

Mom, Dad, Me at I month

There was a war going on and if people saw servicemen dressed in their uniforms trying to get home, they would even go out of their way to take them to their destinations.

I am not sure how many different rides my Dad had or how long it took him to get to the hospital, but from what I was told, he arrived right around the time I was born.

When I was born, the name I inherited was, Roland Earl Bailey, Jr after Dad, however, they didn't want me to be called Jr., so they nicknamed me Ronnie and as I grew older it was later shortened to Ron.

Grandma Bailey

Psalm 37:23 reads, "The Lord directs the steps of the godly. He delights in every detail of their lives." To me this meant, He knew I would be the first-born son of Roland and Ruth Bailey and He had a special plan for my life. The plan now documented in the story you are about to read.

Chapter 3

"Above all, love each other deeply, because love covers over a multitude of sins." 1 Peter 4:8

Setting the Stage For My Life

Mom and Dad were best friends and dated each other during high school. They grew up during the years of the great depression and after graduating from high school, my dad joined the Navy.

Mom and Dad's wedding

In July of 1943 Dad was involved in the invasion of Sicily, one of the most important invasions of the War, up to that time. It was the biggest air and sea operation ever conducted by any country, defeating Italy's alignment with Germany during WWII.

After being away from each other so long during the war, they got engaged when Dad came home on leave, and were later married on December 4th, 1943. Shortly thereafter, my dad was transferred to the Naval Base at Virginia Beach, Virginia. Mom joined him – but according to the Navy, she should have stayed in Leominster with her family, as Dad was destined to be away for a while, involved in the most daring military event ever – the invasion of Normandy Beach, better known as D-Day.

Me at about 1yr old

He was assigned to the mine sweeper, the "USS Staff."

Mine sweepers went in ahead of the other ships to clear explosive mines and make a safe environment for their invading ships. It was one of the few boats in the Navy made mostly out of wood

The "USS Staff" was the leading ship in the invasion on D-Day. They went in under enemy fire, but while completing the mission, they hit a mine. Many of my dad's shipmates were killed; with many more badly injured.

During the explosion, my dad too was hit by shrapnel and injured his back while manning the engine room.

The "USS Staff" was completely disabled, and while the invasion continued, the survivors on the "USS Staff" were rescued by other ships in the area.

Within a few days, Dad, his shipmates and other casualties of the war, were on the great ship "Queen Elizabeth;" headed to the United States for medical care and R & R.

As history revealed later on, the invasions of Normandy Beach and Sicily were the two major events responsible for ending the war in 1945.

After the war, Mom, Dad and I lived in California for a year before moving back to Leominster; to live out their dreams.

Within a couple of years, my parents bought a home and soon after that, my brother Donnie was born.

Donnie and I did everything together, up until we got into school and started developing our own sets of friends.

We were boys and we did what boys did. We got into a lot of mischievous activities.

As an example, one time we were playing together and decided to play a prank on Mom. We tied a string around two lamps located across the room from each other in the living room and pretended to be fighting. Donnie began yelling, as if I was hurting him and Mom came running in to break us up. What happened next was classic. She ran in to break us up and hit the strings like we had planned, causing the two lamps to come crashing to the floor. The lamps both shattered making a mess, but what we didn't know; these were wedding presents and perhaps two of her most favorite items in the house. She was upset and rightfully so. We were then spanked and sent to our room to think about what we did and wait for Dad to come home to deal with us. The waiting on Dad was the worst part of it.

Mom was the first line of punishment, followed by Dad who provided his own punishment to reinforce Mom; when he came home from work.

When we were older we tried to convince our parents their type of punishment was called "Double Jeopardy" and was against the law. They reminded us — we were in their house — they made the rules and they were the law.

Proverbs 29:15 "A rod and a reprimand impart wisdom, but a child left undisciplined disgraces its mother." We learned from the earliest ages, "Children obey your parents."

Chapter 4

"Whoever spares the rod hates their children, but the one who loves their children is careful to discipline them." Proverbs 13:24

Growing Up in The 40's & 50's

I grew up in Leominster, MA, a small town 32 miles west of Boston.

Leominster was settled by Europeans around 1653 and incorporated in 1740; almost 36 years before the United States became a Nation. By 1944, the year I was born, Leominster's population had grown to nearly 23,000 people.

I lived at 98 Orchard Street in Leominster for most of my youth — in a large three-story home my grandfather had designed back in the early 1900's. He originally designed the home as a single residence, and later it was changed into an apartment house. My dad liked the house and bought it using the GI Bill after he was discharged from the Navy. We lived on the first floor and rented out the second and third floors. It was a grand old home complete with a carriage house; which was later converted to a stand-alone three car garage. We had a long wide driveway with a big yard; great for football and other outside sports. It was perfect for neighborhood activities, but in the summer, it needed to be mowed and a long wide driveway that had to be shovel in the winter. It

Nearly 2 years old

was hard work and back then everything had to be done by hand.

First Christmas with Donnie

We mowed the yard with an old steel-bladed push mower that weighed a ton and just pushing it was challenging. It was heavy, and the blades would get rusty and stick; unless lubricated every month.

Mowing the yard was hard work and usually took a couple of hours each week for my Dad to get it done.

On June 24th, 1947, my younger brother Donald M. Bailey was born and soon became my best friend. We did everything together as toddlers and kept Mom and Dad busy with the mischief we would get into.

One time, when I was about seven and Donnie was five, we decided to have a contest to see who could pee the furthest. The old house we lived in had large steam radiators in all the rooms to provide heat during the cold weather. We decided to stand at one end of our bedroom and pee all the way to the radiator. When the pee hit the radiator, it would make a hissing noise followed by the sweet smell of urine. We both laughed and thought it was funny each time we hit the radiator, but one day Mom caught us in the act. The fun was over! We got a spanking from Mom and when Dad got home, we were again reprimanded by him. I think we even went to bed without our supper. Dr Spock hadn't written his book yet on how to parent children, so the remedy for discipline was a good spanking, which worked; because we never peed on the radiator again.

While we had many spankings during those growing up years, Dad was never angry when he spanked us. He usually discussed what we did wrong and followed it saying; "this will hurt me more than it will hurt you." We knew then what was coming next.

Mom, Donnie and me

I was about 8 years old when Dad started teaching me about my responsibilities as a family member. He wanted to pay me an allowance and help me learn about the value of money. My allowance was 25 cents a week with part of the allowance predicated upon mowing the yard. This became a lesson in work ethic and showed me the virtues of hard work. My allowance was then increased to 50 cents a week during the wintertime for the extra work I was expected to do.

In Massachusetts we got a lot of snow during the wintertime, and in some weeks I had to shovel the driveway and entranceways more than just once a week. In fact, when we had a North Eastern snow storm, I would end up shoveling every day due to the heavy snow-fall and drifting caused by the wind. In New England they didn't measure snow just in inches. It was common for us to get a foot or more of snow and have drifts well over five feet in a storm. Irregardless of the amount of snow we got, the driveway and walks still had to be maintained. We had renters and they had to be able to park their cars and have accessibility into the house.

We all worked together in those early years. Mom and Dad even helped out when they had time. Later on, my younger brother Donnie would also get an allowance and do his fair share of the work.

Our house was located about a mile from our school and whether we had thunderstorms or heavy snow, we still walked to school and back every day. We were expected to be in school and that's just the way it was. We didn't know any difference. In fact, back then I don't ever remember any school closings due to a snow storm.

Adjacent to our home and part of the original property was the caretaker's house. It was a separate structure located about ten feet away from the main house. Between the two structures was a narrow walk-way that went from the front yard to the back yard, over to the carriage house; which was later converted to the garage.

The caretaker's home became a separate property and was owned by Mrs. Edith Latchis. She had four children; Terri, James, Peter and John. Edith or as we affectionately called her, "Auntie E", was a widow. Her husband had been killed in an accident. He was the co-owner and a major partner with the Latchis Theaters, which were located through-out Massachusetts and New Hampshire.

Before the Latchis family moved next door, they lived in a large Greek style mansion just down the street from us. Their home was spacious and was decorated with a lot of European and Greek antiques. The move had to have been a huge adjustment for them. After all, she lost her husband to an accidental death and was a widow saddled with four young children to raise by herself. In addition, she had moved her family from their large home to a home of around 1200 square feet. Still, we never saw the pain they must have felt at the time. We just enjoyed them as our neighbors and over time we became one big family.

James and Peter were twins. They were born on March 13, 1944 and were eight-months older than me. I actually met them in kindergarten before they moved next door and through the years we became the best of friends. They were bigger and stronger than me growing up and I often took the brunt of their physicality. We were competitive as young kids and would often end up playing pretty rough. We were just like brothers and got into real knock-down drag-out fights; ending up with cuts and bruises to prove our toughness. We were just guys trying to earn a little respect from each other; going from being best friends one minute, to worst enemies the next; then back to being best friends again the next day.

When we became teenagers we started our growth spurt. I tried my best to keep up with them physically and we lifted weights and worked out together. They seemed to be getting much stronger, while I was just getting taller.

It was during that time, I realized Auntie E gave the boys a special elixir every day. I thought that was the reason they were so much stronger than me. I asked her if I could be included in their daily routine and she gave me a table spoon of the magic formula right along with them.

The elixir was sort of brown and tasted horrible, but if this was going to make me stronger, I thought it would be worth it.

I was taking it every day until eventually my mom started getting it for me. It was then, when I found out this magic elixir was non other than Castor Oil. It had nothing to do with getting stronger or putting on weight — that was something I envisioned myself. At least it was healthy.

During this time my brother Donnie was hanging out with John Latchis. They were best friends, and when they were around ten years old, they also got involved with us in a number of neighborhood altercations. Donnie was like a bantam rooster. He was small but tenacious. He liked to get right in the middle of the action. He was sort of a scrapper, and over time earned respect; even from the bigger kids.

If we wanted to do something other than just play in the neighborhood, we would go to the movies.

The Latchis family owned the Metropolitan Theater in Leominster and on the weekends we would go to the movies with the Latchis boys for free. We would usually go a couple of times a month, depending on what was going on in our lives and what was playing at the theater. We liked Tarzan or Lone Ranger movies the best and if we had been to a Tarzan movie, everyone near us would soon hear our best Tarzan yells; as we walked back home. I had the loudest and best yell of all of us. It was so loud — it was obnoxious!

In May of 1954 my youngest brother Bradford C. Bailey was born. He was both curious and adventuresome. As a toddler, he took Mom's alarm clock apart — just to see how it worked. On another occasion, Mom had Brad tied up outdoors in our yard and she quickly ran into the house to get something, but when she came back out; he was gone. Brad was only two years old and Mom thought someone had kidnapped him. She panicked, and after searching the neighborhood; called the police. This was on a Saturday and I was playing baseball at the Little League park down the street. Mom sent Donnie to inform Dad and me of Brad's disappearance. News reached us that Brad had disappeared, maybe was kidnapped and the police were trying to find him. The Little League game was immediately canceled and both teams were sent out to look for him.

Later in the day, Mom received a phone call from the police department letting her know they had found Brad. Apparently he took his tricycle and rode or walked over two miles, across the main streets of downtown Leominster, to where my dad's company office was located. It was next to where the trains parked their cars for loading and Brad decided for himself, he wanted to meet Dad and see the trains. Well, my parents didn't know whether to hug him or spank him. Well of course they hugged him and convinced him to never do that again. It's still a mystery how he was able to go all the way to Dad's office at only two years old?

OVERCOMING FEARS AND BUILDING CONFIDENCE

When school was out our family went camping. First at Beamon Pond and later at St. Laurent Point, located on Lake Dennison, in Winchendon, MA. All of the camp grounds there had camping sites located near private beaches and play areas for kids. It was a perfect place for families to enjoy their lives during the summer. Especially, for someone 8 to 10 years old like me. The only problem with me was; when it came to enjoying the beach, I was afraid of the water.

Both my parents and the life guard tried to teach me how to swim during the summer, but I wouldn't put my head under the water. I was content to put my feet in the water and play in the sand on the beach. Putting my head all the way under the water scared me.

Mom, Donnie, Brad and I stayed at camp for the entire summer, while Dad came up on the weekends. Dad was a lineman for Worcester County Electric. He had to be available for emergencies or electrical outages during the week and occasionally be on call during the weekends.

The weekends were special for us, especially at St. Laurent Point; a place where our family had ownership in an association that owned and developed the camp grounds at Lake Dennison. At St. Laurent Point, in addition to all of the great lakeside activities, we had outdoor movies on Friday night and local entertainment performing for us on Saturday night. These activities were usually over by 9:00 or 9:30 for the younger kids, while the adults and teenagers stayed up later – dancing to the music being played over the loud speakers near the stage.

Our campsite was located fairly close to the stage area and I remember many nights, just lying in our tent listening to the songs being played over the loud speakers. It was a great way to relax, while reminiscing about the fun we had during the day. It also started me thinking about singing and being on that stage. I could actually visualize it! I was too young be involved, but my time would come soon enough.

When the summer ended Mom and Dad enrolled me in a swimming class at the Leominster Recreation Center. I was nearly 9 years old and it was time for me to learn how to swim.

Members of the swim team

I resisted my instructor at first but he was patient and soon had me blowing bubbles in the shallow end of the pool. He won my trust and before long I was putting my entire face in the water. My next step was to learn how to float, and when I started paddling; I was off like a rocket! I was really enjoying the water now and couldn't get enough of it.

The swimming instructor got excited about my progress over the next couple of weeks and invited me try out for the swim team. I tried out and was soon traveling with the Leominster Recreation Center City's Swim Team;

competing at my age level and winning medals. This was great for confidence building. I was being recognized by Bob Gross my coach, my team mates, my parents and my friends as a winner on the city's swim team. The local newspaper released pictures and wrote articles in the sports page about the team's success in the State Finals and also had an article about me winning in my age group. I loved competitive swimming and when I turned 12 my coach signed me up to swim in the Amateur Athletic Union; better known as the (AAU). It was a program designed to develop Olympic champions. The practice was intense and in addition to the sprints we swam, my coach had me swimming over 250 laps a day in the pool for conditioning.

Bob was an innovative coach and worked with me personally to develop a different style of kick for the backstroke. We developed a way to generate more thrust by kicking a certain way underwater and since Bob was working personally with me, every so often he would have someone come by during practice to witness what he was accomplishing with me. I loved having Bob Gross as my swimming coach but I was also money motivated, so when I was 13 years old, I bought a newspaper route. My coach had just moved to California to help coach the Olympic Swimming Team, so I decided this was as good a time as any to put swimming on hold and make money as a paper boy.

It may have not been the best decision long term with the prospects of college scholarships in the future, but it was what I wanted to do at the time. I felt I could work on the scholarships later — when I was in High School.

I had heard about a paper route for sale with about 125 papers. I think I paid around $40 for the route. It would have been equal to about two month's earnings of the person who had it before me. I was now an entrepreneur. I owned my own business and I was motivated to build it!

First, I provided the best service to my customers; in the hope they would brag about me to their neighbors. Then after three months, I would approach the homes around them and solicit their neighbors. That worked pretty well.

I loved most of my customers and they showed their appreciation for my service by the tips I received at the end of each week. At the end of the week, I collected for the papers I delivered during the week. Collections were done while delivering the papers during the day and the larger my paper route grew, the more I tried to work out special payment arrangements with my customers. I had some paying monthly, some bi-weekly and some weekly. I worked to convert as many as I could to pay monthly or bi-weekly to make it easier on me. To help accomplish that, I used a small ledger book to keep track of everything.

Christmas was when my paper route really paid off! I received over $100 in tips plus other gifts. In 1958 that was a lot of money but I wanted to build my route up even more.

I wasn't afraid to call on new people and leverage the relationships of their neighbors to open doors for me. That paid big dividends for building my paper route. Likewise, in growing my business, I discovered not just prospecting, but also; networking, advertising and how to handle money. The skills I learned as a paper boy — helped me even more, when I got into the insurance business.

By the Spring of 1959 I had built my paper route to over 250 papers and had hired my brother Donnie to help deliver them. We each had two large delivery bags saddled across the back of our bikes, consisting mostly of the Leominster Enterprise and Fitchburg Sentinel, to provide the local news. We also each had an extra bag, on our front handlebars for the New York Times, The Boston Globe, Boston Traveler and the Boston Herald.

The New York Times were heavy and at Christmas time it was like delivering Sears and Roebuck's catalogues. Those papers put a strain on us, but as we found out; the people who bought those papers were also the best tippers.

By that next Spring, I had built the paper route as big as I wanted it to be. The winter brought us a lot of snow and at times it was tough to get everyone's paper to them by suppertime. To help accomplish that, I bought a toboggan to carry the papers. My brother and I would then walk the 4 or 5 miles in the deep snow, up and down the steep hills of Leominster, to deliver all of the papers. Some days Mom even drove us around. The snow plows did a pretty good job cleaning the snow off of the roads but we had to travel up and down sidewalks to deliver the papers and most were covered from snow the plows pushed off of the street, or from the drifted snow that hadn't been shoveled.

Finally it was time! I was faithful to my customers and they were good to me but it was time for to make a change in my life. With that in mind, I split my paper route into two routes and sold both of them.

My brother Donnie had first choice for the part he wanted and I sold the other one to a friend, netting a nice return on my original investment of $40.

Those early years as a paper boy taught me a lot about the discipline of being self-employed, the importance of having a good work ethic, how to handle money and how to build confidence in a competitive work place. I liked winning and my confidence was increasing. I loved the recognition I was receiving and rewards I was getting, but I still had this void in my life. I was 15 years old and starting to think of myself as an adult. I was no longer just a teenager; I was searching for the meaning of life, and who or what is God.

GROWING UP UNITARIAN

I was baptized and brought up in the Unitarian Church. Actually, I was sprinkled and welcomed into the family of the church as an infant. My parents were pretty active, so I was there a lot. I went to kindergarten and Boy Scouts there, as well as, attended all of my Sunday school classes with perfect attendance, all the way through High School. The attendance pin I had was represented by a bar for each year of perfect attendance and by the time I finished High School, it was about 7 inches long. Mom was proud of my perfect attendance pin.

The fact was, even with perfect attendance, I had never read the Bible – nor was I ever taught about Jesus. Something else unique to our church was; the church closed its doors in June when school let out and didn't open up again until school started in September. It was convenient for us. We were at our camp all summer; making perfect attendance even easier.

The First Unitarian Church of Boston was founded in 1630 and was the oldest church in Massachusetts. The First Unitarian Church in Leominster was established in 1743. Some famous Unitarians were; John Quincy Adams, Louisa May Alcott, Ralph Waldo Emerson and P.T. Barnum from Barnum and Bailey's Circus.

The Unitarian's were established as an Old Testament Church, but in 1960 they merged with the Universalists movement and became known as the Unitarian Universalists Church. The Universalists embraced all forms of beliefs from; Christianity, Hinduism, Buddhism, Islam, Humanism to Wiccans and even Atheism. With the merger of the two denominations in 1960, the Unitarian Universalists became an all-inclusive church.

In my childhood, I attended Sunday School but didn't learn anything about the Bible. Instead, I studied, Aesop's fables and lessons learned from reading books like; "The Fox and the Grapes" or "The Lion and the Mouse." I also learned about different religions, but I never had any discussions about the Trinity, eternal life or Jesus being God.

As a Unitarian, we celebrated Christmas with Santa Claus; not Jesus, and our Christmas was actually centered around the Festival of Lights – a pagan holiday. Basically Unitarians could believe what ever they wanted to about God: it was confusing. Some referred to God as a Higher Power, some equated God as Mother Nature or Mother Earth and some felt God was a female. It was easy to be confused trying to figure out who or what God was?

My saving grace was that I had wonderful parents and they lived a clean unadulterated life, loving each other and loving us kids. They were wonderful role models in nearly every way possible. They, even did their best to be spiritual leaders in the family. Mom in fact, considered herself to be very spiritual. She would often put different religious sayings on the refrigerator for us to see. They were uplifting and encouraging, but I still had this emptiness. I just knew there had to be more; as to who or what God was.

As a young person I was afraid of the dark and I had to leave my bedroom door open to reveal some light before I could go to sleep at night. This was normal for young kids but I was 8 years old. Why was I still afraid of the dark? Well, part of the reason may have been due to the following prayer I was taught to pray every night.

"Now I lay me down to sleep, I pray the Lord my soul to keep. If I should die before I wake, I pray the Lord my soul to take. God bless Mom, Dad and my brothers. Amen"

Since most Unitarians didn't believe in either heaven or hell, the idea of dying in my sleep concerned me. Why would I even want to pray that prayer? If God, whoever God was, took my soul, what would he do with it? Why do we even have to die? The idea of dying was concerning and the darkness from the closed door represented death to me.

My parents tried to help me understand death by telling me it was just a process of life and I shouldn't be concerned at my age, but the explanations they gave didn't satisfy me, so my mom made an appointment to talk to Reverend Earl Stevês.

Reverend Steves was a sweet, gentle older man who my mom looked up to for his wisdom and leadership in the church. Mom made him aware of my concerns in advance, so he started the session by asking me what questions did I have for him?

I began by asking him about heaven and hell. I told him my friends were Christian Scientists and they believed when we die, we will either go to heaven if we are good or hell if we are bad. They believe it is an actual place we will go, to be with God after we die. They called it having eternal life. Reverend Steves said, "A lot of people believe that but that is not what I believe." He said, "I believe it's all how you live your life." "Heaven and hell is a state of mind." He went on to say, "That is why it is best to try and live a good life." He continued; "When you do something good for somebody you get a good feeling don't you?" I said, "Yes." He said, "That feeling is you experiencing heaven." He followed up with another illustration of hell, then switched to the subject of death. Basically, he told me the same thing as my parents. Next, I asked him about eternal life. He went on to tell me the cells in our body came from our parents and our children's cells will come from us; therefor our cells will continue to live for eternity. That was his explanation of eternal life and this was coming from the head Pastor.

Needless to say, his explanations were not very comforting and something inside told me there was more to the story of life, death, heaven, hell and who or what God is. I still had questions that I wanted answers to.

It will take years before my questions are answered, but when they are, they will be answered by God Himself; in a most unique way.

DISCOVERING A LOVE FOR MUSIC

My parents loved to sing together while driving in the car, so it was only natural for me to sing along with them when I got older. I learned their songs while listening to them sing, and as I got older learned how to harmonize with them to compliment what they were doing. Sometimes we even had three-part harmonies going on. It was fun!

I loved singing and picking out the harmony parts by ear. I loved music in general and was especially fascinated by sounds played on a piano.

We had an old upright piano at our home that sat against the wall as a piece of furniture. No one ever played it, but every so often as a young child I would walk up and hit some random keys on it to make some noise. However, one day when I was around 8 years old, Mom noticed I wasn't just hitting random keys but I was putting a melody together. Nothing great, but Mom could see I had a genuine interest in music, so she arranged for me to start taking piano lessons at the Fitchburg Music Store. The store was located about 10 miles from where we lived. My lessons would be for one hour and she would have to drive me there once a week. She signed me up, bought my books and the following week I began my lessons.

The lessons were hard at first, playing the same routine repetitively until I got it right. Next, I learned basic scales and how to play some beginner's songs.

I didn't like the songs I had to learn but I promised Mom I would practice an hour a day to learn them. My biggest problem was; Mom usually called me to come in and practice my piano right at the time I was having fun playing with my friends. Piano practice would then bring an end to my fun for the day; for after I practiced Dad would be home and it would be time to eat. Suppertime was family time and we all ate together. After supper I would do my homework for school, and once completed I watched TV until bedtime.

I have to admit, sometimes I lied about finishing my homework when a good program was on TV.

In the summertime we went to camp and I took a break from my music lessons.

It was at camp where I met Ray Brown: a friend of my parents. He was around their age and played the accordion. Ray entertained everyone around the campfire at night with his accordion and they all sang songs from the 40's and 50's well into the night. I was mesmerized by his playing ability and how much fun everyone was having. Ray was popular and fun to be with.

One day I was talking with Ray about the accordion and comparing it to the piano. He said, "if you can play the piano, you could play the accordion." I thought about what he said and talked to my parents about changing my piano lessons over to learning the accordion. This happened at the same time I had become more involved with swimming.

So, between school, swimming practice and music lessons, my schedule was starting to get hectic for Mom. I was busy, but she also had two other children to look after.

We lived about a mile from my school and school was only a couple of blocks to the Rec. Center, where I swam. I would walk to school in the morning and after school I then walked over to the Rec. Center to swim. After practice, if everything went as scheduled, I caught a ride home with Dad, when he got off work. If it didn't, I just walked home. In addition, to make it easier on Mom, I changed my accordion lessons over to Saturday morning.

I played the accordion for about a year and in 1956 I heard a Fat's Domino record called "Blueberry Hill." I loved that song and taught myself how to play it on the accordion. Playing "Blueberry Hill" on the accordion was fun but it just didn't sound the same, so I figured out how to transpose it over to the piano. I wanted to play the piano again, and play songs by Fats Domino, Little Richard or Jerry Lee Lewis. My piano teacher though, wasn't as thrilled as I was with my choice of music, so we ended my piano lessons. From then on, I taught myself to play by ear.

I was 12 years old, fascinated with what was happening on the music scene and starting to go to boy / girl parties. I thought to myself, what could I do to stand out? Ray Brown stood out by playing the accordion and he was very popular at the camp, but I felt accordions were more for old people around camp fires or "The Lawrence Welk Show:" Not for kid's parties.

This was all happening around the time Elvis Presley and Ricky Nelson had come on the scene. They both played guitars, sang songs and were a hit with the girls, so I decided I wanted to play the guitar and sing those songs too.

I had been watching Ricky Nelson on the "Ozzie and Harriet" TV show long before he started singing. He was a couple of years older than me and once he started singing, I knew what I wanted to do. All I needed was a guitar.

LEARNING THE GUITAR

In New England, most houses have large basements and lots of attic space. It was a place where people held on to stuff. Our house even had storage areas for our renters. Most of their storage was in the attic, while ours was in the basement. It was storage for family heirlooms, extra furniture, clothes and whatever else you wanted to store away for a later day.

Every so often my brothers and I would rummage through the stuff in the basement to see what we could find. We found; old post card readers with boxes of old post cards, old hat boxes with the hats in them, and on this one day we found an old guitar. I don't know why we had never noticed it before, but there it was; way back in the corner. It was old and it didn't have any strings, so I took it up stairs to learn more about it. First, I wanted to know if it was ours or if it belonged to one of our renters.

I found out from my dad, it was a guitar my Grandfather Bailey made. The guitar was one of the few items he had from his father. Dad told me his father made it from old cigar boxes. I found that interesting – it looked like a regular guitar to me. I then asked Dad if I could buy guitar strings and learn how to play it? He thought that was a great idea and gave me his blessings.

I brought the guitar to the music store, purchased new strings and had them tune it.

The new strings sat high off of the frets on the neck and were hard to press down. The neck was bowed or twisted due to the construction and time in our basement, but I was determined to play it. A friend of mine showed me four chords and drew them on a piece of paper for me to learn. Once learned, those chords would allow me to play a lot of songs. I learned where to put my fingers and worked on those chords every day. The chords were abbreviated to only use the lighter strings; the first four strings of the guitar.

In the beginning, the tips of my fingers became sore and bled. It was the price I was willing to pay. My finger tips had to become calloused, to get a clear sound, when the strings were pressed down against the neck of the guitar. Once my fingers were calloused, I needed songs to play.

I started learning songs and began to get creative. I thought about playing the Fats Domino's Song, "Blueberry Hill" on the guitar. It was a song I had played on the piano. To make that happen, I played a chord on the piano and then tried to copy it on the guitar. I had a good ear, so just like transposing music from the accordion to the piano, I transposed the piano chords over to the guitar. I also had a record player, so I bought some Ricky Nelson records and worked out the chords to his songs on the guitar to play along with the record. I practiced for hours memorizing his songs and before long, I was able to entertain my brothers, parents and anybody else who wanted to listen. I wanted to be ready to perform on stage at camp in the summer.

Memorial Day was when we set up camp for the summer. We had evolved from living in tents, to tent-trailers, to mobile homes and needed more space to accommodate everything we had.

We owned a large lot with an area full of wild brush that needed to be cleared. While clearing the brush, I heard someone playing an electric guitar at another campsite, so after our camp site was all set-up, I went over to see who was playing. He was a person new to St. Laurent Point, by the name of Russ Rogers.

Russ was about 27 years old, single and played in a Country Western Band. I told him I was just learning how to play the guitar and he took me under his wing. He became like a big brother to me and showed me additional chords to play for the Ricky Nelson songs I was learning.

Trophy fish-camp in back

When I first met Russ, he looked familiar and sure enough, he was part of the entertainment that played on the camp stage the previous year. He asked me if I was going to try to be a part of the program and of course I said yes. We sang and played a couple of songs together. He then asked, "would I like to play with his band on the camp stage and sing the Ricky Nelson songs I was learning?" I got all excited, thinking about singing with his band: I said "sure!"

I practiced with him a lot before we played on stage and got the songs down pretty well. The night we played on stage I felt nervous, but I was ready. His band played a few songs to start the show and then called me up. There were over 100 people in the audience, with around 30 pre-teen or teenagers. Then, when the music started and I began to sing, the girls all rushed the stage screaming and clapping. It was just like what I saw on TV with; Elvis, Frank Sinatra or Ricky Nelson. I was really over whelmed! It was spontaneous and really impacted me. It also made an impact on Russ and his band mates. The band then kept the hype alive by playing the second Ricky Nelson song we had worked on and the excitement continued. That confirmed it. I wanted to become a singer like Ricky Nelson and eventually record my own record.

When the night was over Russ and his bandmates asked me to be a part of their band when they played the camp's stage again? I was only 14 years old, too young to play the places they were playing, but at least I could play the camp's stage with them.

During the summer we played the camp's stage a couple of times a month and I learned more songs by Ricky Nelson, Elvis and the Everly Brothers. In fact, one Saturday morning Russ came over to my campsite and asked if I would like to see a show with him? It was an outdoor show featuring artists on "The Louisiana Hayride" and was being broadcasted over the radio. My parents gave me permission to go and we drove to Manchester, NH, to see the show.

Apparently, Russ knew someone associated with the show and arranged for me to sing in a guest spot. I sang, "Bye bye Love," a song by the Everly Brothers and everyone carried on and made me feel like a star. I loved being in the spotlight. So, at age 14, I sang live over the radio on the "Louisiana Hayride." It was a great boost to my confidence and something to talk about when we got back to camp.

By now my parents realized I was serious about playing the guitar. Before, when taking piano or accordion lessons, they had to call me to come in and practice. With learning the guitar, they were trying to encourage me to take time from practicing to go outside and get some fresh air with my friends. They also overheard Russ tell me if I was serious about performing with any groups in the future, I really needed to get another guitar. The one I had, didn't stay in tune and was hard to play with the strings so far off of the neck..

When I came home from camp that summer, I went to work at the Leominster Public Library. The library was an interesting place to work. It was also where I could meet girls. When I saw a girl trying to locate certain books, I would go up and ask if I could help her. If time permitted, I looked up the book's classification and took her to the isle where the book was stored. (Back then we used the Dewey Decimal System to classify and file all of the books in the library). If the girl I was helping was cute, it would also give me an excuse to talk to her. Having an excuse made it easier for me to approach them.

When November rolled around, my parents surprised me with an electric guitar for my birthday. It was a gold Kay guitar with one pickup. I couldn't believe my eyes. I started playing it and even without an amplifier, it sounded better than the guitar my grandfather made. My dad looked over to me and said, "Let's see what this sounds like with an amplifier." He then stripped a wire and attached one end to the speakers in Mom's stereo cabinet and the other end to the guitar jack. We turned on the stereo and I played the guitar. Wow...I had an electric guitar!

GIRLS - CARS - AND - ROCK-N-ROLL

When I was 15 years old the family moved from our apartment house on Orchard Street, to a single-family home on Wachusett Street, located about 8 miles from my high school and 7 miles from downtown Leominster.

Our new home was situated on top of a high hill and from our living room window, we could see all the way to Boston, where every so often you could see the sun reflecting off the windows of the Prudential Tower. Across the street was a big brown Swiss dairy farm, consisting of the main house, a large barn with silos and several smaller homes where the farm help lived. Then next to the road behind the fence, beautiful brown Swiss cows grazed in amongst the woods, fields and open pastures,.

Across another street we owned 10 acres of open field, while up the street 200 feet more, was a beautiful view of Mt. Wachusett. It was very picturesque...especially in the Fall.

It was in the Fall, when the leaves changed and our view captured the multitude of colors from all of the various trees, for as far as you could see.

Mom used to say we had a home with a Million Dollar View. That was true, but the view I was most interested in at the time, was the open field we owned across the street.

I had saved some money in the bank from my paper route, so I asked Dad if I could buy a car and drive it in the open field we owned? He thought about, said I could and offered to help me find a car.

Within the next few weeks, he heard a friend of his was selling his 1947 Chevy for $40. It had been the family car and well maintained, so Dad thought it would be a good car to ride around the field in. We mapped out the area to to drive the car in and when completed, we basically had mapped out a quarter-mile race track. It was perfect; and for the next year or so, my brothers, friends and I tore up the field with that car. We not only had a lot of fun driving, but from that experience, we also learned how to use the clutch and stick shift pretty well. I was nearly ready to get my driver's license now and drive on the open road!

My next adventure would be to buy a street car. I was tired of riding the school bus and was looking forward to driving my own car to school. I couldn't wait to be sixteen.

Chapter 5

"If you abide in Me and My words abide in you, ask what you desire and it shall be done for you."
John 15:7

The Early 60's

A month before I turned sixteen, I went to work at the Victory Super Market stocking shelves and cleaning floors at night. Once I had my own car, I started working during the day in the back room; packing and loading inventory, as well as carrying out groceries for customers.

I was a good employee and within a year, I was promoted to Assistant Manager of both Dairy and Frozen Foods, under the watchful eye of Norman Charpentier.

Norman was a great guy to work with and one day while working together, we got a shipment of bananas in. He asked me to open the box of bananas and put them on display in the store.

As I was removing a small bunch of bananas from the box, a big black furry tarantula suddenly ran across my hand. When that happened — I threw the bananas and yelled! I thought I was going to have a heart attack. Nothing like that had ever happened to me before: it really scared me! In fact, my heart continued to pound for at least five minutes after that happened. Norman just sat there and laughed at my reaction. Having tarantulas in banana boxes was a common occurrence back then and this was his way of initiating me into the world of produce.

On the day I turned sixteen, my dad drove me to the Department of Motor Vehicles to take my written and driving tests. That afternoon I was happy — for I passed and received my driver's license — then drove my dad home to celebrate my birthday.

One week later I bought my own car. It was a black, 1950 Ford Custom Convertible with pin stripes and red flame accents on the fenders. It was powered with a 1953 Mercury flat head engine. The engine was modified and the car sounded like it wanted to race.

The next day, with a sense of pride, I drove my car to school to show it off and throughout the day I would look out the school windows to see it sitting there waiting for me to get out of school. When school was over, I drove some friends home before going to the local hardware store to buy some white pom-pom's to glue around the dash board and large white fuzzy dice to hang on the rear-view mirror. In addition, I bought some fake wide white walls and large moon disk type hub caps for the tires. Now the car was all dressed up and ready for me to show it off.

Within a couple of weeks all the kids in town knew my car. The only problem was, the police knew my car too. Leominster was a small town and everyone knew everyone back then.

My dad had an inside track on where I went and what I did. He was a lineman for the county but he was also a volunteer fireman with good friends in the police department and they did a lot of things together. In fact, one day I was speeding through town and rather than chase me down to give me a ticket, the policeman just called my dad — I would have rather just had a ticket from the policeman.

I loved having a convertible. It was a real chick magnet, especially in the summertime. There was something special about driving with the top down, the wind blowing through your hair and having the radio blasting.

That summer, I sang with Russ Rogers and his band at the camp's talent night every couple of weeks. Elvis, Ricky Nelson and Roy Orbison were big hit makers back then and those were the artists I emulated the most. I just loved singing and being in the spot light with Russ's band. The girls in the audience also continued to do their part, by rushing the stage when we started performing. Everyone got involved and we had a lot of fun. It also prepared me for working the stage later on when I had my own band.

Life was going along pretty well; then I hit a bump in the road playing baseball at high school. The score was tied and we were at the bottom of the ninth inning. I was up to bat and hit a long ball into centerfield. I knew I had a double for sure, but as I rounded second base, I decided to run to third. Then, when I reached third base, I felt I could make an infield home run and win the game. But, while I was running around third base, the centerfielder threw the ball all the way to the catcher. I hadn't planned on that happening. Now, in order for me to score, I had to run down the catcher. The catcher was Ralph Caisse. Ralph was strong, solid and weighed about 60 pounds more than me. This was now a suicide mission, but I was committed to scoring the winning run. Ralph guarded the plate and put his body towards me, while catching the throw from centerfield. I ran into him, causing him to drop the ball and scored the winning run, but in the process I messed up my right knee. The coach told me to just run it off and it should be ok. Well, I tried to run it off, but I was hurting — my knee didn't feel stable.

I went to Dr. Wheeler's office and had him examine me. After my examination he informed me I had torn my cartilage and I ended up with a cast on my leg from my ankle up to my hip. I was in that cast for about 10 weeks. Oh, I got a lot of sympathy and signatures on my cast but having to wear that cast, caused me to miss out on the Junior / Senior Prom that year.

Later on during the Summer of 1961, my brother Donnie asked me to help him pick up a goat at someone's farm. I said sure, so we drove over and picked up the goat. Donnie put the goat in the back seat of my car with him.

I had the top and the windows up, so the goat couldn't get out. The goat however, didn't like being enclosed or restrained by Donnie and before we traveled too far, the goat put his horns thru my convertible top. I should have known better, thinking the goat would be ok in the back seat with Donnie, but it happened. Needless to say, I was up-set.

When we got home, I repaired the torn areas of the top with black electrical masking tape. Then to add insult to injury, that winter we received a monster snow storm: a big North Eastern blizzard.

My car was parked off the side of the road, in a parking area across from our driveway, safe from any snow removal equipment. The snow from the storm drifted so high it completely covered the car.

We had a dog at the time named Laddie. He was a beautiful full-size collie and he loved to jump in the snow. He would jump about 4 or 5 feet, disappear in the snow and reappear to do it again. I happened to be looking out the kitchen window towards my car watching Laddie jumping in the snow when all of a sudden, I saw him jump and disappear in the snow. I got concerned when he didn't resurface and ran out to the area near my car, where he was jumping. Low and behold when he disappeared, he jumped through the top of my car. This time the top on my car was not able to be repaired with tape. My once beautiful car was now pretty ragged and full of snow. I had a choice; I could buy a new top or I could get a different car. I looked around and found a 1953 Ford Custom-line Convertible with a blown engine. I could buy it for the same price as the new top, so I bought the 1953 Ford and put the 1953 Mercury engine in it from my 1950 Ford. I then put a pair of 1959 Cadillac tail lights on it to give it some customization and the look I wanted.

The Bailey family in 1962

I was a Junior in High School and still trying to figure out who or what God is. That was important to me, so I started attending the Christian Science Church with my neighbors to try and find some answers to my questions. I would go there after the Unitarian Church service was over on Sunday. The classes I attended were primarily about becoming a member of the Christian Science church. I learned about Mary Baker Eddy, the founder of the Christian Science church and her core beliefs on healing with prayer. I was also introduced to the Bible. Well, we didn't actually study it. In my class everyone was assigned to memorize the names of the books in the Bible and the order they were in. I memorized them but didn't have a clue what was in them.

I was given a Bible and tried to read it on my own, but got lost somewhere in Genesis. I then became confused about what I was reading and lost interest in going any further. But memorizing the names and order of the books in the Bible proved to come in handy on one occasion, when I was older — at a Bible study I was invited to attend.

I was finally a Senior in High School with only a few months left until graduation. My big question at this point in my life was; what did I want to do after I graduate? Oh, I knew what I wanted to do. I wanted to join a rock-band, make a record and travel the world. My problem was; if I didn't go to college, I would be drafted into the Army.

Since music was going to play a large part in my decision — I needed a plan.

This then was my plan — I will join the Air Force (rather than be drafted by the Army), let Uncle Sam pay for my college using the G.I. Bill when I get out, see the world while in the Air Force, and play in a band once stationed at a permanent base.

Chapter 6

"Train up a child in the way he should go and when he is old, he will not depart from it." Proverbs 22:6

Life as an Airman

I graduated from High School in June of 1962 and in August joined the Air Force. The drive to the bus station with my parents to begin my life as an Airman was bitter sweet, for I knew life was going to change; once I left home.

I hugged my mom before getting on the bus and she began to cry, starting me welling up with tears too. Dad was proud of me joining the Air Force but even he had a teary look in his eyes. I looked back while stepping onto the bus and saw them holding each other up, as they both waived to me. I found a seat next to the window and took one last look back, as I pulled away from the station. The separation from my parents and leaving the security of home was emotionally tough. I was entering a new phase of life and on my way to Springfield, Massachusetts, to be inducted into the Air Force.

IN THE EYE OF A HURRICANE

I was sworn in, along with a number of other recruits the following day and put on a bus to Logan Airport in Boston, Massachusetts. In the airport we were assembled and placed on a plane going to San Antonio, Texas.

I was pretty excited – this was the first commercial flight I had ever flown on. The plane I was boarding was equipped with four propeller driven engines, with seating for 225 passengers, and as luck would have it; my first commercial flight would have us fly directly into a hurricane. The flight started out pretty normal but after being in the air for a couple of hours, we were told to fasten our seat belts due to an approaching storm. The seat belt sign came on and the Captain told us we should expect some turbulence until we climbed above it. The turbulence however, continued to get worst! In trying to fly above the storm, the pilot flew into large thermal drafts causing the plane to bounce all over the sky. Passengers, (as well as airline stewardesses), were sick from the turbulence, with some needing oxygen. It was scary! We had flown into a hurricane. We were in that mess for a long time before finally landing in the eye of the storm in New Orleans, Louisiana. Once we landed we all cheered: we were on the ground safe! We then went inside the terminal and waited for the rest of the storm to pass over.

Once the storm passed, the plane was checked out and we continued our flight to San Antonio, Texas. Once in San Antonio, the new inductees were separated into groups and put on buses going to Lackland Air Force Base, to begin basic training.

BASIC TRAINING

We arrived at Lackland with our perfectly combed hair and colorful travel attire. The Training Instructors were there to greet us as we got off the bus. They lined us up in true military fashion and started barking out commands. They let us know from the start, they were not there to make friends. They had 13 weeks to turn us into Airmen and the training was designed to separate the men from the boys. Some will wash out and some will want to quit but won't be able to. We were now the property of the U. S. Government and will have limited individual rights until we graduate from basic training.

Our first assignment was to locate the flight squadron we were to be assigned to and be introduced to the barracks we would be in. Once inside the barracks, we were assigned beds and footlockers. We were then escorted to the supply stations and issued all of our government supplies we would need while we were there. Items like; boots, fatigues, dress uniforms, underwear and socks. We were then given a list and a set amount of money for toilet articles to be purchased at the Base Exchange. These were items like; soap, shaving gear and deodorant. Everything we received from the Air Force and on the list purchased at the Base Exchange had a special area of its own in our footlocker. If you had anything more or didn't purchase the article on the list, you would face the consequences from the Training Instructor. When our footlocker was organized we gathered everything we brought from home, such as; books, magazines, cameras and clothing. Those items would be put in a box and placed in storage for us until we graduated from basic training.

The next day at 4:30 a.m. the Training Instructor turned on all the lights in the barracks, blew his whistle and started yelling for us to line up for reveille. This was now going to be our new normal. We lined up for roll call and was given 30 minutes for all of us to get our bathroom details done, be fully dressed, make our beds and be outside the barracks in formation. Once dressed and in formation we did drills and marched over to the mess hall for breakfast.

At breakfast we were ordered not to talk in line. We were instructed to look at a spot on the back of the head of the person in front of us and not make eye contact with anyone while waiting to be served. Once our food was served we found a table and ate our food with minimum conversation. When breakfast was over we took our tray to be washed and got back in formation; in readiness to leave the mess hall area. From the Mess Hall we marched over to the Medical Hall where we would get our shots and vaccination. We marched in columns and broke off into single files. We had the same orders given about finding a spot on the person's head and not making eye contact with anyone. There were hundreds of new GI's getting inoculated and you could hear the shots being administered in different parts of the hall. The shots and vaccines were administered by air guns. It was quick and if you flinched or they missed the mark, it could easily tear your skin. That happened to a few guys in our squadron and it took longer for them to heal. It also left a nasty scar.

Once we received our shots we got back in formation and marched over to get our hair cut. This was 1962, and with the exception of the jocks with their crew cuts, most of us had long hair. My hair was similar to Fabian's or Elvis at the time. I had always had compliments on my hair and it was always neatly combed. It was part of who I was, and to a certain degree, set me apart from the crowd. We were now in military formations — like lambs waiting to be slaughtered. One by one we saw young guys with full heads of hair being sheared like sheep and turned into skin heads. I don't even think the airmen cutting our hair were barbers. It was a five-minute haircut, with no design in mind. When it was over, no one stood out. We all looked about the same. Fortunately, hair grows back in time but for those 8 weeks we looked more like prisoners than soldiers.

Basic training was all about discipline. The Training Instructor would see how far he could push us before we broke. If we failed mentally or physically, he would try and make an example of us to the rest of the squadron. A lot of times this would happen in drilling exercises. If we got out of step or out of formation, we would be called on it. The usual punishment was to give the Training Instructor 30 pushups. If we did it with an attitude, we could end up doing 30 more. Again, he wanted to break us, not have us show everyone how strong we were.

The Training Instructors were masters at doing things to aggravate and intimidate us. More than once, our Training Instructor came to attention in front of me; so close that when he slapped his boots together and arched forward, the bill of his hat hit my forehead. They loved to get in our face with their bad breath and wait for us to flinch or make a remark. Once we did, we were fresh meat on his grill to be barbecued. Nearly everyone got grilled at least once a day. He of course had favorites and they were more than grilled. They were openly toasted.

For an example, one day we were required to go into the gas house fully protected and once inside – remove our gas mask. The gas was so thick we couldn't see anything in front of us and once we took off our mask, our eyes burned so bad that we thought we would be violently ill. We had to stay in the gas house until we were dismissed, and on this one day some decided to exit early. Of course, they were caught leaving the gas house early and had to go back in again. But this time it would be different. They were inside for leaving their assigned post early, while also being reprimanded by the Training Instructor. A type of AWOL. (Absent without Leave). This, now also put a target on their back for further harassment going forward.

By the end of the 8-week period, I was in the best physical shape of my life. I had gained 30 pounds; mostly all muscle. I was able to run a couple of miles fully dressed with field gear and was doing 50 clap pushups every morning along with all the other exercises we did.

During those 8 weeks we had been isolated from everything outside of our basic training. The first couple of weeks we were even isolated from making or receiving phone calls; unless it was an emergency call from home. When we were finally able to make phone calls, we only had 10 minutes to talk. There were only a small bank of phones available for us to use and everyone on base wanted to talk on them. If I remember correctly – I didn't have enough money and had to call home collect. At any point; it was great to spend those 10 minutes talking with my parents. During that time, Mom of course monopolized the phone while giving Dad his minute to say he was proud of me. It was comforting in those minutes to hear my parent's voices and their words of encouragement.

At the end of the 7th week we were given a pass for the day – so, four of us decided to go to San Antonio – to see the Alamo and the Zoo. In 1962 San Antonio was a town where as a young Airman you had to be cautious where you went, and with our skinned head's we all stood out from the crowd. We were told the parts of town that were off limits to us, as well as the safe areas recommended for a day of relaxation.

We decided to go to the Alamo first, and we were amazed at how small the old Spanish Mission fortress was. We all expected it to be a lot larger in size. After the Alamo we went to the Zoo. We entered at the front gate, and by the time the sun was ready to set, we had seen the majority of the Zoo,

Rather than walk back to the front gate, we were told about a side gate near the rear where we could exit. Once through the turnstile, we realized we should have gone back to the front of the Zoo, to catch the bus back to Base. We then realized we were in a part of town that didn't look too friendly. The four of us decided to follow the road we were on to a cross street to see if we could find a more heavily traveled road. The sun was nearly down and as we continued to walk, we noticed a hundred feet or so in front of us was a run-down house with about 10 or 12 Mexican's hanging around on the front porch. As we got closer, we heard a couple of them yell to us, "Hey gringos what are you doing here, are you lost?" Our first thought was to turn around and run but we kept walking. They were sort of heckling us but not aggressively. They stayed on the porch and we kept walking. We finally walked far enough and realized they were not going to be any trouble. For a moment we thought we might have to use our military training — but thankfully we didn't. We finally found the street we were looking for and walked over to meet the bus going back to Base.

Once on the bus, the four of us talked about our adventure on the street outside the Zoo. We really didn't know each other before venturing out on the town together. We were four Airman on a one-day pass who decided to see some of the popular tourist sites in San Antonio and made a mistake thinking we could get back to the bus stop without having to go all the way back through the Zoo; to where we came in. We all agreed we had each other's back. If we would have had an altercation, we were ready to fight. We were all from different flights within our squadron at Lackland, but for that moment we were brothers in arms.

These were just a couple stories about my time in Basic Training at Lackland.

Others would have included the horrors of working K.P. (Kitchen Police), the long marches, fully dressed in 105 degree temperatures included in our physical training, and

Airman Ron Bailey

keeping watch as a sentry in the cold rain outside the barracks all night.

The last week of Basic Training was spent qualifying for graduation and the Training Instructors last chance to break us. At the end of graduation week, we all dressed in dressed blues for our pictures and the finale graduation march.

MY TIME AT KEESLER AIR FORCE BASE

The next day we were given our personal belongings that had been stored, and together with our duffel bag loaded with military items, we boarded the bus for Keesler Air Force Base, in Biloxi, Mississippi. Keesler Air Force Base would be home for the next 7 weeks; where I would finish basic training and start technical training in AC&W. (Aircraft Control and Early Warning)

In Aircraft Control and Early Warning, we learned how to read a radar scope, understand weather patterns and write backwards on a large plexiglass reporting board. Of course, there were many more responsibilities to learn but those would be learned on the job once we reached our permanent station.

At tech school, we were away from the initiation phase of basic training. The Training Instructors were more instructional than confrontational, and after a couple of weeks we began getting free time when we were not working. This could be to hang out on Base and relax or even go into town, if we wanted to.

These were the early days of segregation; and it was in Biloxi, Mississippi where I was educated about racial division. I had never been exposed to segregation in Massachusetts, especially in Leominster where I grew up. In Biloxi however, they had separate every-things; hotels, clubs, water fountains, bathrooms, public swimming pools, seating areas and eating places. It was evident, neither group of people liked each other.

On my first bus trip to Biloxi, I caught the bus outside of the Airbase and immediately went to the back to sit down. Once seated, I felt everyone staring at me. I couldn't figure out why. Finally, this sweet black lady pointed to a sign by the back door of the bus which read, "colored section." I then felt like I was breaking the law and immediately moved to the front of the bus. That was my first personal racial encounter with segregation in the South.

Later in the month riots broke out at the University of Mississippi when James Meredith, a black student attended school there. He was the first black to ever be enrolled at the University and white people didn't approve of it. He was vigilant in his determination and had to be escorted to his classes by the National Guard. Times were changing in the South and no one liked it. Heck, we had black Airmen at the Base but we couldn't go to town together for fear one side or the other would start a riot over their racial bias.

Jerry and me

MEETING MY NEW BEST FRIEND

As I write this, I find it so amazing the way God puts people in your life to help fulfill the desires of your heart.

On my first day of Tech School

after an hour or so of class we were given a break. Some used it for smoking or the bathroom and others used it to get to know each other better. So, during the break I went up to this one guy and said, "Hi, my name is Ron Bailey." I then put my hand out to shake his hand, just like I did when I was building my paper route. He looked at me and said, "So," then laughed and said, "My name is Jerry McClure." Well, Jerry and I started talking and discovered we both played guitars and sang. We learned we liked the same songs, types of music, artists and bands. We were also athletic and liked all types of sports. There was definitely a chemistry between us and we soon became friends. This would become even more evident once we were stationed in Germany.

Ready for work

I don't remember all the things we did together at Biloxi but I do remember when we received our permanent Base assignments — most of our classmates were assigned to the 601st Tactical Squadron in Kassel, Germany. Jerry and I could hardly wait.

We were all excited but we still had a few weeks until our technical training in AC&W was completed. What happened next could have changed all of our lives.

Unbeknownst to mainstream media, during that time there was a large Russian presence being monitored by our government in Cuba. It was near the end of October 1962 and while the rest of the country slept, President Kennedy put all military personnel on alert. I was issued a fully loaded M-1 rifle and ordered to patrol the beach area of Biloxi. We were shown how to march with our weapons in basic training. We were all aware of how to use the weapons but never thought we would be using them to protect our own shores. We were told to watch for submarines or small boats coming to shore. Each Airman had about 50 paces or 150 feet of shoreline to patrol. We walked 50 paces to the left then turned around and walked 50 paces back to the starting point with our weapon on our shoulder. This went on during the night with only the light of the moon to illuminate the area. We were all a little nervous, for we were never told why we were on alert. It was a need to know situation, so we never knew until it was all over, as to why we were on alert and guarding the beach. It wasn't until the next day that we learned about the missile crisis in Cuba and just how close we came to being in a war.

After the crisis was all over, we talked about what happened and jested about how the moon had cast different shadows in the ocean at night. It was easy to get confused about what we were looking at, and what if we did see a submarine or a small boat coming towards shore, would we have shot at it? The general consensus was; we were part of history and glad no one was shot over some mistaken situation we could have caused.

AC&W Class Graduation

Two weeks later I finished Tech School and was certified as an AC&W operator. I said my good byes to Keesler Air-Force Base and went home for a four-week leave; before going to Germany.

Chapter 7

"Sing praises to the Lord, you His holy ones, and give thanks to His holy name." Psalm 30:4

Pursuing My Love for Music in Germany

I was only away from home four months since joining the Air Force, but everyone knew I was different from when I left. When I joined the Air Force I was 6' tall and weighed 128 pounds. When I returned, I was still 6' tall but weighed 158 pounds and carried myself with a certain air of confidence. I left as a young high school graduate and came back a young man.

Mom was amazed how much I filled out in just four months and tried to show me off when I was in my uniform whenever she could,. I preferred to wear my civilian clothes while I was home but I was happy to go along with some of the plans Mom made for family get togethers. I realized I was going to be gone for three years and wanted to make every day count for all of us.

Some of my time home was spent with Dennis Cormier, a good friend from high school. We loved singing and playing our guitars together. It was easy for us to spend hours working on new songs or figuring out harmonizing parts to old songs. I spent time with other high school friends too, but my time home was mostly spent with my brothers and my parents. My family was important to me.

My time at home went by quickly and soon I had to get ready for Germany. I was going to be gone for three years and I needed to pack everything I wanted shipped to my new Base. I didn't have much but I wanted to ship my guitar amplifier, a tape recorder, my radio and some extra clothes. I planned on buying another guitar once I was there.

A week after Christmas I was on a bus headed for McGuire Air force Base in New Jersey. Once at McGuire, we were all placed in a holding area and waited to board our plane to take us to Rhein-Main Airbase in Frankfurt, Germany. Our plane was a C-130 powered by four turbo-jet propellers. It was a cargo plane converted to transport troops. The first thing I noticed was it didn't have many windows. Instead the plane had portholes spaced around 10 feet apart and once inside the plane, you noticed other unconventional things. The seats were facing towards the rear of the plane instead of towards the front. Also, we had cargo nets to hold our belongings and not overhead storage cabinets. Even if you were lucky enough to get a seat next to a port hole, you had very little visibility. The experience was especially different for take offs and landings. For when you were taking off you were seated facing down and while you landed you were facing up. We flew from New Jersey to Greenland where we re-fueled before continuing to Rhein-Main Air Force Base in Germany. The entire flight was about 24 hours long. When we got to Rhein-Main, we were all pretty tired. We were assigned a room at the Base and told to meet outside the barracks at 10:00 the next morning to board a bus that would take us to the Frankfurt Bahnhof. Once at the Bahnhof we would catch a train to Kassel, Germany.

The next morning, we were all allotted German currency to pay our expenses for our trip to Kassel and then went to the bus stop. A large number of Airmen were already at the bus stop at 09:40 when I arrived with my duffel bag. We still had twenty minutes to board the bus before it was scheduled to arrive, so I decided to go to the bathroom. I asked one of the Airmen to watch my duffel bag for me and I would be right back.

I thought I had plenty of time, but when I got back everyone had left, and my duffel bag was sitting by itself next to the post where I left it. I gathered my thoughts and grabbed a taxi that was nearby. I told the cab driver my dilemma and he said he could get me there by the time the bus would arrive there. He spoke very good English and I said we need to get there quick, since I didn't know what time the train would be leaving for Kassel.

I then learned what quick was in Germany. It was the fastest taxi ride I had ever experienced. I looked down at the speedometer and thought at times we were going 120 miles an hour but realized later it was kilometers: still, over 70 miles an hour! By the time we reached the Bahnhof, my knees were weak from the ride. I stood up, held out my hand with my German currency in it, and said, "how much do I owe you?" He took his cab fee from the money in my hand. I then threw my duffel bag over my shoulder and walked into the Bahnhof to find the ticket master. Once inside I recognized some of the Airmen I had been on the plane with. I told them how I missed the bus, along with my crazy taxi cab ride to the Bahnhof, then we all went to purchase our tickets. When we purchased our tickets, we found out we had plenty of time before our train departed the station.

The sights, sounds and activity inside the Bahnhof was just like in the movies. The steam engines came to rest at their place on the platform and once in place, they released the break's pressure causing the steam to come pouring out from under the engine. You could also hear the whistles blowing loudly as each train departed from their place on the platform.

The train ride itself was fun. We sat in old wooden seats and you could feel the train's cadence as you traveled down the tracks. I sat next to a window to see Germany's landscape as we traveled; reminding me of New Hampshire or Vermont, with different style homes.

Every time we came to a road crossing or entered a small town, the engineer would blow the train's whistle. The train whistle became part of the ambience of the ride itself. The sights and sounds of my first train ride in Germany continue to stay with me to this day.

Once we reached Kassel, Germany we all grabbed our duffel bags and were met by other Airmen from the 601st; who transported us to our new Home Base.

Our Home Base in Kassel was located only 10 kilometers from where the Nazis had traps set to guard a top-secret project they were working on during the War.

Kassel was known for its heavily fortified Air Base built by the Luftwaffe and was located inside a mountain. Near the end of War II, the U.S. captured the Air Base and permanently closed the inside of the mountain, sealing the secrets stored inside. In addition – near the end of the War the German Nazis placed a lot of mines and traps around the area to discourage people from treasure hunting. In fact, during the two weeks I was there, someone was killed by tripping a mine while looking for souvenirs.

Two weeks after we arrived at Kassel, we were shipping out. The 601st Tactical Unit was being relocated to Sembach Air Force Base in Sembach, Germany. Our main function during this time was tearing down lockers and placing them in trucks to be taken to our new base in Sembach. There was also an inquiry made as to who could drive a truck. Well, I drove small trucks on a friend's farm and felt I should be able to drive the larger deuce and a half. So, I was selected to drive one of the trucks in the convoy to Sembach. I felt I would be able to drive the truck but I wasn't familiar with German street signage. I didn't think that would be a problem though if I was in a convoy.

Getting the convoy ready

The day of redeployment came. The trucks were all loaded: some with supplies others were troop transporters. In all we had about 35 trucks and a couple of jeeps equipped with radio phones. One jeep with the commanding officer was positioned up front to guide us and the other stationed at the very back for stragglers or roadside emergencies.

My truck was the 10th truck in the convoy. We all started out together but when we came to the town of Kassel, we started getting into traffic. Once entering the busy cross streets our trucks needed to be nearly bumper to bumper, in order to prevent civilian drivers from merging into line with us. And then it happened: at one of the busy intersections, a German driver challenged me and raced in front of my truck. Once in front of my truck, he slowed down and let someone else get in front of him; upsetting me even more , as I watched the convoy pull away from me. When the separation occurred, I was approaching a fork in the road and soon I could no longer see the convoy in front of me. With both roads having the same name, I made a decision to go left at the fork and hoped this was where the convoy had gone. Unfortunately, by taking the road to the left, I ended up taking the remaining 25 trucks down a narrow cobblestone road with clearance for cars only. To make matters worst, the only way for us to meet up with the convoy was to take a one-way street, going the wrong way. The downtown streets were narrow having less than 5 feet of clearance on each side of our trucks and the people on the sidewalks were yelling at us but we continued on. I didn't know what else to do except keep driving and do my best to get back with the rest of the convoy.

Mobile Operations HQs

Around this time the Lieutenant in the jeep from the rear of the convoy showed up mad as hell wanting to know where I was taking his convoy? He reminded me that I had just taken 25 large trucks thru an area of town designated for smaller vehicles only and then down a one-way street the wrong way!

After chewing me out, he radioed ahead to the forward commander in the other jeep and told him what was going on. The Lieutenant then assumed the forward position and we followed him to meet the convoy who stopped to wait for us.

Mobile Radar Site

I now had to do some explaining to the young Lieutenant in charge of the convoy. I'm sure the Base Commander had some explaining to do to the people of

Kassel too. Everything went smooth from then on until we arrived at Sembach.

At Sembach I had a brief meeting with the two officers to explain how the German driver raced in front of me at the busy intersection causing the separation and loss of sight of the convoy in front of me. Then how that was further complicated when I came to the fork in the road and took the left road. They then asked me, "Didn't I notice the signs saying no vehicles over a certain size on that road"? I told them, "I didn't understand all the signs and went with my gut." I apologized and they let me off easy. I heard a lot though from the other truck drivers who were following me. By the end of the week we were all laughing at what it must have looked like to the German people of Kassel. Did they think we were there invading them or liberating them?

We unloaded all the trucks and when the day was nearly over, went into the barracks to find our rooms. We set up our beds and put our lockers together. Once everything was setup in our rooms, we went to the Mess Hall to eat. The Mess Hall was located directly across from our barracks. The 601st Tactical Radar Unit was a mobile radar unit and we were going to share the Base with the 38th Tactical Missile Wing.

We were the first part of the 601st to occupy our section of the Base and it was going to take about a month or so before everything was up and running. Some of the truck drivers went back to aid in the transferring of additional supplies and troops from Kassel to Sembach, while the rest of us stayed behind to help with the new set up. Because we had two locations it wasn't clear to anyone who was in Kassel and who was in Sembach.

The next morning reveille was called and we all went to breakfast. After breakfast we went back to the barracks for roll call. When the roll call was completed my name wasn't mentioned. The Sergeant calling out the roll call, then asked if anyone was omitted? A couple of people added their name to roll call but I didn't add mine. They assigned different duties to the people on roll call and since they didn't have my name, I wasn't assigned to do anything. Instead I went over to the recreation hall and played pool that morning. I then joined up with some of the guys later that afternoon and helped assemble beds and lockers in the barracks. I was operating under the radar so to speak. I actually could come and go as I pleased. No one had a record of me.

As the new recruits came in, their names were added to the roll call. Soon Jerry McClure showed up from Kassel and I told him what was going on. He became my roommate and we began getting reacquainted with each other. The next day when roll call was announced, Jerry's name had not been read and when they asked if anyone's name was omitted, he didn't speak up either. The work assignments were established off of the roll call list and everyone took off to their assigned areas.

Up until now I was sort of a lone wolf, showing up in the afternoon to pitch in where I wanted to. I hadn't gotten too close to anyone for fear that they would figure out the game I was playing. Now I had Jerry with me and when everyone reported to their assigned areas, Jerry and I went to the Recreation Hall to play pool or ping pong for the morning. When noon came, we went to the Mess Hall and decided to just leave the Base for the day. We put on our civilian clothes, caught a ride from someone going to town outside the front gate and went into Kaiserslautern. We were like two tourists walking in a large German town filled with night clubs, restaurants, stores, fountains and other tourist attractions. There were also a lot of pretty German girls to look at.

We spent the rest of the day in Kaiserslautern checking out everything we could and while we were downtown, we met some other GI's. They told us about a corner where the Airmen hung out to catch a ride with people going back to Sembach. Sure enough, later on we went there and caught a ride with a couple of Airman going back to Base.

We continued this charade for a couple of weeks and one day while playing pool, the Sergeant supervising the Recreation Center came over and asked what Squadron we belonged to? We told him the 601st. He then went back to doing whatever he was doing. About 15 minutes later, we were meeting with a Sergeant from the 601st and had some explaining to do. We hadn't shown up on the work manifest and as a result of our freelancing, we were given extra duties to perform, with limited access to town for the next month.

At this point the headquarters of the 601st was getting more organized. The radar station was set up, it was in service, and we were reporting there to work, instead of doing the menial tasks assigned to us in the beginning. By the end of the month, most of the 601st had completely transferred from Kassel to Sembach and we were fully operational. The end of the month was also when we received our pay. On pay day we all went to our mail boxes to get paid. Everyone received their pay checks that day except Jerry and I. We didn't receive one because our names were not on the roster turned into the paymaster. So, we had to take the good with the

Permanent Radar Site

bad, in regards to having all that free time in the beginning.

We were paid every two weeks. So, on our next pay day Jerry and I received the full amount; including the back pay due us. Having the extra money was good, because we now had the money to buy our new guitars. Timing was good as well, for my personal supplies shipped from home arrived; especially my guitar amplifier.

Jerry and I plugged our new guitars into the amplifier and took turns singing the different songs we knew. After a few songs, we started harmonizing together and soon had a room full of Airmen listening to us. We worked up about 25 songs together, and felt we should try and play in some of the smaller German Gasthauses in the area.

Sergeant Razindous liked us and offered to drive Jerry and I around to visit the different Gasthauses. We would go into the Gasthaus, introduce ourselves to the owner or manager and tell them we would love to play and entertain their customers. It wouldn't cost them anything, as we would just play for tips. We did this for a while and soon built up a small following. The costumers loved us and in addition to tipping us they would buy us beer as we played. The first time that happened, due to the high alcohol content, we could only handle a couple glasses of beer. Later though, we were able to handle a couple of pitchers.

Singing at a Gasthause

Where we played, we had the regular customers from town and customers from the Base. When they bought us the beer, they did it out of appreciation, and since we didn't want to appear like we didn't appreciate them buying us the beer, we ended up drinking too much on more than one occasion. It was all about how we would time it. We would play for about forty minutes and then take a ten-minute break. It was during the ten-minute break where we had to pace ourselves with the customers buying us beer. We played two hours top and repeated songs upon request. Many times, when we played the requested songs, we would also have a beer waiting for us when we took our break. We were paying our dues, learning how to work the audience and getting ready to take the next step in our musical journey.

Chapter 8

"For everything in the world; the lust of the flesh, the lust of the eyes, and the pride of life-comes not from the Father but from the world." 1 John 2:16

Building a Legacy with the Stingrays

Jerry and I played together for a couple of months before deciding it was time to start a band. Once we felt ready, we put out feelers for a drummer and a bass player. We preferred they could sing — to allow us to do three-and four-part harmonies.

The first person to join us was Tony Carter. He was a drummer from New Jersey. Jerry met Tony while working out at the Base Gym. The next person was Rick Thompson. I met him in the Recreation Hall while playing pool. Rick was from Connecticut and was another guitar player. Jerry met Robert "Squeaky" Hugel at the same time but he also played the guitar. Squeaky was from Oregon but said, he could also play the bass. The good news was, all of us could sing. The bad news, we had four guitar players. To solve this dilemma Jerry decided to sell his guitar and play bass.

Each player brought a few songs to our expanding catalogue, allowing us to provide a couple of hours of solid music without having to repeat anything. Now all we needed was a name; so, after throwing names around for a few hours, we decided to call ourselves "The Stingrays," named after a new model of Corvette introduced that year.

We practiced a few hours a week at the recreation center. Then, after a couple of weeks, we were hired to play at a German Gesthause. Initially we were each paid around $5.00 a night, a meal, plus all the beer we could drink. It wasn't about the money at this point. We were looking for a place where we could perform and start building a following. In a way we were being paid to practice but after a month the owner agreed to change our arrangement; paying each of us $10 a night, a meal and three large glasses of beer. He realized our band was good for his business and if we were to leave, we were able to make more money in the clubs in Kaiserslautern. He also didn't want us getting drunk on him half way thru the evening. It was a win-win situation.

Playing at an NCO Club

Eventually we started playing other clubs in an around Kaiserslautern. We also started playing at the Army and Air Force clubs in the area. We began playing both Non-Commissioned Officer and Officer clubs through-out Germany. We even played a couple of NCO clubs in France.

At the Sembach Teen Club

We were making good money and having a small taste of what it felt like being "Rock Stars." We were treated like celebrities when we played some of these clubs. This was further amplified when we played the Teen Club on our base.

On the day we were scheduled to play, we went to the club early to set up our equipment. We practiced just enough to get our sound balanced for the room. The doors were closed until showtime and when the show started, the kids all rushed the stage. The girls were only a couple of years younger than us and were throwing themselves at us. This was even more evident when the show was over. We couldn't go anywhere: we still had to breakdown and load our equipment into our vehicles. In all, it was a day to remember. We had a lot of fun and even gave out a few autographs.

Jerry and I were now making more money playing on the weekends than what we were making every two weeks in the Air Force. The guys in the barracks changed our names from, "The Juke Box Boys" to "The Gold Dust Twins" because we always had extra money on us. We made even more money playing pool during the week. Life was good!

WAS I SAVED?

One day, I was playing pool at the recreation center and the guy I was playing with asked me out of the blue, if I was I saved? I thought for a second and responded, "Saved from what?" He sort of laughed at my response and then asked, "Was I a Christian?" I responded and said, "I was." He then said, "I thought so" and he never brought the subject up again. I really didn't know what he meant by being saved and I honestly thought I was a Christian. My rational was; I was a Unitarian — I was neither Catholic nor Jewish — and since Unitarians were Protestants — I thought Protestant was just another name for Christian. Now if he probed a little deeper, he would have discovered I was a Unitarian and most Unitarians don't believe Jesus is God. In fact, it was the first time I heard the expression of being saved.

EXPERIENCING CHANGES

Jerry and I were close. We did everything together and over time it finally took its toll on us. We still played in the Stingrays together but we needed a degree of separation for a while, so Jerry changed rooms when the opportunity presented itself. When Jerry moved on, I was assigned a new roommate by the name of Bob Miller. Bob was from Chicago and new to Sembach. He also liked to sing. He had somewhat of a Broadway or classical sound to his voice. I played the guitar in the room and we tried to sing together but it just didn't work. He had a strong well-trained voice and he was hard to harmonize with. We thought it might work singing in a choir together, so we decided to join the Base choirs. He was Catholic, so I agreed to sing in the Catholic choir with him and he sang in the Protestant choir with me. The Catholic program was different. I was singing in Latin and the service was all conducted in Latin; so I didn't understand what was going on most of the time. The symbolism of the service however, was interesting to me. The Protestant service was pretty generic, held together by an encouraging message. Bob and I sang in the choirs together until I was transferred back to the States. God was preparing me for what was to come, later on in my life.

If there was one thing I learned in the Air Force, everything was subject to change, at any time. Jerry and I were members of the 601st and we came to Germany the same month, for the same three-year commitment. Squeaky on the other hand, was only with us for six months and Rick Thompson was discharged shortly after that. We made those adjustments pretty easy but our next challenge would be Tony Carter. He was our drummer. What we didn't realize was, while we were in the process of reorganizing our band, another band playing the same clubs in the area, lost a couple of their players. So rather than try and find new talent when Tony left, Jerry and I merged with the other band and we kept the name, "The Stingrays." With the new "Stingrays" we had an even bigger repertoire of songs to play. We were playing top 40 songs plus a number of old standards. We played songs from all the different artists of the day, like; Ricky Nelson, Elvis, Roy Orbison, The Everly Brothers, The Beatles, The Rolling Stones, The Kinks, Otis Redding and James Brown. We did some Country Songs and even some original songs I had written.

One of our favorite places to play was the Stadt Vein. It was one of Kaiserslautern's most popular night clubs at the time. We played there a week or two at a time. In addition to playing, we met bands from all over the world there. In fact, I bought a 1959 Fender Jazz Master guitar from one of the players in a band from Liverpool, England.

It was also a great place to meet girls. German women loved Americans and they especially liked the guys who played in a band. Suffice it to say, we never had a shortage of women to share our time with.

Jerry and I harmonizing

Jerry and I had planned on completing our tour of duty with the 601st in Germany for the full thirty-six months, however we received an offer, (along with a number of other radar operators), to complete just nine more months in Germany and get an early release from the Air Force, or we could elect to be reassigned to a Base in the United States for the remaining 16 months. We were given a month to make our decision. During the month we also received another offer. It was an opportunity to be promoted to a Warrant Officer and become a helicopter pilot.

While making our decision, a booking agent we worked with, asked us to stay in Germany to work with him. He wanted to handle all our booking arrangements, once we were released from the Air Force, plus play on some of the ocean cruises he had contacts with. We had a lot to think about.

First, we decided against becoming helicopter pilots. That was easy. Vietnam was heating up and helicopter pilots were in high demand. They also had a very high mortality rate. We knew we wanted to get back to the States, put another band together, record a record and become Rock Stars. That was all we ever talked about since establishing the Stingrays. We had a taste of what it could be like and felt it was our destiny.

We agreed to go back to the States and finish our four years, if we could be stationed together. We felt staying in the Air Force would give us the time we needed to establish the new band.

We notified the First Sergeant to tell him what we would like and he made it happen. He cut orders for Jerry and I to be stationed together at a radar site in Waverly, Iowa. We were hoping for a base in California but Waverly was the only site he was aware of that needed two radar operators.

Over the next few months we shipped our personal effects to our next Base in Waverly, Iowa and headed home for a two week leave before reporting in Iowa.

This next move was Providential. Up until this moment in my life, I didn't realize how much God was guiding me. It was only later, after looking back over my life, where I saw how different situations ultimately shaped my future; and this was one of them.

They say the Lord works in mysterious ways. This was one of them. I didn't know it at the time but His plan included me going to Iowa – so I could meet my soulmate.

Chapter 9

"For my thoughts are not your thoughts, neither are your ways my ways, declares the Lord. As the heavens are higher than the earth, so are my ways higher than your ways and my thoughts higher than your thoughts." Isaiah 55: 8-9

My Move to Iowa & the Birth of the Je-Rons

Having a couple of weeks at home before moving to Iowa was just what I needed after being in Germany for two years. I had grown up since graduating from high school and joining the Air Force. There was a lot of change at home too. Not so much with my parents, but my younger brother Donnie was now serving in the Navy near Viet Nam and my youngest brother Brad had just turned eleven years old. Time wasn't waiting for anyone. I was twenty years old and ready to put my dream of recording a record in motion. I was ready to leave home and put together the band I would eventually record with.

The Waverly radar site was a small remote Air Force base, located about four miles from the town of Waverly, Iowa and twenty miles from the towns of Cedar Falls and Waterloo. Jerry and I both arrived at the Waverly radar site together. We were given a couple of days to receive the personal items sent from Germany and set up our room, before reporting to work. We were looking forward to unpacking everything, especially our guitars and amplifiers. Everything arrived safe and sound. Once our equipment was all set up, we started playing and singing together. We soon had about ten people in our room listening to us. We made friends fast and met most of the guys in the barracks that week. We then inquired around to see if there were any drummers or piano players on Base.

The Je-Ron's

We found out, we were only five miles from Wartburg College, a four-year liberal arts college. We put a message on the college bulletin board, located in the student hall advertising for a drummer and key board player who can sing. Within a couple weeks, we found two students who met our requirements. The first one was Mel Raatz. He had a great personality, played multiple instruments, sang harmony well and owned his own keyboard. Mel had a friend by the name of Randy Elbe, who also sang and played the drums exceptionally well. Mel and Randy both had the chemistry we were looking for in the band. All we needed now was a name. We spent time tossing names around and finally ended up with "The Je-Rons," after Jerry and myself.

The Je-Rons had a few practices and soon we were playing clubs in Cedar Falls and Waterloo. It didn't take us very long before we had the sound we were looking for, so we contacted an agent and he started booking us all over Central Iowa.

We were almost to the point where we could record a couple of the songs I had written, when Randy, our drummer, quit college and joined the Air Force. We never saw that coming. Finding a new drummer and getting him up to speed was going to set us back!

We expected at least a month's delay but within a couple of weeks, we auditioned and hired Steve Bracken as our new drummer. We were back playing the clubs and on schedule again to record our record. Steve fit in perfectly. He had a great personality; he sang and was a good drummer. Soon our agent was booking us not just into clubs, but also into; colleges, fairs and larger coliseums. This all happened while Jerry and I were still in the Air Force.

During that same time, the Air Force had a talent contest. We couldn't enter the band, because everyone wasn't in the Air Force, so Jerry and I decided to enter the contest as a duet. The talent contest had a lot of different categories to compete in but only the top two finishers would go on to the Nationals in Kansas City. Jerry and I won the local talent contest and finished second at the Nationals, singing the Righteous Brother's version of Unchained Melody.

We now were ready to record our record. We had a financial backer and our agent worked out a deal for us to record with a producer he knew in Illinois. We decided to record, "I'm Going Home," on side A, an original song I wrote and "Chains," a cover song on side B, to show our harmony.

Russo's - Cedar Rapids, IA

On the day of the recording we drove to Studio One in Rock Island, Illinois and set up our equipment. The producer wanted to record us live and set up his microphones accordingly. We didn't know anything about recording and just went along with everything he suggested. Our agent/manager didn't know anything either.

We recorded both songs that morning on a high-quality tape recorder and the records were pressed later the following week. By the end of the month we had three - hundred vinyl records in our possession to sell. We put some records in music stores on consignment, sold some at the NCO Cub on Base and gave some to the local radio stations in hopes they would play them. The rest we sold at the different venues we were playing.

My twenty-first birthday was in November and Jerry arranged to have a small gathering of friends over to his apartment for a party in my honor. My mom was going to call me at eight-o-clock that night to sing happy birthday to me. Singing happy birthday to each other on our birthday was a family tradition and eight-o-clock was a convenient time to call. What I didn't know, was Jerry had another arrangement at ten minutes after eight with a local disc jockey to play our record for the first time on the radio. So, while I was talking to my mom, our song played over the radio. I went crazy sharing the moment with my mom and everybody there broke into a round of applause. It was a wonderful surprise!

Our Record

Another great surprise came shortly after that. Jerry and I were riding in my car, with the top down, listening to the radio in Cedar Rapids, IA, when our record came on over the radio. I got excited, pulled the car over to the side of the road and turned the volume up high. We were shouting, "that's the Je-Rons, that's us!" What a thrill to hear our song being played over the radio again. The first time was on my birthday and it was very special to have shared it with my mom. Every time we heard it played over the radio since then was a realization of a dream come true.

Playing live at Russo's

The following week; Jerry, Mel and I took a day and drove to Chicago to promote our record. We met with a few radio people and they brought to our attention a small problem we weren't aware of. Our record was thirty-seconds longer than customary for conventional radio play. The thirty-seconds represented another spot for a paid commercial and could limit our record's exposure with the major radio stations. Jerry and I were upset! We felt our agent and his producer friend should have known better. Even so, our record ended up performing well in the medium size market and local stations.

One of the first local radio personalities to embrace us, was a Disc Jockey by the name of Chris Bailey. He had a daily radio program on KWWL and a TV program on Saturday morning. He ran a contest allowing the public to vote on new records being introduced on his station each week. Each day four new records were introduced and voted on. On Friday, the winners from each day were voted on and the winners from each week carried over to be voted on at the end of the month. The winning record at the end of the

A Promotional Photo

month, won the opportunity to play live on Chris's TV program. Our record won the contest and as a result, we played on Chris's TV program. During this same time, Chris was putting together a program in Altoona, PA to feature the long-awaited live performance of *The Monkees. The Monkees* were a successful band made up of actors, chosen to perform on a TV program called *The Monkees*. The TV executives hired top song writers and worked with the best studio musicians in the industry to make their records. The actors played their parts on TV and the songs became big hits. In fact, for a while they were bigger than the Beatles. Now it was time for *The Monkees* to play live. This event was going to happen in August of 1967. Chris mentioned that he would like us be one of the opening bands for the show. This was our big opportunity: the break we had hoped for: we all got excited!

MY LOVE FOR MUSIC VS MY LOVE FOR A WOMAN

We were selling our records wherever we played. We had a lot to look forward to over the next year and as luck would have it, we started to lose focus on our musical goals. Steve was married when we brought him into the band. Mel and Sharon were the next to get married. Soon afterwards, Jerry got married to Nancy. I was the only one not married, but I found a girl who I became madly in love with.

Joanne was special. I had been with a lot of different girls by now but not anyone quite like her. She was very pretty, easy to talk too and fun to be with. I told her I liked her, but my music would come first before I considered having any sort of long-term relationship; so she knew where my priorities were. I also knew I liked her a lot and with everyone else getting married, I could easily tie the knot with her. In fact, on one of my phone calls with my mom, I told her I met a great girl, who I really liked a lot.

From the time I met her, we saw each other nearly every day. She lived in a house with several other girls, close to Mercy Hospital; where she worked. One day when I was visiting her, we were sitting in the parlor or family room when someone knocked on the door and was yelling for Joanne to come outside. She had a strange look on her face and told me to sit in the family room while she went out to see what he wanted. She left and soon I heard an argument followed by a sound of someone being slapped. I immediately went outside and saw this guy had slapped Joanne. He then went into a crouch position, like he knew martial arts. He was in a rage and while yelling at me, he hit me in the side of my head. I responded by charging him, picking him up and throwing him over the porch railing into the hedge below! After I threw him over the railing, Joanne grabbed me and pulled me back into the house. We no sooner were in the house with the door closed, when he was pounding on the door and screaming at us. He stood there screaming and pounding on the door for about ten minutes before he finally left. He was crazy and we were afraid he was going to either break down the door or go through a window to get to us — when he left it was a quite a relief. In the meantime, while he was pounding on the door, I

Finding true love

asked Joanne who he was and why was he so angry? She sheepishly told me he was her fiancé. She told him everything was over between the two of them and was trying to give him his ring back. She didn't expect him to come over while I was there and when she went out on the porch to give him his ring, an argument ensued. It got over heated and he slapped her. He was insanely jealous.

It was a good thing he was in a rage, for Joanne told me he was a former Marine and was into martial arts. His rage kept him from thinking straight, allowing me the opportunity to pick him up and throw him off the porch the way I did.

Now, the fight was over but Joanne had some explaining to do. I had seen her with a diamond ring before but she told me it was from her grandmother. Joanne never told me she was engaged. She told me she had second thoughts about getting married to him even before she met me but didn't know how to break it off. Joanne knew he wouldn't understand and would get mad when she gave him his ring back. She apologized for lying and not telling me about being engaged in the beginning. She thought it might have hurt our relationship and didn't want to chance it. I now understood why her fiancé was so upset, but he didn't have a right to hit her. With everything settled, we jumped into my car and headed down the road to the night club in Cedar Falls, where I was playing that night.

With everyone in the Je-Rons married except me, Joanne and I started spending more time together. I really enjoyed being with her and felt we were right for each other. On the nights the band wasn't playing we would just hang out together and enjoy each other's company. One night we were sitting together on the couch in her parent's home when the movie, "Blue Hawaii" came on TV. I was a big Elvis fan and he was the star of the movie. Joanne's parents weren't home and we were watching the movie by ourselves. In the movie Elvis got married and when he started singing "The Hawaiian Wedding Song," I looked over at Joanne and asked her to marry me. I got caught up in the movie and felt this was as good a time as any to ask her. She said "yes," and the rest is history. If I had planned it, I would have asked her Dad for his permission first and then bought her a ring. We could hardly wait until her parents came home to tell them. After we told Joanne's parents we called my parents. We hadn't set a date yet but when we called my parents, my mom asked, "Have you set a date?" Before I could respond, Joanne said, "we are thinking the end of January." I told them, "we are not sure yet but will let them know once we get a handle on everything." I was thinking of having a longer engagement period than two months, especially since our record was out and opening doors to larger venues for us to play. After discussing it over, we decided, why wait? We were compatible and good for each other. She knew she only had two months to plan everything, so she needed to get organized. First, she checked with her church to see what dates were available. They gave her a couple of options and we decided on the 28th of January. Next, I called my parents to tell them our plans. I told them I would bring Joanne to Massachusetts during the week of Christmas to meet them. Next, was to visit with her Pastor for premarital counseling. We had three one-hour meetings with him. I told him I was a Unitarian and he told me, he felt we were compatible and in alignment with each other.

Driving to Massachusetts was a long drive. The Interstates were still under construction and back then it took us around 28 hours to drive from Iowa to my parents' home in Leominster. My parents were happy to see me and finally meet Joanne. It snowed while we were there and

Joanne had a chance to experience a white Christmas in New England. We drove around and met my grandmother, then spent some time shopping for stocking gifts. Mom and Dad liked Joanne and could see how comfortable she and I were together. Dad could tell we were in love, where Mom couldn't get used to the idea that her first born son was going to be getting married in less than two months, to someone who lived over 1,000 miles away.

On Christmas Eve we all went to the Unitarian Church to celebrate the festival of lights. It was a different experience for Joanne. We sang Christmas songs, yet there was no message about Jesus. The service was about spiritual enlightenment and the meaning of life. Joanne told me the service was cold and weird. I told her as a Unitarian, she was entitled to worship anyway she wanted too and we left it at that.

On Christmas day, we exchanged gifts and Joanne met some of my extended family. Joanne and I also opened our gifts to each other, which were the wedding bands we bought to be exchanged on our wedding day. They were white gold with three small diamonds on each band. Later in the week, Mom arranged a wedding shower for Joanne, which gave her a chance to meet more family and friends.

Our time in Leominster went by quickly and the day we were supposed to leave, we were hit with a lot of snow. We felt once we got off the hill and onto the main highways we would be ok. We put snow chains on the rear tires of my car and started on our trip back. We made it to the Massachusetts Turnpike when one of the chains broke and rapped around the rear axle. I had to pull off of the road and crawl under the car to unwrap the chain. It was cold, I was lying in slush, (which is melted snow); traffic was going by us at around 50 miles per hour and every truck going by, splattered me with more slush. My fingers were numb and I had to take my gloves off to unwrap the chains. I was miserable but finally I unraveled the chain from the rear axle, as well as, removed the chain from the other tire. I was wet and cold. I changed shirts but continued driving through the snow until we got to Ohio. In Ohio we started driving in sleet, which was a mixture of ice and snow. This was a dangerous road condition. So many cars were sliding off the highway and nothing could be done to help them. In fact, a car in front of us started sliding off of the highway into a ditch which ran along the side of the road, and when I applied my brakes to help them, my car started heading in the same direction as theirs. I immediately took my foot off of the brake. That corrected the direction we were headed in and we continued driving down the road.

I had driven in icy conditions growing up in Massachusetts but this was different. In all, we counted over fifty Winnebago's and countless cars and trucks in ditches by the time we made it to Iowa.

We drove nearly 32 hours non-stop back to Iowa in constant heavy winds, snow, ice and blizzard like conditions. By the time we reached Joanne's parents' home we were completely worn out but happy to be back home. I thanked God for getting us back safely. I still didn't know who or what God was, but I believed in a higher power and felt we were protected on our trip back from Massachusetts. God was at work with me and once married my life was going to radically change.

Chapter 10

"For where your treasure is, there your heart will be also." Matthew 6:21

Marriage/Move/New Beginnings

It was the last week in January. I had been playing in the band all week; up until the day before our wedding. It was snowing in Iowa and many states to the east were under severe weather conditions. Flights were canceled into Chicago and very little transportation was going into Iowa. My parents knew they had to get to Cedar Rapids by the 28th for our wedding and they were frantic! They were traveling not just with their luggage, but also with a couple of wedding gifts and my younger brother Brad.

They managed to make a flight out of Boston to Chicago, but were told nothing was going to Iowa on that day. My dad inquired about other modes of transportation going into Iowa and was told, maybe he could get there by train. He called the train depot in Chicago and they told him Amtrak was scheduled to go to Muscatine, Iowa later in the day but it would still leave them over eighty miles from Cedar Rapids. My dad called Joanne's dad, (Mel) and told him their situation. Mel told him, "If you can get to Muscatine, I will drive down there and pick you up."

My parents took a taxi from the airport to the train station and purchased tickets for the three of them, to go to Muscatine, Iowa on Amtrak. My dad called Mel back and gave him the information on when they should arrive. Mel then called Ernie Beanblossom, a friend of his; to see if he would make the drive with him. It was still snowing and the fastest way to Muscatine from Cedar Rapids was on secondary roads. The roads were covered with snow: they were dark and narrow too, but after the two plus hour drive, they made it to Muscatine.

Neither Mel nor my dad had met before. There were a lot of people getting off the train and Mel didn't know which couple in the crowd were my parents, until my dad happened to say to my mom, "I'll be glad when I can put these damn wedding gifts down." Mel heard my dad and said, "Did you say wedding gifts?" They laughed a sigh of relief, introduced themselves to each other and drove back to Cedar Rapids to get settled in for the night. My brother Donnie had also flown in from Hawaii, where he was stationed in the Navy. They all stayed in the one room efficiency apartment Joanne and I would call our home, after we were married.

It was funny. The snow had fallen all around Eastern Iowa but not much in Marion, where we were getting married. The next day the sun was out, the roads were clear and the church was all set up for the wedding. The guys in the band were the ushers. Donnie, my brother was the Groom's Man and Jerry was my Best Man. Joanne's sister, Kathy was the Maid of Honor and her best friend Donna Caldwell was the Brides Matron. The candle lighters were; my youngest brother, Brad and Joanne's brother, Jim.

Mr. and Mrs Bailey

The wedding went off without a hitch and afterwards there was a light reception dinner in the church. We didn't have any plans for a honeymoon, so Joanne's parents, sister and brother along with my parents and brothers, went with us to a famous restaurant in the Amana Colonies to celebrate the occasion.

A new Chapter begins

Joanne and I drove in a separate car, so when the meal was over we could get away whenever we wanted to. After the meal we spent time with the family talking about the wedding and then drove back to the Town House in Cedar Rapids, where we stayed for our honeymoon night. The Town House was a moderately priced hotel with very few amenities. We found our room and put the Don't Disturb sign on the doorknob. Once inside the room, Joanne decided she wanted a diet coke before settling in for the night. I called down to the front desk for room service, to see if someone would bring us two cans of diet coke. About ten minutes later the bellhop knocked on our door and gave us the two cans of diet coke. I told him thanks and gave him a five-dollar tip. That was a lot of money for a tip back then but it was my wedding night and I wanted everything to be special.

The very next day, as we left our room we noticed a coke machine only fifteen feet away from the door to our room. We started laughing and thought about giving the bellhop the five-dollar tip for something I could have done for just fifty cents. Fifty years later, we still laugh about it.

When the weekend was over my parents and Brad left to fly back to Massachusetts. My brother Donnie also left at the same time to go back to Hawaii and Joanne and I set up house in our one room efficiency apartment.

With all the changes going on in the band and me wanting something to do during the day, I got a full-time job in Cedar Rapids with a company called Dearborn Brass. My job was to strip the old chrome plating off of bathroom plumbing fixtures and get them ready to be plated with new chrome. I was working with different types of acids and after a couple of weeks I noticed how the chimneys by the acid bins, (where we de-chromed the bathroom fixtures) were all eaten away. I began thinking, I was breathing those fumes too. I knew breathing those fumes couldn't be very healthy, so at the end of the week I quit my job at Dearborn Brass.

What was ironic, at this stage of my life my biography could have read; shortly after being married, I was a singer in the band during the evening and had a job as a stripper during the day.

The next week I applied for and got the job as an expeditor at Collins Radio, in Cedar Rapids. It was a clean environment and the pay was good. I also got a lot of exercise by walking at least five miles a day taking materials to press operators throughout the plant.

Hanging with Donnie

With everyone in the band now married and working during the day, the band began to suffer. Jerry was the first one to leave and soon after we had to get a new drummer. We didn't practice like we used to, so we didn't introduce any new songs to our play list. Without Jerry, we went from a four-piece band to a trio and was losing the excitement we had just three months earlier.

It was the Je-Rons keeping me in Iowa and I began to see the handwriting on the wall. We were just a shell of who we once were. We no longer had the commitment we used to have and it was time to call it quits. With this decision we also gave up on our dream of opening for *The Monkees* in August. The big opportunity we had been waiting for was only four months away and just like that, we walked. The days of the Je-Rons were over. So, what do we do now?

Joanne and I talked about our options and decided to move to Massachusetts to start our new beginnings. I called my parents and told them of our plans to move back to Leominster and how we would probably need to live with them for a few weeks until we found an apartment. They were excited about our decision to move back and could hardly wait for us to get there.

In May, Joanne and I packed our belongings in a U-Haul trailer and headed to Leominster, Massachusetts to start our new life together. The U-Hall was packed mostly with my musical equipment, some household goods and our clothes. Once on the road, we drove all night and through the next day — arriving in Leominster in the early evening. Mom had my old bedroom made up for us and we unpacked our stuff. We put the majority of our stuff in their basement with the exception of our clothes.

Initially, I wanted to finish college. I had taken courses in Business, Psychology and German while I was in the Air Force to help me with my promotions. I was accepted by the University of Massachusetts, matriculated and was going to use the G.I. Bill to pay for it. I thought I wanted to be a child psychologist. I could go to school during the week and maybe even play in a band on the weekends for additional money.

During this time, I was visited by John Erdman, my life insurance man. He told me I should convert my G.I. insurance. I said, "I would as soon as I had extra money." I knew I had 120 days in which to exercise my conversion option. He asked me, "What was I going to do now that I was back home?" I told him, "I thought I would go back to school with the hopes of becoming a child psychologist someday." He then asked me, "What made me decide on becoming a child phycologist?" I said, "I think I would like to have a career where I can help people solve problems early in life to prepare themselves for a better future." He then told me, "I needed to talk to his sales manager at Prudential." I agreed to meet with his sales manager and John set up an appointment for me, for the following week. I still didn't know what I wanted to do and up until now, the only thing I ever thought of, was making it in the music business.

The next week, I met with John's sales manager, Rocky Pandiscio. Rocky and I hit it off right from the start. John had shared with Rocky, the conversation I had with him about wanting to be a child psychologist.

In the process of getting to know a little about each other, Rocky said, "John told me you were interested in becoming a child psychologist to help people solve problems while they were young, to help them become better citizens when they were older; is that right?" I said, "I think so, I'm still not sure." Rocky then asked me, "What if you could help young adults solve some of their financial problems while giving their families peace of mind? Would that appeal to you?" I said, "that sounds interesting too." He went on to say, "At Prudential, what I have explained to you, is what we do and the one thing to think about is; at Prudential we will pay you to become a successful counselor where in college you will pay them in the hopes of finding success on your own." That statement intrigued me. He then asked me if I would be willing to take a test to determine if I would qualify to work with them? I spent the next hour taking the personality profile test Prudential used to screen their applicants. Rocky graded the test and told me I passed with flying colors. He then told me, the next step would be to visit with the District Manager, who would have the final word. Rocky then scheduled me to see him in three weeks for a personal interview.

Over the next three weeks I had other job interviews too, but decided after talking to Rocky; to work with Prudential if the District Manager liked me. I also learned a few sales strategies during the job selection process. I had an interview with one other insurance company and took their personality profile test as well. It also proved I was suited for insurance sales, but this company had no base salary to work with. I could work with them but only on straight commissions. I wasn't too hot on that idea!

I met with Rocky's District Manager the next week. His name was William Robinson. He had a lot of questions for me. Many of the questions were about my time playing in the band. We talked about the possibilities of my finishing college and the thoughts I had of being a child psychologist. While this was all going on, Rocky waited for me in the conference room.

When my meeting with Mr. Robinson concluded, Rocky was called into the room with us. Mr. Robinson told us although I was suited for the position they had open, he was hesitant to hire me because of my past history in music. He went on to say the money Prudential pays to support new agents was substantial over five years and his income was directly tied to making the right decisions in the hiring process. I looked at Mr. Robinson and said, "that's ok." "I have been accepted by another insurance company and can start anytime with them." "I just wanted to give Prudential a chance, since my personal insurance has always been with them." Mr. Robinson then spoke up and said, "Well, let's not make any snap decisions just yet." I then said, "Let me think about this for a week." "I want to compare the opportunities I have and I'll let you know what I decide." Mr. Robinson told me he was going to be up at his summer place in Maine during the week but for me to call him there collect, when I have made my decision. What I discovered in that moment; was since I told him another insurance company wanted me; in his mind I now became more desirable to employ. I was the one who now had control and it was now my decision to make, not his. His decision would actually be made once I've made mine.

Rocky and I drove back from the District Office going over the interview I had. He told me he was hoping my decision would allow the two of us to work together with Prudential in the future. I knew in my mind I wanted to work for Prudential; they were the ones who were going to pay me to learn. I didn't say anything to Rocky about my thought process until I told Mr. Robinson my final decision. When I got back home I told Joanne I thought I had a job and will know more by the end of next week. When the end of next week rolled around I called Mr. Robinson at his summer home in Maine and told him I made my decision. I told him I would love to have the opportunity to work with Rocky and be one of the top sales people in the District. I couldn't believe what happened next; he got all excited and told me I made a great decision. We talked about five minutes more on how much Rocky wanted this to happen and how the two of them were really looking forward to seeing great things from me in the future. He then told me to report to Rocky the following Monday at 9:00 a.m. to complete my paperwork and start my training.

I met with Rocky on Monday as instructed and after completing my paperwork we started my training program. I was told — since I only had a small number of clients assigned for me to service — I would have a special contract with Prudential; to give me incentives or an additional bonus to write business — not already associated with the policyholders on the books. We discussed how I could maximize my contract by writing my friends or relatives and getting referred leads from them; or from any other sales I made. It reminded me of when I was building my paper route. Over the next couple of days, I put together a list of the people I knew for Rocky and I to call on. The first week Rocky also introduced me to some of the policyholders on the route assigned to me. I had about 100 families on the books to service and collected their premiums each month. While we were collecting their premiums, we were able to set up some sales appointments, which resulted in a couple of small sales. I was beginning to catch on. I was reading everything I could about the types of policies I could offer, learning the rate book and how to figure out what applications went with what products. By the end of my second week I decided I would try and sell something on my own, without Rocky. I didn't tell Rocky, I just went ahead and set up an appointment with my good friend Dennis Cormier. We sang and did a lot together in high school.

He was in a show band called "The Soul Survivors" and was home in between bookings. He was married and his wife was expecting their first child. I sat down with Denny and his wife Lynda at the supper table in their apartment. I explained what I was doing and made a pretty convincing presentation as to why he needed to buy life insurance on he and his wife. I had put together a presentation using a family policy to insure Denny, Lynda and any children they had in the future. The policy would also provide extra term coverage on Dennis to help Lynda raise the children should Dennis die while the children were young. I asked Dennis if he would like to have that extra coverage on Lynda too? He told me "No, but go ahead and write the policy as you explained it, without the extra coverage on Lynda."

I was excited, I wrote my first policy on my own and I could hardly wait until I could call Rocky and tell him. It was my first policy — and it would also become my first claim!

Dennis and I were very close. When the policy came back I delivered it and went over everything with him. After I delivered the policy, he wanted to talk to me. It seemed the rhythm guitar player was drafted into the Army and Denny thought maybe I might be interested in trying out for his spot in the band. I got excited and said I would love to try out and see if there was a fit. They were one of the top bands in New England at the time, complete with great choreography and topped off with a soulful brass section. I tried out and everything looked good, but now I needed to make a decision. I was doing well with Prudential and the band was doing a lot of traveling. They could be gone weeks at a time on tour. Being on tour would have been my dream a year ago but now I was married.

Joanne and I were living in our own apartment now. I usually left our apartment around 8:00 a.m. and worked up until 10:00 at night. Much of my selling would be at night to both the husband and wife after suppertime. Joanne started a job working as an assistant to a doctor in Leominster and was usually home by 5:00 p.m. Sometimes I would eat supper with her but many times I would not come home until I was done for the night. This one night I decided to sit in and play a set with the "Soul Survivors", at a night club in Fitchburg. When I came home, Joanne was still up and was upset because I didn't call her. Back then we didn't have cell phones and I relied on pay phones or the phones at the people's homes I was at. I didn't want to call her from the night club and thought she would be in bed by the time I got home. Well she wasn't, and she let me know if this was the way we were going to live, she would just as soon be back in Iowa. She knew I had been singing; my voice was a little hoarse, and the suit I was wearing smelled of smoke. It wasn't like I did anything wrong but she was upset over my choice of singing in a club, instead of coming home after work. I knew right then, I had to make a decision. I had to either be married to music or to Joanne. I couldn't have both, so I chose to be married to my wife and that night, I divorced music! The next day, I told Denny I wasn't going to play with the "Soul Survivors" but I will continue to be his insurance man. I made my decision and there was no looking back. I put all my efforts into being a sales leader in the District and my income rose accordingly.

Part of my strategy was to develop a survey to help me talk to people about their need for life insurance. I developed a survey about insurance needs and reached out to the people living in the same area I was servicing. I then developed a presentation to work with the new survey and was soon getting a lot of additional sales. In addition, I went to the court house and got the names of people discharged from the Military; eligible to convert their G.I. Insurance. It was a good way to use my daytime hours efficiently.

By the end of my first year I was one of the leading sales people in the District and my income was now where we could afford to buy a home. We found a nice house on a lake with a circular driveway. It was priced at $8200. We went to the bank and bought it. The banker told us, since we both were working, there was no reason why we shouldn't qualify for the loan.

Joanne's 21st Birthday

We qualified for the loan, made our down payment and bought the house. We moved our furniture from our apartment and was all settled in by the end of the month. During the month we had some additional news. We found out Joanne was pregnant and if we had waited just a couple more weeks to buy the house, we may not have qualified for the loan. Timing was everything and it was a good thing we applied for the loan when we did.

Joanne and I didn't see much of each other during the week due to our busy work schedules. On the weekends though, we tried to do something fun, like getting together with my old friends; who were now becoming her friends too. Many of those weekends were spent with Denny and Lynda: when Denny was not playing in the band. By this time, they had a daughter, and so much of their free time was spent with her. It was on one of those weekends, we learned Lynda was having some medical issues and during the next week was diagnosed with Hodgkin's disease. Later that month she had surgery and they felt confident the cancer was eradicated.

Later Dennis called and asked me to add the extra insurance coverage to Lynda's policy. The coverage I had talked to him about when he first purchased the insurance. I had to tell him, we would have to wait five years before additional insurance could be looked at, due to her having the cancer. He understood, as sometimes cancer cells hide somewhere in the body and come back later. Unfortunately, that is what happened in Lynda's situation. Her cancer came back, she went on chemo and eventually passed away. Now Dennis had the responsibilities of raising his daughter by himself. Family and friends helped, but raising her as a single parent was going to be hard.

As a life insurance man, this taught me more than any training Prudential could have given me. I learned first-hand the need for life insurance on both the husband and wife. I saw how life insurance provided a level of financial support along with the emotional support at the time of need. With my new conviction, I now designed insurance plans to provide more than just basic coverage on both the husband and wife. I also designed the plans to help them accumulate extra money for the future, when they no longer needed the protection.,.

Working with the families originally assigned to me, my weekly surveys, chasing after newly-weds and soldiers being discharged from the service was keeping me pretty busy. I was working nearly every day of the week, plus at this point, we were getting ready to have a baby of our own.

Everything was going well and then we received word Joanne's mom was having problems with double vision and weakness in her legs. She had gone through a battery of tests to determine the cause and when the results came back, she was diagnosed with Multiple Sclerosis; a progressive and disabling disease. We read up on the disease and saw how debilitating M.S. could be. This was serious and there was no cure! We felt terrible but life had to go on.

In New England the Fall was spectacular and where we were living, all we had to do was look across the street to see all the different colors of nature casting her image on the

Digging out from the plow

lake water. I loved riding around New England in the Fall. Especially near the lakes or up to my parents', where you could see forever. It was a special time of the year for me. That was the fall; but when winter came — it could be brutal.

The first year in our new home when winter came — we were hit with a huge snow storm. I hired a snow removal service to plow my driveway because the snow was too high and too heavy for me to shovel by hand. We had a circular driveway so all they had to do was start on one side of the driveway and push the snow back out on the street. Once on the street they could push it off to the side of the road.

The night before the storm, I pulled my car up on the front lawn away from the driveway. About halfway through the storm I noticed the snow accumulating and drifting to the point of where I couldn't see my car, so I put a broom at the end of my bumper. It was sticking out of the snow to show the driver of the snow plow where my car was. I then called the snow removal service to let them know what I did. The snow plow came through later and cleared my driveway, but I still ended up having to dig my car out from where I parked it on the lawn. I could shovel out my car, I just didn't want to shovel the whole driveway when we had a big storm.

The broom marks my car

By the end of the year I hit my goal to qualify for Prudential's Sales Leader's Convention and was recognized as the District's "Rookie of The Year." I had worked hard and was getting recognized for the work I did. I was even asked to speak at the year-end awards banquet that January. I was flying high!

Joanne had stopped working a few months earlier and with the winter upon us, she was feeling house bound. We were expecting another large round of snow to hit, so she wanted to take a ride out to my parents' home before the snow hit us too hard. She just wanted to get out of the house and take a nice ride. The snow was starting to fall pretty hard and I knew it would probably be heavier where my parents lived. When we got to my parents' home, the snow was already beginning to accumulate and drifts were forming across the road. The wind was blowing hard and when we reached the top of the hill where my parents lived, we stopped on the side of the road to gaze at the view before turning onto my parent's street. In just the short time we stopped to look at the view, we got stuck. The snow and the wind was picking up. I knew I better get Joanne into my parents' home before getting the car free from where I was stuck. When we walked into their house, my parents were shocked to see us, especially with Joanne eight months pregnant and in the middle of a blizzard. Dad went outside with me. Together we freed my car from where it was and I drove it into their driveway. Once inside the house safe, Dad began telling me how stupid it was for us to be out driving around in this storm, with Joanne eight months pregnant. All I could do was agree with him.

Dad was a volunteer fireman and he called Wayne Schofield, another fireman who lived up the street from them, to formulate a backup plan in case Joanne needed to see the doctor before the streets were cleared. Both my Dad and Wayne had snow mobiles to transport her if the snow wasn't passable by cars or trucks. Thankfully Joanne was fine up on the hill, for we were stranded there for four days before the streets were cleared enough to drive on. We were glad we never had to use the backup plan. Joanne also had a little taste now of what it was like for me living on Wachusett Street in the wintertime as a teenager.

We got a lot of snow that winter and February wasn't letting up either. Even with all the snow, I was still making my calls, having appointments and selling insurance; while waiting for Joanne's delivery date to arrive. Every night I was out, but I would try and call home every couple of hours to check with Joanne to see how she was doing. On February 13th, I was on an appointment about an hour away from home and I realized I hadn't checked in with Joanne. I was in the middle of writing an application for insurance on this young couple, when I asked them if I could use their phone to make a quick call to see how my wife was doing? When I called, Joanne was frantic: she didn't know how to get in touch with me! Her water had broken and she called my mom. I told her I was on my way! I told the young couple my wife was in labor and I needed to come back and finish everything at a later time. I ran out of their house and drove my car as fast as I could on those icy roads to get to Joanne! Dad was the first person to show up and wanted to take Joanne to the hospital in his company's truck. Joanne would have nothing to do with that. Next a friend showed up and she wanted to take her to the hospital in her Corvette. Joanne told her thanks but she was waiting for me. When I finally arrived, everyone there was telling me she was having contractions and I needed to get her to the hospital at once! I helped her into my car and drove as fast as I could to the

Leominster Hospital. Her pains were now less than ten minutes apart and we knew in a few hours we were going to have a baby. When I got to the hospital the attendants met us in the emergency room. They took Joanne to another part of the hospital, while I filled out the insurance forms. In those days, you weren't permitted to be with your wife in the birthing area, and in our case Joanne didn't go right into the birthing room. She was put in a holding area all by herself located in the hallway near the birthing room; because no rooms were available for her to wait in on that side of the hospital.

The attendant located me back in the waiting room to advise me to go home and get some rest; for she could be in labor a few hours or more. The waiting room was full of old and stiff furniture. To try and sleep there would have been very uncomfortable; so I went home to get some rest. I no sooner got home when the hospital called to let me know I was about to become a father. I called my parents, as well as Joanne's parents, to let them know what was going on and I went to the hospital. When I got to the hospital Mom was also just getting there. We went into the maternity ward together and with Mom being a nurse, she marched back to where the delivery room was. We got there just as a friend of Mom's was cleaning my daughter, wrapping her in swaddling cloth and putting a ribbon in her hair. All I could think of was, wow...she was so beautiful. Mom and I just looked at each other with tears in our eyes, as we celebrated this new branch on our family tree. The nurse then carried my daughter back to Joanne, where she was waiting to hold her. When we walked in to see Joanne, she was lying in bed with a big smile on her face holding our daughter next to her chest. She was so proud of what she was showing me. We named our daughter Kimberly, the name we both decided on

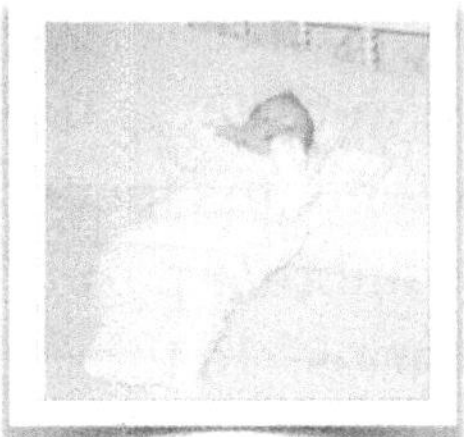
Kim at 2 weeks

if we had a girl. One other thing to note; she was born on Valentine's Day, which was special in itself but this was also my dad's birthday. So, as a special birthday present, we gave Dad his first grandchild.

Over the next couple of days in the hospital, Joanne and Kim saw my family a lot: especially Mom, Dad and my brothers. On the third day I picked up Joanne and Kim and took them home. Joanne had Kim all dressed up in pink and lace from some clothes she received from one of her baby showers. It was a Kodak moment and Kim was the star of the show!

A few days later Joanne's mom and grandmother flew out from Iowa to be with us tor a few days. Life was getting a lot more exciting with Kim around. We were sleeping less but we were having lots of fun.

The next week I called the couple I was visiting with when Joanne's water broke and set up another appointment to finish writing their applications for life insurance. They told me I was in such a hurry to leave after talking to my wife on the phone, that I left everything with them, including my briefcase and unfinished applications on the table. I told them I hadn't even thought about my briefcase until then. We laughed and I told them all about my life as a new dad. I then saw them the following day, picked up my briefcase and completed their applications .

Great-Grandma Meggers

Joanne's Mom and Grandmother were soon back in Iowa and now it was just the three of us. I was back into my work schedule but had to be more flexible knowing I might be needed to run an errand or two during the day.

With Kim as a new born baby, we didn't go out much. This was during the winter so when we did go somewhere, just dressing her to go outdoors was a major event. It was just easier to stay at home. One cold weekend while Joanne was playing with Kim, I decided to sit down and write a song. It had been a long time since I had written any songs or even picked up my guitar. Music and I were estranged from each other, but seeing Joanne and Kim together like that motivated me to write this song.

Kim

KIMBERLY'S SONG

A little girl came home to me
Wrapped up in a baby bunting
She turned her head and looked at me
I knew that she was something
Now baby's clothes of pink and lace
Showed me how my family's growing
And watching smiles on my wife's face
Meant she's proud of what she's showing
It was just nine months ago she was just a dream
But she's been sent from heaven
to make her presence seen
As parents now our lives have changed
And a new routine's begun
We're changing pants and sleeping less
Still having lots of fun
Yes life can be oh so wonderful when you raise a family
And if you have a girl why don't you do what we did
And call her Kimberly
Yes if you have a girl you can do what we did
And call her Kimberly

It was a personal song that I had written about Kim but in a month it will become a special key to open up additional opportunities for me with Prudential.

Chapter 11

"And my God will meet all your needs according to His riches of His glory in Christ Jesus."
Philippians 4:19

Early Success/Music Open Doors

Kim was only two months old when I went to Prudential's Sales Leaders Convention at the Diplomat Hotel in Miami, Florida, in April of 1969. To begin my adventure, Rocky, my Sales Manager, picked me up and we drove to Logan Airport in Boston. On our way to the airport we stopped at a neighborhood bar Rocky was familiar with and he introduced me to eating clams on a half shell. He said, "You can't eat the clams on a half shell without having a drink to wash it down," so he ordered a drink consisting of Seagram Seven whisky and seven-up for himself. He then asked me, "What would you like to drink?" I said, "I will have the same." I never was much of a drinker, except for my time in Germany, where I acquired the taste for drinking German beer. I was now with Rocky and if he had a seven and seven, I was going to have one too. Before the clams were finished, Rocky ordered another round for us and by the time we got to the airport, I was starting to feel the drinks I just had. We got on the plane and found our seats. When we were in the air, the stewardess came around and Rocky ordered two more Seagram Seven and seven-ups for us. Rocky fell asleep and when the stewardess came around again she asked me if

I would like another drink. I said sure and when she asked me what I was drinking, all I could think of was Cutty Sark and seven. Oops, novice drinkers should never mix scotch and whisky together. I noticed that drink had a different taste to it but I drank it anyway. That drink plus the altitude did it. I was officially drunk. I went to sleep and when I woke up we were in Miami. My stomach was upset and I also had a horrible headache. I told Rocky about my experience ordering my drink and he just laughed. I was actually, still a little tipsy when I got off the plane. Rocky and I then managed to get our luggage and navigate through the airport where everyone from Prudential going to the Diplomat Hotel was supposed to meet.

At the hotel, we met up with Mr. Robinson our District Manager who came down a day early. That evening we enjoyed a fantastic meal with a welcome from the President and Senior Executive Vice President of Prudential's Home Service Division. The first day of the convention was great and I met sales leaders from around the country.

The next day we had meetings in the morning and had the afternoon to ourselves. For me, I just wanted to go to the beach and after lunch as I was headed to the beach, I was approached by Rocky and Mr. Robinson, my District Manager. I guess my name came up in a conversation Mr. Robinson had with the Senior Executive Vice President. They were talking about the various backgrounds of the new sales leaders and Mr. Robinson mentioned I used to be a singer in a Rock Band. In the course of the conversation the Executive Vice President asked Mr. Robinson if he thought I might be interested in playing at a party they were having for the Home Office executives and wives that night. Mr. Robinson then handed me a formal invitation from the Senior Vice President, inviting me to attend and play for the

Home Office party that night. I told Mr. Robinson I would be happy to play at their party, as long as I was just playing back ground music and they provided the guitar. I told them I preferred playing a Gibson acoustic guitar if possible.

I was nervous about playing by myself in this format but I went to the party. When I got there, I met the Senior Vice President and before the night was over, I met nearly all of the different Home Office executives and their wives. I was given a nice Gibson acoustic guitar to play and I positioned myself on a stool in an area of the room where I could be heard but not in the flow of everything. The men were all over by the bar smoking cigars, drinking their drinks and talking business. The women on the other hand were at the tables talking to each other, most likely about their children. I felt a little strange but I started singing and playing an assortment of songs I felt appropriate for the event. When I started singing songs by Elvis and Ricky Nelson the women started leaving their tables and started gathering around me. They started making requests and I did my best to accommodate them. Pretty soon we were all singing Beatle songs and having a good time. In between the songs I would talk and allow the atmosphere to be more intimate. As an example, I told them I proposed to my wife while watching the Elvis Movie “Blue Hawaii” on TV and this next song was one of the songs that inspired me. I then sang, “Wise Men Say” followed by, the “Hawaiian Wedding Song.” I also told them I was a new father and I wrote a song for my daughter. I then asked them if they would like to hear it and they all said yes. I told them the back story to the song and started singing it. When I finished the song, they were all crying and coming up to hug me. By now the men were all wondering what was going on? They slowly came over and started joining in on the fun we were having. The party was only two hours long and when it was over, the Senior Executive Vice President came over to me and said, "My wife told me you are a brand-new father and you sang an original song you wrote for your daughter." He went on to say, "She suggested I make a place in the program for you to sing your song to the attendees at the convention tomorrow." He then asked me, if I would be interested in doing that? I told him, "It would be an honor."

The next day I couldn't wait to tell Rocky and Mr. Robinson what went on at the party and my inclusion in the convention's program. Mr. Robinson told me I was really making a great impression with the right people and he was excited about my playing for the convention attendees. When my time came to do my song, I was introduced as; Ron Bailey, "Rookie of The Year" for The Worcester East District and a brand-new father who wrote a song for his new daughter.

There were over 4,000 people in attendance and it was just me with a couple of microphones. One for the guitar and one for my voice. Fortunately, the acoustics were great and the song went over well. I received a lot of good feedback from the Home Office people I met the previous night, as well as, the different sales leaders who were there as attendees.

I didn't know it at the time but because of sharing my music at the party, my career with Prudential was about to go into overdrive.

Chapter 12

"Hope deferred makes the heart sick, but desire fulfilled is a tree of life." Proverbs 13:12

Fast Track Into Management

After coming back from the convention, Mr. Robinson wanted me to talk to the District Agents about why they should make every effort to qualify for the next convention. I shared the fun I had, my impressions of the convention and the knowledge I gained from being there. When I finished speaking, Mr. Robinson challenged us to make next year's sales leader's convention our goal and announced the location for the next one.

A couple of weeks later I received a call from Mr. Robinson to let me know I was selected to be a part of a new management training program Prudential was developing. The training program would take place twice a month at the Home Office in Boston. Mr. Robinson told me this was a tremendous opportunity for me, especially since I've already met some of the people involved with the program at the convention.

Everything was coming together. My sales continued to stay strong, I continued to build a steady stream of prospects and I was rubbing shoulders with all the right people to insure my future with Prudential.

In June, Lori Bailey was born and my brother Donnie became a father. Now our parents had two granddaughters to show off and spoil. Lori and Kim were only four months apart and were so cute together. Life was good!

In July, Joanne and I took a trip to Iowa to show off Kim to Joanne's family. I could tell Joanne really missed her family and with her mom having multiple sclerosis, she felt torn not being around to help her. I could also see how Kim brought happiness to Helen, Joanne's mom. Joanne and I began talking about possibly moving back to Iowa so Joanne could be involved with helping her mom. We felt having Kim there would help Helen in her fight against MS.

I was torn but I agreed to meet with Prudential's District Manager in Cedar Rapids, Iowa to see what opportunities were available; if we decided to make a move. The District Manager's name was Chester Affeldt. He was a nice, very professional looking older man. I told him about myself and what I had been doing since joining Prudential. I shared with him the special contract I had with Prudential for writing business and the new management program I was participating in. Mr. Affeldt seemed interested in my story and then he said, "timing is everything in life." "You being here at this particular time could be good for both you and for the District." He went on to tell me, Perry West, one of his twenty plus year veterans was on disability and will be retiring the end of the year. If I moved there, I will be able to inherit his book of business to service. He has one of the best books of business in the office and everyone he works with loves him. He is "Mister Insurance Man" to the community and highly thought of in the office. I thought that was worth considering. Mr. Affeldt told me he would check with his Home Office for their guidance on everything and see what steps needed to be taken, if I were to make a move.

I told Joanne about my meeting with Mr. Affeldt, what my impressions were of the office and what he told me about the possibility of inheriting a well-established book of business; if we moved there. She got all excited about the prospects of moving back to Iowa but now I had to figure it all out in my mind. How was I going to break the news to my parents...especially my mom? What was this going to do to them? Next, how was I going to explain this to Rocky and Mr. Robinson, who have been in my corner ever since I joined Prudential? How was my moving going to affect my management opportunities with Prudential? Finally, we would need to sell our home and start over in an area less familiar to me. I would have a lot to think about once I knew how Prudential felt about me moving from Massachusetts to Iowa. In making decisions my thought was, I will make my decision based on my understanding of the situation and then work hard to make the choice I make the right one.

Today, this decision would have been a lot easier to make. My first action would be to pray about it. I would tell the Lord the desires of my heart and ask Him to give me wisdom to make the right decisions. I would then wait for His peace to help guide me in my decisions.

In the Bible it says in Philippians 4:6 NIV. "Do not be anxious about anything, but in every situation, by prayer and supplication, with thanksgiving, let your requests be made known to God, and the peace of God which transcends all understanding, will guard your heart and your mind in Christ Jesus."

As I look back, this was another time when it was apparent, God was aligning me with the plans He had for my life. I had to be in Iowa for all the pieces of my life to come together.

MOVING BACK TO IOWA

When we got back to Leominster, I received a call from Mr. Affeldt. He told me the North Central Home Office in Minneapolis checked with New England's Home office in Boston and have worked out the details; if I make a move. Mr. Affeldt told me he was excited to have me on board, if we move and to feel free to call him for any reason.

Joanne and I spent a lot of time weighing the pluses and minuses of the move before actually making our final decision. With Prudential's approval given, we sat down with my parents and told them our plans. We explained about the opportunity waiting for me in Cedar Rapids with Prudential and Joanne's concern for her mom's health. Mom took it pretty hard but tried to understand it from Joanne's point of view. Dad knew I was supporting Joanne and understood the position I was in. We had a few more months yet before we moved and a lot of decisions that still needed to be made. I felt relieved after talking to my parents. I was torn but I knew Mom and Dad still had Lori there to love on.

Next, I set up a meeting with Rocky and Mr. Robinson to explain my situation to them. They were surprised but understood how my decision was made and where my mind was at. They told me I had a job there as long as I wanted it. I really appreciated their understanding my situation and supporting me through my next step, which was to sell my house. I continued to sell insurance but my focus now was on spending as much time as I could with my family while getting prepared to move.

We had a few road blocks trying to sell the house but managed to sell it in September with the possession date of November 1st. My contract with Prudential in

Massachusetts would end on October 31st, meaning we had to move by October 31st: my mom's birthday!

The weekend before my last day at work, the guys in the office scheduled a deep-sea fishing trip, as a going away party for me.

We took the fishing boat out of Boston Harbor and spent the day fishing, telling stories and drinking beer. I caught a 30-pound Cod fish while out to sea. The Captain of the boat gutted it, packed it in ice and put it into a Styrofoam cooler for me. My plan was to take it back to Iowa with me. While on the boat the guys from the office also presented me with a going away gift. When I opened it I saw they had bought me a pair of bib overalls as a joke, to use on my business appointments in Iowa. We all had a great laugh and it was a bitter sweet moment. It was sad leaving Rocky and all the guys I worked with.

The last week in Leominster was sad for me. Even though Don and his wife would still be there with Lori, their other granddaughter, I felt my parent's sadness of our moving over 1,000 miles away. Leaving this time was harder for me than when I first went into the Air Force, but our decision was made and we knew what we had to do.

On our way out of town, we stopped at my parents' house one last time, to give Mom her birthday gift and wish her a happy birthday before starting our long road trip to Iowa. I knew the move was making Joanne happy but at the same time, I knew it was tearing my mom's heart to pieces.

Once on the road we settled into our trip to Iowa. We had the Cod fish on ice in a large ice cooler in the U-Haul trailer and I was excited to show my father-in-law what I had caught. After driving for a couple of hours, we stopped to change Kim's diaper and to go to the bathroom. We had continued on down the Interstate when Joanne realized she didn't have her purse. She left it in the rest area. Panic set in! All the money from the sale of our house and all of our savings was in her purse and we couldn't just turn around to go back. We had to wait until we got to the next exit before going back. All the way back I had a sick feeling in my stomach. It took us about twenty minutes to get back to the rest stop we were at. I parked the car and Joanne ran into the Ladies Room where she left it. I remained in the car with Kim praying for Joanne to find her purse intact. Luckily for us, the purse and its contents was still where she left it.

She came back to the car waving her hands and thanking God for protecting us. Wow, we were so thankful for His protection! I felt a higher power was at work in our lives protecting us.

We drove to Ohio before checking into a hotel for the night. In spite of the delays, we were making pretty good time. I checked the trailer to see if any of the contents had shifted and to put more ice on the Cod fish. When I opened the cooler to put more ice on the fish, I could smell it beginning to decay. I put all new ice in the cooler and hoped it would prevent it from spoiling anymore.

We spent the night at the hotel and in the morning I checked on the Cod fish before continuing our drive to Iowa. Much to my dismay the smell had gotten worse and I ended up throwing it away. Now I wished I would have had the Cod filleted by the Captain of the boat we were fishing on. We could have eaten some during the week and left the rest with my parents to eat later.

After driving for another ten hours we arrived at Joanne's parents' home; where we would be staying until we bought our own home in Marion.

Chapter 13

"This is the confidence we have in approaching God; that if we ask anything according to His will, He hears us." 1 John 5:14

Working Thru The Transition

My contract in Massachusetts with Prudential ended October 31,1969 and my new contract wouldn't start in Iowa until I was licensed. We didn't recognize it at the time, but that would become a problem in Iowa. Both my new manager and I, thought I would receive the same income in Iowa as I had in Massachusetts while in transition. We were wrong! I had a special contract in Massachusetts: different from the one I would have, once I was licensed in Iowa. I could still operate on a non-resident license in Iowa until I passed my resident's test, but it could present problems qualifying for a house loan. This move was going to present a few more challenges than we initially expected.

During this time Joanne and I continued to look for a house with a realtor. After looking for a couple of weeks, we found one we liked, but now our next step was qualifying for the loan. Thc bank needed to know we were able to afford the mortgage payments and with my contracts up in the air with Prudential, we couldn't show how we could. So, we had Prudential write a letter to the bank for some assurance of my income over the next twelve months, based on my past sales results. Fortunately, the bank accepted Prudential's letter and we were able to buy the house.

Our home in Marion, IA

The next few months were tough. I passed all my licensing requirements but operating on a non-residents license kept me from receiving extra income from servicing the clients assigned to me.

I continued to service them, with the hope of receiving retro-active pay when my Iowa contract with Prudential was completed. That never happened due to the legal language written into the contracts, and once licensed, I had to wait another 13 weeks to complete my pay cycle.

Money was scarce for us during those weeks. One of the areas we scrimped on was the way we ate. Joanne was creative and learned how to make different types of soup to get us through those weeks. She would go to the butcher at the grocery store and ask if they had any bones for our dog to chew on. Well, we didn't have a dog; it was for us. With those bones she made different types of soup, by adding different vegetables to the broth. Sometimes when we were lucky, the bones even had meat on them. At any rate; we made it through those days, and once my pay cycle was completed, we were back to normal.

I had to be focused on sales! I was given the files and collection details on the clients assigned to me. I set up appointments as before, but this time it was different. Perry West, the agent who was supposed to be on disability, was also calling on these same people. He had been their agent for over twenty years and was; "Mr. Insurance Man" to them. I was performing client reviews and making insurance planning recommendations, but before they did anything, they called Perry to get his opinion. He would then visit with them about the recommendations I made and write the insurance. He had been told I was the new insurance man for those clients and just couldn't understand why he wasn't allowed to sell insurance to the clients he had built up over the years. The problem was – Prudential didn't care. He wouldn't be paid the service fee for servicing those clients but he was still licensed and in Prudential's eyes, he could still sell insurance. Fortunately, my District Manager talked to Perry and made him realize the situation I was in. We had a few more instances in the first six months, where we bumped heads, but soon I was winning friends and building a good clientele. I worked hard and each month my goal was to be on pace for the convention. I wanted to be the top salesman in the District.

By the end of 1970 I reached my goals, qualified for the "Sales Leader's Convention" and ended up being named the "Rookie of The Year" for the Northeast Iowa District.

I started off 1971 with the news Joanne was pregnant. We were excited knowing we were going to have an addition to our family, come September. Kim was two years old and we thought it was perfect timing to have another child. The pregnancy went well with the exception of having to go through Iowa's hot summer, and everyone was taking bets on whether we were going to have a boy or a girl. Joanne was carrying this baby different than she carried Kim, so we felt we were going to have a boy this time.

During the summer I didn't play as much golf on Friday afternoon's due to the high heat. Instead, I played on Saturday morning. We would usually get a tee time around 6:30 or 7:00 am and be done by around noon to beat the heat. On September 4th, Joanne was asleep when I left to play golf. I had just finished the second hole when I saw a golf cart racing down the cart path to join up with us. It was being driven by my father-in-law. He yelled to me, "Hop in the cart, we need to get you home right away! You're going to have a baby today." My friends told me they would take care of my clubs and I jumped into the golf cart with Mel. Apparently, her water broke after I left the house, so she called her parents. Her mom came over to take care of Kim while Mel drove to the golf course to pick me up. When we got back to my house, Joanne was all packed and ready to go. The hospital was only twenty minutes away, but since it was Saturday with very light traffic, I probably made it in ten. The labor pains she was having, motivated me to drive fast and by the time we reached the hospital, her pains had intensified even more. They immediately took her into delivery and I went to the waiting room.

In less than two hours, Dr. Orcutt came out from the delivery room and told me, "Congratulations, you have a beautiful baby boy." I cried with tears of joy and asked "How is Joanne doing?" He said "she's doing great and you should be able to see her shortly." When I went in to see her she was all smiles and she had our son tucked up under her arm. He was wrapped in swaddling and on his arm was a little bracelet with his name, Todd Bailey, spelled out in beads. It was such a beautiful sight to behold. Todd Roland Bailey was the name we decided on if we had a boy. Roland, was named after my dad and me. We now had a boy and a girl. What a blessing!

I wanted to do something special to show Joanne my appreciation for giving me a son, as well as, let the town of Marion know we just had a baby boy.

I was friends with the manager of the local Hardy's hamburger place in Marion and they had a large sign on the main street coming into town for advertising the daily specials. I wanted everyone to know we had a boy, so he allowed me to use the sign for a week. The sign read,

"Joanne, thank's for my son — Todd Roland Bailey — born September 4, 1971." Joanne was moved when she saw the sign and thought it was really special.

Everyone was excited to greet Todd except his big sister Kim. Up until now she had been the queen bee and the center of attention. Now she had to share the spot light and initially be over shadowed by the attention her little brother was getting. Initially, she got upset being upstaged by her younger brother and told us to take him back to the hospital where we got him.

My parents drove up from Massachusetts to join the celebration and they were with us for a week. They loved being in Iowa with us and loving on their grandchildren. Kim was getting a lot of attention from them and they loved playing with her. Kim was their first grandchild and they hadn't seen her for over a year.

While my mom and dad were still in Iowa, Mel, Dad and I got to talking about how fast time flies. Mel and Dad were remembering back to when they were my age and that in just six months, my dad would be turning 50. My dad went on to explain why he never thought he would live to be 50. It seemed his dad had died at 42 and his only brother at 47. They both died from issues relating to the heart. My dad then made the comment, "I am the oldest surviving male in my family." Mel and my dad talked about turning 50 and joked about me being in my twenties. The emphasis was on how fleeting life was.

Our family is growing

We had a great week with my parents, but soon they had to go back to Massachusetts and I had to get back to work. As a commissioned sales person, I had work piling up and waiting for me back at the office. I had planned my work schedule ahead of time, knowing I was going to take a week off, once the baby was born and everything went as planned. In fact, even though I took the week off, I still made phone calls from home to set up selling appointments for the following week, to try and stay on schedule for my goals.

Todd and Kim

I was now hitting on all cylinders again! I was doing a lot of client reviews, seeing the newlyweds and converting the SGLI insurance on soldiers being discharged from the service. I was also doing joint sales with other agents in the office. In addition; I introduced my way of prospecting, using the survey I had developed back in Massachusetts, to the District agents; to make selling fun!

Up until this point, church wasn't much of a priority to us. But, Joanne and I both felt with Kim getting older, it should be important, so we decided to attend the Marion Christian Church, where we got married. This was the church Joanne had grown up in, so we already knew people there. I also looked at church as an additional prospecting source for my insurance business.

Attending church on Sunday became part of our life and after a few months we were asked to join. We said sure and were brought before the congregation to repeat our vows before the congregation. It felt like I was getting married to the church. We stood in front of the congregation and the pastor said, "If you except Jesus as your savior and want to join the Marion Christian Church say I do." I then said "I do." It was more rhetoric than anything personal. As a Unitarian, I didn't know any difference. I wasn't trying to be born again, I was joining the church. My born-again experience was still a few years away.

In November of 1971 my grandmother, Sadie Bailey passed away. She lived to the age of 82 and died of colon cancer. Apparently she had been ill for some time but never told anyone, except maybe my dad. My dad was very close to her and I called to talk to him about whether or not I should come home for her funeral. He said it was up to me. The funeral was just going to be a small family get together and with us just having a new baby, he would certainly understand if we didn't come. I felt bad not going back for her funeral but with the year-end and holidays approaching, I didn't think I could give up the time, as well as, endure the extra expense to go back. Besides, I wanted to remember her as the fun loving, sweet grandmother; who let me stay up late to play cards with her when I was a young kid.

By the end of 1971, in spite of some of the setbacks I had, I was named the "Salesman of The Year" for the District, qualified for the "Sales Leaders Convention" again and was a recipient of the "Northern Star Award" for being one of the leading agents in the Region. My hard work was paying off.

DIVING INTO MANAGEMENT WITH PRUDENTIAL

Chester Affeldt, my District Manager was proud of me and in 1972 he promoted me to the Sales Manager's position. This completed my first goal in management. I had a nice corner office where I could proudly display my awards and seven agents were assigned to me.

Selling insurance though is a high turnover business and soon I had a couple of openings to fill. I was learning first hand why Sales Managers got discouraged and burned out. If I had an open agency, I had to either service the agency myself or pay another agent to service it for me. I also had to work with the agents assigned to me, as well as provide sales training to the new agents in the office. Inheriting agents was also challenging. I had a couple of veteran agents who had been in the business ten or more years and were just set in their ways. I had to win them over and help them increase their income, without applying undo pressure to them. The young agents were fun to work with but they could run you ragged, taking you to a lot of unqualified prospects. My goal was to try to work with each of them to increase their sales.

My staff of seven agents was soon full again and we were all working together. I set goals for the agents each week and if we met those goals by Thursday, we could play golf on Friday afternoon, after the morning meeting. The old veterans even got involved and by the end of the year we had nearly sixty percent of my sales team qualifying for the "Sales Leaders Convention," and as a manager I qualified for the Region's "Northern Star Award."

Having balance in our lives was essential, so in addition to working hard and raising a family, we were now regular church attendees. We went to Sunday school, as well as, the regular church services each week. There we met Ray and Nancy Hild and their family. They were new friends and we looked forward to being in church with them each week.

At the end of the summer I was asked to be a Deacon by one of the Elders – and I accepted. I really didn't have to do anything as a Deacon, except attend a meeting once a quarter. It felt good to be gaining influence in the church we were married in. Joanne said she was proud of me.

In the Fall of 1972 my District Manager, Chet Affeldt had become disabled and was replaced by Orrin Smith. Orrin was a nice guy but was more of a hands-on manager. In his first month, he wanted the sales managers to put together a sales plan for the rest of the year and an action plan to support it. I got excited and wrote down the goals I had for my sales team. I was a big thinker and my goal was simple. I wanted everyone on my staff to qualify for the "Sales Leaders Convention" by the end of 1973. However, when I sat down with Orrin to present my goals to him, he looked at them, handed them back and told me to make them realistic. I thought they were realistic. I felt if I could lead my team by selling with them, we could all qualify for the convention. He didn't think it was reasonable and burst my bubble. I rewrote the goals to satisfy his requirements and by the end of the year; had two agents promoted to Sales Manager positions with nearly eighty percent of the remaining agents on my staff qualifying for the "Sales Leaders Convention." I again qualified for the "Northern Star Award" for management. I have to admit, at this point in my life I was proud of my accomplishments and maybe even a little arrogant. I felt I worked hard and was deserving of the recognition I was receiving. I thought of myself as the Captain of my ship and the master of my fate with my mantra being, "If it was going to be, it was up to me!"

In April of 1973 we got word from a realtor friend that a house was going to be for sale in the Marion Country Club. This home was owed by a personal friend of the realtor and wasn't on the market yet. The realtor said, if we were interested, she would call the owner and arrange a time for us to look at it. We went over and I fell in love with it. Buying this house was going to be a stretch for us, for this home was twice the price of the one we were presently in but it was just what I wanted for our family and to show everyone how successful I was becoming. It was situated on the eighth fairway adjacent to the tee box and from the back porch you could see the majority of the Marion Country Club's back fairways. The house was immaculate and the location was perfect; so we put an offer on it. The owner accepted our offer subject to the sale of our house and a closing in June.

In the first week of June I received a horrifying phone call from my mom. Dad was in the hospital! He had a stroke and was having additional strokes since he had been admitted. I thought about the comment my dad had made about his family's health history and how he was the oldest surviving male in his family. It scared me! I called the doctor to see what the prognosis was and if he thought I needed to be there. He told me my dad had suffered ten strokes and he still didn't know what was causing it. The doctor told me he put my dad on the blood thinner Coumadin and hoped he would be able to tell me more in a few hours. When I was finished talking to the doctor, I prayed for God to heal my dad and comfort my mom.

At this point, I didn't know if I should go to Massachusetts or not. I wanted to be there for Mom but if the Coumadin worked, I would be flying there and back for an expensive visit. A quick visit like that would have cost me over a thousand dollars and I was supposed to close on our new home in a couple of weeks. On the other hand, if my dad died, I would never see him again and would always regret not going. I called the doctor again. He told me he thought the Coumadin was going to be the answer for my dad, but we would know more over the next twelve hours. I asked the doctor, "if he were me, would he fly there to be with his dad or would he wait?" He told me, "that is entirely up to you but if it was him he would wait." He went on to tell me, "each one of his strokes were reversible; meaning he had no signs of long-term paralysis."

I called my mom and told her of my discussion with the Doctor. She told me she had a lot of support from my brother Donnie, plus her sisters who were there with her. But even with all of her close support, she had been on pins and needles all day because of my dad's family history. I was on pins and needles too, as I awaited my dad's prognosis the next day. The next day came, the Coumadin was working and my dad was doing fine. I was relieved. I thanked God for healing my dad and for protecting him from any paralysis. I believed in prayer but I still didn't know who or what I was praying to.

As a Unitarian, we never discussed the New Testament. Now as a member of the Disciples of Christ Church, I was learning more about the stories of Jesus and the power of prayer. I was also learning; prayer was important in all circumstances not just in emergencies.

In 1973 I was evaluated by Prudential to become a "Regional Training Consultant." This was a Home Office position designed to learn the "District Manager's" responsibilities. The only problem was, if I excepted the promotion, we would have to move to Minneapolis, Minnesota.

My career with Prudential would be set once I became a District Manager but moving away from Joanne's mom, who still had issues with Multiple Sclerosis was not an option at this time. Besides, my income at this point was only two thousand less than my District Manager's income. So, life was good.

Mom, Dad & grands

In January of 1974 I was feeling good. In 1973 I had recruited some really good people and I was receiving good bonuses from working with the new agents. In fact, I was working with a new agent and had just closed the biggest sale I was ever a part of in my career, when I had a life changing event happen. The sale involved a farm estate tax issue. The sale's commission for the agent was around $5,500 and I was pumped. It took us a couple of interviews to actually close the sale and the agent learned a lot from the experience. I felt like I was at the top of my game. What could alter my course? What happened next – was another God thing!

Me and the kids

The next day I received a phone call from a man named Larry Wedeking. The call went something like this: "Hi, is this Ron Bailey? My name is Larry Wedeking." "I know the name Larry Wedeking doesn't mean anything to you but I just visited with a friend of yours by the name of Denny Couchiera." "I met Denny at a meeting I was speaking at in Boston and when he found out I was from Iowa he asked me if I knew you?" We talked for a while and then I told Denny "I was developing the State of Iowa and was looking for strong leadership in different areas of the state." Larry then told me, "Denny thought you might know of some strong leaders in the insurance industry who would like an opportunity to make a six-figure income." I asked Larry to tell me what he was looking for. He went on to try and set up an appointment with me. I then said, "Larry be honest with me, you're just trying to recruit me aren't you?" He said "Ron, I really don't know you, so I don't know if you would be someone who could handle or even qualify for this opportunity. I'll be happy to go over it with you and if it's not right for you, perhaps you may know someone else I can talk to while I'm in Cedar Rapids." I told him, "I was pretty busy and really not interested in making any changes myself but maybe I could come up with a name from someone in the

Life Underwriters Association I belonged to." He then asked, "Do you have a good opportunity with Prudential?" I told him, "I believe it is one of the best opportunities in the Insurance industry today." He said, "well let's do this, you show me your opportunity and I'll show you mine and if your opportunity looks better than mine, I'll go to work with you." I thought to myself this guy is smooth. Maybe I can learn something by sitting down with him. So, I told him, "let's do that."

I agreed to meet Larry for lunch the following day and I called the agent I was working with to let him know I wouldn't be working with him the next day. Besides if everything was issued and placed on the farm estate sale the way we wrote it; he had his sales quota more than met for the next three months. I then told him, "Surprise me and write something on your own." He laughed and said he would try.

The next day I met with Larry Wedeking. He was impressive and I found out he was only two years older than me. He was dressed to the nines, wore an expensive gold watch and had a charismatic presence about him. I commented on his watch and he told me it was an award he received from Franklin for qualifying for an honor club called "The Key Club." That really impressed me! We exchanged small talk establishing a brief relationship and then he said, "Dennis told me what he knew from working with you in Massachusetts but didn't have much to tell me since you moved to Iowa." He said he thought you were very successful and in some sort of special management program. I told Larry I was in a special management program in Massachusetts but I had to give that up and start over in Iowa. He asked me "How is that going?" I then started bragging about the success I've had in Iowa to impress him. I told him I won all these awards, was the third highest paid person in the office and was being considered to go into Prudential's Home Office as a "Regional Training Consultant." He then said, "That is very impressive." "You mentioned you were the third highest paid person in the District." "How much did you make last year?" I was very proud and told him, "Last year I made $23,400." He said, "that is impressive!" He continued to inform me, he was two years older than me and has been in the insurance business two years longer than me. He went on to say, "last year I made $72,000 but enough about me – tell me about the opportunity you have at Prudential." I then said, "enough about Prudential – tell me about the opportunity you have at Franklin Life." He had my attention and showed me the most interesting presentation I had ever seen for selling insurance! When it was over he asked me if I thought I could increase my sales with a system like this to work with? I told him it looked really good. He then explained how the system was also designed as a recruiting tool. I could recruit unlimited numbers of people into my own sales organization while selling and everyone recruited would be promoted by performance predetermined by a contracting pattern, not politics. He went on to illustrate; if I recruited just five people and helped them to recruit five more, with each of us just writing two sales a week, a year from now, my income would be more than what I was presently making at Prudential. When he was finished with his example, he looked me straight in the eyes and said, "If you are good enough, you could even have my position and I would be happy for you." "For along the way we would both have made a ton of money."

I thought to myself; Larry was good. He was really good; but not three times better than me. The reason he was making three times more money than me had to be the system. As I was thinking these thoughts, he pulled out a packet from his briefcase containing trade journal advertisements of different Franklin Life Agents. These advertisements didn't brag about the products or company's history, they bragged about the income these agents were making.

Franklin Life was one of the oldest insurance companies in the industry. They had the top ratings, great products and great client service record but they highlighted their agents. People younger than me were making a six-figure income. That was impressive! Larry had my attention! The next step was to see what Joanne would think.

MAKING ANOTHER LIFE CHANGING DECISION

I called Joanne and told her about my interview with Larry. I asked her if it would be ok if I invited him for dinner so she could hear what he told me. She was hesitant but said it would be ok. Larry showed up around 6:30 and rang the doorbell. He had a bouquet of flowers in one hand and a bottle of Chianti in the other. He greeted Joanne like she just won the Publisher's Clearing House lottery. She was really taken with him, as was I. We had a nice meal and then Larry started sharing with Joanne what he shared with me earlier in the day. He showed Joanne the insurance presentation he had shared with me and asked her what she thought? Joanne's response was, "I knew Ron sold insurance but this was the first time I ever really understood what it was." I understood where she was coming from, for with me it was about facts and figures. With Larry it

The Bailey Family

was about telling stories and painting pictures. Joanne could visualize what Larry was talking about. He then proceeded to tell Joanne about the opportunity available to head up the entire Northeastern Iowa portion of the Iowa Region. Larry told us he was impressed with both of us and felt this would be a great career move if we decided to take advantage of the opportunity. We told Larry this was something we needed to think about. He said, "Take a couple of days or weeks if you like." "If you are seriously considering this opportunity, I will stop looking for any other candidates to fill this position; for the time being." He thanked us for our hospitality and as he was leaving he said, "if you do decide to take this position, I will personally work with you to help you build your own Agency."

When Larry left Joanne looked at me and said, "Was he talking reality with us or was he just blowing smoke?" I had the materials he had given me from the afternoon's meeting and the presentation he had made to Joanne. I looked back at Joanne and said "everything looked like it was on the up and up to me."

I was starting to weigh what I had with Prudential versus what I could have with Franklin Life. I was going to turn down the Home Office position with Prudential because I would have to move. With Franklin I could build my own Agency, control my own destiny and not have to move. That had a lot of appeal to us. I thought about wearing a fancy Omega Gold watch like his and Franklin's selling system he showed me. I started thinking about different questions I should ask him.

On Friday I had my regular District meeting with Prudential and my sales team was recognized for having another outstanding week. The farm estate sale was celebrated and the young agent I sold it with was put on a hero's pedestal. When the meeting was over I went back into my office and all I could think about was the opportunity I saw with Franklin Life. With my door closed, I called Larry at his office and after making sure he was free to talk, asked him questions about the following; "If I made a change to Franklin how would my pay work, what kind of salary would I start at and what were the company benefits?"

Larry told me to put together a list of anything I would have questions on and he would make a special trip to Cedar Rapids to address them with me. We decided to meet the next week on Wednesday. I told Larry most of the questions Joanne and I had, regarding; making sure we would have enough money to make the payments on our new house and keep us from having any financial pressures during the transition. We didn't want to experience any unknown setbacks like we experienced at Prudential.

Larry asked how much would we need to make this transition work? I replied around $500 a week. He told me he would put together a game plan for me, based on the income I would need during my transition and longer if needed. He again reminded me to make a list of all the concerns or questions we could think of, to address when we got together the following week.

When Wednesday came, I had my list of questions ready and was looking forward to visiting with Larry about the opportunity with Franklin. We met at a restaurant on the other side of town away from my office. We ate a late breakfast and then went over my concerns for having a steady income through my transition to Franklin. Larry asked me what I expected from my agents at Prudential each week and I told him to try and have two sales a week. He then asked me if I thought I could make two sales a week using Franklin's selling system? I told him I felt confident I could do at least that. He showed me the commission schedule I would be on as a General Agent with Franklin Life. It was 60% higher than Prudential's. He explained how I would receive 80% of the commissions on the business I submitted every two weeks and as long as I did my part, he would make sure the Home Office did theirs. He told me the money I would be receiving the first year would be considered a loan collateralized by the business I was writing, and would have little or no tax impact on me the first year. Franklin did have a group hospitalization plan but the cost would be my responsibility. He answered all of my questions, gave me more pamphlets about agents who joined Franklin Life and what their income was just five years later. I went home after my meeting with Larry and shared all of the information with Joanne. This would be another major change if we went to Franklin.

I started to think of how all of this started. Larry ran into an old Prudential colleague of mine while speaking in Boston at an insurance function. Dennis asked Larry if he knew or heard of me. Larry got my information from Dennis and contacted me the week I made my largest sale ever! I sat down with Larry because I felt I could learn something from him, not because I would actually be interested in leaving Prudential. I'm feeling good about my future with Prudential and Larry showed me a better opportunity if I were willing to take a risk. Joanne and I both make a decision to look into the opportunity for ourselves. Now we were at that point where we were into it emotionally and needed to make a choice.

It was the end of January in 1974. I have all seven agents on board with the idea of qualifying for Prudential's Leaders Convention and we started the year with the largest sale I have ever been a part of. I was having mixed emotions about what I should do; so I called my dad.

I told my dad about my meeting with Larry and the opportunity I was being presented. He asked me, “son, I have never asked what kind of money you are making but you have been quite successful so I imagine it is more than $15,000 a year.” The average income in 1973 was around $7,200 and my dad was making around $12,000 a year, so he knew I was doing pretty well with Prudential. I told my dad “I made $23,400 last year.” With that he asked me what the new company was going to pay me? I told him I would be on straight commissions with no salary, other than a loan collateralized by the sales I made to help me get started. He then wanted to know if I would have the same fringe benefits as Prudential? When I told him, I would be self-employed and have to establish my own benefit program, there was silence on the other end of the phone. He finally said, “I don’t know son. You are making more money than I ever have, you have great fringe benefits with Prudential and your career seems to be a perfect fit for you right where you are at. Why would you risk all that on something with little or no guarantees?” I told Dad, “I see where people are at with Prudential 20 or 30 years down the road and I’ve seen some examples of people with Franklin during the same time frame. For some reason, the road with Franklin has more appeal to me.” We continued to talk about different things and before we hung up, I thanked him for helping me think through my situation. I still hadn’t decided 100% to make a change but the more I talked about the Franklin opportunity the more excited I got about it.

A couple of weeks passed and Larry was wanting to know where we were on our decision? I told him we were on the fence. Everything looked good with Franklin but I would be giving up a lot to make this move. He told me he was taking a few people to Franklin's Home Office in Springfield, Illinois and wanted to know if Joanne and I could join them? I told him I thought we could make it work but I would need to talk to Joanne and see what she thought.

Joanne and I talked about the trip to Franklin's Home Office and I called Larry the next day to tell him we would love to join his group. Larry set everything up with the Home Office and added my wife and I to the guest list. The trip was set for Thursday and Friday of the next week. I arranged to have those days off at Prudential and Joanne got the baby sitting set up.

The following week we met everyone in Iowa City and rode with Larry and his wife, along with another couple, to Springfield, Illinois. The other couple were new to Franklin and had been in the insurance business for around five years. Roger had only been with Franklin for six months but was already making more money than what he made with his other company after four years. He was also starting to build his own Agency. He was all excited and we talked the entire trip about the Franklin opportunity.

At the Home Office we were greeted and entertained like royalty. Franklin's Home Office really rolled out the red carpet for us. During our stay at the Home Office, Larry also carved out time with a few very successful people with Franklin who were once General Agents with their own agencies and were promoted to Vice Presidents and Superintendent of Agencies. They shared their stories with us and made Joanne and I feel much more secure about the opportunity with Franklin. We ate in the private dining room with the President and he even spent time getting to know us. It was a special trip and we were glad we went.

Signing with Franklin

Joanne and I began feeling the opportunity with Franklin was as good or maybe even better than Larry was telling us. We prayed about our decision and with all the new information we gained, as well as, the emotions still present from the trip, we felt more at peace now about making the change. My next move was to sit down with Orrin Smith, my District Manager at Prudential and let him know I was leaving.

I set up a meeting with Orrin Smith the next week. He was still all excited about the estate case I had written with the new agent a few weeks earlier. He also shared information given to him regarding Prudential's assessment on my candidacy for the Regional Training Consultant's position. He told me the ball was in my court. The promotion with Prudential was a big step and could lead to great things for me and my family. He understood why we moved to Iowa in the first place, so he knew it would be a hard decision to move away from Joanne's mom and the family again. He went on to tell me that this opportunity doesn't come around too many times and if I want to go up Prudential's management career path, timing is everything.

I told Orrin how much I enjoyed working with him as a sales manager and I was ready to make a change but it wasn't going to be with Prudential. I told him I was going to become a General Agent with Franklin Life. As I was telling him that, I developed a lump in my throat. It was emotional for both of us. He spent a few minutes trying to convince me to stay with Prudential but at the end realized I had made up my mind on this change. I gave him a month's notice and told him I would help him clean up any loose ends during that time. Orrin asked me to keep everything under my hat about my leaving. He would announce it in a couple of weeks and would have my replacement by that time. I understood and agreed to not say anything. I was also hoping the estate case would get issued during those last few weeks so I could get paid on it but since larger cases take longer in underwriting; it didn't happen. Well, after giving my notice, I felt a big relief. I called Larry right away and told him I gave my notice to Prudential and would be ready to join Franklin Life the 15th of March.

My life was going to change but not all for the better right away. I found out I was going to have to take two steps back before I was able to take one step forward. My faith was about to be tested.

Chapter 14

"Commit to the Lord whatever you do and He will establish your plans." Proverbs 16:3

Leaving Prudential to Become Self Employed with Franklin Life

In March, the District Manager announced my leaving and introduced the new sales manager. I was excited and ready to make the change to Franklin. As a sales manager with Prudential, I sold most of the people I sat down with. With Franklin, I thought all I needed were qualified prospects to sit down with and I would do the same. I was comfortable with my presentation skills so my selling should be a no brainer. So, on March 15th I left Prudential and was ready to make it happen with Franklin.

Larry told me to set up as many selling appointments as I could in a three-day period and he would work with me. He said to include people I hadn't been able to sell in the past, so he could show me the magic of Franklin's President's Plan in action.

I had a number of people lined up for the week but as hard as we tried, we had no results from our efforts. I started to get concerned. That never happened to me before when I had the security of Prudential policyholders to fall back on. Larry was also surprised.

I knew sales was a numbers game — sooner or later I was bound to make a sale. I just had to keep a positive attitude and not worry about my first week. I committed to memorizing the President's Plan presentation word for word and made a goal to make at least three presentations a day.

I went on fifteen interviews before I made my first sale! I couldn't eat, my stomach was upset and I had a problem sleeping. I started questioning my decision about leaving Prudential and if I had let my ego get ahead of my common sense. Eventually I made a few sales in March but I thought I should be closing two out of the three people I saw instead of maybe one out of four.

April came and I received my first check from Franklin. It was for $1,000 just like Larry said. I signed the promissory note and sent the copy to Larry. I didn't have the financial pressure yet but I needed better sales results to maintain my end of the bargain. I decided I would make a commitment to go after "The Diplomat Club", one of Franklin's honor clubs. I was goal orientated and this had a nice reward attached to it. I would have to make twenty sales over the next thirty days. If I have to work seven days a week and have four appointments a day, I will do whatever it takes. I prayed for God to help me. I wanted to make this work. I didn't know what else to do. I still didn't know who God was, but felt I should at least pray.

I started making more sales and God gave me the endurance to make the twenty sales I needed in April. I found myself growing in confidence and recruited a couple of sales people to join the agency. Larry told me if I was going to build an agency, I needed to get an office outside of my home. I was hesitant at first, for that would cost me more money each month. I talked to the other agents I recruited and we all agreed to share in the office expenses.

Larry helped me pick out the office and the office furniture we needed. We settled on a basement office without any windows in a new office building. I wasn't crazy about not having any windows but it was in a great location and affordable for us. We also had to get phone lines installed and office equipment. I leased the office furniture, typewriter and copy machine. I then signed for everything and explained the details to the other agents.

Larry helped me set up the contracts and financial agreements with the new agents. He told me the Home Office wouldn't allow me to finance the new agents, since I was on financing myself, so he put the financing responsibilities under himself and we agreed to split the override fifty-fifty. He went on to explain, I would be better off recruiting agents part-time.

He said to look for people of influence in the community who would like to supplement their income, while seeing if the insurance business would be a good career fit for them. He also mentioned part time agents wouldn't present as many financial concerns to me.

The Franklin had a motto: "To be a successful agency builder you had to lead from the front." I was all about being a leader and I wanted to be a leader at Franklin.

Franklin had four major honor clubs to set the Franklin leaders apart from the rest of the pack. Less than one hundred Franklin agents had the distinction of qualifying for all four major honor clubs from the inception of the honor club system. It was those agents who set the standards for selling and agency building in the Franklin. I challenged the new agents in my agency to qualify for "The Key Club" with me. I felt it would set us apart as an agency, if we all qualified for the beautiful Omega gold watch together. I told Larry about our agency plans and he told us he would take us all out to dinner with our wives when we accomplished it. In addition to the recognition, the watch and the dinner, we would have each earned over $7,000 in commissions for those two months. We were all pumped and ready! We gave ourselves two weeks to gather up prospects, send out mailers and set up our initial appointments to kick off the sixty-day contest period.

We were into the third week of our contest when I got a phone call asking me to come to Des Moines for a meeting with Larry. I thought this was strange because Larry and I discussed the importance of not having any distractions during that sixty-day period. He said, every day would be important to me. I wondered what was going on? I felt something was wrong! His secretary told me Larry wanted me there Friday morning at 10:00 for an important manager's meeting. Larry was always there for me so I told her "I will be there."

On Friday I got up and drove three hours to be in his office by 9:45. When I arrived, the other managers were going in to see Larry one on one. We all sat in a separate waiting room for our turn. My name was called and I sat down with Larry. Larry didn't look like himself and I asked him if he was ok? He said, "no...this has been something I haven't been looking forward to!" I could feel the resignation in his voice. I got concerned. This wasn't the Larry I thought I knew. He then told me he was leaving Franklin and had accepted a Vice President's position with another insurance company in Des Moines. I asked him how long had he been contemplating the change? He told me he was in contention for this position over the last three months. He went on to tell me how impressed he was with me and started emphasizing the benefits of working with a local insurance company. He was now talking about the importance of having an office allowance and company benefits. The very things I gave up with Prudential. He told me if things didn't work out with me at Franklin, he would offer me an Agency Manager's position with his new company. He went on to tell me I would be building a scratch agency, the same as Franklin but I would have more financial support with his new company. I told Larry, "Thanks for the opportunity but right now I'm committed to make it work at Franklin."

I was devastated! How was I going to tell Joanne? I got in my car and started to cry! I called out to God for help! I was in debt with promissory notes to Franklin Life and the person I was trusting to mentor me was no longer with me. I had a long drive home!

I was exhausted by the time I got home from my meeting in Des Moines and Joanne could immediately tell something was wrong. I wasn't my happy go lucky upbeat self. I told her Larry was leaving Franklin and going with another company. We both felt like we had been deceived and became nervous about our future with the Franklin. I thought Larry was as solid as a rock with Franklin and I basically hooked my car to his train, confident he knew where the train would take us. Now I felt stranded without any direction or a map to guide me.

I had a special meeting on Saturday morning to tell my new agents. We talked about the success we experienced as an Agency and for us to make this work we had to stick together. We had to focus on our goals and stick to the game plan we established.

On Monday I called the Home Office to make sure we could still depend on receiving our pay checks every two weeks, based on the original agreement signed with Larry. They assured me, as long as we continued to submit good business, nothing would change for now. They also felt confident the new Regional Manager would honor the financing arrangements Larry made.

Reminding me of a quote by Thomas Paine, an English born American Revolutionary War hero, a deist and a part of the Unitarian movement; "These are the times that try men's souls."

At this point in my life today, I would again refer to Philippians 4:6-7 "Don't be anxious for anything, but in everything by prayer and supplication with thanksgiving let your request be known to God. And the peace of God which surpasses all understanding, will guard your hearts and minds in Christ Jesus."

MEETING THE POLISH PRINCE

At church I was learning about trusting God but I have to admit, I was concerned. I prayed everything would continue to go well but I was concerned about the decision I made to change from Prudential to Franklin, without Larry's leadership. I didn't have any peace and my soul was being tested.

The next month I received a phone call from Ed Wilmowski, the new Regional Manager. He told me he reviewed all my contracts and financing agreements. He said he was impressed with my accomplishments since coming to Franklin Life and was excited about the roll I would play in developing the Region. He asked me how everything was going and I told him the truth; "My wife and I are concerned about our situation." We talked for a while over the phone and set up a time to meet each other the next week and go over everything together.

The next week I met Ed at my office. He was a tall athletic looking guy with a lot of enthusiasm. He had on a nice-looking three-piece suit and was wearing the Franklin's signature gold Omega watch I so admired. He was also wearing "Franklin's Million Dollar Club" gold ring. The Franklin jewelry showed me he had some of the credentials I was looking for in a mentor, to help me build my Franklin business. During my morning meeting I learned Ed was a successful head football coach from the suburbs in Chicago. He started with Franklin part/time and later went full-time when his Franklin income exceeded his teaching salary. He told me how he would help me build an agency with teacher/ coaches and gave me some examples using reasonable production numbers. I was starting to feel better but was still anxious about my situation. Ed asked me to call my two associates and have them meet us for lunch. We drove to downtown Cedar Rapids in his new Mercedes and met at Bishops Cafe'. Ed bought us lunch and assured everyone the financing agreements would continue as originally set up. He said the Home Office will do their part, as long as we do ours. When the meeting was over everyone left feeling more at ease. Ed then invited Joanne and me to join him for dinner that evening. He said he would pick us up at 6:30 pm. I called Joanne and she set up the baby sitters for the evening. We had a wonderful meal and Ed assured Joanne that we made the right decision joining Franklin. We talked about how I would play a major part in developing the Region and how excited he was to be on the journey with us. We thanked him for the evening and for setting our mind at ease. A few days later he sent us a letter reemphasizing his confidence in us for the development of the north eastern section of the Region and signed it, Sincerely, Ed Wilmowski, Regional Manager. "The Polish Prince"

EARLY YEARS WITH FRANKLIN LIFE

Like the way Larry wanted to help me get started selling with the Franklin's sales system, Ed wanted to help me recruit teacher/coaches. I was excited: my father-in-law was a teacher/coach and he knew a lot of coaches in the area.

I started off by visiting the local schools and meeting the coaches on their free periods. I told them I was building an agency of teacher/coaches and would like to extend an opportunity for them, to see what I was doing. I also told them we would have pizza and beer at the function for them; while they learned about the opportunity. Twenty coaches showed interest in being at the opportunity meeting, so I sent out invitations to all of them and followed up with phone calls. I did everything Ed coached me on.

Ed told me he would pick up the tab on the opportunity meeting, so all I had to do was get the coaches there. I reserved the entire bottom room in a pizza place, normally used for parties and large gatherings. I told the manager of the restaurant; we would have between ten and twenty people at the event. We figured if we had ten we would probably need five pizzas and if we had twenty we will probably need ten. I asked if we could hold off ordering until everyone showed up? He said, "It would be fine." We also agreed it would be best to buy a small keg of beer, rather than be charged for individual glasses.

On the day of the opportunity meeting, Ed met me at the pizza place and we set up the room for fifteen people. Ed said, "It is better to look full and add more tables and chairs if we needed them." The program was scheduled to start at 7:00 pm. At 6:45 one coach arrived. We put his name tag on him and started talking to him. At 7:00 another coach arrived and that was it. We waited another fifteen minutes and then walked the two coaches down to the large party room, set up with fifteen chairs around three tables. We ordered three pizzas and a couple of pitchers of beer. We were told we could dispense our own beer from the keg and we would only be charged by the pitchers, not the keg as was originally planned. I poured the beer while Ed shared his personal story of how the Franklin opportunity worked for him and his family.

It seemed the coaches drank their beer rather quickly, and every time their glass was empty, I filled it up. I was also a little nervous, so every time I filled theirs, I filled mine. The first part of the presentation took thirty minutes.

During that time we had the lights on, so we could eat the pizza while listening to the presentation. The second part of the presentation was a slide show, containing stories of successful Franklin agents who came to work at Franklin part/time, while still teaching. For that part of the presentation I turned the lights out. Ed went through the slides and success stories for the next thirty minutes of the program. When we turned the lights back on at the end of his presentation, the pitchers of beer were empty and the two coaches were feeling pretty good. I know because I even had a buzz.

I thought the meeting was a disaster. I knew with the room rental, pizza and beer, Ed had spent a couple hundred dollars presenting the opportunity to only two coaches; one went home drunk, and the other started working with me part-time.

A couple of months later Ed and I looked back on that evening and laughed about it; for that night was the beginning of my teacher/coach recruiting efforts.

This is how that night played out. The one coach who came to work with me ended up writing business and introduced me to a couple more teacher/coaches. He got his insurance license and when the football season started, he decided insurance wasn't his game. However, one of the coaches he introduced me to became one of my best agents and later transitioned to full time.

I knew recruiting was a numbers game. I learned that from my time at Prudential, but I never had any personal financial responsibilities for agents before. Two months after Larry left, one of my full-time agents also left. We now had to pick up his share of the office expense, creating more expenses to me and the other full-time agent I was sharing the office with.

The remaining agent was a good producer and was matching me nearly sale for sale. My override on him was very small because I was splitting it with Ed. We always had small sales contests between us and thought we were good for each other – until I discovered he was writing bad business. The Home Office alerted me that he had a Ponzi scheme going and was writing a lot of quarterly business. He would send in the first three months premium with the application and was paid eighty percent of the full annual commission, but the business was never issued. The business was supposed to be the collateral for the loan. In short we had to fire him and Ed was responsible for his debt to Franklin. It was a couple thousand dollars and Ed, the co-signer on the promissory note, had to collect from the agent. That situation didn't go well and Ed had to take him to court. I learned a very valuable lesson from that situation.

I now had to pay the entire office expense myself. This was not the dream I had envisioned. I had a couple of coaches working with me part-time and I was all alone in a basement office in Cedar Rapids.

I would drive to my office without any windows and sit there by myself, remembering the nice corner office I used to have with Prudential. What had I done to myself and my family? I was sort of depressed and having my own private pity party, so I started reading motivational books. I needed to change my thinking. I determined, "If it was going to be, it was up to me." I read that, made a poster and posted it on the wall in my office. I also posted, "Whether you think you can or whether you think you can't, you are absolutely right." I believed, "I was the master of my own fate" and in order to survive, I needed to get out of my office and see the people.

Selling was a numbers game. I was starting to do more joint sales with the coaches I recruited, and that was good. Ed also challenged me to qualify for another one of Franklin's honor clubs. I changed my goal from trying to qualify for the gold watch and instead, I decided to go for Franklin's "100 Million Club." It was a club recognizing writing one million dollar's-worth of insurance in 100 days. The prize was a pair of diamond studded gold cufflinks. Ed told me, when I qualified he would sweeten the pot fifty dollars, so I could buy a nice French cuff shirt to show them off in. Ed was living up to his name, "The Polish Prince."

OUR WEEKEND AT CHESTNUT MOUNTAIN

It was the end of the year and Joanne's family decided it would be fun to rent a couple of rooms at the Chestnut Mountain Lodge for New Years. It would consist of my two brothers-in-law and their families, my father and mother-in-law and my family. In all there was 13 of us.

Driving to Chestnut Mountain everyone was talking about skiing and I told them I grew up on skis in Massachusetts. In fact, I had merit badges in both downhill and cross-country skiing through the Boys Scouts. They were all impressed. When we got to the Lodge we checked in and went down to the area where we were all assigned our skis. I noticed everyone was getting small four or five-foot skis. When it came my turn I asked the guy handing out the equipment if they had any six or seven-foot skis? He looked at me kind of funny and said, "I think we do in the back room." I said, "I would prefer those if you have them." He came back with the skis I asked for and was wiping them down with a towel. He then asked, "What size boot do you need?" I told him "Size 12." Since the bindings were different on the skis than the newer skis they were issuing everyone else, he couldn't find the right size boot. All he could find was a size 13 but said it should work ok. I checked everything out and proceeded to go to the warm-up area. I skied in the warm-up area for about 15 minutes and thought I was ready to get on the tow to go up the hill. I wasn't really steady on my feet but felt it would be just like riding a bicycle once I started going down the slope. On the top of the hill I positioned myself to do snow plows to control the speed and to make slow turns. As I started down the hill I turned my feet to make the snow plow but I kept going straight. My shoes were too big for my feet — my feet turned inside the boots — but the boots wouldn't turn the skis. I continued going straight and now I was picking up speed. I couldn't turn and I couldn't stop. All I could do was fall down!

As I was doing all of these moves, I was being watched by someone on the ski patrol and when I fell, he came over and asked, "Are you ok?" I said "I was." He then asked, "Are those your skis?" I told him, "These are the skis I rented." With that he told me to follow him. I took the skis off and he carried them to where they were issued to me and began chewing the attendant out for issuing me this old equipment.

I tried to tell him it was my idea to have the seven-foot skis but it was too late. He had the attendant get the standard skis for me with the proper sized boots. I explained to the ski patrol person helping me, "Having the longer skis was my idea." He just looked at me and said "He should have known better" and walked off.

I skied much better after that, but it still wasn't as easy as I thought it would be. I had to admit, it had been over twenty years since I had last skied and I wasn't as limber as I used to be. So much about me growing up on skis in Massachusetts as a kid. With that incident — I became the butt of my family's humor and lost my credibility of having a couple of mcrit badges in skiing.

The next day we all decided to hit the swimming pool after skiing. Todd was about four years old and liked to have me to toss him in the air when we were in the swimming pool. Once in the pool I began tossing both Todd and Kim into the air and catching them. Kim was heavier than Todd and when it was Todd's turn, I decided to see how far I could toss him. This time when I tossed him into the air, I threw him so hard that his bathing suit came off in mid-flight. It was funny to see Todd's facial expression when that happened. After all, we were in a swimming pool filled with a lot of people. Initially he was embarrassed but I tied his bathing suit back on him and we continued to have fun in the pool.

Over the next couple of days, I was sore from skiing and from tossing the kids in the pool but my heart has been full from all those wonderful memories since then.

Well, my first full year with Franklin Life was no cake walk, but by the end of the year I qualified for three of the four major honor clubs, I was wearing Franklin's signature gold Omega watch I so admired, I qualified for Franklin's

Million Dollar Conference and was named the Iowa Region's, "Rookie of the Year." My hard work was paying off.

CAMPING IN THE RAIN

I had been working hard and my schedule consumed nearly all seven days of the week, so Joanne thought it would be fun to take the kids camping one weekend. We owned a Volkswagen pop-up camper and used it when we would go back to Massachusetts to see my family. It was self-contained and since the kids were still small, it would sleep all four of us. It had a stove, sink, refrigerator and nearly everything you would need. The only thing it didn't have was a toilet. We felt we could improvise and use a bucket for that. So, that next Friday we packed the camper with food, drinks, games, extra blankets, fishing gear and headed out to Palisades Park to go camping for the weekend. We found a nice camping area once we arrived and set up camp. We no sooner set up our campsite when it started raining. We stayed in our camper, ate sandwiches prepared ahead of time and played games until we went to bed.

During the night the kids had to go to the bathroom, so we had them use the bucket and I put the bucket back under the camper to keep from stinking up the place. The rain continued throughout the night and into the morning. By the middle of the morning, the walls were closing in on us from being in the camper for so long. We tried playing games but after a while with it still raining, we decided to go home. We were all in agreement. I started the camper, pressed down on the gas to leave but just spun the tires. Apparently I had parked in clay and when it became wet from the rain it had become slippery. Well, luckily our camper was light and I could get behind it and push. I figured, with Joanne driving and me pushing, we should be able to get the camper moving. The rain started to let up a little but not enough to keep us hanging around the wet muddy camp ground we were at. I rolled down the window on the driver's side of the camper so Joanne could hear what I was saying when I got behind the van to push. I told her, "When I yell hit it, put it in drive and press down on the gas pedal." I wanted the shifter in neutral to begin with so I could push the van off of the area where I had spun the tires earlier; before she hit the gas. I rocked the van a little and then I yelled "Hit it." When I did she put the van in gear and hit the gas. The camper lurched forward and the spinning tires hit the bucket of bathroom waste; throwing the contents all over me. I had toilet paper and waste covering me from head to feet. I wiped my face off with my shirt and then got into the van. My wife couldn't help but laugh and as mad as I was at the time, I also laughed at the thought of what just happened. The kids didn't know what to think, they just knew I didn't smell very good. We went camping a few times after that but this was our first camping experience and our most memorable.

The next year I moved my office to Marion, where I was living. My new office had a nice large room with a store front window over-looking the street. Once we moved all the office furniture in, Joanne helped me decorate and we hung all of my Franklin awards on the wall. We had four nicely matted picture frames on the wall immediately behind my desk. Three of the picture frames were filled with honor club certificates, leaving one picture frame empty. It would be a constant reminder to me of what I had to do to have all four. The last honor club was called the "Sixty Club." I had to write insurance policies on over sixty different people during sixty calendar days. I then had to have all sixty sales issued and delivered to officially qualify. It was the honor club most agents didn't have.

I tried to qualify for the "Sixty Club" a couple of times but ended up short each time. My main focus was on Agency Building now. I wasn't going to give up on the "Sixty Club" but I had full-time agents in key areas and was helping them build their agencies. Ed was helping me with the full time recruiting and I was concentrating on bringing in teacher/coaches.

I worked hard into the summer months recruiting teacher/coaches and selling with new associates. I decided it would be fun to take a three-day vacation and go fishing in the Great Lakes. I talked to my father-in-law and my two bothers-in-laws. I also wanted to take my son. Todd was about 6 years old and I thought this would be a great experience for him. Mel knew where to go and planned the trip for all of us. We all stayed in one room at the Red Roof Inn, which proved to be pretty disastrous after all of us ate spicy food that evening. We all participated in the room's atmosphere that night and in the stories told the next day.

The next day we got up early and met the Captain of the fishing boat Mel reserved for us. The water was pretty calm that day and after reaching the designated area we let out our fishing lines. We were not disappointed. Within the hour, we were all catching fish. It was exciting watching Todd's expression each time he caught a fish. We all wanted to help him but he wanted to do it himself. He was excited and was proud of all the fish he caught on his own.

By two o' clock we had each caught a number of large lake trout and salmon. We then went through a dry spell for about an hour, so the Captain took us to another area. We started catching fish again and then Todd had another strike. This time the fish on his line kept the fight up for a long time.

Todd wanted to land the fish himself but was getting tired. The fish was getting tired too. As Todd was reeling him, the fish came close to the boat and then took a run for it. When we saw the size of the fish on the end of Todd's line we all got excited and Todd had a new rush of adrenalin go through him. He kept the line tight and slowly reeled this monster fish in. When he brought the fish next to the boat again, the Captain took his net and aided Todd in landing the fish. Once in the boat we all marveled at the size of the fish Todd caught. It was nearly as big as him! He was overwhelmed with joy over the fact that he not only caught a lot of fish without much help from anyone but he also caught the largest one.

Todd's big fish

It was now time to go back to the docks and have our pictures taken with our catch. As we were headed back to shore, the Captain informed us that the brown trout Todd caught was a trophy size fish and nearly a record, based on its size and weight. Something to be really proud of!

After our pictures, the Captain filleted the fish and wrapped them in tin foil, to be put in our ice coolers. We were excited then to get home to share our stories and have a big fish fry.

We had put in a full day of fishing and were all totally excited. Especially over Todd's fishing experience. I am excited all over again re-living this moment in my mind.

Catch for the day

When we got home, we had our fish fry and invited some of the neighbors over to eat the freshly caught fish with us. We had a lot to talk about. Especially, Todd's big fish story.

On Monday it was back to work; doing my best to personally produce and grow the Agency's production. I was determined to stay on pace with my goals, and it paid off.

By year end, I again qualified for "Franklin's Million Dollar Club" and was recognized at the Regional awards banquet, as Iowa's Regional "Sales Leader" and "Agency Builder" of The Year.

I was also a speaker at the meeting and talked about the importance of time management. I also talked about keeping the right attitude through the ups and downs of the business. When I finished my talk, the Senior Executive Vice President of Franklin returned to the microphone and challenged me to do the "60 Club" again. He then announced, in addition to the award from the company of a diamond and gold women's Omega watch for my wife, he would give my family the use of his condo in Arizona for a week. When he finished, he asked Ed if he would add anything to the reward? Ed said he would chip in $500, which would cover most of our airfare. So, in front of everyone I took the challenge and I told Joanne, "When we go to Arizona, it will be a well-deserved family vacation; for it will have taken its toll on all of us."

I blocked off the months of February and March on my calendar to accomplish the task. By the end of March, I had submitted applications on sixty-five lives, enough to satisfy the initial qualifications. Next, they all had to get approved, issued and delivered.

I was so fired up when April came, I thought I would try and do another honor club; while I still had the momentum. I got up early the next Monday morning and walked on to a work site to see a construction worker about disability insurance. It had snowed over the weekend and the area I walked into was icy; covered by a light snow. When I hit the ice I fell, breaking both the tibia and fibula; the major bones in my right leg. The construction work stopped and the workers took me to the hospital. I messed up their day and mine with that fall. I showed them why disability insurance was needed. I just hadn't planned on making my presentation so vivid.

With full leg cast

With that fall, I was laid up for the next ten weeks with a cast on my leg from my foot up to my hip. All I could do was make phone calls. Some of the guys came over to the house to see me and others kept in contact with me over the phone. It was a long ten weeks.

During my time of mending I also went to "FMDC", Franklin's Million Dollar Conference. The Conference was in Myrtle Beach and by the time of the convention, my cast was reduced to cover just my foot to my knee. With the smaller cast, I was able to get around much better.

I didn't spend much time on the beach for fear of getting sand fleas inside my cast but I did manage to climb to the top of a lighthouse with it. The hardest part of the whole cast situation was flying on the airplane with the limited leg space and having that cast on my leg.

At "FMDC" it was confirmed! I officially qualified for the "60 Club" and now had all four of Franklin's Major Honor Clubs. The Executive Vice President gave me the keys to his condo in Arizona and Ed gave me the $500. Now, all we had to do was decide when we wanted to go.

When I got my cast off, we made plans to fly to California to see friends and drive to the Camel Back Resort Area where the condo was.

While in California, we went to; Disneyland, Knott's Berry Farm, The Queen Mary and the San Diego Zoo. We then headed off to Arizona and saw a lot of interesting sights there. We brought the kids with us and we really enjoyed our time together, but I was anxious to get back to work. I had a lot of catching up to do.

I had been off for a total of three months but during that time, my needs were still taken care of by the commissions earned from sales on the "60 Club," agency overrides on my agents, plus I had a small disability income plan I had purchased when I first started with Franklin.

The "60 Club" certificate now filled the empty frame over my desk and I beamed with pride at having all four honor club frames filled. Franklin Life also placed a nice article in the local newspaper commending me on qualifying for the "60 Club" and for being in the top 1%, out of over 5,000 sales people with Franklin, for having all four major honor clubs since the clubs were started.

By year end, the agency was the top agency in the Region and at the awards banquet I was again recognized as the "Agency Builder of the Year." My income was nearly double what it was at Prudential just three years earlier and I was beginning to see how my Franklin dream was coming true.

NEW PROMOTION AND ANOTHER MOVE

Shortly after the awards banquet I was invited to come to the Home Office to speak with the Senior Officers of the company about another opportunity with Franklin. Ed accompanied me on the trip, as well. The Home Office wined and dined me and made me an offer to join the Home Office team as, Vice President and Superintendent of Agencies.

The position and program was designed to be a training ground for Franklin's Regional Managers, the company's top field position and the company's largest income earners. I was honored and listened to everything but by the time I got back to Iowa, I decided against making a change.

Ed had a lot of influence over my decision. He told me I was being promoted to the Area Manager's position in the region which would pay me at a higher commission level and give me a greater override on my associates. It was the second highest field position in the company and I wouldn't even have to move. After all, the reason we moved to Iowa in the first place was because of my mothers-in-law's struggle with Multiple Sclerosis and my wife's desire to help her when needed. That still hadn't changed. My wife and I talked about what the company was offering us and decided we were better off where we were for the time being.

A couple of months went by and I was again invited to come into the Home Office. This time with my wife. We met with the company's top executives, as well as, other Home Office people and their wives in the evening. Joanne was very comfortable during the entire process and felt she had even made a few new friends. We also met with a couple of newly appointed Vice Presidents and heard about their impressions of the Superintendents Program I was being offered. By the end of our visit we decided it was worth thinking about again. We went home and just like my move from Prudential, I made a list of the positives and negatives of making the move. I prayed that God would give me wisdom to make the right decision for me and my family.

After a few weeks, a Home Office representative came and visited with Joanne and myself to see where we were at in our decision-making process. He told us it was unusual for the Home Office to pursue someone once they have turned down a Home Office promotion like I did and if I turned it down this time, he doubted I would ever have this opportunity presented to me again. I appreciated him taking the time to personally counsel with us and I told him I would have an answer for him by the end of the week. I felt in my heart we won't make a right or wrong decision. We will just make the decision together and then work to make it right.

At the end of the week Joanne and I both agreed, if we were ever going to make this type of a move, now would be the best time in our life to do it. The kids were young and at this stage of their lives it wouldn't disrupt their schooling or friendships. We knew it would be disappointing to Joanne's mom and dad but knew they would understand our situation. It was a career move and at this time in our lives, it was necessary to move to reach the pinnacle of my success with the Franklin.

I never thought of it back then, as a move God was orchestrating; to move us into a position of influence and total surrender to Him. God had been guiding us all this time and had us right where He wanted us.

Even though I still hadn't personally asked Him into my life yet, He knew my heart and He knew I needed His help on this decision.

There is nothing worse than sitting on the fence when it comes to making decisions. One day you're all in, the next day you're not, and the uncertainty of everything creates additional unwanted stress. There were still a few things we wouldn't know even after we made the move. We wouldn't know how long we would be in the Home Office before a Region would become available and we wouldn't know where it would be located once available? It could be anyplace inside the United States or even Alaska. Of course, we wouldn't be forced to take a Region we didn't want. The

Home in Springfield

question was, would we ever be able to live within a reasonable distance to Joanne's family again?

Once our minds were made up to take the promotion, the Home Office set up a Realtor for us to work with in Springfield and we went house hunting for a week. By the end of the week we narrowed our house hunting down to one house that was much too big and one too small. We were nervous over the two options we were left with. We thanked the Realtor and told him we would get back to him.

We then decided to drive around on our own. We didn't know where we were going, but ended up driving into a new subdivision. There we found a house for sale by owner. It was the perfect size, in a great location and even located on a small lake. We talked to a few of the neighbors and they told us how great the neighborhood was.

We knocked on the door to inquire about the house for sale and they let us in to see it. We liked the house and made them an offer on the spot. They accepted the offer that afternoon and I notified the Home Office we bought a home for sale by owner and didn't use their Realtor for the sale. The Home Office assured us we were ok in doing what we did and approved a bridge loan for me equal to the price of the house we bought, until my home in Iowa sold. We set the date of possession for November 15th, so we could be all moved in by the holidays.

Looking back, we can see God's fingerprints all over us finding and buying that house in Springfield, Illinois. Everything was going as well as could be planned. Now, all we had to do was sell our house in Iowa. We put our house up for sale in Marion, Iowa and listed it with Tom Davis, my other brother-in-law. He was a hard worker and one of the top Realtors in Marion. Everything was set, God was putting all the pieces together; we were ready to make the move.

Chapter 15

"Trust in the Lord and do good; dwell in the land and befriend faithfulness." Psalm 37:3

In the Home Office With Franklin Life

As of November 1 we have a new Superintendent of Agencies . . . . Roland F. Bailey, Jr. Ron comes to us from Marion Iowa where he was General Agent for several years. We welcome Ron, his wife Joanne and their two children to Springfield.

October 1st was my starting date in the Home Office. The closing date on our new house In Springfield, was the 15th of November. This meant I would be in Springfield a month before Joanne and the kids could join me. This type of move was common for new Home Office executives at Franklin. To accommodate us; the Home Office owned an exclusive apartment complex and reserved a few apartments for temporary housing needs. Home office management also allowed us to spend time with our families when we could. They knew the importance of family support in this type of move. So, if I had my work done by Friday morning, I could leave early and drive back to Iowa to be with Joanne and the kids for the weekend. It was a five-hour drive one way for me, so I could only do that every other week.

On the first day in the Home Office, I met Brady Creel, who I would be sharing the apartment with until November. He was a former teacher/coach who went full-time with Franklin Life after a few years of successful selling and agency building in Dalton, Georgia. Brady and I hit it off right from the start. We talked about our families, our backgrounds and our accomplishments with Franklin Life.

That evening, we decided to find a nice place to eat. I drove my car, so I could get acquainted with the area and on our way to the restaurant, Brady asked me if we could stop and pick up his dry cleaning. He had been in Springfield a week longer than me and had some clothes to pick up.

On the way over to the dry cleaners Brady got really jumpy and screamed under his breath like he was being attacked by something. He tried to calm down and then he did it again swatting at his pant leg. I didn't know what to make of it. I had just met him and he was acting like a nut. He told me he felt something run up his pant leg. I thought this was strange behavior coming from a grown man. I really wasn't sure what I thought. All I knew was; we were going to be roommates for a month.

We stopped at the dry cleaners and Brady left to pick up his clothes. It was starting to get cold so I turned up the heat in the car. When I did a little mouse ran out, stood on the car mat, looked up at me and then ran up behind the dashboard. I knew then why Brady had exhibited such strange behavior earlier. When Brady came back to the car with his dry cleaning, I told him what had happened. We laughed and I drove to find a place where I could buy a mouse trap.

The next day we were supposed to turn in our weekly expense sheets and I added the mouse trap to mine. The Home Office said it was the first time they had ever had a mouse trap as an expense item and after sharing our story, they paid it under miscellaneous moving expense.

Apparently the mouse crawled up behind my dashboard in Iowa to stay warm and on the way to the dry cleaners it dropped down to the floor and ran up Brady's pant leg. The next day the mouse was found dead in the trap. Mission accomplished!

Being in the Superintendents program was a unique experience. We were the main liaison between the Home Office and the field. Our job was to build relationships with the Regional Managers through working in their region as mentors to their managers and salespeople. We would help train their associates while working in the field and encouraged them to reach the specific goals they had made with their Regional Manager. We also took them out for a nice meal after working with them. For us it was a chance to spend time with successful Regional Managers and see first-hand why they were successful. It was a great learning experience for me.

During my time at the Home Office I worked with regions throughout the country and I recruited two of Franklin's top "National Sales Award Winners," as well as a few top "Regional Sales Award Winners," for a couple of the regions I worked in. I was very proud of that.

My plan was to be in the Home Office for a couple of years but in less than a year, Ed Wilmowski, my old Iowa Regional Manager, resigned and moved his family to Arizona.

The Iowa Region was open once again and I felt I was the best candidate to fill it. I told Joanne and she became ecstatic! This would allow us to be within a couple of hours driving distance to her parents and for me, the chance to work with people I already knew. I petitioned the Home Office to give me the Iowa Region and after some discussion they said yes.

I had about a month to sell my home in Springfield and move to Des Moines, Iowa where the regional office was

RM contract signed

located. I needed to be there as soon as possible, to hold it together!

Des Moines was like the hub of the insurance industry in the Mid-West, and when companies faced uncertainty, or word of management changes hit the street, other agencies would immediately try to recruit the best agents from that company.

The Home Office immediately put out a bulletin letting the Iowa regional associates know I was being promoted and would be taking over the Regional Managers position; effective immediately!

I still had one last trip scheduled before I officially left the Home Office. It was to work with the Regional Manager in San Francisco.

WHAT IS A PENTECOSTAL CHURCH?

I had a very successful trip working with the managers in the San Francisco area and on Wednesday morning the Regional Manager asked me if I would like to join him and a few of his managers for a Bible Study that night. He told me he had ten to twelve managers attend the study with him each week and they follow a curriculum usually lasting an hour. I told him, "I would love to join them." We ate supper together, then went back to his home for the Bible study.

He set up twelve chairs in his living room and put Bibles on each chair. He told me his study was designed to be interactive, as well as fun. He said he follows a curriculum and calls out the Bible verse to be discussed. The first person to find the verse in his Bible then raises their hand to be recognized, stands up and reads it. This format created friendly competition and kept everyone alert. I told him I thought it was a creative way to have the study.

Everyone showed up around eight o'clock and found a seat. The Regional Manager opened in prayer and then introduced me to everyone in attendance. We all had Bibles in our laps and when the Bible verse was called out, I immediately found it. Everyone was still searching when I raised my hand and asked if I should read it? I stood up and read the verse and then there was a small discussion about how the verse pertained to the subject being studied. The next verse was called out and again I found it right away. I looked up to see if anyone else was there yet and the Regional Manager saw me looking around. He asked me if I had found it and if so to read it. This happened a few more times and after that; everyone had fun trying to beat me in locating the verses being selected. Because I was so quick in locating some of the versus, a few even thought I had advanced knowledge of the scriptures we were looking up. I assured them it was all on the up and up. When it was over we all agreed it was a meaningful hour and everyone left feeling uplifted. Now it was just the Regional Manager and me.

He told me he was blown away by how quickly I found the various verses used in the study. He went on to say, "You really know your Bible." What he didn't know was, I only knew where the books of the Bible were located. I didn't have a clue what was in them. I kept that to myself. We then talked about the opportunity I had ahead of me with the Iowa Region.

He told me running a region was going to put a lot of demands on both me and my family in the formative years. It could be a seven day a-week job if I let it. He went on to say — I needed to make a decision from the beginning to run the Region and not let the Region run me. He said "You need to align yourself with a good Attorney, a good CPA for obvious business reasons and most importantly, you need to find a good church – a solid Bible believing based church but be careful – don't end up in a Pentecostal Church!" I asked him, "What's a Pentecostal church?" He said, "You will know it if you ever attend a Pentecostal service. The congregation acts very boisterous and they shout out words of encouragement while the pastor is preaching. It's very disruptive! They also do strange things like dance in the isle, raise their hands at different times during the service and speak in a strange language. It's a language that has to be interpreted by someone to get any meaning out of it." I said, "I would definitely stay away from that." Little did I know what God had in mind for me!

MOVING BACK TO IOWA AGAIN

While in San Francisco on assignment from the Home Office, I received a phone call from my wife. We had our Springfield home on the market for sale by owner and she had two people bidding on it. I told her to contact our neighbor across the street. He was an attorney and I had discussed handling our closing for us when we sold our home. He had agreed to help us. I knew Joanne was in over her head and we didn't want to get into any real estate issues that could come back and bite us.

Our attorney friend handled the situation and called me for my decision on the specifics of what we wanted to do. By the time I came back home, I found out my wife was involved in a bidding war and our house sold for $10,000 more than what we were asking for it. With that, we set the closing and date of possession to correspond with our move back to Iowa.

New home in DSM Iowa

Looking back, we saw how God put His stamp of approval on our move back to Iowa. For timing is everything and God's timing is perfect. We lived in Springfield a little less than a year and made a $12,000 profit on our home in Springfield after expenses. We now were faced with finding a home in West Des Moines, Iowa and hopefully take possession within a few weeks. In my mind it had to be a home worthy of my position as Regional Manager. This meant I was going to have to spend more on this home to create the image I wanted for myself and family.

The Home Office allowed Joanne and me a week to go house hunting in Des Moines. We found a top realtor in the area and started the process of finding our next home. During that week we found a three-level home with a swimming pool that we fell in love with and bought it while we were there. We were also able to have the date of possession fall perfectly in line with the time of my taking over the Region. Little did we know how God specifically picked out this house for us during our time of transition. This would become perfectly clear in about a year when new neighbors move in next door.

Backyard view with pool

My first job as Regional Manager was to find a personal assistant to help me with the regional back office support and until I found one, Joanne would have to help me. I also wanted my wife to be involved with the interview process of selecting my personal assistant so she would be comfortable with who we hired and also because she was a good judge of character. We interviewed a dozen or so people and found an amazing woman by the name of Gail. She was married, with children and was looking for a job with flexible hours. She also had all the office and personal skills I was looking for. She was perfect!

After getting the regional office squared away, I set up a manager's meeting to see who was still on board and create the synergy needed to get the Region up and going.

Ed had been gone nearly three months. We were down a few people since he left and production was also down. I proposed a contest for the regional associates and introduced it to my management team. They liked it and we decided to have a regional picnic to kick everything off. I then announced the name of the Region was changing from the Iowa Region to the Central Plains Region. This was something I had discussed with the Home Office before I left and they liked the idea of the new identity created by a new name.

At the August picnic we served soft drinks and beer, along with; different types of salads, desserts, hamburgers, hotdogs and bratwurst with all of the fixings.

A number of teacher/coaches in the Region were beer drinkers so I ordered a large keg of the beer for the event. By the end of the day we all had a good time. We kicked off the sales contest and not only finished off the keg but we also made another beer run before it was all over. I was amazed at how much beer this group drank.

There were a lot of disappointments my first year. Two months after my move back to Iowa, a seasoned veteran with

Franklin Life passed away from a heart attack. He was excited about me being the new Regional Manager and we had great plans for his involvement with the region. He was only 48 years old. I also lost a number of agents due to lack of production. They were recruited by Ed and sort of lost interest when he departed. I knew attrition would be a problem but it seemed when I took one step forward, I was taking three steps backwards. This forced me to work even harder. I had to personally sell insurance in order to keep my family's cash flow up. I knew, if I personally produced business at Franklin's Million Dollar Conference level for five years, the regional overrides should be able to take care of my family needs from then on. That was my goal but could I do that and still have a life?

In May the following year, I lost another great Franklin veteran to a heart attack. He was a good personal producer, had a history of 25 years with Franklin Life and had one of the top agencies in the region. He was a 59-year-old long distance runner whose heart exploded after finishing one of his daily runs. We were all shocked! We thought he was in great health.

Having lost two older key players to heart attacks, I needed to restructure the region. When I did, we again began to come together as a team. We started recruiting more and our sales began to pick up. By the end of the year the Central Plains Region, in spite of our set-backs, won National recognition for the amount of new insurance coverage sold: I felt we were back on our way to doing great things. But the question was...was I running the Region or was the Region running me?

Chapter 16

"Brethren, I do not regard myself as having laid hold of it yet; but one thing I do: forgetting what lies behind and reaching forward to what lies ahead, I press on toward the goal for the prize of the upward call of God in Christ Jesus."
Philippians 3:13-14

Chasing Jesus

The Central Plains Region garnered recognition for the hard work we had done, but in terms of recruiting, we were taking three steps back for every one step going forward. I was back to working six and seven days a week trying to keep everything moving forward. I needed to build additional agencies with strong leadership.

Before leaving Iowa to work in the Home Office, I recruited my brother-in-law, Jim Meggers into the Franklin and put him with the agency manager in Dubuque. Jim was a teacher/coach and a hard worker. He had been working a number of jobs at the time to make the extra money he wanted. After working with Franklin Life for a few months, Jim saw where he could make more money and have more time with his family by selling insurance instead of working his other jobs. Jim had great sales leadership skills and I knew when the time was right he would make a great agency manager.

Unfortunately for me, the Iowa Region's territory was re-designed by the Home Office before I became the new Regional Manager and I lost the agency in Dubuque to the Central Illinois Region based in Chicago. That meant, I also lost my brother-in-law.

Before I went into the Home Office my office was located in Marion, Iowa. It was where my brother-in-law was from. He knew a lot of people there and had a number of friends who were coaches there as well. He would be a natural to take that over.

In 1980, I sat down with Jim and his wife Chris, and told them about a plan I wanted to discuss with them. I pointed out, if he stayed living where he was, he would always be in the Central Illinois Region with Franklin Life, but if he moved back home to Marion, he could be back with me. We talked about giving up the security of his teaching income for the uncertainties of being self-employed. I laid it all out for them to see and in the end they knew I was offering them a great opportunity. I told them if they moved to Marion, he would be the agency manager and I would help him build his agency. I also told him I would assign a couple of seasoned agents to him to begin his new agency and together we would develop a game plan to meet his income goals.

After a couple of weeks and a lot of soul searching, they decided to move back home to Marion, Iowa and be a part of the Central Plains Region with me. It proved to be a great move for all of us. With his moving, I knew I had a good leader in place for that area of the region.

In the Spring of 1980, Linda and Rick moved into the house next door to us, in West DesMoines. They were our age and had children the same ages as ours. We soon discovered we had a lot in common with each other and became great friends. We would go out to dinner every so often and even started going to church together. Joanne and I had been attending this one church I liked because of their music, so one day we invited them to join us.

We had been going to church together for about a month, when one of their children said, "Why can't we ever go to our old church again?" Linda said, "We are with the Bailey's and we are going to church with them." Then their son said, "I miss Royal Rangers and my friends there." Rick then said, "Maybe next week." Linda spoke up and said, "There is a music program this Saturday at the First Assembly of God Church, in Des Moines. It is a program called Good Ole' Gospel. Would you like to see it with us?" It sounded like it would be fun for all of us, so I said, "We would love to."

I really enjoyed the program and didn't realize it was being performed by their church choir, until it was over. I thought it was a group of professional singers performing at the First Assembly of God Church over the weekend.

When the performance was over, I asked our neighbors to let us know when the show will be back in town, for I would love to see it again. Linda told us the program was put on by the music department at their church and invited us to join them on Sunday, if we wanted to see more.

MY ENCOUNTER WITH THE HOLY SPIRIT

We went to their church on Sunday and I was really moved by the music, but something else also happened on our initial visit to the First Assembly of God Church in Des Moines. Something I wasn't prepared for. I had a supernatural encounter with God! It was a taste of what I would experience later on in my journey to find Jesus.

When the church service started I was immediately ministered to, by the choir. The music was captivating and I hung on every word. These were songs about welcoming the Holy Spirit, talking about God's faithfulness and finding Jesus. I had never heard songs like this before. After a few worship songs, Pastor Crabtree called people to come forward for prayer and the laying on of hands for healing. The choir then sang, "Rise And Be Healed In The Name Of Jesus." People started praying out loud all around me and my mind went back to what I was told about the Pentecostal movement. Should I be on guard about this? Was this a Pentecostal Church?

As I was having this thought, someone from the back of the sanctuary started making a noise. It was like they were having an epileptic fit. I started to turn my head in the direction of the noise and noticed everyone had their heads bowed. Instinctively I bowed my head too. The pastor then gave the interpretation of what was said and while the pastor gave the interpretation, I immediately felt a warm electric like sensation go through me. The feeling started in my feet and traveled up my legs all the way through my body, to my head. I could feel my body completely filled with something unbelievably wonderful. In the middle of this encounter I had to open my eyes. I truly thought I was levitating. As soon as I opened my eyes and saw I was still standing on the floor, I closed them again to bask in the moment. I was warm and tingly all over and when I sat down I immediately turned to Linda to ask her, "What just happened?" She looked at me with concern and said, "What happened was Biblical." I then asked her, "Did you feel that?" She asked back, "Feel what?" I was confused. She then said, "We can talk about this when church is over?" I looked over at my wife and I asked her, "Did you feel anything just now?" She also asked, “Feel what?” I couldn’t believe it. Neither my wife nor Linda felt anything. Was I the only one who felt anything at all? What was going on with me? I knew what I felt was real. I could hardly wait until church was over to ask Linda about what happened to me.

When church was over, I tried to get Linda to talk with me about what happened. She was lost for words. She didn’t know what I had experienced. All she knew was someone in the sanctuary gave a message in tongues followed by an interpretation from the Pastor. She thought I was uncomfortable about what went on in the service and didn’t want to try and address it. She walked from the sanctuary, down the hallway to the parking lot with me on her tail trying to talk to her. When she got to her car, she looked at me and said, “Let’s have dinner and we can talk about the service.”

We went to Mr. Steaks, a restaurant in West Des Moines. We sat in a table near the back where we could talk. After we ordered our food, I asked the question, “Did you feel anything when the pastor gave his interpretation of the noise we heard during the service?” Again, Linda told me “I didn’t feel anything, why was that important to you?” I then told her what I had experienced. Rick, Linda and my wife all were sitting there in the service next to me but I was the only one to receive this revelation. Now, I was more curious than ever about what I experienced. Linda then said, “I can’t tell you anything about what you experienced personally but I have a book you can read, to help understand the Holy Spirit and the gifts of the Spirit.”

Later in the day Linda found the book about understanding God’s Holy Spirit and gave it to me. I opened the book and noticed the book was written by a pastor who used to be with the Disciples of Christ Church. The same church Joanne grew up with and we were married in. The book told a story about this pastor going to a Pentecostal service at another church and being baptized in the Holy Spirit. Up until then he had always thought the gifts of the Spirit were only used during the time of Pentecost and the early church. Once he received the baptism of the Holy Spirit, he spoke in tongues and knew his life was being supernaturally transformed.

Because of his personal transformation, he wanted others he knew and trusted to experience this new transformation too. A few were leaders in his own church. He started teaching them about the Baptism and the gifts of the Holy Spirit.

Word reached the Headquarters of the Disciples of Christ Church about what he was doing and soon found himself out of a job. They didn't condone this action and terminated not only his pastoral responsibilities but also his membership in the Disciples of Christ Church. In other-words he was excommunicated.

In his book, while being out of work and losing his credentials with the Disciples of Christ Church, miracles occurred to help him pay his bills just in time. Money showed up just in time, to keep his house and pay for his utilities while supporting this new supernatural walk with God. The book explained how this deeper spirit filled walk with God was available to everyone and at the end of the book was a prayer with added scriptures, to help someone receive this supernatural spiritual baptism. I wanted that!

Over the next few weeks Pastor Crabtree preached on salvation and the gifts of the Holy Spirit. The timing was perfect and the book I was reading confirmed everything Pastor Crabtree said. Jesus was tugging on my heart strings.

Being raised Unitarian from my childhood, I never gave salvation any thought. When I was questioned about being saved while in the Air Force; I didn't know I needed to be saved. Saved from what? Think about it — most Unitarians didn't believe in heaven or hell, so what difference would it make? Well, I learned later on, I was a sinner whether I wanted to admit it or not.

Romans 3:23 "For all have sinned and fall short of the glory of God."

Later in Romans 6:23 "For the wages of sin is death, but the gift of God is eternal life through Jesus Christ our Lord." Yes, I needed a savior and His name is Jesus.

I decided if Jesus was truly God, I wanted to be supernaturally touched by Him. I was ready, but I still hadn't accepted Jesus as my Lord and Savior yet. I had a taste of His goodness and wanted Jesus to be a part of my life more than ever!

I had been to different churches, studied different religions and even though I hadn't accepted Jesus in my heart, I was starting to believe He was the Son of God. The question was, did I need to go to church and go down front to be saved, or — could I do this in the quiet of my own bedroom? I determined, Jesus didn't care where I gave my life to him; He just cared that I do it. With that in mind, I bowed my head and prayed a simple prayer asking Jesus to forgive me of my sins, come into my life and make me a new person. I then felt a sense of relief, knowing I was no longer searching for God, but from this point forward; I was walking with Him and making Him Lord of my life.

I really didn't feel anything other than a sense of well-being when I prayed to receive Jesus into my heart. I felt I was no longer just me. I had Jesus with me. Next, I wanted to pray the prayer in the book and receive the Baptism in the Holy Spirit.

In the book the author explained, when I received the Baptism in the Holy Spirit, I would be given a new prayer language. I would speak in an unknown tongue used to glorify God. I wanted that to happen now more than anything. If it was a supernatural gift and it was from God; I wanted it!

Just like God had prompted me to seek Him as a young boy, I believed He wanted me to take a deeper walk with Him and be baptized in the Spirit. I believed it was part of His plan for my life. He just had to get my attention.

In His word He tells us He has a plan for us.

Jeremiah 29:11 "For I know the plans I have for you declares the Lord. Plans to prosper you and not harm you. Plans to give you hope and a future." He also wants us to ask.

James 4:2-3 "You do not have because you do not ask." He wants us to ask but with the right motives. God has a plan to prosper us, but we often don't receive it because we ask to satisfy our own desires.

For months I prayed to receive the baptism of the Holy Spirit and the gift of speaking in tongues; as the evidence of my receiving it. I wanted to speak in tongues and experience a deeper walk with Jesus more than anything. So much so that it became an obsession with me.

Around the same time I started seeking the baptism of the Holy Spirit, I was also approached by Dawn Crabtree, the Pastor's wife and choir director — to see if I would be interested in joining the choir. Linda, our neighbor told her I was a singer and loved the choir's worship music.

When invited, I asked Mrs. Crabtree; "How much time would I need to devote to the choir if I were to join?" She told me, "We practice on Wednesday night after the Wednesday night service and we sing both the morning and evening services on Sunday. I then told her my work schedule and why joining the choir wasn't possible at the time. I told her I was honored to be considered and would love to be a part of the choir someday in the future; but at this point in my life, I needed to concentrate on building my insurance business. I ended our conversation letting her know; "When I reach a certain point in the Region's production, I would love to revisit singing in the choir with you."

Dawn was very persistent in a good way and asked me every couple of months; if I was ready to join the choir? I was totally covered up with work and just kept giving her the same answer; "I haven't reached that point in my business yet, where I can take the time to be active in the choir."

A few months later, Pastor Crabtree gave a sermon on trusting God for our provision. My mantra then was, "If it's going to be – It's up to me" and the pastor was saying, "Let go and let God." He talked about how the Israelites had to first step into the Jordan River in faith, before the river receded; allowing them to cross. He said, by faith we needed to surrender everything; our life, our business, our future to God and trust Him for our provision. It seemed impossible to do, but it was a great message.

When the service was over Dawn stopped me and asked, "What did I think of the message?" I said, "It was pretty inspiring." She then asked me, "Do you believe God is able to meet all your needs?" Well after hearing Pastors message on trusting God, what could I say? I said, "Sure I do." She then said, "Why don't you join the choir and trust God to meet your business needs?" She went on and told me the Christmas Program was finished but they will start work on the Easter Program in January. Could I join them in January? Wow...I had never been challenged like that!

I told her, "I will pray about it." I knew as a young Christian, that answer could buy me more time.

I did pray about my desire to serve Him singing in the choir, but I was praying mostly to receive the Baptism in the Holy Spirit with the evidence of speaking in tongues. It had been a number of months now from the first time I started reading the book on "The Baptism in the Holy Spirit." I thought all I had to do was read the book, pray the prayer and I would receive the Baptism; followed by speaking in a new heavenly language. But it didn't happen that way.

Initially, I read the book and Bible verses mentioned and prayed to receive the Baptism in the Holy Spirit but nothing happened. I read the book a second time to see if there was something I was missing and again prayed to receive the Baptism but still nothing happened. I didn't know what to expect. All I knew was when the pastor in the book received the Baptism in the Holy Spirit, he spoke in tongues and I wanted to receive the gift of speaking in tongues; as evidence of my receiving the Baptism.

Night after night I prayed and night after night nothing happened. Then one night while I was praying — I resigned myself to the fact that maybe the baptism wasn't for me. I decided just to concentrate on Jesus and I prayed; "Lord Jesus, I don't care if I get the Baptism or if I speak in tongues: I just want to let you know, I love you with all of my heart and now that I've found you, I am happy you are my Lord and Savior."

As I was telling Jesus how much I loved Him, I started feeling a warm sensation come over me. The same feeling, I experienced in the church a few months earlier, except this time it was more intense. I felt my feet start to tingle and get warm. The warm tingly feeling continued to travel up my legs, like a slow moving electrical current and while this was going on, I heard the sound of wind rushing around me. I then felt my tongue getting hot, as if it was on fire and then it began to move uncontrollably and with everything else going on I felt like I was having an out of body experience. It was incredible! The power that created the Universe and raised Jesus from the dead was in me! All this was happening while I was telling Jesus how much I loved Him.

I was relaxed and yet I had the greatest rush of love I had ever felt going on inside of me! There was also an increased pressure building up inside of me during this whole experience. When all of this increased pressure and rush of love reached my head, the endorphins all kicked in. I was high on the love of Jesus! I don't know how else to explain it. It was better than any honeymoon night could ever be! It felt like every part of my body was radioactive and it was all from the love of Jesus!

I stopped trying to figure out what was happening and just totally surrendered myself to the Lord. This was more than I had ever imagined it would be. For months I had been seeking the gifts of the Holy Spirit, and all along I should have been seeking the giver of the gifts.

I tried to remain calm while everything was taking place: my wife was asleep next to me and I didn't want to wake her.

Up until this time I kept my praying in the Spirit under my breath. I was high on Jesus! I just wanted to continue to pray in the Spirit and experience that special moment the Lord had arranged for me. I also wanted to hear what I was saying. My tongue was taking me on a trip and I wanted to hear the new prayer language I was given.

I raised my voice just a little more to hear what I was saying and when I did my wife woke up. She heard me saying words that didn't make any sense and became concerned; remembering what my mom told her about our family's health history; all my wife could think was – I was having a stroke.

I finally took control of myself, long enough to tell her, "I just received the Baptism in the Holy Spirit and I was ok." I told her to go back to sleep but she just laid in bed, confused about what was going on with me. I was too...I was happily confused; and I stayed that way for the next three days.

Before this had happened, it was hard for me to pray for a few minutes, much less pray for hours; and in my initial phase of praying in the Spirit; it was three days!

Romans 8:18-27 "The Spirit helps us in our weakness. We do not know what we ought to pray for, but the Spirit Himself intercedes for us through wordless groans."

I had been asking for the gift of tongues, as a sign of being baptized in the Holy Spirit. All along, I should have been seeking a relationship with Jesus first, and then ask to be filled with His Holy Spirit.

As great as that evening was; I never could have realized what was going to happen next.

The first experience of my new walk with the Lord was His salvation. By faith, I welcomed Jesus into my heart, to give me a new life, cleanse me from my sins, and seal me for the future; with the promise of eternal life.

My second experience was Him baptizing my soul, filling me with the Holy Spirit, and empowering me to be a witness for Christ.

This was evident in Acts1:5 where Jesus says, "John baptizes with water, but before many days you shall be baptized with the Holy Spirit." He then says in Acts 1:8 "You shall receive power when the Holy Spirit has come upon you; and you shall be my witnesses." This came true on the day of Pentecost and the days to follow.

Acts 2:2-4 "And suddenly a sound came from heaven like the rush of a mighty wind, and it filled all the house where they were sitting. And there appeared to them tongues as of fire distributed and resting on each one of them and they were all filled with the Holy Spirit and began to speak in other tongues as the Spirit gave then utterance."

Galatians 2:20 "I have been crucified with Christ, and I no longer live, but Christ Jesus lives in me and the life I now live in the flesh I live by faith in the Son of God who loved me and gave himself for me."

Yes, Jesus was alive! He was in me, and soon by faith, He will give me a glimpse into a supernatural way of living!

Chapter 17

"Do not be anxious about anything, but in everything by prayer and supplication, with thanksgiving; let your requests be made known to God and the peace of God which surpasses all understanding will guard your hearts and your minds in Christ Jesus." Philippians 4:6-7

Three Days of Isolation

Once my wife knew I wasn't in danger of having a stroke, she eventually went back to sleep. However, I was undeterred in my Spirit filled adventure and continued basking in the wonderful love of Jesus. I was in a holy windstorm. The Holy Spirit was in me, around me and through me. It was intoxicating!

I was never part of the drug culture so I couldn't compare my feelings with anyone on drugs, but one time I received a hard hit to my head playing baseball and saw stars. Well, I was seeing lots of stars while caught up in this heavenly euphoria praying in the Spirit. I had heard the expression of being high on Jesus and thought it was just a metaphor but right then, I was literally high on Jesus.

I spent the entire evening praying in the Spirit while experiencing God's love and when the morning came, I didn't even want to get out of bed. All I wanted to do was stay in my bedroom and pray. This behavior wasn't like me and it really concerned my wife. So, out of her concern for me, she called Pastor Roger Lane and talked to him about what was happening. She had never had any experience with anything like this before and needed to be assured everything was alright. He assured her; if I had received the baptism in the Holy Spirit I should be okay.

I stayed in my bedroom the entire day and by evening when Joanne came to bed I was still praising God in the spirit. Time was not a factor to me.

Looking back, the nights and days all blended together. I really don't remember what went on. I was caught up in something wonderful and didn't want it to end. Joanne, on the other hand, did remember.

She didn't sleep very well the next night and while trying to go to sleep, she said I was glowing in the dark on my side of the bed while praying in the spirit. That freaked her out and made her wonder even more what was going on?

On the beginning of the third day, which was Monday, I called Gail, my secretary to let her know I wouldn't be coming in. I told her I wasn't feeling like myself and needed the day to recover. I couldn't tell her I had a radical change in my life the other night and was high on the love of Jesus. Up until a few days ago I wouldn't have understood what that meant either.

I asked Gail to call the managers and get the production numbers for the month. In 1980 we did everything over the phone and posted the numbers on a large production board in our conference room for everyone to see. I let her know I would be in on Tuesday to put together the meeting's itinerary and in the meantime she can start organizing the handouts for everyone.

After talking to her I went back to my room and continued my time with the Lord. This was my third day and I was starting to think about what was going on. My wife thought I was going crazy. I knew something had to give and

I needed to get back to work. I even began to ask God if this was really Him, or if it was me? How could I know?

It was just too easy to slip back into my new prayer language and be high on Jesus again. I started questioning my sanity. I remember even asking God to please prove this was Him and not something my subconscious was conjuring up. Was I weak and delirious due to lack of food and sleep? I really didn't feel sleep deprived but I didn't feel normal either. I was just in a wonderfully confused state of mind and what happened the next day completely changed my life forever!

Chapter 18

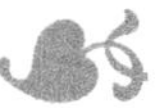

"Trust in the Lord with all your heart, and do not lean on your own understanding, but in all your ways acknowledge Him and He will make straight your paths." Proverbs 3:5-6

A Message To Me From Jesus

It was Tuesday. I had very little sleep for the last 40 hours and had eaten very little food. I was high on Jesus and nothing else mattered. My wife was concerned and thought maybe I was losing it. I even began to question how much was me and how much was God.

When I arrived at the office that Tuesday, I asked Gail to call the managers again and prepare all the additional handouts we would need for Friday's meeting, while I work on the itinerary. I told her I didn't want to be disturbed, unless it was from my wife or an emergency. I went into my office, shut the door, and sat down at my desk to start organizing the Region's year-end meeting.

I no sooner sat down at my desk, when I again felt the rush of God's Holy Spirit all over me. I experienced such a high on Jesus' love that I was compelled again to open my eyes to see where I was. I wasn't out of my body — it was wild! I was numb to everything except praying in my new prayer language. I was experiencing the peace of God people talked about in the Bible; which surpasses all understanding. God's supernatural peace also surpasses all human logic and while experiencing it nothing else mattered.

Philippians 4:7 “The peace of God, which surpasses all understanding, will guard your hearts and minds in Christ Jesus.”

I lost track of time enjoying my time with the Lord and at 1:00 PM, Gail knocked on my door to ask me if I was ok? When she did, it took me a couple of seconds to gather my thoughts before I could tell her I was fine and I was still working on the itinerary. She told me she had completed all the tasks I had given her and unless I needed her for anything else, wanted to know if she could take off early to pick her daughter up at school. I told her she could and I would see her the next day.

I was now alone in my office. Up until this time I had been praying mostly under my breath, but with no one around to hear me, I could now pray louder and hear what I was praying. In my mind I was telling Jesus how much I loved Him and wanted to serve Him but what I was hearing was a language I couldn’t understand. I didn’t know what I was actually telling Jesus but I was over joyed with having this time of worship. Just Jesus and me in my own private sanctuary.

I continued to pray in the Spirit until around 3:30 PM and looked at the empty legal pads sitting on my desk waiting to be filled out. I had a lot of work to do, to finish my itinerary before tomorrow; for Friday’s manager’s meeting!

My office was located on the third floor in an upscale office building in West Des Moines, Iowa. It was home to a number of professional people and was complete with a work out room, sauna, jacuzzi and even an indoor heated swimming pool. At this time of day people would come to the office building to work out or they would be leaving work early to beat the traffic.

My office was dimly lit with the exception of the light over the writing area on my desk. I had closed the window shades to the keep people from seeing me walking around in my office, as I'm sure I looked pretty animated.

Then it happened! I was in my own sanctuary filled with the love of Jesus, praying in this new angelic language when suddenly...God appeared to me!

In a split second, the purest, brightest, whitest, blinding light I had ever encountered emerged from the ceiling in my office and penetrated my forehead. The energy from the light was warm and like an electrical current traveled down the right side of my neck, across my shoulder and down my arm until it reached my hand. Once this feeling reached my hand, my arm began to shake uncontrollably. I was somewhat, like in a state of shock. What just happened? Had I pushed the limits of my body too far? After all, I was going on my fourth day without sleep since my initial spiritual encounter.

I began to wonder if my lack of sleep was driving me insane or if I was developing a neurological problem? I had heard of people going off the deep end due to a lack of sleep. What was happening to me and why was my hand and arm trembling? I started to get concerned.

I walked back to my desk and sat down. When I did, intuition or something else led me to put a pen in my hand. With the empty legal pads still on top of the desk waiting for me to organize Friday's meeting, I began to write something. I couldn't believe what happened next! Like my old IBM typewriter; God, Jesus, The Holy Spirit, someone other than me, took control and began writing something that looked Arabic or some other Middle Eastern language, likening itself to a form of hieroglyphics. It was definitely not anything I could have written on my own. These symbols or writings were penned starting on the right side of the paper. They continued to the left and then dropped down to the next line; where this time I wrote from the left back to the right until the end; dropping once again to write from the right to the left. This created three separate lines; filling the entire area with these symbols or writings; one right under the other.

I wrote like this for over an hour and filled several legal pads. I had no control over my hand during this time. I just continued praying in the spirit and wrote in this unknown language. My hand was now getting sore and I was low on legal pads.

To my amazement, when I stopped writing long enough to analyze what had been written, the symbols all lined up from top to bottom, even though I wrote from right to left, left to right and then back from right to left. I also noticed the writing pattern changed slightly after each three lined segment. What just happened? Was there something significant to what was written?

I called our church and set up a meeting that afternoon to talk to Pastor Roger Lane about this. He said to come over and he would fit me into his schedule. I sat in the wedding chapel outside his office until he was able to see me. When his scheduled counseling secession was finished, he invited me to come into his office. I was still feeling God's presence all over me. He shared with me how Joanne had called him the other day out of concern for me and wondered how everything was going? I told him about my latest encounter with the Holy Spirit and he just listened. I showed him what I had written on the legal pads and he asked me, "Can you write more so I can see it?" I told him my hand was shaky and I was still feeling God's presence, so we prayed and I started to write in the Spirit again. After I stopped writing, he looked at what was written, gave me some counseling concerning receiving the baptism in the Holy Spirit and passed on the details of what he saw to Pastor Crabtree.

Pastor Crabtree had been out of town all week and when he got back, I met with him for lunch. He asked me about the details of my initial baptism of the Holy Spirit and my three days of isolation. He then asked me about my experience in the office with the bright light and mysterious writings. He looked at the writings and confirmed what I experienced was a genuine encounter with God's Holy Spirit. He then said what I experienced in my office was a type of "Damascus Road Experience." I was a new Christian and didn't even know what that meant, so we discussed it as well. He looked at the mysterious writings on the legal pads again and said, "Most likely the language written here was a form of writing in tongues." Then what Pastor Crabtree said next was key! He said "These writings of yours will be more meaningful to you if you can get the interpretation." Together we agreed for and prayed to receive the interpretation of what was written; hoping God would reveal something to us. But nothing happened right then.

I went home and organized my desk. I placed the tablets with the hieroglyphics on one side and the empty legal pad on the other. I looked at the tablets with the writings and placed my pen down on the empty one. I prayed and again I started writing in symbols as before. My arm and hand continued to shake as I prayed for the interpretation, but I kept writing in those mysterious symbols. During this time more legal pads were filled up with these symbols. This went on for over an hour and finally with my arm hurting from the continuous shaking, I put my left hand over my right arm to calm it down. Again, another miracle happened! With my right hand immobilized, the pen pulled my hand across the legal pad and began writing in

English. The interpretation was being revealed. God was speaking to me. He called me by my name, He told me he loved me and He answered questions I had as a child growing up in the Unitarian Church.

One of my questions growing up was; who and what is God? Unitarians believed in all forms of religions. Most believed in some form of a higher power. Some in reincarnation, some in Mother Nature, some in witch craft and some even believed in atheism. For a person seeking who God was, it left a lot of options.

The very first interpretation was; "God is love." It repeated the same statement three times. Followed up with; "Jesus is love." The next interpretation was; "The Holy Spirit is love." Each one of those statements were penned three times. The next statement was; "God, Jesus and the Holy Spirit are one." That was penned three times. Then God said; "God loves you Ron Bailey," "Jesus loves you Ron Bailey," and the Holy Spirit loves you Ron Bailey." Also penned three times. There was something special about everything being in threes.

God was love, Jesus was God and the Holy Spirit was living in me. This also revealed the structure of the Trinity to me.

I was seeing not only who God was and what God was but I also learned He knew me personally. This was huge to me!

I was excited feeling the pen pull my hand over the legal pad revealing these questions I

Writing in the Spirit

had growing up but then the interpretation revealed, "I must die." I became concerned and momentarily picked my hand up off of the paper wondering what He was going to say next: I put my hand back down and the interpretation continued with, "to yourself." "For you are called according to my purpose:" "I want you to sing." I was simply blown away! He knew the conversations I was having with Dawn Crabtree about joining the choir, the work schedule I was faced with and my prayers desiring to serve Him.

My questions answered

I was interested now to see how God was going to make all of this work. By now I had experienced a couple of weeks dealing in the supernatural; and believed if Jesus asked me to walk on water; I would be willing to give it a shot. I was ready: all I had to do, was to surrender everything over to Jesus and adopt the principal of "Let go and let God."

As the Regional Sales Director for a major insurance company I traveled most of the state of Iowa; recruiting, training and had the responsibility of developing salespeople into managers. In addition to my

1 page from10+ legal pads

A closer view of writing in the Spirit with interpretations.

managerial responsibilities, I was expected to personally produce insurance sales at a high level to generate my family's cash flow. As a leader at Franklin Life, I needed to be what I wanted from my managers and that was to lead from the front by example.

I always had a strong work ethic, working nearly seven days a week and this was my schedule for the week. My days started at 7:00 in the morning when I got up and would usually end around 10:30 at night. I did my planning on Sunday afternoon with early evening phone calls to set up my week. On Monday and Tuesday, I traveled to the eastern part of the state to work with my managers located there. On Wednesday I would be back in the office during the day and in the evening I would either write personal sales and stay home in the evening or I would arrange to be in another part of the state working with another manager. I would usually come home on Thursday night, be in my office on Friday morning to wrap up the week and handle any problems or concerns that developed during the week. On Saturday morning I conducted training for the new agents and Saturday afternoon was with the family. This was my schedule projected for the first five years.

I told God I was letting go to join the choir and was trusting Him for the Region's production. I was serious about surrendering everything to Him after He revealed His instructions to me during the interpretation. My only question now was, how do I do it?

Up until then, the biggest production month for the Region had been around $38,000 of commission income. With me not personally producing and working just on overrides from my associates, the region would need to generate around $50,000 in commissions to make everything work. That would be nearly 30% more! I knew I had to take a huge step of faith.

The following is a testimony of God's faithfulness in providing my provisions.

In January, I rearranged my schedule to do my planning on Monday and have one day trips to work with my managers on Tuesday and Thursdays. That would give me Wednesday and Sunday nights for the choir.

With this new schedule I spent more time at home, delegated more to my managers and by the end of January when all the production totals were added up, I found out we did slightly over $60,000 of commissions, without any personal production from me. The results were way over my expectations! I did my part and I joined the choir. God showed up and supernaturally provided more than I was even asking for. He also increased my faith in the principal of "Letting go and letting God."

My faith was about to be tested again and my work schedule modified once more. In February, Phil Pfaltzgraff, the assistant director of music asked me if I would get involved with a musical he had written. He had heard me sing and in addition to the regular program, he wanted me to take the lead on a couple of other songs he selected. I told him I would love to and asked him when would they have practice? He said they were planning on Monday night. I rearranged my schedule again agreeing to sing in his program and by the end of February the production for the Region jumped to $62,000 of commissions. I truly was involved with the concept of, "Letting Go and Letting God." Something supernatural was going on here!

During this time, we had been working on the Easter Musical and Dawn, the pastor's wife, mentioned to me how she wanted to have a small representation of the choir perform our Easter Musical program at some of the smaller churches in the area. She then asked me if I could take part in it? Of course, the next thing I asked her was; "When do you plan on practicing?" It really didn't surprise me when she said "Tuesday night" but now I was faced with rearranging my work schedule once again.

During the month I even recruited a couple of new agents who were looking for an opportunity in the insurance industry and heard about our region's training program. By the end of March, we had another record-breaking month with commissions totaling over $64,000. By now different managers from around the country were calling me to see what we were doing to get the results we were getting!

By the month of April, I had all my nights except Thursday occupied by either the church choir or other church related singing activities and when April ended the Easter musical was finished but it was quickly replaced with "Good Ole' Gospel," another musical the choir performed during the Summertime. I knew the impact "Good Ole' Gospel" had on the community. That was the first program I was introduced to a couple of years earlier by our neighbor.

So how was this "Let go and let God" principal working? Well let's just say, every month was a record breaker over the previous month and Jesus was in charge of running the Region; while I was busy singing.

By June we did nearly $80,000 of commissions and numbers of new recruits were up all around the Region. In addition to my fellow Regional Managers around the country, now the Home Office was also calling to find out what we were doing to have such amazing growth? It wasn't prudent for me to tell them I joined the choir and let Jesus have control of the Region. They just wouldn't have understood. What I did say was, "I have been working with my management team and was delegating more responsibilities to them."

In June, Pastor Crabtree asked me if I would take a leadership role in a new evangelizing program the church was interested in called, "Evangelism Explosion." First Assembly had just built a new sanctuary and was committed to this new evangelizing program scheduled to be rolled out in October. I told him my plate was pretty full with the choir activities and my work but I would pray about it.

I did pray and I petitioned God — if the Region did $100,000 in commissions in August — I would join the leadership team of "Evangelism Explosion" in October. The $100,000 was a dream number I hoped the Region would accomplish one day.

Well, August came, and by the end of the month, the Region did $107,000 of commissions. It was nearly three times more than the highest monthly production we had the previous year and $7,000 more than what I was asking for. I was blown away!

The Region continued to have great months afterwards but never as high as when I petitioned God for the month of August. But here is what happened: October came and went then November came and I never joined "Evangelism Explosion." I couldn't justify the money I was making by singing in the choir and only being a part-time Regional Manager for Franklin Life. The control I had given God over my life, I was now taking back. I guess I had unconsciously reverted back to my old self and the concept of, "If it's going to be — it's up to me." What a ride and what lessons Jesus taught me during that time!

He taught me; Seek Him first and not material success. If material success came, it would be a by-product of my first serving Him and His faithfulness to meet my needs. I

Accepting The Awards

learned He loved me and I desired to have an intimate relationship with Him. He truly was my first love.

In January of 1982, I was home when I received a phone call from the Home Office. Des Moines had just been hit with a major snow storm: the outside temperature was 20 degrees below zero; with the wind chill factor of nearly 72 degrees below zero. Interstate 80 was shut down and there were warnings for everyone to stay off the roads. The phone call was to inform me the Central Plains Region was officially ranked number one in every major category measured for National recognition. We took every award! They, also told me I had two candidates in the running for "National Rookie of the Year." I was pumped and even though it was cold outside — I was warm and excited from the phone call I just received. The results (at the end of the year) for "Letting go and letting God" were in: The Region had qualified to win every major National Award available and it would be official when announced at FMDC. The awards were presented by Bill Alley, President & CEO.

As I received each of the awards given to the Region, I thanked God in front of everyone at Franklin's Million Dollar Conference, for His blessings and I recognized all of my managers and agents who were part of the Region's success.

This was also the first time in the history of Franklin Life; a Region ever produced two "National Rookies of the year." Both were awarded due to excelling in different areas. Jim Meggers, my brother-in-law was named the "National Rookie of the Year" for all of Franklin for the great job he did

Our new home in West DSM

in agency building and Bob Headley, a new agent I recruited from the insurance industry, was named the "National Rookie of the Year" for personal production.

God blessed them both that year with His favor but in a few years the winds of change will hit and when it does, they will both cost me a small fortune. Still, through it all; God remained faithful.

During this time, I continued to sing in the choir and special music programs when asked. The managers and agents continued to grow their business and I was able to spend more time with my family. God gave me supernatural favor for a season and I wanted to be obedient to Him. Even in spite of my short comings and failed promise, He showed Himself faithful to me.

When the next "Evangelism Explosion" session started, I took a leadership role but production levels never reached the August record of $107,000 again. What did I learn from all that? When I was obedient and practiced His principal's set-up for us in the Bible, God blessed me. He gave me the desires of my heart, like singing and having more time with my family. But he also blessed me materially.

Back yard with heated pool

Over the next year my income nearly doubled. With that extra income, I purchased a new Mercedes right off the show room floor, while also building a 3,850

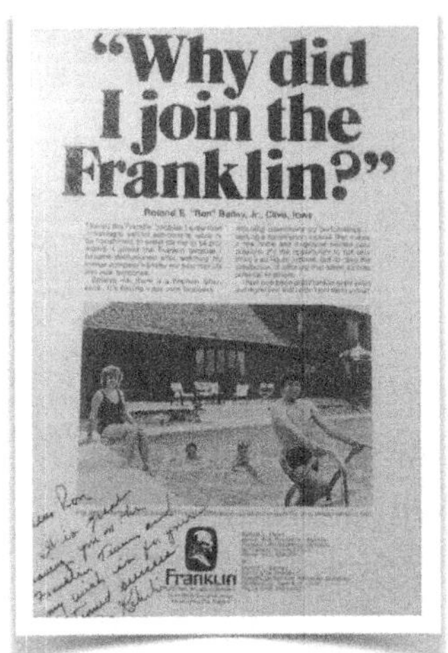

Trade Journal Ad

square foot home with another 2,400 square feet of unfinished space in the basement. In addition it had an in-ground heated swimming pool and we were living in Ashland Estates; a new up-scale sub-division in West Des Moines.

Our success was also the subject of trade journal advertisements and I was featured in multiple insurance magazines during that time. In addition, my associates all benefited financially from God's favor on them. But most importantly, God was showing me just how real He was and how much He loved me. He proved His faithfulness to me and was teaching me about servanthood. He was also showing me how to be responsible with the blessings He had given me.

Luke 12: 48 "To whom much is given, much will be required as well. All during this adventure I was learning God's principals both in church and in practical experiences. One truth was in the principal of tithing.

Throughout the Bible in both the New Testament and Old, we are reminded that God is the source of everything we have. If our source is in our self, we are limited but if our source is God, we are joint heirs with Christ and our potential is limitless. He is our Father and He wants to share His wealth, His strength and His power with us.

Malachi 3:10-12 God is actually asking us to test Him when He says; "Bring the full tithe into the storehouse, that there may be food in my house and thereby put me to the test, says the Lord of hosts, if I will not open the windows of heaven for you and pour down a blessing until there is no more need. I will rebuke the devourer for you so it will not destroy the fruits of your soil and your vine in the field shall not fail to bear, says the Lord of hosts."

When the Israelites obeyed the Lord and gave their first fruits, they experienced an overabundance of provision and freedom from want. Their abundance became proof that God was in Israel and made them the envy of all nations.

Over the years God has taken care of His people through tithes and generous giving. I learned this principal early as a new Christian. I was becoming used to the gifts of the Holy Spirit and discovered this was another supernatural principal that ran counter to human logic.

When I first started tithing I was giving about $100 a week and as my income grew my tithing grew. By the end of the next year my tithing had grown right along with my income. I was a happy giver! In the years following my giving was more than just the tithe. There were always causes like supporting missionaries, expanding the church facilities or gifts of appreciation, to name a few. Like the gifts of the spirit, there was something supernatural about tithing and I learned you can't out give God.

I was learning how to grow and mature in my walk with God. Having an intimacy with Jesus through His Holy Spirit gave me supernatural faith. It was a faith built on love and trust. His desire was for me to trust Him with all my heart, all my soul, all my mind and all my strength. I needed to Trust Him in all things and pray to Him on all occasions.

What I learned from my pastors at First Assembly of God in Des Moines, Iowa was; when I was baptized the first time in the Holy Spirit, I had an infilling of His Spirit. When I had my second encounter with Him in my office, I had a fresh re-filling of His Spirit but also received supernatural unmerited favor. With His favor He not only blessed me but everyone in the Region. He was honoring our work as we were honoring Him.

Once put into action, I found His principals still work today, as much as they did over 2,000 years ago. I also learned to be content in all situations and take the good with the bad. At this point in my life the sea was set for smooth sailing, but In a few years the winds of change will hit and the seas will get choppy. That is when I will need Jesus as my anchor.

Chapter 19

"But seek first the kingdom of God and His righteousness and all these things will be given to you as well." Matthew 6:33

Joining Evangelism Explosion

When the Evangelism Explosion program started back up in the Spring, I volunteered and took a leadership role. However, in spite of my new involvement with E.E. we never exceeded the production we had that past August. I did capitalize on the program and from it, learned how to effectively witness to people for Christ.

After I received the baptism in the Holy Spirit, I had a passion for helping people understand the gospel message and for leading them to the Lord. I even called some of my old friends from High School and witnessed to them over the phone. One was a friend who just had a heart attack. He was very open and accepted Jesus as his Lord and Savior over the phone. I also led my mom and one of my brothers to the Lord.

My friends knew me and they knew I was sincerely interested in them. Even though we were over a thousand miles away, we were able to share our lives together and be reconnected to our old high school days. In the process of reconnecting, it was easy for me to share my story with them. I would also tell them about the love of God and then ask them two questions. I asked; "If you were to die today, would you know for sure you would go to heaven?" If they said I think so or they weren't sure, I would then ask, "Let's just say you died and were standing in line to get into heaven and you were asked, "Why should I let you into my heaven, what would you say?" If they answered with anything other than by God's GRACE, or the blood of Jesus, I would say, "Would you like to know how you can know for sure?" Because of the relationship I had with them, they would trust me to lead them even further.

I taught this method of witnessing to my key managers in the region and developed a presentation to be used at their discretion, at the close of each insurance sale.

Most of the sales made back then were plans involving a combination of cash value life insurance and term insurance. When we were ready to leave after the sale was made, we would say, "In our lives four things will happen to us and the policy you are applying for tonight will take care of three of those four: dying too soon; living too long and becoming disabled along the way." This plan you are qualifying for helps you and your family if anyone of those situations occur while you're here on earth, but let me ask you a question; "If you were die tonight, would you know for sure that you would go to heaven?" It was non evasive and easy to witness to people with that approach. The results were very gratifying to say the least and we posted them for our associates to see.

On our production board in the regional conference room we added a category for "DFJ." People who made a decision for Jesus. The calls coming in at the end of the month were now going something like this; we had thirty sales for the Franklin and five sales for the Lord.

Through our active involvement with Evangelism Explosion, over the next couple of years we were able to lead well over 100 people to the Lord and introduce them to good churches. We had a mission to lead people to the Lord but we also felt it was important to get them into a good church once they made their confession of faith.

Nothing lasts forever and the insurance industry was going to be involved in a major shift in the way insurance policies were to be sold. I also began feeling the need to spend more time with my son. My daughter was going off to college and my son was now a teenager. I had made a point to be at all of his activities growing up but between the insurance business and church, I wasn't spending as much quality time with him as I would have liked.

TIME WITH MY SON

When I turned 40 years old, I began to reevaluate my life and decided I wanted to slow down and spend more time with my son. Time was flying by and I wanted to have some special time with him while there still was time.

Todd was interested in biking and when he was around 14 years old, he heard about RAGBRI, a large bicycling event taking place across the State of Iowa. It was sponsored by the Des Moines Resister, the local news-paper. In fact, RAGBRI stood for, Register's Greater Bike Ride Across Iowa. The total bike ride for the week, would cover about 540 miles.

Todd had just purchased a Cannondale Bike made with an aluminum cast frame and he was itching to ride it, so he asked me if he could participate in this road event?

I asked around and found out it was a week-long event made up of mostly adults, so rather than discouraging him, I told him, "Let's do it together." When I checked further into the event, I found out it was also a big party event for older kids.

I talked with my biker friends at church about riding RAGBRI and discovered they too had an interest in the event. We then decided, it would be a good way to use "Evangelism Explosion." The church liked the idea and said we could use their van as a shag wagon; for people injured or too tired to bike, as well as, to hold spare bike parts. Since this would be a church sponsored event for E.E., the church also provided us with team shirts; reflecting two large question marks on our back; designed to cause people to inquire about the meaning of question marks; allowing us to share our faith with them. In addition, the church gave us Bibles to hand out. We now had a plan in place for the event.

This was March and I had less than four months to prepare. What I needed next was a bike. I looked around and ended up buying a used 18 speed Schwinn bicycle from one of my biking friends at church. Once I had my bike, Todd and I started practicing for the big ride to come.

On the first day Todd and I had only ridden around 15 miles before I broke my chain climbing a high hill. Fortunately, someone in a truck going to West Des Moines was driving by when it happened. He stopped to see if we were okay and gave us a ride back to our house. We felt God was watching over us. We would have had a long walk back.

Todd and I ready to ride

It snowed a lot between March and April, so we didn't practice as much as we would have liked but we still managed to have a few 40 miles or more rides in before RAGBRI.

On the day RAGBRI began, we dipped our back tires into the

Missouri River and set out to reach the Mississippi River six days later. Then once we had reached the furthest town to the east, we dipped our front tires in the Mississippi River to complete our ride.

Todd and 15,000 plus bikers

During the bike ride; all the small farm towns along the way had bake sales and we stopped occasionally to fill up on homemade cookies, fruits or pastries. Then at night, we ate heavy carbs like; pizza, spaghetti or pancakes. We averaged over 60 miles a day, with one day being a 100-mile challenge, so we had big appetites.

On the day of the 100-mile challenge, I wanted to ride the longer route and my son didn't, so at the junction, my son went one way and I went the other. Well, to both of our dismay, he ended up riding the 100-mile challenge and I did the 70 mile plus trip. He was upset, but after receiving his special recognition patch for completing the challenge, he was happy he did it and I was proud of him for completing it.

We usually started riding at sun-up which was around 5:30 a.m. We wanted to get as much accomplished as we could while the sun was not beating down on us. Most of the days we rode, temperatures were in the high 90's accompanied with high humidity. Over those days we even rode through a few thunderstorms. The wind was a big factor. It was fine when it was at your back but we had a couple of days when the head wind was so strong, we had to pedal just to go down the hills. Those days were brutal! RAGBRI was not for beginners or the poorly conditioned.

On riding RAGBRI, I learned about how the water towers were positioned in the small towns we rode through. I never thought much about it before, but water towers were placed in the highest areas in town so the water could be distributed easily by gravity. The town's water towers were picturesque in Iowa and said something about the communities they were in but when it came to riding a bike, it usually meant get ready, you are approaching a steep hill.

One day before the rain hit us, I was pedaling hard going up a hill gasping for air, when out of nowhere, a big juicy fly flew down my throat and almost knocked me off of my bicycle! I had swallowed it, choked and finally coughed it back up! My son was riding beside me and asked me if I was ok? I then told him what happened. He laughed, and as we rounded the corner of the hill we saw this big pig farm. The smell was horrible! He laughed again and said, "I bet I know where that fly came from." It was a sick thought and we both laughed at the visual it painted.

Todd and I both felt we were in pretty good shape when we started RAGBRI but by the end of the ride, we knew we were in great physical shape. We were tired but we felt a great sense of satisfaction knowing we rode the entire ride. Some of the hills we rode up drained us of every drop of energy we had in reserve but we did it. Many people ride only a day or two to just say they rode in RAGBRI. They came from around the world to ride in the adventure we were on.

As a biking event, RAGBRI was actually one of the pre-conditioning rides professional bikers participated in before competing in the "Tour de France." The premier biking event in the world of biking; ranking up there with the Olympics for bikers.

It was a challenging week, where the average biker lost about 10 pounds over the course of the ride. But it was different for me. I ended up gaining around 10 pounds riding RAGBRI; probably due to all the carrot cake and oatmeal raisin cookies I ate along the way.

RAGBRI was a great experience for Todd and me. In addition to our personal accomplishments, a number of people asked us about the question marks on our team shirts. So, in addition to a great father-son adventure, we both had an opportunity to witness a number of people give their hearts to the Lord. That in itself was worth the price of admission. Our biking team from the church also invited everyone who made a confession of faith, to visit our church in Des Moines to learn more about what it meant to be born again. We also gave each of them a Bible.

Todd and I, both look back on the adventures we shared and the memories we have, of the week we rode RAGBRI together.

After riding RAGBRI, physically we were both in great shape so a few months later we decided to ride the MS-150 challenge together. It was a two-day bike riding event totaling 150 miles, to raise money and awareness for Multiple Sclerosis.

The day we left Des Moines, we rode into a head-wind nearly the entire way. It was a long gruesome ride with a lot of unhappy bikers trekking their way across the State of Iowa. The only consolation was, we should have a tail wind coming back, making our ride back to Des Moines easier.

The next day we woke up early to hit the road before the sun rose in the sky. Once on the road headed back to Des Moines, we started riding into the head wind again. This was horrible! Going back to Des Moines, the wind was in our face the entire time. Again, it was so strong that we had to

Our Custom Franklin Van

pedal while going downhill. At this point, Todd and I were both tired! If either of us had been riding by ourselves, we probably would have called it a day and taken the shag wagon back. Riding together, challenged us to keep on biking and finish strong.

Finally, when we were within 20 miles of our destination, we were so worn out we just wanted to cry: instead we made a joke out of it and laughed all the way to the finish line in Des Moines.

If we hadn't been in such good condition from riding RAGBRI, we probably never would have made it all the way. Well...we made it: it was for a good cause and we both have lasting memories from it. Most importantly, we experienced it together.

Chapter 20

"Be glad for all God is planning for you. Be patient in trouble and prayerful always." Romans 12:12

Winds of Change

The insurance industry was changing and computers were becoming the key player in the sales process. It was, who ever showed the best returns on their print-outs won the sale. The days of selling guarantees in life insurance was becoming a thing of the past. The new universal life sales were sold using smoke and mirror tricks with no guarantees. Computer illustrations could now be manipulated to show anything.

Over time, my agents became discouraged continually losing business to this new hybrid method of selling. We were selling traditional guaranteed whole-life plans with dividends, to further increase values at retirement. Our competition was using computers to separate the life insurance protection portion from the retirement component and illustrating hypothetical cash values to retirement, using non-guaranteed historical stock market returns instead of fixed interest rates. People believed what thcy saw on the print-outs and we lost business.

There were over 50 insurance company home offices located in Des Moines. Many of the insurance companies were ahead of the curve on technology and saw how the computer was becoming a key factor in the sales of life insurance. They armed their agents with computers and many of them gave their agents a bonus, on top of regular commissions to harvest cash values out of other companies' policies. Some companies even paid their agents to replace their own business.

Up until this time, wholesale replacement of policies in other companies was illegal but now it was excepted and Franklin had a target on its back because of the rich cash value plans we sold.

Computers also gave birth to companies like A. L. Williams whose philosophy was, buy term insurance and invest the difference. They made a campaign out of destroying any and all cash value type policies through multi-level marketing organizations. A. L. Williams worked in large churches and recruited the pastors; the pastors recruited church leaders and they in-turn recruited the congregation.

Des Moines was a huge insurance town and First Assembly was one of the largest churches in the area. It was a perfect breeding ground for a leader in A.L. Williams to set up shop in. That is exactly what happened. One of the leaders in A.L Williams from Atlanta, GA moved to Des Moines and started working the First Assembly congregation. He never recruited any of the pastors but he was replacing our business and trying to recruit everybody he talked to. All of this together was making my life a living hell.

Through all of this, I was praying for God to help me. Why was this happening? It was just three years ago I was in God's favor and now it seemed like I was being punished. My Region was hemorrhaging and I didn't know how to stop it! I sort of felt like Job.

I petitioned the Home Office for help! We needed to understand how to compete against these new forces. I began losing my key managers and their agents to other companies. One of the key managers to leave was my brother-in-law; the leading agency builder, a top producer and one of my best friends. In addition, he was family. He finally gave up on Franklin and went with another company to sell the new plans.

Our presentations allowed us to sell with the best in the business, but other agents could easily replace our business using their computers. Replacement activity was high in Iowa and my agents were losing confidence in what they were doing. That's what happened with Jim. I did my best to convince him to stay, but he lost confidence in selling Franklin's guaranteed whole life plans. I had given him all of my old clients when he moved to Marion, helped him build his agency and now he will become my biggest adversary working in another company!

When Jim left, it sent shock waves through-out the Region. He not only left, but a number of his agents left with him. I was now spending most of my time doing damage control, trying to conserve business instead of sales management. I was crushed! My blood pressure was affected and I was put on a new medication where one of the side effects heightened my emotions. The Region was in a downward spiral and I was going down too. I was doing my best to keep everyone encouraged while needing to be encouraged myself.

With all of these new changes in the insurance industry, the government got involved. There was a crisis going on! New laws and regulations were passed that the insurance industry had to abide by. With new regulations came continuing education and in preparing for the new changes, I became certified by the state of Iowa to teach continuing education classes. This also gave me a chance to meet other insurance agents in Iowa. I also introduced business ethics into the class to build agent relationships and try to slow down the replacement activities from other companies.

I got tired of the rat race I was running; so, to relax I took my family to Florida for a nice vacation. We visited my parents, went to Disneyland and played in the ocean.

While relaxing in Florida, I started thinking about the prospects of retiring. I was only 41 years old but the idea of moving to Florida started growing on me. I talked about it with Joanne and she also thought it had some merit. She saw how the business was affecting me and after getting back from vacation we continued to talk about the possibilities of moving there. What was going on?

In 1985 I probably averaged receiving from the Home Office 20 replacement notices a month; of people dropping their insurance. They were sent in envelopes throughout the month by regular mail. A year later, I was receiving three or four large boxes of replacement notices a week from the home office and they were delivered to me by U.P.S. Hundreds of clients were leaving Franklin a week and most of them now were being replaced by my former agents.

Joanne and I talked about moving to Florida again to semi-retire: to work when I wanted to and not have the stress of running the Region.

At the annual Regional Manager's meeting in the Home Office, I made an appointment with the Senior Executive Vice President of Franklin to discuss the situation I had in Des Moines. He knew I was getting hit with a lot of negatives but didn't know how bad it was affecting me. I told him "Joanne and I were thinking about moving to Florida to slow down but I would continue to work with Franklin in Florida, if the Home Office helped us with our move."

The Home Office now understood my situation and after a lot of discussion, they agreed to move us to Florida. They saw — what was happening in the Region — was costing me time, money and my health.

I never stopped to think about it being God's plan to move us to Florida, for what needed to come next. In my mind, I just wanted to slow down and spend more time with my family. With God though — it was aligning me with my destiny.

I had one more obligation to take care of before moving to Florida. I had promised the Regional Manager in Wyoming I would speak at his quarterly regional meeting in April. The meeting date was set and he made reservations for us at a lodge near the area of Mt. Rushmore. I saw Mt. Rushmore as a kid and wanted to take my wife and son there, so they could see it too.

I decided to drive so we could see all the sights along the way. When we reached Rapid City, South Dakota it started to snow. It was in the early evening and the snowflakes were large and fluffy in the light from my headlights. As the sun started to fall behind the Mountain, the snow continued and in the distance we could see something glowing. The light grew more evident the closer we got to Mt. Rushmore. We were excited! We will see Mt. Rushmore all lit up. We continued driving while looking at the glow coming off of the mountain. Every so often we could catch a better view of the faces in the distance. We were close! It was just around the bend and we'll see the faces all lit up. Then; when we were within a mile of seeing the Presidents faces, the lights were shut off and Mt. Rushmore went dark.

With the mountain dark, we were all bummed out. We not only missed Mt. Rushmore all lit up but we now realized we were driving in deep snow! There were no other cars on

Near Mt. Rushmore

the road and the snow was not letting up. I gripped the steering wheel tighter and concentrated on keeping the car in the middle of the road, as we drove deeper into the mountains. It was dark and scary, but in-spite of what we faced, we finally arrived at the Lodge safe and sound.

In the snow storm God gave me a picture of my life: and the revelation He gave me became part of my closing comments at the end of the meeting.

The message was; as long as I stayed focused on my goal, all I thought about was my vision — which was to see Mt. Rushmore all lit up. When the lights went out — I lost my vision and then, all I saw were the problems around me.

For the agents I was talking to; it meant, keep your eyes on your goals and not on the replacement problems or the negatives of the business. Have a vision, keep the lights on, stay positive and make your goal — to qualify for Franklin's Million Dollar Convention next year.

God's message to me was; follow the light (Jesus) and put your trust in Him. Let the Holy Spirit guide you. You may have a lot of negatives around you clouding your vision, but if your eyes are fixed on Jesus, He will guide you through it all to your destination.

At Mt. Rushmore

I was moving to Florida to change our lives but God was moving us to align us with His purpose for our lives.

RETIRING TO FLORIDA

The Home Office agreed to pay for my wife and me to fly to Florida to help us decide where we wanted to live. While we were there, I also visited with the managers in those areas to see who I wanted to be associated with once we moved.

After exploring the area and visiting with the different Area Managers; we decided on the Tampa Bay area. We worked with a realtor who drove us around and helped us narrow our search down to a choice between Clearwater or Sarasota. The Home Office then sent us a second time to look at homes in Sarasota and Clearwater.

After looking at all of the homes the realtor picked out for us on our return visit, we decided to buy a 5-bedroom, ranch-styled home with an enclosed swimming pool under construction, in Clearwater. It was a Rutenberg Home situated in Countryside which was in a perfect location for us. Countryside High School was one of the top high schools in the area. That was important to us, not only for our son but also for resale when the time came.

Once our house in Iowa sold, it was time to move. The new Regional Manager was appointed and we said good-bye to our friends and Franklin associates.

I was tired of the rat race and climbing the corporate ladder. Money and position wasn't as important to me now. I was ready to live a life of leisure with my wife and son; while my daughter headed off to college.

Looking back, God's timing was perfect in directing our move to Florida. The area we bought in, was exactly where we needed to be for Kim to meet her future husband and it was also there where the path of her life-long career would begin.

Todd and me in FL

We drove our car from Des Moines to Clearwater and when we showed up for our walk-through inspection before our closing, we found our home was still a couple of weeks away from being finished. I was livid! I was also upset about the changes I had made to the house over the phone; that hadn't been carried out. I had called from Iowa before we left to make sure everything was on schedule and going as planned. This was going to complicate things a little.

I notified the Home Office of our dilemma and the agreement we had with them was that they would pay our moving expenses until we closed on our home. We thought it would probably cover only a few days of hotel and food expenses but they surprised us and paid the bill for the entire month, as well as storage for our furniture.

We stayed at the Holiday Inn Surf, a popular hotel right on Clearwater Beach. Every-day we ate in the hotel and went to the beach just like we were tourists. It was wonderful.

The first week we were there Kim, who hadn't left for college yet, met a young man named George Chambers at our hotel, and later called us from his home. She said "Dad, you're not going to believe this. I'm standing in a ballroom of the biggest house I have ever been in; over-looking Clearwater Bay." "It is a mansion located in a private compound on Clearwater Bay and it's so spectacular it was even used in a couple of movies." She went on to explain this house was owned by Dr. Chambers, the father of this young college kid she met. Dr. Chambers was a famous hair transplant surgeon who pioneered the hair transplant industry.

New home in Clearwater

Kim and George became good friends and when Kim came home on break from college, they would see each other as friends. When the next summer came around Kim was looking for a way to earn extra money and George suggested maybe working for his dad as a receptionist.

Kim applied for the job and was hired. In addition to being a receptionist, on occasion she also had a chance to observe the surgeries. She saw first-hand what the technicians were doing and decided she could do that too. So, when the summer ended, Kim didn't go back to college at Evangel. Instead she attended The University of Tampa and received a degree as a surgical assistant. Now, she was able to assist in the surgeries. Kim was a fast learner and soon became part of Dr. Chamber's traveling team. By this time, he was doing surgeries all over the State of Florida. Later on, Dr. Chambers started franchising his business and opened up a school to train the doctors. In addition to assisting him on surgeries, Kim became one of his instructors at the school. All that happened because she met George when we were staying at the Holiday Inn Surf waiting for our house to be completed. God was aligning Kim up with her destiny.

Chris-Craft Scorpion

When we moved into our house I found additional issues to deal with the builder on, but in time everything was taken care of. I soon realized Florida people moved at a different pace than what I was used to up North.

One of the first things I did once we were settled, was to buy a life-time family membership to American Fitness. I worked out nearly every day and after a few months I was really feeling good. I was enjoying working out, going to the beach and adjusting to my new lifestyle.

I enjoyed this new life of leisure for about six months but the problems up North didn't go away. My income was dropping drastically due to the insurance replacement activity still going on in Iowa. I also knew I had to get all new licenses in Florida before I could make any sales to build-up my income, and keep my end of the bargain with the Home Office. In addition, we wanted to find a good church.

One of the largest and most popular churches at the time was the Clearwater Baptist Church. It was in downtown Clearwater near Clearwater Beach. They had a great music program and once we got settled in the church I joined the choir. I wanted to continue singing for the Lord. I enjoyed singing in the choir and also singing as a solo-artists with back up tracks. Life and singing for the Lord was good.

One day, Kim was running around with Sherry, a girl who lived across the street from us and they decided to go to a club where Sherry's boyfriend hung out. It was there where Kim met Ken Lee. He was a golf pro and instructor at Countryside Country Club. She and Ken hit it off and soon were dating quite regularly. I liked Ken. He was a gentleman and treated Kim good.

One day I received a phone call from Ken to see if we could get together. When he came over to the house I noticed he was a little nervous. We spent a few minutes talking about golf and living in Clearwater, then he looked me in the eyes and said; “I really love Kim and I would like your permission to marry her.” Wow, I thought for a minute and all I could say was; “I’d be proud to have you as my son-in-law.” He relaxed and told me how nervous he was trying to figure out how he would ask me. I then told him, “Once you marry her she will be your responsibility and there is no giving her back.” I said it tongue in cheek and we both laughed. He then said, “Don’t say anything to Kim. I plan on asking her this week.” We talked some more and then he left. After he left, I told Joanne about my talk with Ken and she started to cry. We were happy for them, yet it was hard to comprehend; our little girl was going to be getting engaged to be married.

When the end of the week came, Ken popped the question to Kim and presented her with a diamond ring. Kim could hardly wait to tell us she was engaged and show us her ring.

When the time came, she had a beautiful beach wedding at the Sheraton Sand Key Resort Hotel on Clearwater Beach. Our friend and pastor from First Assembly of God Church in Des Moines, Iowa, Phil Pfaltzgraff performed the wedding ceremony and it was a very special day!

Kim was now married and Todd was off to college. Time had flown bye. I sold a little insurance now and then to maintain my part of the agreement with the Home Office but I wasn’t working very hard. I was doing what I wanted when I wanted to. The Area Manager, however, wanted me at the office in Tampa with him, to be more involved in building the agency. He had a nice office in Tampa but for me, driving the causeway every morning was a

Mr. and Mrs. Lee

pain. The drive was pretty but the traffic was horrible. It was easier for me to drive to where the agents were working than being in the office in Tampa. This became an issue with the Area Manager and soon we were at odds over it. I didn't want a controlling office schedule, I wanted contentment.

Lauren's welcoming party

During this time, I became active in the Life Underwriters Association in our area. I was content in giving back to the industry and was enjoying the fellowship with agents from various companies in the area. I soon rose to the rank of President of the Association. I was excited about the work I was doing and worked hard to make a difference. The hard work paid off and when the Florida State Association Chairman recognized the State's local associations that year; the Clearwater Association was ranked number one in the four major categories they recognized. I was then asked to speak at the National Association of Life Underwriter's Convention in Nashville, TN.

While in Nashville, I connected with Brady Creel, my friend and associate from the days in the Home Office. We shared what was going on in our lives and he told me if I ever thought about moving, he would love for me to work with him in Nashville.

I never thought much about that until a year later. It was when

Lauren Patricia Lee

Kim and Ken presented us with Lauren Patricia Lee, our new grand-daughter. We enjoyed spending our time with her. Then one day Kim told us, Ken was being transferred to New Jersey to take over management of a golf course and they would be moving. We were heart broken and I thought back to how my mom felt when we moved from Massachusetts to Iowa with her first grand-daughter.

The winds of change was starting to move again. I was being fulfilled with my involvement in the Life Underwriters Association but I was still having control issues with the Area Manager. In the meantime, Joanne was feeling the empty-nest syndrome with just the two of us living in this five-bedroom home. With those feeling being real, we started talking about downsizing.

It was 1994 and the real estate market in Clearwater was stagnant. Interest rates were high and a lot of homes were in foreclosure. A friend of mine living down the street from us, was having a garage sale. He was down-sizing to get back to living in an apartment. He and his wife divorced and had to sell their home. He tried to sell it by owner first and then went with a realtor. Their home was on the market for over six months and they ended up selling it for $46,000 below what they originally paid for it. I had gone to his garage sale just to say hi and while I was there he asked me if there was anything I would like. I said "No" and then I saw his for sale by owner sign. I said "Maybe this sign." He said, "It's yours." I took the sign home, bought some new numbers at Home Depot to place on it and put the sign in our front yard on my mother-in-law's birthday. I did it as a joke. I really didn't expect it to sell. What was I thinking?

Joanne and I decided to leave the sign in the yard to see if we would get any hits. After all, we had started to think about down-sizing. We prayed; "Lord, if it is your will for us to sell this house; this is what we will sell it for." We figured if we sold our house for the amount we were praying about, it was God's will for us to sell it. We didn't have to sell, and I sure wasn't planning on selling it for less than what we paid for it.

I knew the market was not conducive to selling it on our own — it was; "Let go and let God." There were homes all around us for sale, with some on the market for nearly a year. Florida was in a recession.

Later that week, while my wife and I were eating supper, we received a phone call from someone who wanted to look at our home. They told us they were calling from their car phone in our driveway. (Back then very few people had mobile phones). We told them they could and we let them in to see it. He owned restaurants in the malls around the area and his wife was a realtor. They looked through the house and made us a full price cash offer, subject to having a home inspection and with a possession date in November. It wasn't subject to the sale of their home or anything: it was as clean an agreement as you could possibly have. We accepted their offer with earnest money to bind the agreement and his wife drew up the paper work. When they left, Joanne and I both looked at each other in amazement. What just happened? We had to be out of our house in two months, then we'll be homeless. We were told our house selling for cash at the full price so quickly was truly a miracle. What was God doing?

There were a lot of homes on the market but did we want to live in Florida full time? We started thinking about our options. Because there were so many homes on the market, there were great corporate lease programs available. We could live in million-dollar homes on the water for just $750 a month, subject to us allowing the homes to be shown to prospective buyers. We qualified for the program and our furniture qualified for the staging, but we could not have any pets. Well, we had a dog. Ashley had been with us for five years and was part of our family. She was a beautiful Lhasa Apso and with our kids out of the house, she was our companion.

We decided to look at the executive leased homes to see what options we had. We had a friend who said they would take care of Ashley — we could visit her whenever we wanted and when we found a permanent home, we could have her back. With that situation solved, we felt better about pursuing the leased executive homes.

Most of the large homes on the water were located away from everything we were familiar with so we opted to look at homes closer to Clearwater. We narrowed the search down to a smaller home on Lake Tarpon and a larger home in Tampa, near the office. With the smaller home we would have to sell some of our furniture and with the larger home we would have to leave a lot of the upstairs rooms empty. We prayed — “Lord this is your move — what do we do?”

I then had a thought come to me. What if we lived in Florida for six months and lived somewhere else for six months? That way we could enjoy the four-seasons of the year and be closer to our families when we wanted to get together for the holidays.

I called Brady to see if he would be open to working with me on a six-month basis, if we chose to live in the Nashville area? Brady said he would love it and asked Joanne and I to come to the regional picnic they were having the end of September. He said he would love for me to be their guest speaker, and if so, the regional fund would pick up all of our expenses; while also giving us a chance to look over the area. How could I refuse that offer?

I spoke at the regional picnic and Brady drove us around Franklin to see the different things of interest. I never realized how many famous people in the entertainment business lived in Franklin. I was very impressed with the area.

When we got back to Clearwater, I needed to talk to the Area Manager to see how the six-month arrangement would work with him or see if it would be better to stay in Florida and just do the executive lease program.

I called his office to try and set up an appointment with the Area Manager but I was told he was in sequester for a couple of weeks and didn't want to be disturbed by anyone. He was in his office but was working on the fall meeting. I called again the next week and asked to have him call me but was again told the same thing.

During this same time, I had talked to my son-in-law about what we might do and he gave me the name of a realtor who was a friend of his sister. (He and his sister grew up in Knoxville, TN) and she had a friend who was a realtor in Franklin. I called her friend and told her we were looking for a place to rent six-months out of the year, in or around Franklin. We knew of plenty of places like that in Florida so didn't think there would be a problem. On the other hand, she said it would be next to impossible for an arrangement like that in Franklin. Even so, she would look for us.

GOD'S MOVING US TO FRANKLIN

It was the middle of October and I still hadn't heard anything from the Area Manager in Florida. I was running out of time and needed to make a decision!

While contemplating my options, I received a phone call from the realtor in Franklin. She said she couldn't find anything for us to lease or rent for six-months but she had a lead on an attorney who was getting a divorce. He was trying to sell his home but would be willing to rent it to us until he sold it. His divorce would be final in December and we could move into it in January if we were interested. It was basically like the executive lease program in Florida except we would be able to keep Ashley. We asked her to send us some pictures and room sizes to see if our furniture would work. When we received the information, we saw where everything would work. Now it was a question of what do we do? God was up to something. He sold our home; now we need to see how He's going to orchestrate our move and with the Area Manager still not contacting me – I figured I really wasn't that important to him after all.

New home in Franklin, TN

Joanne and I began thinking more about the rental home in Franklin and the chance to work with Brady. In the back of my mind, I even thought about possibly getting involved with the music business once we got to Nashville. I could sing and still work in the insurance business.

I checked with different moving companies and found a reputable company who would pack us, hold our furniture in storage and move our stuff to Franklin in January. In the meantime, we had friends in Iowa

Back of home - koi pond

who would allow us to live in their home until January. They would be visiting their son in California through the holidays. It was all coming together. We will move to Franklin, stay in Iowa over the holidays and meet the moving van at our new rental in January.

The Bailey's & Lee's

Now, looking back, I realize the situation with the Area Manager was all a part of God's plan for us to move.

We enjoyed our time in Iowa and drove to Franklin on New Year's Day. The next day we met the moving van and set up house. We knew we would have to make another move in a few months, so stored a lot of boxes in the garage and unused bedrooms. We figured we would have at least six months to check out the area before we would need to move again.

By the second week though, we were having a couple of showings a day. It was hard on Joanne to keep the house show-room ready and with that much activity we thought it could be sold at any time. We felt if that were to happen; we needed to find something sooner than originally planned.

We called our realtor to start showing us homes in our price range — in and around the Franklin area. We looked at new and used homes for a couple of weeks and settled on a new house being built by the Carbines. The home we liked was located next to Denzel Carbine's home, one of the owners of the company and across the street from his project superintendent. It was being built as a model home and they were only a month away from finishing it. It was a perfect fit for our situation: plus if we had any problems, we lived right next door to the guy who could take care of them. So, by

March 1, 1995 we found a local moving company and moved into our new house.

By the middle of March, I completed all of my insurance and securities exams for the State of Tennessee. I was now ready to help Brady build his region.

In August of 1995 my grandson, Kyle Bai Lee was born and Joanne went out to New Jersey to help Kim. A few weeks later Kim and the kids came to be with us in Franklin; while Ken stayed in New Jersey to prepare for them to move. Ken was being transferred to take over the management of "The Gauntlet," a golf course near Greenville, South Carolina. Kim and the kids stayed with us a week and then we all drove to Greenville to see their new home. It was very nice and I could see where I could even live there. It was such an improvement over New Jersey for them.

We stayed for a week and then drove eight hours back home to return to work; training and working with Brady's top managers around the region.

I originally met Brady's top agents and managers when I spoke at the regional picnic a year ago. I was now working and helping them build their agencies, while building my own personal clientele closer to home.

At the time, I knew Franklin Life was looking for a company to buy them. Franklin hadn't put any money into new technology and weren't willing to give in to the changes going on in the industry. This meant they had to find a suitable partner or be sold to the highest bidder. Well, Franklin Life was bought by American General and life was going to change for Franklin agents.

American General was corporate and Franklin Life was entrepreneurial. It was an oil and water mixture; very toxic and not very compatible. American General tried to create more structure in Franklin's agency system, while at the same time they terminated a lot of people in Franklin's Home Office. This created additional strife with Franklin agents. To solve this dilemma, someone from Franklin needed to be a mediator to this calamity. Brady Creel was the person chosen for the job. He moved to Franklin's Home Office as the Chief Marketing Officer and became the liaison between Franklin and American General. With Brady gone, I was now alone to fend for myself. God knew my situation though – He had other plans for me. Part of His plan included me finding Christ Church in Brentwood.

Joanne had gone to Iowa for a couple of weeks to help her parents and I stayed home to take care of our dog, Ashley. On Sunday; I thought I would visit a new church.

I decided to try Christ Church in Brentwood rather than go to the one we had been attending in Franklin. I heard Christ Church had a great choir and a lot of people in the music industry considered it to be their home church.

It just so happened the day I went they had a guest speaker. The speaker spoke about health issues they faced earlier in their life and how they found a non-profit Christ-centered facility in Nashville that ended up saving their life. The facility she spoke about was free and had a high success rate for those who completed the program. I knew someone who suffered from the same condition as the speaker did and had been close to death a couple of times. The person I knew was involved in another program. It was expensive and had a low success rate.

I picked up information on the facility being discussed and shared it with my friend. We checked into the program and they were accepted. God was intervening. This was no coincidence. This was God's perfect timing. The program worked for my friend and they became a testimony to God's healing power. It was a miracle for me to have been there when I was. God knew what had to be done and He used me at that moment to do it. He also introduced me to the wonderful worship music of the Christ Church Choir.

I knew I wanted to sing for the Lord again. Up to that point, Joanne and I had stayed in Franklin attending different churches but were not active. When I went to Christ Church and heard the choir, I knew I wanted to be a part of the their worship program. I told Joanne about everything and when she came home the following week, we went there to church. She loved Christ Church too. I inquired about how I could join the choir and was told I would have to try out. I found out the Christ Church Choir was a world-famous choir and many people in the choir were in the music industry. I just knew I wanted to sing for the Lord again; so I auditioned and joined the choir the following week.

The Christ Church Choir was under the leadership of Joy and Landy Gardner. Joy was a Grammy nominated singer and Landy was a gifted director. I sang first tenor and loved being part of the choir.

A lot of the songs we did were written or arranged by Joy and Landy with the help of Grammy winning producers. One person on staff was a young college graduate by the name of Bradley Knight. He was a very gifted musician, as well as, a producer and arranger. His songs were amazing and they always tested my vocal range. Bradley was fun to work with too, but after a couple of years he left Christ Church and answered the call to become the Director of Music at Prestonwood Baptist Church, a large church in Dallas, Texas. Bradley then moved to Dallas but would come back to Nashville to record many of his arrangements.

Meanwhile, with all the confusion going on with Franklin Life, I decided to change companies. At first I tried

Painting of The Christ Church Choir

to align myself with top management positions near where my daughter and her husband were living, so we could be close to the grandchildren; but Ken kept getting transferred. I was driving my head-hunter crazy. Just about the time he found something for me, Ken would move to another location and we had to start all over again.

I loved singing in the Christ Church Choir and I loved living in Franklin. So, we decided rather than try and chase the kids we would just stay put. With that in mind, I accepted the Agency Branch Manager's position for Prudential in Brentwood, TN. It was a position my head-hunter found for me. As Prudential's Branch Manager, I had around twenty-five agents and three staff people to supervise. I began to feel a sense of contentment come over me. I loved recruiting and training new agents.

I joined up with Prudential in September of 1997 and one day while walking to my office I noticed a new company had moved into an office suite down the hall from me. I went in to inquire about the type of business it was and to see if they would be interested in getting a quote on group insurance. I found out it was a site acquisition company, who acquired properties to build cell-towers on, for the wireless communication industry. In my questioning, I asked the manager if they would be interested in talking to my son about working there? I told him Todd had graduated from FSU with a double major in Finance and Real Estate. He told me to have my son send him his resume'. Todd was working for a mortgage loan company at the time and wanted to find a job involving real estate. He had been looking at different commercial real estate opportunities to get into but couldn't find anything that would pay him above $24,000 a year to start.

He sent his resume' to the person I had talked to and they called him for an interview. His interview went well and he was able to start the job almost immediately. His starting salary was around $32,000 and the rest is history.

I was at Prudential for around a year. When I took over the Branch it was ranked in the bottom ten percent of Branches in the company. A year later we were ranked in the top twenty-five percent. I felt good about our improvement but the winds of change were moving again. Prudential was going public and they started closing smaller offices and consolidating their managers. Prudential was looking for different ways to cut expenses and show more profitability to investors. In the process of all that, I was caught up in the reorganization.

Looking back, I think the reason I became the Branch Manager of Prudential was God's plan for me to help Todd find his life long career. With that — His timing was perfect.

With the winds of change happening at Prudential, I was visited by a Vice President from Met Life. He was following what was going on with Prudential and wanted me to join Met's management team in Nashville. He asked me to show him my results while Prudential's Branch Manager in Brentwood and the income I had been earning. I showed him how the Branch went from the bottom ten percent to the top twenty-five percent under my leadership and gave him a copy of my income statements. When I did, he – along with the Managing Partner of the Met Life office in Nashville – put together a compensation plan to equal my present income with Prudential. In addition; they gave me an additional incentive to sell business with new Met Life Agents, by appointing me as a Functional Manager. In essence, they were making me a deal I couldn't refuse.

I went to work for Met Life in 1999 but soon they were also positioning themselves to go public and the same thing happened. Six months later, the Vice President who made the deal with me was replaced and the new Region we were a part of; was increased from five states, to eight states: eliminating the jobs of five Vice Presidents. The new Vice President sat down with the Managing Partner and me and discussed the contract I had with Met Life. The new Vice President said, "Met Life couldn't support that rich a contract" and he took away my Functional Manager part in the contract. I really thought that was a cheap shot. Met Life is worth Billions and they needed to reduce my income by a couple thousand a month. The Managing Partner came to me after the Vice President left and apologized to me. He reminded me, he was there when my contract was initially negotiated and approved by the former Vice President. He went on to tell me he tried to convince the new Vice President to leave everything alone because of the value I was bringing to the Agency. He said, "He didn't listen to me and

Carnegie Hall Marquee

under the circumstances I wouldn't blame you if you left; but if you are going to leave, I expect you to give me 100% while you're here." I agreed I would.

CMA Pass

God gave me the ability to make choices in the midst of uncertainty. He gave me the courage to believe in those things that were unseen and hard for me to grasp. I also discovered; overtime — all things do eventually work out for good — to those who love the Lord — according to His will. I felt content: what more could I ask for?

Maybe over time I lost my competitive edge. Maybe it was the continued infilling of the Holy Spirit, the move to Florida or just being caught up in the winds of change, but at this point in my life the only real fulfillment I had was singing in the choir.

Jesus had proved Himself real to me and after all of those years of searching for Him, I wanted to sing for Him more than ever. After all that is what He asked me to do.

With the choir, I was not only ministering to others but I was being ministered too. When I learned the words to the songs I was singing, I was learning scripture. I was feeling His presence. I didn't expect my life to ever be like it was when I first gave God my business. He was training me back then to trust Him. I trusted Him and He was faithful to me. He continued to exceed my expectations up until I broke my promise to Him about joining Evangelism Explosion. I now know I can trust Him in the good times and in the bad. I no longer need to have the material success I had. I was content with having the Holy Spirit's balance in my life and singing in the choir.

1 hour before show

In the Christ Church Choir, I had an opportunity to sing in different venues such as; the Grand Ole Opry, the Ryman Auditorium, Bridgestone Arena, RCA Stadium and many other large churches around the country. We also sang and recorded with such artists as; Wynona, Lee Greenwood, Amy Grant, the Gaither Vocal Group, Vestal Goodman, Jake Hess, Buck Rambo, Dolly Parton, along with many others. Of those, one of my favorite memories was when a few of us in the choir had the opportunity to sing back-up to Dolly Parton at the Country Music Awards in 2002. It was televised and a few of my friends back in Massachusetts saw the program and commented on it.

Another great memory was singing in the city choir at Billy Graham's revival in Nashville at the Nissan Stadium; with over 50,000 people in attendance that day.

Finally, in May of 2018; I was asked by Bradley Knight to join him and others to sing his music at Carnegie Hall. The choir that sang at Carnegie Hall was made up from choir members of: Christ Church in Brentwood, Prestonwood Baptist Church in Dallas and people from different choirs from around the country Bradley had worked with. It was an awesome experience and another great memory.

Show Time

When God asked me to sing for Him back in 1980, He opened all the doors necessary for me to serve Him throughout my life. He also gave me an opportunity to glorify Him while He was fulfilling the desires of my heart.

Psalm 37:4 "Delight yourself in the Lord and He will give you the desires of your heart."

Chapter 21

"And we know that all things work together for good to them that love God, to them that are called according to His purpose." Romans 8:28

Connecting the Dots

This story started with my search to know who or what God was. Then at age thirty-six – I found God in Jesus Christ – through the person of the Holy Spirit.

It was confirmed again after I had a personal "Damascus Road Experience." In that moment; God supernaturally answered questions I'd had since childhood and asked me to sing for Him.

A number of miracles followed – all with perfect timing to further increase my faith – how could I not believe in Him after all that?

I believe God has a plan for all of us and He has given each of us gifts to build-up the body of Christ for His glory. We are made to have fellowship with Him and to discover His will for our lives. The question is, how?

I further believe, once we seek to serve the true God of the Bible, the choices we make throughout our life are directed by divine intention and not just our own free will.

Our God, is a God of order and intentionality. He created us for the season we live in right now – to help Him build His kingdom. His plans for us started before we were in our mother's womb and He has made a way for us to complete them. He has saved us, protected us, equipped us and has empowered us to be ambassadors for Jesus and there-in lies our true purpose.

Jeremiah 29:11 - "For I know the plans I have for you, declares the Lord. Plans to Prosper you and not to harm you. Plans to give you hope and a future."

Looking back early on in my life — He gave me a desire to know Him and the gift of music to worship Him with. Over time — He put those two elements together fulfilling His purpose for my life, while giving me the desires of my heart.

As a young man He filled my mind with questions I wanted answers to — along with a love for music. The questions He placed in my subconscious, prompted me to want to know more about who or what God was. On the other hand, my love of music grew into an infatuation with wanting to be popular and later on, desiring to be famous. It was In that process where God continued to show up in my life. His timing was perfect; not just coincidental.

From the time I found the guitar my grandfather made in the basement of our home, to joining the Air Force; many choices were made for me to be where I needed to be, when I needed to be there. Choices I believe, inspired by God.

In my youth I sought fame and fortune. As I grew older, I found what I really wanted, was to have an intimate relationship with Jesus.

Looking back; I am amazed how everything came together to make that happen.

The following is a sample of events to prove my point. First, was the timing involved in joining the Air Force. Then it was the friendship developed with Jerry McClure in basic training that allowed us to form the Stingrays; the rock-band we had in Germany. It was our desire to write and play music together that caused us to be stationed together in Iowa.

In Iowa we established the Je-Rons, a popular rock-band in the Mid-West — while playing in a night club there, is where I met Joanne — my soulmate and the girl who later would become my wife.

Once married, Joanne and I then move back to Leominster, Massachusetts, where I am originally from; to begin our married life.

In Leominster, my love for Joanne caused me to re-evaluate music as a career and work in the life insurance industry with Prudential. I found success with Prudential in Massachusetts but God needed me back in Iowa to fulfill His plans for me.

I was doing exceptionally well with Prudential in Iowa when God arranged for me to meet Larry Wedeking through Dennis Couchiarra; an old Prudential associate I had worked with back in Massachusetts. Dennis just happened to meet Larry on a weekend day in Boston; while attending an insurance opportunity meeting that Larry was the guest speaker at.

Some would say my meeting Larry was just another random event — a coincidence, but for me to have been impacted so deeply — I know it was part of God's plan and His perfect timing for my life. Look closer to see exactly what happened!

The meeting I had with Larry was only secured by using Denny Couchiarra's name. Larry was only in Boston speaking for one day. Larry only had my name because Denny asked him if he knew me and while they were talking, Denny told him about my moving to Cedar Rapids, Iowa with Prudential. On top of that — Larry talked to me when my future was secure with Prudential; yet I felt impressed to make a life changing move to Franklin Life when I did. Then three months after I started working with Franklin, Larry left and went with another company. Larry had to have talked to me when he did — God's timing again was perfect!

Over the next three years, I had success with Franklin and then was promoted into Franklin's Home Office. There, I was a roommate with Brady Creel for a month, while waiting to close on the new home we had bought. Seventeen years later we end up working together in Tennessee.

I then move from the Home Office in Illinois back to Iowa and we buy a home in West Des Moines. A year later a young family moves into the house next to ours and invites us to go to their church. It is there, where I have my initial encounter with Jesus.

From there — I question my neighbor about my experience and she gives me a book — she just happened to have — on receiving the Baptism in the Holy Spirit.

I read the book, discover who God is through Jesus Christ and later receive the baptism in the Holy Spirit.

Then — God speaks to me in the person of the Holy Spirit and asks me to sing — at the same time Dawn Crabtree, the Pastor's wife, was asking me to join the choir.

I knew — when God asked me to sing — He had heard my prayers and I joined the choir.

I then took a step of faith — turned my business over to Jesus and trusted God for a specific amount of income needed from the Region's overall sales production to make-up for the absence of my personal sales production. God then rewarded my trusting Him and showed me His faithfulness — working every thing together for my good.

I continue to have more opportunities for me to sing for Him, pulling me further away from my responsibilities as the Regional Sales Director, and He continued to give me favor for putting Him first in my life. That was — up until the day I broke my promise to Him and I took back the responsibilities I had given Him of running the Region.

Dolly at the CMA's

Unconsciously, I gave up my stress-free life of letting God do His thing. I broke my promise to Him and took back the stress of running the Region myself — why did I do that?

The winds of change had now kicked in and at age forty-two I move to Florida to retire. There, my daughter meets her husband and establishes her career. I then move to Tennessee and work with Brady Creel — my old roommate from the days we spent together at Franklin's Home Office.

Franklin is sold a year later; Brady moves and I become the Branch Manager for Prudential. During that same time my son feels unfulfilled working for a loan company and I introduce him to the manager of a company moving into the office next to mine at Prudential,. Todd sends in his resume and the rest is history. He goes to work with them and finds his life-long career, working in wireless communications. God not only took care of me, He took care of my family too. Through it all — I continued to sing.

Over the next ten years, I only worked when I wanted to in the insurance industry and sang all over the country with the Christ Church Choir.

In addition to singing in the regular weekly church services, we sang back up to legends like; Dolly Parton — who we sang with on the televised "Country Music Awards" show and most recently in May of 2018 — I sang at Carnegie Hall — highlighting the music of Bradley Knight.

Todd, Abby, Blake & Holly

Once I answered His call, God opened up a lot of opportunities to fulfill the desires of my heart; while worshiping Him in music.

Today my son, my daughter and their families all live within ten miles of Joanne and me. We all get together for holidays, birthdays, sporting events and other occasions; as they present themselves. We are blessed to be this close to each other.

My daughter, Kimberly Bailey Lee, today is a hair-transplant surgical assistant with PAI Medical Group. Ken Lee, her husband, is a former golf professional and part owner and Vice President of Trophy Suits. They met because we moved to Florida.

My oldest grandson Kyle Bai Lee, is a senior at Williamson Baptist College on a wrestling scholarship, with the goal of being a wrestling coach after graduation.

My granddaughter, Lauren Lee Hungate, graduated from Lee University and is pursuing a career as a song-writer. Her Husband, Mickey Hungate also graduated from Lee University and is working for Dave Ramsey. Had we not moved to Franklin, Tennessee; chances are they would not have met at Lee University.

Mr. & Mrs Todd Bailey

My Son, Todd Roland Bailey, is Director of Business Development & Strategy for Crown Castle International. His wife, Holly Bradley Bailey is retired from Sales

Management with Sprint. Had we not moved to Franklin; chances are they wouldn't have met either.

My two youngest grandchildren; Blake Roland Bailey and Abby Elizabeth Bailey, are students in the City of Franklin's school system. We especially enjoy being around them for their school and sporting events. Being a part of our grand-children's lives is important to us. Life with God is intentional. Connect your own dots and see how it works!

Our lives here on earth are temporary. It is like a blink of the eye when compared to eternity: for once we are born again – the Bible tells us we are citizens of Heaven and will reign with the Lord forever. I now know, without a shadow of doubt, when I die – I will be with the Lord for eternity. Can you say that too? The following is how you can.

LIFE'S TWO MOST IMPORTANT QUESTIONS

(1) If you were to die today, do you know for sure you would go to Heaven?

(2) If so, why should God let you into His Heaven?

TO KNOW FOR SURE

John 3:16 "For God so loved the world that He gave his only begotten Son, so that anyone who believes in Him shall not perish but shall have eternal life."

Romans 3:22-24 "This righteousness is given through faith in Jesus Christ to all who believe. There is no difference between Jew and Gentile, for all have sinned and have fallen short of the Glory of God, and all are justified freely by His grace through the redemption that came by Jesus Christ."

Romans 6:23 "For the wages of sin is death but the gift of God is eternal life through Christ Jesus."

Romans 10:9 "That if you confess with your mouth the Lord Jesus and believe in your heart that God has raised Him from the dead, you will be saved."

Romans 10:13 "For whoever calls on the name of the Lord shall be saved."

THE SINNER'S PRAYER

"Lord forgive me of my sins for I know I am a sinner. Come into my life and make me a new person. Cleans me from all unrighteousness, fill me with your Holy Spirit and help me to be more like you. In Jesus name I pray."

When you pray this prayer and mean it. You now know for sure – when you die you will go to Heaven. Congratulations and welcome to the "Body of Christ." You are now born again.

Being born again is worth celebrating and you will soon become more spiritually aware of your surroundings. Next, you need to find a bible believing church. Not a progressive church that is all inclusive or heavily opinionated but one that preaches what the Bible says. Once you find the right bible believing church you should be baptized as a public declaration of your new found faith in Jesus Christ as your Savior. You then need to be a part of a Sunday School or Cell Group that meets outside the church walls with other Christians for teaching and support.

Soon you will discover your biggest battles won't be against flesh and blood but against spirits in the spirit world. This was hard for me to initially grasp but when I joined forces with Jesus I became a threat to Satan and as a born-again believer you have enlisted into God's Army. So, to be effective for His Kingdom, you need to put on the full armor of God to protect yourself and to defeat the enemy. You then need to grow closer to the Lord and pray to be filled with His Spirit."

RECEIVING THE BAPTISM IN THE HOLY SPIRIT

Once we are born again, we need to grow in Christ. Growing as a Christian means becoming closer and developing a more intimate relationship with God. It begins with the forgiveness of our sins and the reading of His Word in the Bible. His Word will instruct us how to live, serve and grow closer to God. By drawing closer to Jesus and having the right intentions to serve Him, we can experience even more through the infilling of His Holy Spirit.

Asking Jesus to come into our lives and making us new in Him is where it starts; for in our declaration of faith He seals us for eternity. When we ask Him to Baptize us in the Holy Spirit, He fills us with Himself.

We are all empty vessels waiting to be filled with the presence of Jesus through the power of the Holy Spirit and He wants us to desire Him more than anything else in our lives. For we are His children created for His glory and the glory of His kingdom. Because we are His children, His desire is for us to trust Him in all things and pray to Him about all things.

When we were saved and born again our experience with Jesus could be compared to drinking a glass of water and having the water we drank inside us. When we are baptized in the Holy Spirit it is like us trying to drink all the water out of a lake. It is too much to consume, for it is in us, through us and all around us. For when we are filled with

His living water, we are filled with the love of Jesus, as well as, the ministry of Jesus.

Many times, this is followed by signs and wonders. One sign is speaking in a new heavenly language, better known as speaking in tongues.

Once we are ready to receive the baptism of the Holy Spirit, we should desire to have a deeper relationship with Jesus and pray for the infilling of the Holy Spirit — while believing by faith we are receiving it. He wants us to receive His gifts.

Luke 11:11-13. Words spoken by Jesus regarding receiving the gifts of the Holy Spirit; "You men who are fathers, if your son asks for a piece of bread, do you give him a stone? If he asks for a fish, do you give him a snake? If he asks for an egg, do you give him a scorpion? Of course not! And if even sinful persons like yourselves give children what they need, don't you realize your heavenly Father will do at least as much, and give the Holy Spirit to those who ask Him?"

This is my prayer to help you. "Dear Heavenly Father, I come to you in the precious name of Jesus Christ my Lord and my Savior. I thank you Lord Jesus for saving me and sealing me for all eternity, through the grace of God and the gift of eternal life. I now pray for your Holy Spirit to completely fill me with your love. Lord Jesus, baptize me in the Holy Spirit, fill me with your love and let your anointing, glory and power come upon me. I love you Lord with all of my heart, all of my mind, all of my soul and with all of my strength. Thank you Lord for loving me and baptizing me in your Holy Spirit." AMEN

After you have prayed your prayer — keep telling Jesus how much you love Him and worship Him with all of your mind, soul, heart and strength. When you feel a sense of something happening — surrender yourself completely to Him — keep praising Him and let Him have His way with you. For if you truly desire to have an intimate relationship with Jesus, He will fill you with His Holy Spirit and give you supernatural gifts to glorify Him.

God is closer to us than the air we breathe. He knows us and He is worthy of all our praise. Surrender yourself to Him, experience His infinite love and pray to receive a taste of heaven and "A Glimpse Behind Heaven's Veil."

Mickey, Blake & Lauren along with Joanne, Abby & Kyle

Made in the USA
Monee, IL
04 October 2021

79020038R00144

MW01632208

GULLIVER'S TRAVELS

PAPER MILL PRESS CLASSICS

The Arabian Nights	Andrew Lang
Black Beauty	Anna Sewell
Dracula	Bram Stoker
Great Expectations	Charles Dickens
Oliver Twist	Charles Dickens
A Tale of Two Cities	Charles Dickens
Jane Eyre	Charlotte Bronte
Robinson Crusoe	Daniel Defoe
Wuthering Heights	Emily Bronte
The Great Gatsby	F. Scott Fitzgerald
The Secret Garden	Frances Hodgson Burnett
The Phantom of the Opera	Gaston Leroux
Madame Bovary	Gustave Flaubert
Moby Dick	Herman Melville
The Call of the Wild	Jack London
The Last of the Mohicans	James Fenimore Cooper
Emma	Jane Austen
Persuasion	Jane Austen
Pride and Prejudice	Jane Austen
Sense and Sensibility	Jane Austen
Gulliver's Travels	Jonathan Swift
A Journey to the Center of the Earth	Jules Verne
Around the World in Eighty Days	Jules Verne
20000 Leagues Under the Sea	Jules Verne
The Wonderful Wizard of Oz	L. Frank Baum
Alice's Adventures in Wonderland	Lewis Carroll
Little Women	Louisa May Alcott
The Adventures of Huckleberry Finn	Mark Twain
The Adventures of Tom Sawyer	Mark Twain
The Prince and the Pauper	Mark Twain
Frankenstein	Mary Shelley
The Scarlet Letter	Nathaniel Hawthorne
The Picture of Dorian Gray	Oscar Wilde
Treasure Island	Robert Louis Stevenson
The Jungle Book	Rudyard Kipling
The Adventures of Sherlock Holmes	Sir Arthur Conan Doyle

JOHNATHAN SWIFT

GULLIVER'S TRAVELS

PAPER MILL PRESS

Paper Mill Press
Published by Book Depot, Inc.
67 Front Street North
Thorold, ON L2V 1X3

This 2019 Book Depot, Inc. edition
published by arrangement with Atlantic Publishing.

Cover and endpaper design by Yvonne Fetig Roehler

ISBN: 978-1-7740-2168-2

Printed and Bound in China
23 22 21 20 19 • 5 4 3 2 1

CONTENTS

PART I

A Voyage to Lilliput

CHAPTER I

The author gives some account of himself and family. His first inducements to travel. He is shipwrecked, and swims for his life. Gets safe on shore in the country of Lilliput; is made a prisoner, and carried up the country.

My father had a small estate in Nottinghamshire: I was the third of five sons. He sent me to Emanuel College in Cambridge at fourteen years old, where I resided three years, and applied myself close to my studies; but the charge of maintaining me, although I had a very scanty allowance, being too great for a narrow fortune, I was bound apprentice to Mr. James Bates, an eminent surgeon in London, with whom I continued four years. My father now and then sending me small sums of money, I laid them out in learning navigation, and other parts of the mathematics, useful to those who intend to travel, as I always believed it would be, some time or other, my fortune to do. When I left Mr. Bates, I went down to my father: where, by the assistance of him and my uncle John, and some other relations, I got forty pounds, and a promise of thirty pounds a year to maintain me at Leyden: there I studied physic two years and seven months, knowing it would be useful in long voyages.

Soon after my return from Leyden, I was recommended by my good master, Mr. Bates, to be surgeon to the Swallow, Captain Abraham Pannel, commander; with whom I continued three years and a half, making a voyage or two into the Levant, and some other parts. When I came back I resolved to settle in London; to which Mr. Bates, my master, encouraged me, and by him I was recommended to several patients. I took part of a small house in the Old Jewry; and being advised to alter my condition, I married Mrs. Mary Burton, second daughter to Mr. Edmund Burton, hosier, in Newgate-street, with whom I received four hundred pounds for a portion.

But my good master Bates dying in two years after, and I having few friends, my business began to fail; for my conscience would not suffer me to imitate the bad practice of too many among my brethren. Having therefore consulted with my wife, and some of my acquaintance, I determined to go again to sea. I was surgeon successively in two ships, and made several voyages, for six years, to the East and West Indies, by which I got some addition to my fortune. My hours of leisure I spent in reading the best authors, ancient and modern, being always provided with a good number of books; and when I was ashore, in observing the manners and dispositions of the people, as well as learning their language; wherein I had a great facility, by the strength of my memory.

The last of these voyages not proving very fortunate, I grew weary of the sea, and intended to stay at home with my wife and family. I removed from the Old Jewry to Fetter Lane, and from thence to Wapping, hoping to get business among the sailors; but it would not turn to account. After three years expectation that things would mend, I accepted an advantageous offer from Captain William Prichard, master of the Antelope, who was making a voyage to the South Sea. We set sail from Bristol, May 4, 1699, and our voyage was at first very prosperous.

It would not be proper, for some reasons, to trouble the reader with the particulars of our adventures in those seas; let it suffice to inform him, that in our passage from thence to the East Indies, we were driven by a violent storm to the north-west of Van Diemen's Land. By an observation, we found ourselves in the latitude of 30 degrees 2 minutes south. Twelve of our crew were dead by immoderate labour and ill food; the rest were in a very weak condition. On the 5th of November, which was the beginning of summer in those parts, the weather being very hazy, the seamen spied a rock within half a cable's length of the ship; but the wind was so strong, that we were driven directly upon it, and immediately split. Six of the crew, of whom I was one, having let down the boat into the sea, made a shift to get clear of the ship and the rock. We rowed, by my computation, about three leagues, till we were able to work no longer, being already spent with labour while we were in the ship. We therefore trusted ourselves to the mercy of the waves, and in about half an hour the boat was overset by a sudden flurry from the north. What became of my companions in the boat, as well as of those who escaped on the rock, or were left in the vessel, I cannot tell; but conclude they were all lost. For my own part, I swam as fortune directed me, and was pushed forward by wind and tide. I often let my legs drop, and could feel no bottom; but when I was almost gone, and able to struggle no longer, I found myself within my depth; and by this time the storm was much abated. The declivity was so small, that I walked near a mile before I got to the shore, which I conjectured was about eight o'clock in the evening.

I then advanced forward near half a mile, but could not discover any sign of houses or inhabitants; at least I was in so weak a condition, that I did not observe them. I was extremely tired, and with that, and the heat of the weather, and about half a pint of brandy that I drank as I left the ship, I found myself much inclined to sleep. I lay down on the grass, which was very short and soft, where I slept sounder than ever I remembered to have done in my life, and, as I reckoned, about nine hours; for when I awaked, it was just day-light. I attempted to rise, but was not able to stir: for, as I happened to lie on my back, I found my arms and legs were strongly fastened on each side to the ground; and my hair, which was long and thick, tied down in the same manner. I likewise felt several slender ligatures across my body, from my arm-pits to my thighs. I could only look upwards; the sun began to grow hot, and the light offended my eyes. I heard a confused noise about me; but in the posture I lay, could see nothing except the sky. In a little time I felt something alive moving on my left leg, which advancing gently forward over my breast, came almost up to my chin; when, bending my eyes downwards as much as I could, I perceived it to be a human creature not six inches high, with a bow and arrow in his hands, and a quiver at his back. In the mean time, I felt at least forty more of the same kind (as I conjectured) following the first. I was in the utmost astonishment, and roared so loud, that they all ran back in a fright; and some of them, as I was afterwards told, were hurt with the falls they got by leaping from my sides upon the ground. However, they soon returned, and one of them, who ventured so far as to get a full sight of my face, lifting up his hands and eyes by way of admiration, cried out in a shrill but distinct voice, *Hekinah degul*: the others repeated the same words several times, but then I knew not what they meant.

I lay all this while, as the reader may believe, in great uneasiness. At length, struggling to get loose, I had the fortune to break the strings, and wrench out the pegs that fastened my left arm to the ground; for, by lifting it up to my face, I discovered the methods they had taken to bind me, and at the same time with a violent pull, which gave me excessive pain, I a little loosened the strings that tied down my hair on the left side, so that I was just able to turn my head about two inches. But the creatures ran off a second time, before I could seize them; whereupon there was a great shout in a very shrill accent, and after it ceased I heard one of them cry aloud *Tolgo phonac*; when in an instant I felt above a hundred arrows discharged on my left hand, which, pricked me like so many needles; and besides, they shot another flight into the air, as we do bombs in Europe, whereof many, I suppose, fell on my body, (though I felt them not), and some on my face, which I immediately covered with my left hand.

When this shower of arrows was over, I fell a groaning with grief and pain; and then striving again to get loose, they discharged another volley larger than the first, and some of them attempted with spears to stick me in the sides; but by good luck I had on a buff jerkin, which they could not pierce.

I thought it the most prudent method to lie still, and my design was to continue so till night, when, my left hand being already loose, I could easily free myself: and as for the inhabitants, I had reason to believe I might be a match for the greatest army they could bring against me, if they were all of the same size with him that I saw. But fortune disposed otherwise of me.

When the people observed I was quiet, they discharged no more arrows; but, by the noise I heard, I knew their numbers increased; and about four yards from me, over against my right ear, I heard a knocking for above an hour, like that of people at work; when turning my head that way, as well as the pegs and strings would permit me, I saw a stage erected about a foot and a half from the ground, capable of holding four of the inhabitants, with two or three ladders to mount it: from whence one of them, who seemed to be a person of quality, made me a long speech, whereof I understood not one syllable.

But I should have mentioned, that before the principal person began his oration, he cried out three times, *Langro dehul san* (these words and the former were afterwards repeated and explained to me); whereupon, immediately, about fifty of the inhabitants came and cut the strings that fastened the left side of my head, which gave me the liberty of turning it to the right, and of observing the person and gesture of him that was to speak. He appeared to be of a middle age, and taller than any of the other three who attended him, whereof one was a page that held up his train, and seemed to be somewhat longer than my middle finger; the other two stood one on each side to support him. He acted every part of an orator, and I could observe many periods of threatenings, and others of promises, pity, and kindness.

I answered in a few words, but in the most submissive manner, lifting up my left hand, and both my eyes to the sun, as calling him for a witness; and being almost famished with hunger, having not eaten a morsel for some hours before I left the ship, I found the demands of nature so strong upon me, that I could not forbear showing my impatience (perhaps against the strict rules of decency) by putting my finger frequently to my mouth, to signify that I wanted food.

The *hurgo* (for so they call a great lord, as I afterwards learnt) understood me very well. He descended from the stage, and commanded that several ladders should be applied to my sides, on which above a hundred of the inhabitants mounted and walked towards my mouth, laden with baskets full of meat, which had been provided and sent thither by the king's orders, upon the first intelligence he received of me. I observed there was the flesh of several animals, but could not distinguish them by the taste. There were shoulders, legs, and loins, shaped like those of mutton, and very well dressed, but smaller than the wings of a lark. I ate them by two or three at a mouthful, and took three loaves at a time, about the bigness of musket bullets. They supplied me as fast as they could, showing a thousand marks of wonder and astonishment at my bulk and appetite.

I then made another sign, that I wanted drink. They found by my eating that a small quantity would not suffice me; and being a most ingenious people, they slung up, with great dexterity, one of their largest hogsheads, then rolled it towards my hand, and beat out the top; I drank it off at a draught, which I might well do, for it did not hold half a pint, and tasted like a small wine of Burgundy, but much more delicious. They brought me a second hogshead, which I drank in the same manner, and made signs for more; but they had none to give me.

When I had performed these wonders, they shouted for joy, and danced upon my breast, repeating several times as they did at first, *Hekinah degul*. They made me a sign that I should throw down the two hogsheads, but first warning the people below to stand out of the way, crying aloud, *Borach mevolah*; and when they saw the vessels in the air, there was a universal shout of *Hekinah degul*. I confess I was often tempted, while they were passing backwards and forwards on my body, to seize forty or fifty of the first that came in my reach, and dash them against the ground. But the remembrance of what I had felt, which probably might not be the worst they could do, and the promise of honour I made them, for so I interpreted my submissive behaviour, soon drove out these imaginations. Besides, I now considered myself as bound by the laws of hospitality, to a people who had treated me with so much expense and magnificence. However, in my thoughts I could not sufficiently wonder at the intrepidity of these diminutive mortals, who durst venture to mount and walk upon my body, while one of my hands was at liberty, without trembling at the very sight of so prodigious a creature as I must appear to them.

After some time, when they observed that I made no more demands for meat, there appeared before me a person of high rank from his imperial Majesty . His Excellency, having mounted on the small of my right leg, advanced forwards up to my face, with about a dozen of his retinue; and producing his credentials under the signet royal, which he applied close to my eyes, spoke about ten minutes without any signs of anger, but with a kind of determinate resolution, often pointing forwards, which, as I afterwards found, was towards the capital city, about half a mile distant; whither it was agreed by his Majesty in council that I must be conveyed.

I answered in few words, but to no purpose, and made a sign with my hand that was loose, putting it to the other (but over his Excellency's head for fear of hurting him or his train) and then to my own head and body, to signify that I desired my liberty.

It appeared that he understood me well enough, for he shook his head by way of disapprobation, and held his hand in a posture to show that I must be carried as a prisoner. However, he made other signs to let me understand that I should have meat and drink enough, and very good treatment. Whereupon I once more thought of attempting to break my bonds; but again, when I felt the smart of their arrows upon my face and hands, which were all in blisters, and many of the darts still sticking in them, and observing likewise that the number of my enemies increased, I gave tokens to let them know that they might do with me what they pleased. Upon this, the *hurgo* and his train withdrew, with much civility and cheerful countenances.

Soon after I heard a general shout, with frequent repetitions of the words *Peplom selan*; and I felt great numbers of people on my left side relaxing the cords to such a degree, that I was able to turn upon my right, and to ease myself with making water; which I very plentifully did, to the great astonishment of the people; who, conjecturing by my motion what I was going to do, immediately opened to the right and left on that side, to avoid the torrent, which fell with such noise and violence from me. But before this, they had daubed my face and both my hands with a sort of ointment, very pleasant to the smell, which, in a few minutes, removed all the smart of their arrows. These circumstances, added to the refreshment I had received by their victuals and drink, which were very nourishing, disposed me to sleep. I slept about eight hours, as I was afterwards assured; and it was no wonder, for the physicians, by the emperor's order, had mingled a sleepy potion in the hogsheads of wine.

It seems, that upon the first moment I was discovered sleeping on the ground, after my landing, the emperor had early notice of it by an express; and determined in council, that I should be tied in the manner I have related, (which was done in the night while I slept;) that plenty of meat and drink should be sent to me, and a machine prepared to carry me to the capital city.

This resolution perhaps may appear very bold and dangerous, and I am confident would not be imitated by any prince in Europe on the like occasion. However, in my opinion, it was extremely prudent, as well as generous: for, supposing these people had endeavoured to kill me with their spears and arrows, while I was asleep, I should certainly have awaked with the first sense of smart, which might so far have roused my rage and strength, as to have enabled me to break the strings wherewith I was tied; after which, as they were not able to make resistance, so they could expect no mercy.

These people are most excellent mathematicians, and arrived to a great perfection in mechanics, by the countenance and encouragement of the emperor, who is a renowned patron of learning. This prince has several machines fixed on wheels, for the carriage of trees and other great weights. He often builds his largest men of war, whereof some are nine feet long, in the woods where the timber grows, and has them carried on these engines three or four hundred yards to the sea.

Five hundred carpenters and engineers were immediately set at work to prepare the greatest engine they had. It was a frame of wood raised three inches from the ground, about seven feet long, and four wide, moving upon twenty-two wheels. The shout I heard was upon the arrival of this engine, which, it seems, set out in four hours after my landing. It was brought parallel to me, as I lay.

But the principal difficulty was to raise and place me in this vehicle. Eighty poles, each of one foot high, were erected for this purpose, and very strong cords, of the bigness of packthread, were fastened by hooks to many bandages, which the workmen had girt round my neck, my hands, my body, and my legs. Nine hundred of the strongest men were employed to draw up these cords, by many pulleys fastened on the poles; and thus, in less than three hours, I was raised and slung into the engine, and there tied fast. All this I was told; for, while the operation was performing, I lay in a profound sleep, by the force of that soporiferous medicine infused into my liquor. Fifteen hundred of the emperor's largest horses, each about four inches and a half high, were employed to draw me towards the metropolis, which, as I said, was half a mile distant.

About four hours after we began our journey, I awaked by a very ridiculous accident; for the carriage being stopped a while, to adjust something that was out of order, two or three of the young natives had the curiosity to see how I looked when I was asleep; they climbed up into the engine, and advancing very softly to my face, one of them, an officer in the guards, put the sharp end of his half-pike a good way up into my left nostril, which tickled my nose like a straw, and made me sneeze violently; whereupon they stole off unperceived, and it was three weeks before I knew the cause of my waking so suddenly.

We made a long march the remaining part of the day, and, rested at night with five hundred guards on each side of me, half with torches, and half with bows and arrows, ready to shoot me if I should offer to stir. The next morning at sunrise we continued our march, and arrived within two hundred yards of the city gates about noon.

The emperor, and all his court, came out to meet us; but his great officers would by no means suffer his Majesty to endanger his person by mounting on my body.

At the place where the carriage stopped there stood an ancient temple, esteemed to be the largest in the whole kingdom; which, having been polluted some years before by an unnatural murder, was, according to the zeal of those people, looked upon as profane, and therefore had been applied to common use, and all the ornaments and furniture carried away. In this edifice it was determined I should lodge.

The great gate fronting to the north was about four feet high, and almost two feet wide, through which I could easily creep. On each side of the gate was a small window, not above six inches from the ground: into that on the left side, the king's smith conveyed fourscore and eleven chains, like those that hang to a lady's watch in Europe, and almost as large, which were locked to my left leg with six-and-thirty padlocks. Over against this temple, on the other side of the great highway, at twenty feet distance, there was a turret at least five feet high. Here the emperor ascended, with many principal lords of his court, to have an opportunity of viewing me, as I was told, for I could not see them. It was reckoned that above a hundred thousand inhabitants came out of the town upon the same errand; and, in spite of my guards, I believe there could not be fewer than ten thousand at several times, who mounted my body by the help of ladders. But a proclamation was soon issued, to forbid it upon pain of death.

When the workmen found it was impossible for me to break loose, they cut all the strings that bound me; whereupon

I rose up, with as melancholy a disposition as ever I had in my life. But the noise and astonishment of the people, at seeing me rise and walk, are not to be expressed. The chains that held my left leg were about two yards long, and gave me not only the liberty of walking backwards and forwards in a semicircle, but, being fixed within four inches of the gate, allowed me to creep in, and lie at my full length in the temple.

CHAPTER II

The emperor of Lilliput, attended by several of the nobility, comes to see the author in his confinement. The emperor's person and habit described. Learned men appointed to teach the author their language. He gains favour by his mild disposition. His pockets are searched, and his sword and pistols taken from him.

When I found myself on my feet, I looked about me, and must confess I never beheld a more entertaining prospect. The country around appeared like a continued garden, and the enclosed fields, which were generally forty feet square, resembled so many beds of flowers. These fields were intermingled with woods of half a stang, and the tallest trees, as I could judge, appeared to be seven feet high. I viewed the town on my left hand, which looked like the painted scene of a city in a theatre.

I had been for some hours extremely tired, however, so I crept into my house, and shut the door after me. But I had to come out again, and to get a little change by stepping backwards and forwards as far as my chains allowed.

I soon found that the emperor was already descended from the tower, and advancing on horseback towards me, which had like to have cost him dear; for the beast, though very well trained, yet wholly unused to such a sight, which appeared as if a mountain moved before him, reared up on its hinder feet: but that prince, who is an excellent horseman, kept his seat, till his attendants ran in, and held the bridle, while his Majesty had time to dismount. When he alighted, he surveyed me round with great admiration; but kept beyond the length of my chain. He ordered his cooks and butlers, who were already prepared, to give me victuals and drink, which they pushed forward in a sort of vehicles upon wheels, till I could reach them. I took these vehicles and soon emptied them all; twenty of them were filled with meat, and ten with liquor; each of the former afforded me two or three good mouthfuls; and I emptied the liquor of ten vessels, which was contained in earthen vials, into one vehicle, drinking it off at a draught; and so I did with the rest.

The empress, and young princes of the blood of both sexes, attended by many ladies, sat at some distance in their chairs; but upon the accident that happened to the emperor's horse, they alighted, and came near his person, which I am now going to describe. He is taller by almost the breadth of my nail, than any of his court; which alone is enough to strike an awe into the beholders. His features are strong and masculine, with an Austrian lip and arched nose, his complexion olive, his countenance erect, his body and limbs well proportioned, all his motions graceful, and his deportment majestic. He was then past his prime, being twenty-eight years and three quarters old, of which he had reigned about seven in great felicity, and generally victorious.

For the better convenience of beholding him, I lay on my side, so that my face was parallel to his, and he stood but three yards off: however, I have had him since many times in my hand, and therefore cannot be deceived in the description. His dress was very plain and simple, and the fashion of it between the Asiatic and the European; but he had on his head a light helmet of gold, adorned with jewels, and a plume on the crest. He held his sword drawn in his hand to defend himself, if I should happen to break loose; it was almost three inches long; the hilt and scabbard were gold enriched with diamonds.

His voice was shrill, but very clear and articulate; and I could distinctly hear it when I stood up.

The ladies and courtiers were all most magnificently clad; so that the spot they stood upon seemed to resemble a petticoat spread upon the ground, embroidered with figures of gold and silver.

His imperial Majesty spoke often to me, and I returned answers: but neither of us could understand a syllable.

There were several of his priests and lawyers present (as I conjectured by their habits), who were commanded to address themselves to me; and I spoke to them in as many languages as I had the least smattering of, which were High and Low Dutch, Latin, French, Spanish, Italian, and Lingua Franca, but all to no purpose.

After about two hours the court retired, and I was left with a strong guard, to prevent the impertinence, and probably the malice of the rabble, who were very impatient to crowd about me as near as they durst; and some of them had the impudence to shoot their arrows at me, as I sat on the ground by the door of my house, whereof one very narrowly missed my left eye. But the colonel ordered six of the ringleaders to be seized, and thought no punishment so proper as to deliver them bound into my hands; which some of his soldiers accordingly did, pushing them forward with the butt-ends of their pikes into my reach. I took them all in my right hand, put five of them into my coat-pocket; and as to the sixth, I made a countenance as if I would eat him alive. The poor man squalled terribly, and the colonel and his officers were in much pain, especially when they saw me take out my penknife: but I soon put them out of fear; for, looking mildly, and immediately cutting the strings he was bound with, I set him gently on the ground, and away he ran. I treated the rest in the same manner, taking them one by one out of my pocket; and I observed both the soldiers and people were highly delighted at this mark of my clemency, which was represented very much to my advantage at court.

Towards night I got with some difficulty into my house, where I lay on the ground, and continued to do so about a fortnight; during which time, the emperor gave orders to have a bed prepared for me. Six hundred beds of the common measure were brought in carriages, and worked up in my house; a hundred and fifty of their beds, sewn together, made up the breadth and length; and these were four double: which, however, kept me but very indifferently from the hardness of the floor, that was of smooth stone. By the same computation, they provided me with sheets, blankets, and coverlets, tolerable enough for one who had been so long inured to hardships.

As the news of my arrival spread through the kingdom, it brought prodigious numbers of rich, idle, and curious people to see me; so that the villages were almost emptied; and great neglect of tillage and household affairs must have ensued, if his imperial Majesty had not provided, by several proclamations and orders of state, against this inconveniency. He directed that those who had already beheld me should return home, and not presume to come within fifty yards of my house, without license from the court; whereby the secretaries of state got considerable fees.

In the mean time the emperor held frequent councils, to debate what course should be taken with me; and I was afterwards assured by a particular friend, a person of great quality, who was as much in the secret as any, that the court was under many difficulties concerning me. They apprehended my breaking loose; that my diet would be very expensive, and might cause a famine. Sometimes they determined to starve me; or at least to shoot me in the face and hands with poisoned arrows, which would soon despatch me; but again they considered, that the stench of so large a carcass might produce a plague in the metropolis, and probably spread through the whole kingdom.

In the midst of these consultations, several officers of the army went to the door of the great council-chamber, and two of them being admitted, gave an account of my behaviour to the six criminals above-mentioned; which made so favourable an impression in the breast of his Majesty and the whole board, in my behalf, that an imperial commission was issued out, obliging all the villages, nine hundred yards round the city, to deliver in every morning six beeves, forty sheep, and other victuals for my sustenance; together with a proportionable quantity of bread, and wine, and other liquors; for the due payment of which, his Majesty gave assignments upon his treasury: for this prince lives chiefly upon his own demesnes; seldom, except upon great occasions, raising any subsidies upon his subjects, who are bound to attend him in his wars at their own expense. An establishment was also made of six hundred persons to be my domestics, who had board-wages allowed for their maintenance, and tents built for them very conveniently on each side of my door.

It was likewise ordered, that three hundred tailors should make me a suit of clothes, after the fashion of the country; that six of his Majesty's greatest scholars should be employed to instruct me in their language; and lastly, that the emperor's horses, and those of the nobility and troops of guards, should be frequently exercised in my sight, to accustom themselves to me. All these orders were duly put in execution; and in about three weeks I made a great progress in learning their language; during which time the emperor frequently honoured me with his visits, and was pleased to assist my masters in teaching me.

We began already to converse together in some sort; and the first words I learnt, were to express my desire that he would please give me my liberty, which I every day repeated on my knees. His answer, as I could comprehend it, was, that this must be a work of time, not to be thought on without the advice of his council, and that first I must *lumos kelmin pesso desmar lon emposo*; that is, swear a peace with him and his kingdom. However, that I should be used with all kindness. And he advised me to acquire, by my patience and discreet behaviour, the good opinion of himself and his subjects.

He desired I would not take it ill, if he gave orders to certain proper officers to search me; for probably I might carry about me several weapons, which must needs be dangerous things, if they answered the bulk of so prodigious a person. I said His Majesty should be satisfied; for I was ready to strip myself, and turn up my pockets before him. This I delivered part in words, and part in signs. He replied, that, by the laws of the kingdom, I must be searched by two of his officers; that he knew this could not be done without my consent and assistance; and he had so good an opinion of my generosity and justice, as to trust their persons in my hands; that whatever they took from me, should be returned when I left the country, or paid for at the rate which I would set upon them.

I took up the two officers in my hands, put them first into my coat-pockets, and then into every other pocket about me, except my two fobs, and another secret pocket, which I had no mind should be searched, wherein I had some little necessaries that were of no consequence to any but myself. In one of my fobs there was a silver watch, and in the other a small quantity of gold in a purse. These gentlemen, having pen, ink, and paper, about them, made an exact inventory of every thing they saw; and when they had done, desired I would set them down, that they might deliver it to the emperor. This inventory I afterwards translated into English, and is, word for word, as follows:

Imprimis: In the right coat-pocket of the 'Great Man-Mountain' (for so I interpret the words *quinbus flestrin*,) after the strictest search, we found only one great piece of coarse-cloth, large enough to be a foot-cloth for your Majesty's chief room of state. In the left pocket we saw a huge silver chest, with a cover of the same metal, which we, the searchers, were not able to lift. We desired it should be opened, and one of us stepping into it, found himself up to the mid leg in a sort of dust, some part whereof flying up to our faces set us both a sneezing for several times together. In his right waistcoat-pocket we found a prodigious bundle of white thin substances, folded one over another, about the bigness of three men, tied with a strong cable, and marked with black figures; which we humbly conceive to be writings, every letter almost half as large as the palm of our hands. In the left there was a sort of engine, from the back of which were extended twenty long poles, resembling the pallisados before your Majesty's court: wherewith we conjecture the Man-Mountain combs his head; for we did not always trouble him with questions, because we found it a great difficulty to make him understand us. In the large pocket, on the right side of his middle cover (so I translate the word *Ranfulo*, by which they meant my breeches,) we saw a hollow pillar of iron, about the length of a man, fastened to a strong piece of timber larger than the pillar; and upon one side of the pillar, were huge pieces of iron sticking out, cut into strange figures, which we know not what to make of. In the left pocket, another engine of the same kind. In the smaller pocket on the right side, were several round flat pieces of white and red metal, of different bulk; some of the white, which seemed to be silver, were so large and heavy, that my comrade and I could hardly lift them. In the left pocket were two black pillars irregularly shaped: we could not, without difficulty, reach the top of them, as we stood at the bottom of his pocket. One of them was covered, and seemed all of a piece: but at the upper end of the other there appeared a white round substance, about twice the bigness of our heads. Within each of these was enclosed a prodigious plate of steel; which, by our orders, we obliged him to show us, because we apprehended they might be dangerous engines. He took them out of their cases, and told us, that in his own country his practice was to shave his beard with one of these, and cut his meat with the other. There were two pockets which we could not enter: these he called his fobs; they were two large slits cut into the top of his middle cover, but squeezed close by the pressure of his belly. Out of the right fob hung a great silver chain, with a wonderful kind of engine at the bottom. We directed him to draw out whatever was at the end of that chain; which appeared to be a globe, half silver, and half of some transparent metal; for, on the transparent side, we saw certain strange figures circularly drawn, and thought we could touch them, till we found our fingers stopped by the lucid substance. He put this engine into our ears, which made an incessant noise, like that of a water-mill: and we conjecture it is either some unknown animal, or the god that he worships; but we are more inclined to the latter opinion, because he assured us, (if we understood him right, for he expressed himself very imperfectly) that he seldom did any thing without consulting it. He called it his oracle, and said, it pointed out the time for every action of his life. From the left fob he took out a net almost large enough for a fisherman, but contrived to open and shut like a purse, and served him for the same use: we found therein several massy pieces of yellow metal, which, if they be real gold, must be of immense value.

"Having thus, in obedience to your Majesty's commands, diligently searched all his pockets, we observed a girdle about his waist made of the hide of some prodigious animal, from which, on the left side, hung a sword of the length of five men;

and on the right, a bag or pouch divided into two cells, each cell capable of holding three of your Majesty's subjects. In one of these cells were several globes, or balls, of a most ponderous metal, about the bigness of our heads, and requiring a strong hand to lift them: the other cell contained a heap of certain black grains, but of no great bulk or weight, for we could hold above fifty of them in the palms of our hands.

"This is an exact inventory of what we found about the body of the Man-Mountain, who used us with great civility, and due respect to your Majesty's commission. Signed and sealed on the fourth day of the eighty-ninth moon of your Majesty's auspicious reign.

"Clefrin Frelock."

"Marsi Frelock."

When this inventory was read over to the emperor, he directed me, although in very gentle terms, to deliver up the several particulars. He first called for my scimitar, which I took out, scabbard and all. In the mean time he ordered three thousand of his choicest troops (who then attended him) to surround me at a distance, with their bows and arrows just ready to discharge; but I did not observe it, for mine eyes were wholly fixed upon his Majesty . He then desired me to draw my scimitar, which, although it had got some rust by the sea water, was, in most parts, exceeding bright. I did so, and immediately all the troops gave a shout between terror and surprise; for the sun shone clear, and the reflection dazzled their eyes, as I waved the scimitar to and fro in my hand. His Majesty, who is a most magnanimous prince, was less daunted than I could expect: he ordered me to return it into the scabbard, and cast it on the ground as gently as I could, about six feet from the end of my chain.

The next thing he demanded was one of the hollow iron pillars; by which he meant my pocket pistols. I drew it out, and at his desire, as well as I could, expressed to him the use of it; and charging it only with powder, which, by the closeness of my pouch, happened to escape wetting in the sea (an inconvenience against which all prudent mariners take special care to provide,) I first cautioned the emperor not to be afraid, and then I let it off in the air. The astonishment here was much greater than at the sight of my scimitar. Hundreds fell down as if they had been struck dead; and even the emperor, although he stood his ground, could not recover himself for some time. I delivered up both my pistols in the same manner as I had done my scimitar, and then my pouch of powder and bullets; begging him that the former might be kept from fire, for it would kindle with the smallest spark, and blow up his imperial palace into the air. I likewise delivered up my watch, which the emperor was very curious to see, and commanded two of his tallest yeomen of the guards to bear it on a pole upon their shoulders, as draymen in England do a barrel of ale. He was amazed at the continual noise it made, and the motion of the minute-hand, which he could easily discern; for their sight is much more acute than ours: he asked the opinions of his learned men about it, which were various and remote, as the reader may well imagine without my repeating; although indeed I could not very perfectly understand them. I then gave up my silver and copper money, my purse, with nine large pieces of gold, and some smaller ones; my knife and razor, my comb and silver snuff-box, my handkerchief and journal-book. My scimitar, pistols, and pouch, were conveyed in carriages to his Majesty's stores; but the rest of my goods were returned me.

I had as I before observed, one private pocket, which escaped their search, wherein there was a pair of spectacles (which I sometimes use for the weakness of mine eyes,) a pocket perspective, and some other little conveniences; which, being of no consequence to the emperor, I did not think myself bound in honour to discover, and I apprehended they might be lost or spoiled if I ventured them out of my possession.

CHAPTER III

The author diverts the emperor, and his nobility of both sexes, in a very uncommon manner. The diversions of the court of Lilliput described. The author has his liberty granted him upon certain conditions.

My gentleness and good behaviour had gained so far on the emperor and his court, and indeed upon the army and people in general, that I began to conceive hopes of getting my liberty in a short time. I took all possible methods to cultivate this favourable disposition. The natives came, by degrees, to be less apprehensive of any danger from me. I would sometimes lie down, and let five or six of them dance on my hand; and at last the boys and girls would venture to come and play at hide-and-seek in my hair.

I had now made a good progress in understanding and speaking the language. The emperor had a mind one day to entertain me with several of the country shows, wherein they exceed all nations I have known, both for dexterity and magnificence. I was diverted with none so much as that of the rope-dancers, performed upon a slender white thread, extended about two feet, and twelve inches from the ground. Upon which I shall desire liberty, with the reader's patience, to enlarge a little.

This diversion is only practised by those persons who are candidates for great employments, and high favour at court. They are trained in this art from their youth, and are not always of noble birth, or liberal education. When a great office is vacant, either by death or disgrace (which often happens,) five or six of those candidates petition the emperor to entertain his Majesty and the court with a dance on the rope; and whoever jumps the highest, without falling, succeeds in the office. Very often the chief ministers themselves are commanded to show their skill, and to convince the emperor that they have not lost their faculty. Flimnap, the treasurer, is allowed to cut a caper on the straight rope, at least an inch higher than any other lord in the whole empire. I have seen him do the summerset several times together, upon a trencher fixed on a rope which is no thicker than a common packthread in England. My friend Reldresal, principal secretary for private affairs, is, in my opinion, if I am not partial, the second after the treasurer; the rest of the great officers are much upon a par.

These diversions are often attended with fatal accidents, whereof great numbers are on record. I myself have seen two or three candidates break a limb. But the danger is much greater, when the ministers themselves are commanded to show their dexterity; for, by contending to excel themselves and their fellows, they strain so far that there is hardly one of them who has not received a fall, and some of them two or three. I was assured that, a year or two before my arrival, Flimnap would infallibly have broke his neck, if one of the king's cushions, that accidentally lay on the ground, had not weakened the force of his fall.

There is likewise another diversion, which is only shown before the emperor and empress, and first minister, upon particular occasions. The emperor lays on the table three fine silken threads of six inches long; one is blue, the other red, and the third green. These threads are proposed as prizes for those persons whom the emperor has a mind to distinguish by a peculiar mark of his favour. The ceremony is performed in his Majesty's great chamber of state, where the candidates are to undergo a trial of dexterity very different from the former, and such as I have not observed the least resemblance of in any other country of the new or old world. The emperor holds a stick in his hands, both ends parallel to the horizon, while the candidates advancing, one by one, sometimes leap over the stick, sometimes creep under it, backward and forward, several times, according as the stick is advanced or depressed. Sometimes the emperor holds one end of the stick, and his first minister the other; sometimes the minister has it entirely to himself. Whoever performs his part with most agility, and holds out the longest in leaping and creeping, is rewarded with the blue-coloured silk; the red is given to the next, and the green to the third, which they all wear girt twice round about the middle; and you see few great persons about this court who are not adorned with one of these girdles.

The horses of the army, and those of the royal stables, having been daily led before me, were no longer shy, but would come up to my very feet without starting. The riders would leap them over my hand, as I held it on the ground; and one of the emperor's huntsmen, upon a large courser, took my foot, shoe and all; which was indeed a prodigious leap.

I had the good fortune to divert the emperor one day after a very extraordinary manner. I desired he would order several sticks of two feet high, and the thickness of an ordinary cane, to be brought me; whereupon his Majesty commanded the master of his woods to give directions accordingly; and the next morning six woodmen arrived with as many carriages, drawn by eight horses to each. I took nine of these sticks, and fixing them firmly in the ground in a quadrangular figure, two feet and a half square, I took four other sticks, and tied them parallel at each corner, about two feet from the ground; then I fastened my handkerchief to the nine sticks that stood erect; and extended it on all sides, till it was tight as the top of a drum; and the four parallel sticks, rising about five inches higher than the handkerchief, served as ledges on each side. When I had finished my work, I desired the emperor to let a troop of his best horses twenty-four in number, come and exercise upon this plain.

His Majesty approved of the proposal, and I took them up, one by one, in my hands, ready mounted and armed, with the proper officers to exercise them. As soon as they got into order they divided into two parties, performed mock skirmishes, discharged blunt arrows, drew their swords, fled and pursued, attacked and retired, and in short discovered the best military discipline I ever beheld. The parallel sticks secured them and their horses from falling over the stage; and the emperor was so much delighted, that he ordered this entertainment to be repeated several days, and once was pleased to be lifted up and give the word of command; and with great difficulty persuaded even the empress herself to let me hold her in her close chair within two yards of the stage, when she was able to take a full view of the whole performance.

It was my good fortune, that no ill accident happened in these entertainments; only once a fiery horse, that belonged to one of the captains, pawing with his hoof, struck a hole in my handkerchief, and his foot slipping, he overthrew his rider and himself; but I immediately relieved them both, and covering the hole with one hand, I set down the troop with the other, in the same manner as I took them up. The horse that fell was strained in the left shoulder, but the rider got no hurt; and I repaired my handkerchief as well as I could: however, I would not trust to the strength of it any more, in such dangerous enterprises.

About two or three days before I was set at liberty, as I was entertaining the court with this kind of feat, there arrived an express to inform his Majesty, that some of his subjects, riding near the place where I was first taken up, had seen a great black substance lying on the around, very oddly shaped, extending its edges round, as wide as his Majesty's bedchamber, and rising up in the middle as high as a man; that it was no living creature, as they at first apprehended, for it lay on the grass without motion; and some of them had walked round it several times; that, by mounting upon each other's shoulders, they had got to the top, which was flat and even, and, stamping upon it, they found that it was hollow within; that they humbly conceived it might be something belonging to the Man-Mountain; and if his Majesty pleased, they would undertake to bring it with only five horses.

I presently knew what they meant, and was glad at heart to receive this intelligence. It seems, upon my first reaching the shore after our shipwreck, I was in such confusion, that before I came to the place where I went to sleep, my hat, which I had fastened with a string to my head while I was rowing, and had stuck on all the time I was swimming, fell off after I came to land; the string, as I conjecture, breaking by some accident, which I never observed, but thought my hat had been lost at sea. I entreated his imperial Majesty to give orders it might be brought to me as soon as possible, describing to him the use and the nature of it: and the next day the waggoners arrived with it, but not in a very good condition; they had bored two holes in the brim, within an inch and half of the edge, and fastened two hooks in the holes; these hooks were tied by a long cord to the harness, and thus my hat was dragged along for above half an English mile; but, the ground in that country being extremely smooth and level, it received less damage than I expected.

Two days after this adventure, the emperor, having ordered that part of his army which quarters in and about his metropolis, to be in readiness, took a fancy of diverting himself in a very singular manner. He desired I would stand like a

Colossus, with my legs as far asunder as I conveniently could. He then commanded his general (who was an old experienced leader, and a great patron of mine) to draw up the troops in close order, and march them under me; the foot by twenty-four abreast, and the horse by sixteen, with drums beating, colours flying, and pikes advanced. This body consisted of three thousand foot, and a thousand horse. His Majesty gave orders, upon pain of death, that every soldier in his march should observe the strictest order.

I had sent so many memorials and petitions for my liberty, that his Majesty at length mentioned the matter, first in the cabinet, and then in a full council; where it was opposed by none, except Skyresh Bolgolam, who was pleased, without any provocation, to be my mortal enemy. But it was carried against him by the whole board, and confirmed by the emperor. That minister was *galbet*, or admiral of the realm, very much in his master's confidence, and a person well versed in affairs, but of a morose and sour complexion. However, he was at length persuaded to comply; but prevailed that the articles and conditions upon which I should be set free, and to which I must swear, should be drawn up by himself.

These articles were brought to me by Skyresh Bolgolam in person attended by two under-secretaries, and several persons of distinction. After they were read, I was demanded to swear to the performance of them; first in the manner of my own country, and afterwards in the method prescribed by their laws; which was, to hold my right foot in my left hand, and to place the middle finger of my right hand on the crown of my head, and my thumb on the tip of my right ear. But because the reader may be curious to have some idea of the style and manner of expression peculiar to that people, as well as to know the article upon which I recovered my liberty, I have made a translation of the whole instrument, word for word, as near as I was able, which I here offer to the public.

"Golbasto Momarem Evlame Gurdilo Shefin Mully Ully Gue, most mighty Emperor of Lilliput, delight and terror of the universe, whose dominions extend five thousand *blustrugs* (about twelve miles in circumference) to the extremities of the globe; monarch of all monarchs, taller than the sons of men; whose feet press down to the centre, and whose head strikes against the sun; at whose nod the princes of the earth shake their knees; pleasant as the spring, comfortable as the summer, fruitful as autumn, dreadful as winter: his most sublime Majesty proposes to the Man-Mountain, lately arrived at our celestial dominions, the following articles, which, by a solemn oath, he shall be obliged to perform:-

"1st, The Man-Mountain shall not depart from our dominions, without our license under our great seal.

"2nd, He shall not presume to come into our metropolis, without our express order; at which time, the inhabitants shall have two hours warning to keep within doors.

"3rd, The said Man-Mountain shall confine his walks to our principal high roads, and not offer to walk, or lie down, in a meadow or field of corn.

"5th, If an express requires extraordinary despatch, the Man-Mountain shall be obliged to carry, in his pocket, the messenger and horse a six days journey, once in every moon, and return the said messenger back (if so required) safe to our imperial presence.

"6th, He shall be our ally against our enemies in the island of Blefuscu, and do his utmost to destroy their fleet, which is now preparing to invade us.

"7th, That the said Man-Mountain shall, at his times of leisure, be aiding and assisting to our workmen, in helping to raise certain great stones, towards covering the wall of the principal park, and other our royal buildings.

"8th, That the said Man-Mountain shall, in two moons' time, deliver in an exact survey of the circumference of our dominions, by a computation of his own paces round the coast.

"Lastly. That, upon his solemn oath to observe all the above articles, the said Man-Mountain shall have a daily allowance of meat and drink sufficient for the support of 1724 of our subjects, with free access to our royal person, and other marks of our favour. Given at our palace at Belfaborac, the twelfth day of the ninety-first moon of our reign.

I swore and subscribed to these articles with great cheerfulness and content, although some of them were not so honourable as I could have wished; which proceeded wholly from the malice of Skyresh Bolgolam, the high-admiral: whereupon my chains were immediately unlocked, and I was at full liberty. The emperor himself, in person, did me the honour to be by at the whole ceremony. I made my acknowledgements by prostrating myself at his Majesty's feet: but he commanded me to rise; and after many gracious expressions, which, to avoid the censure of vanity, I shall not repeat, he added, that he hoped I should prove a useful servant, and well deserve all the favours he had already conferred upon me, or might do for the future.

The reader may please to observe, that, in the last article of the recovery of my liberty, the emperor stipulates to allow me a quantity of meat and drink sufficient for the support of 1724 Lilliputians. Some time after, asking a friend at court how they came to fix on that determinate number, he told me that his Majesty's mathematicians, having taken the height of my body by the help of a quadrant, and finding it to exceed theirs in the proportion of twelve to one, they concluded from the similarity of their bodies, that mine must contain at least 1724 of theirs, and consequently would require as much food as was necessary to support that number of Lilliputians. By which the reader may conceive an idea of the ingenuity of that people, as well as the prudent and exact economy of so great a prince.

CHAPTER IV

Mildendo, the metropolis of Lilliput, described, together with the emperor's palace. A conversation between the author and a principal secretary, concerning the affairs of that empire. The author's offers to serve the emperor in his wars.

The first request I made, after I had obtained my liberty, was, that I might have license to see Mildendo, the metropolis; which the emperor easily granted me, but with a special charge to do no hurt either to the inhabitants or their houses. The people had notice, by proclamation, of my design to visit the town. The wall which encompassed it is two feet and a half high, and at least eleven inches broad, so that a coach and horses may be driven very safely round it; and it is flanked with strong towers at ten feet distance. I stepped over the great western gate, and passed very gently, and sidling, through the two principal streets, only in my short waistcoat, for fear of damaging the roofs and eaves of the houses with the skirts of my coat. I walked with the utmost circumspection, to avoid treading on any stragglers who might remain in the streets, although the orders were very strict, that all people should keep in their houses, at their own peril. The garret windows and tops of houses were so crowded with spectators, that I thought in all my travels I had not seen a more populous place. The city is an exact square, each side of the wall being five hundred feet long. The two great streets, which run across and divide it into four quarters, are five feet wide. The lanes and alleys, which I could not enter, but only view them as I passed, are from twelve to eighteen inches. The town is capable of holding five hundred thousand souls: the houses are from three to five stories: the shops and markets well provided.

The emperor's palace is in the centre of the city where the two great streets meet. It is enclosed by a wall of two feet high, and twenty feet distance from the buildings. I had his Majesty's permission to step over this wall; and, the space being so wide between that and the palace, I could easily view it on every side. The outward court is a square of forty feet, and includes two other courts: in the inmost are the royal apartments, which I was very desirous to see, but found it extremely difficult; for the great gates, from one square into another, were but eighteen inches high, and seven inches wide. Now the buildings of the outer court were at least five feet high, and it was impossible for me to stride over them without infinite damage to the pile, though the walls were strongly built of hewn stone, and four inches thick. At the same time the emperor had a great desire that I should see the magnificence of his palace; but this I was not able to do till three days after, which I spent in cutting down with my knife some of the largest trees in the royal park, about a hundred yards distant from the city. Of these trees I made two stools, each about three feet high, and strong enough to bear my weight.

The people having received notice a second time, I went again through the city to the palace with my two stools in my hands. When I came to the side of the outer court, I stood upon one stool, and took the other in my hand; this I lifted over the roof, and gently set it down on the space between the first and second court, which was eight feet wide. I then stept over the building very conveniently from one stool to the other, and drew up the first after me with a hooked stick. By this contrivance I got into the inmost court; and, lying down upon my side, I applied my face to the windows of the middle stories, which were left open on purpose, and discovered the most splendid apartments that can be imagined. There I saw the empress and the young princes, in their several lodgings, with their chief attendants about them. Her imperial Majesty was pleased to smile very graciously upon me, and gave me out of the window her hand to kiss.

But I shall not anticipate the reader with further descriptions of this kind, because I reserve them for a greater work, which is now almost ready for the press; containing a general description of this empire, from its first erection, through along series of princes; with a particular account of their wars and politics, laws, learning, and religion; their plants and animals; their peculiar manners and customs, with other matters very curious and useful; my chief design at present being only to relate such events and transactions as happened to the public or to myself during a residence of about nine months in that empire.

One morning, about a fortnight after I had obtained my liberty, Reldresal, principal secretary (as they style him) for private affairs, came to my house attended only by one servant. He ordered his coach to wait at a distance, and desired I would give him an hours audience; which I readily consented to, on account of his quality and personal merits, as well as of the many good offices he had done me during my solicitations at court. I offered to lie down that he might the more conveniently reach my ear, but he chose rather to let me hold him in my hand during our conversation.

He began with compliments on my liberty; said he might pretend to some merit in it; but, however, added, that if it had not been for the present situation of things at court, perhaps I might not have obtained it so soon.

"For," said he, "as flourishing a condition as we may appear to be in to foreigners, we labour under two mighty evils: a violent faction at home, and the danger of an invasion, by a most potent enemy, from abroad. As to the first, you are to understand, that for about seventy moons past there have been two struggling parties in this empire, under the names of *Tramecksan* and *Slamecksan*, from the high and low heels of their shoes, by which they distinguish themselves. It is alleged, indeed, that the high heels are most agreeable to our ancient constitution; but, however this be, his Majesty has determined to make use only of low heels in the administration of the government, and all offices in the gift of the crown, as you cannot but observe; and particularly that his Majesty's imperial heels are lower at least by a *drurr* than any of his court (*drurr* is a measure about the fourteenth part of an inch).

"The animosities between these two parties run so high, that they will neither eat, nor drink, nor talk with each other. We compute the *Tramecksan*, or high heels, to exceed us in number; but the power is wholly on our side. We apprehend his imperial highness, the heir to the crown, to have some tendency towards the high heels; at least we can plainly discover that one of his heels is higher than the other, which gives him a hobble in his gait.

"Now, in the midst of these intestine disquiets, we are threatened with an invasion from the island of Blefuscu, which is the other great empire of the universe, almost as large and powerful as this of his Majesty . For as to what we have heard you affirm, that there are other kingdoms and states in the world inhabited by human creatures as large as yourself, our philosophers are in much doubt, and would rather conjecture that you dropped from the moon, or one of the stars; because it is certain, that a hundred mortals of your bulk would in a short time destroy all the fruits and cattle of his Majesty's dominions: besides, our histories of six thousand moons make no mention of any other regions than the two great empires of Lilliput and Blefuscu. Which two mighty powers have, as I was going to tell you, been engaged in a most obstinate war for six-and-thirty moons past. It began upon the following occasion. It is allowed on all hands, that the primitive way of breaking eggs, before we eat them, was upon the larger end; but his present Majesty's grandfather, while he was a boy, going to eat an egg, and breaking it according to the ancient practice, happened to cut one of his fingers. Whereupon the emperor his father published an edict, commanding all his subjects, upon great penalties, to break the smaller end of their eggs. The people so highly resented this law, that our histories tell us, there have been six rebellions raised on that account; wherein one emperor lost his life, and another his crown. These civil commotions were constantly fomented by the monarchs of Blefuscu; and when they were quelled, the exiles always fled for refuge to that empire.

"It is computed that eleven thousand persons have at several times suffered death, rather than submit to break their eggs at the smaller end. Many hundred large volumes have been published upon this controversy: but the books of the Big-endians have been long forbidden, and the whole party rendered incapable by law of holding employments.

"During the course of these troubles, the emperors of Blefusca did frequently expostulate by their ambassadors, accusing us of making a schism in religion, by offending against a fundamental doctrine of our great prophet Lustrog, in the fifty-fourth chapter of the Blundecral (which is their Alcoran). This, however, is thought to be a mere strain upon the text; for the words are these: *That all true believers break their eggs at the convenient end*. And which is the convenient end, seems, in my humble opinion to be left to every man's conscience, or at least in the power of the chief magistrate to determine.

"Now, the Big-endian exiles have found so much credit in the emperor of Blefuscu's court, and so much private assistance and encouragement from their party here at home, that a bloody war has been carried on between the two empires for six-and-thirty moons, with various success; during which time we have lost forty capital ships, and a much a greater number of smaller vessels, together with thirty thousand of our best seamen and soldiers; and the damage received by the enemy is reckoned to be somewhat greater than ours. However, they have now equipped a numerous fleet, and are just preparing to make a descent upon us; and his imperial Majesty, placing great confidence in your valour and strength, has commanded me to lay this account of his affairs before you.

I desired the secretary to present my humble duty to the emperor; and to let him know, that I thought it would not become me, who was a foreigner, to interfere with parties; but I was ready, with the hazard of my life, to defend his person and state against all invaders.

CHAPTER V

The author, by an extraordinary stratagem, prevents an invasion. A high title of honour is conferred upon him. Ambassadors arrive from the emperor of Blefuscu, and sue for peace. The empress's apartment on fire by an accident; the author instrumental in saving the rest of the palace.

The empire of Blefuscu is an island situated to the north-east of Lilliput, from which it is parted only by a channel of eight hundred yards wide. I had not yet seen it, and upon this notice of an intended invasion, I avoided appearing on that side of the coast, for fear of being discovered, by some of the enemy's ships, who had received no intelligence of me; all intercourse between the two empires having been strictly forbidden during the war, upon pain of death, and an embargo laid by our emperor upon all vessels whatsoever.

I communicated to his Majesty a project I had formed of seizing the enemy's whole fleet; which, as our scouts assured us, lay at anchor in the harbour, ready to sail with the first fair wind. I consulted the most experienced seamen upon the depth of the channel, which they had often plumbed; who told me, that in the middle, at high-water, it was seventy *glumgluffs* deep, which is about six feet of European measure; and the rest of it fifty *glumgluffs* at most. I walked towards the north east coast, over against Blefuscu, where, lying down behind a hillock, I took out my small perspective glass, and viewed the enemy's fleet at anchor, consisting of about fifty men of war, and a great number of transports: I then came back to my house, and gave orders (for which I had a warrant) for a great quantity of the strongest cable and bars of iron. The cable was about as thick as packthread and the bars of the length and size of a knitting-needle. I trebled the cable to make it stronger, and for the same reason I twisted three of the iron bars together, bending the extremities into a hook.

Having thus fixed fifty hooks to as many cables, I went back to the north-east coast, and putting off my coat, shoes, and stockings, walked into the sea, in my leathern jerkin, about half an hour before high water. I waded with what haste I could, and swam in the middle about thirty yards, till I felt ground. I arrived at the fleet in less than half an hour. The enemy was so frightened when they saw me, that they leaped out of their ships, and swam to shore, where there could not be fewer than thirty thousand souls. I then took my tackling, and, fastening a hook to the hole at the prow of each, I tied all the cords together at the end.

While I was thus employed, the enemy discharged several thousand arrows, many of which stuck in my hands and face, and, beside the excessive smart, gave me much disturbance in my work. My greatest apprehension was for mine eyes, which I should have infallibly lost, if I had not suddenly thought of an expedient. I kept, among other little necessaries, a pair of spectacles in a private pocket, which, as I observed before, had escaped the emperor's searchers. These I took out and fastened as strongly as I could upon my nose, and thus armed, went on boldly with my work, in spite of the enemy's arrows, many of which struck against the glasses of my spectacles, but without any other effect, further than a little to discompose them.

I had now fastened all the hooks, and, taking the knot in my hand, began to pull; but not a ship would stir, for they were all too fast held by their anchors, so that the boldest part of my enterprise remained. I therefore let go the cord, and leaving the looks fixed to the ships, I resolutely cut with my knife the cables that fastened the anchors, receiving about two hundred shots in my face and hands; then I took up the knotted end of the cables, to which my hooks were tied, and with great ease drew fifty of the enemy's largest men of war after me.

The Blefuscudians, who had not the least imagination of what I intended, were at first confounded with astonishment. They had seen me cut the cables, and thought my design was only to let the ships run adrift or fall foul on each other: but when they perceived the whole fleet moving in order, and saw me pulling at the end, they set up such a scream of grief and despair as it is almost impossible to describe or conceive. When I had got out of danger, I stopped awhile to pick out the arrows that stuck in my hands and face; and rubbed on some of the same ointment that was given me at my first arrival, as I have formerly mentioned. I then took off my spectacles, and waiting about an hour, till the tide was a little fallen, I waded through the middle with my cargo, and arrived safe at the royal port of Lilliput.

The emperor and his whole court stood on the shore, expecting the issue of this great adventure. They saw the ships move forward in a large half-moon, but could not discern me, who was up to my breast in water. When I advanced to the middle of the channel, they were yet more in pain, because I was under water to my neck. The emperor concluded me to be drowned, and that the enemy's fleet was approaching in a hostile manner: but he was soon eased of his fears; for the channel growing shallower every step I made, I came in a short time within hearing, and holding up the end of the cable, by which the fleet was fastened, I cried in a loud voice, Long live the most puissant king of Lilliput! This great prince received me at my landing with all possible encomiums, and created me a *nardac* upon the spot, which is the highest title of honour among them.

His Majesty desired I would take some other opportunity of bringing all the rest of his enemy's ships into his ports. And so unmeasureable is the ambition of princes, that he seemed to think of nothing less than reducing the whole empire of Blefuscu into a province, and governing it, by a viceroy; of destroying the Big-endian exiles, and compelling that people to break the smaller end of their eggs, by which he would remain the sole monarch of the whole world. But I endeavoured to divert him from this design, by many arguments drawn from the topics of policy as well as justice; and I plainly protested, that I would never be an instrument of bringing a free and brave people into slavery. And, when the matter was debated in council, the wisest part of the ministry were of my opinion.

This open bold declaration of mine was so opposite to the schemes and politics of his imperial Majesty, that he could never forgive me. He mentioned it in a very artful manner at council, where I was told that some of the wisest appeared, at least by their silence, to be of my opinion; but others, who were my secret enemies, could not forbear some expressions which, by a side-wind, reflected on me. And from this time began an intrigue between his Majesty and a junto of ministers, maliciously bent against me, which broke out in less than two months, and had like to have ended in my utter destruction. Of so little weight are the greatest services to princes, when put into the balance with a refusal to gratify their passions.

About three weeks after this exploit, there arrived a solemn embassy from Blefuscu, with humble offers of a peace, which was soon concluded, upon conditions very advantageous to our emperor, wherewith I shall not trouble the reader. There were six ambassadors, with a train of about five hundred persons, and their entry was very magnificent, suitable to the grandeur of their master, and the importance of their business.

When their treaty was finished, wherein I did them several

good offices by the credit I now had, or at least appeared to have, at court, their excellencies, who were privately told how much I had been their friend, made me a visit in form. They began with many compliments upon my valour and generosity, invited me to that kingdom in the emperor their master's name, and desired me to show them some proofs of my prodigious strength, of which they had heard so many wonders; wherein I readily obliged them, but shall not trouble the reader with the particulars.

When I had for some time entertained their excellencies, to their infinite satisfaction and surprise, I desired they would do me the honour to present my most humble respects to the emperor their master, the renown of whose virtues had so justly filled the whole world with admiration, and whose royal person I resolved to attend, before I returned to my own country.

Accordingly, the next time I had the honour to see our emperor, I desired his general license to wait on the Blefuscudian monarch, which he was pleased to grant me, as I could perceive, in a very cold manner; but could not guess the reason, till I had a whisper from a certain person, that Flimnap and Bolgolam had represented my intercourse with those ambassadors as a mark of disaffection; from which I am sure my heart was wholly free. And this was the first time I began to conceive some imperfect idea of courts and ministers.

It is to be observed, that these ambassadors spoke to me, by an interpreter, the languages of both empires differing as much from each other as any two in Europe, and each nation priding itself upon the antiquity, beauty, and energy of their own tongue, with an avowed contempt for that of their neighbour; yet our emperor, standing upon the advantage he had got by the seizure of their fleet, obliged them to deliver their credentials, and make their speech, in the Lilliputian tongue.

And it must be confessed, that from the great intercourse of trade and commerce between both realms, from the continual reception of exiles which is mutual among them, and from the custom, in each empire, to send their young nobility and richer gentry to the other, in order to polish themselves by seeing the world, and understanding men and manners; there are few persons of distinction, or merchants, or seamen, who dwell in the maritime parts, but what can hold conversation in both tongues; as I found some weeks after, when I went to pay my respects to the emperor of Blefuscu, which, in the midst of great misfortunes, through the malice of my enemies, proved a very happy adventure to me, as I shall relate in its proper place.

The reader may remember, that when I signed those articles upon which I recovered my liberty, there were some which I disliked, upon account of their being too servile; neither could anything but an extreme necessity have forced me to submit. But being now a *nardac* of the highest rank in that empire, such offices were looked upon as below my dignity, and the emperor (to do him justice), never once mentioned them to me.

CHAPTER VI

Of the inhabitants of Lilliput; their learning, laws, and customs; the manner of educating their children. The author's way of living in that country. His vindication of a great lady.

Although I intend to leave the description of this empire to a particular treatise, yet, in the mean time, I am content to gratify the curious reader with some general ideas. As the common size of the natives is somewhat under six inches high, so there is an exact proportion in all other animals, as well as plants and trees: for instance, the tallest horses and oxen are between four and five inches in height, the sheep an inch and half, more or less: their geese about the bigness of a sparrow, and so the several gradations downwards till you come to the smallest, which to my sight, were almost invisible; but nature has adapted the eyes of the Lilliputians to all objects proper for their view: they see with great exactness, but at no great distance. And, to show the sharpness of their sight towards objects that are near, I have been much pleased with observing a cook pulling a lark, which was not so large as a common fly; and a young girl threading an invisible needle with invisible silk. Their tallest trees are about seven feet high: I mean some of those in the great royal park, the tops whereof I could but just reach with my fist clenched. The other vegetables are in the same proportion; but this I leave to the reader's imagination.

I shall say but little at present of their learning, which, for many ages, has flourished in all its branches among them: but their manner of writing is very peculiar, being neither from the left to the right, like the Europeans, nor from the right to the left, like the Arabians, nor from up to down, like the Chinese, but aslant, from one corner of the paper to the other, like ladies in England.

They bury their dead with their heads directly downward, because they hold an opinion, that in eleven thousand moons they are all to rise again; in which period the earth (which they conceive to be flat) will turn upside down, and by this means they shall, at their resurrection, be found ready standing on their feet. The learned among them confess the absurdity of this doctrine; but the practice still continues, in compliance to the vulgar.

There are some laws and customs in this empire very peculiar; and if they were not so directly contrary to those of my own dear country, I should be tempted to say a little in their justification. It is only to be wished they were as well executed. The first I shall mention, relates to informers. All crimes against the state, are punished here with the utmost severity; but, if the person accused makes his innocence plainly to appear upon his trial, the accuser is immediately put to an ignominious death; and out of his goods or lands the innocent person is quadruply recompensed for the loss of his time, for the danger he underwent, for the hardship of his imprisonment, and for all the charges he has been at in making his defence; or, if that fund be deficient, it is largely supplied by the crown. The emperor also confers on him some public mark of his favour, and proclamation is made of his innocence through the whole city.

They look upon fraud as a greater crime than theft, and therefore seldom fail to punish it with death; for they allege, that care and vigilance, with a very common understanding, may preserve a man's goods from thieves, but honesty has no defence against superior cunning; and, since it is necessary that there should be a perpetual intercourse of buying and selling, and dealing upon credit, where fraud is permitted and connived at, or has no law to punish it, the honest dealer is always undone, and the knave gets the advantage. I remember, when I was once interceding with the emperor for a criminal who had wronged his master of a great sum of money, which he had received by order and ran away with; and happening to tell his Majesty, by way of extenuation, that it was only a breach of trust, the emperor thought it monstrous in me to offer as a defence the greatest aggravation of the crime; and truly I had little to say in return, farther than the common answer, that different nations had different customs; for, I confess, I was heartily ashamed.

Although we usually call reward and punishment the two hinges upon which all government turns, yet I could never observe this maxim to be put in practice by any nation except that of Lilliput. Whoever can there bring sufficient proof, that he has strictly observed the laws of his country for seventy-three moons, has a claim to certain privileges, according to his quality or condition of life, with a proportionable sum of money out of a fund appropriated for that use: he likewise acquires the title of *snilpall*, or legal, which is added to his name, but does not descend to his posterity. And these people thought it a prodigious defect of policy among us, when I told them that our laws were enforced only by penalties, without any mention of reward. It is upon this account that the image of Justice, in their courts of judicature, is formed with six eyes, two before, as many behind, and on each side one, to signify circumspection; with a bag of gold open in her right hand, and a sword sheathed in her left, to show she is more disposed to reward than to punish.

In choosing persons for all employments, they have more regard to good morals than to great abilities; for, since government is necessary to mankind, they believe, that the common size of human understanding is fitted to some station or other; and that Providence never intended to make the management of public affairs a mystery to be comprehended only by a few persons of sublime genius, of which there seldom are three born in an age: but they suppose truth, justice, temperance, and the like, to be in every man's power; the practice of which virtues, assisted by experience and a good intention, would qualify any man for the service of his country, except where a course of study is required. But they thought the want of moral virtues was so far from being supplied by superior endowments of the mind, that employments could never be put into such dangerous hands as those of persons so qualified; and, at least, that the mistakes committed by ignorance, in a virtuous disposition, would never be of such fatal consequence to the public weal, as the practices of a man, whose inclinations led him to be corrupt, and who had great abilities to manage, to multiply, and defend his corruptions.

In like manner, the disbelief of a Divine Providence renders a man incapable of holding any public station; for, since kings avow themselves to be the deputies of Providence, the Lilliputians think nothing can be more absurd than for a prince to employ such men as disown the authority under which he acts.

In relating these and the following laws, I would only be understood to mean the original institutions, and not the most scandalous corruptions, into which these people are fallen by the degenerate nature of man. For, as to that infamous practice of acquiring great employments by dancing on the ropes, or badges of favour and distinction by leaping over sticks and creeping under them, the reader is to observe, that they were first introduced by the grandfather of the emperor now reigning, and grew to the present height by the gradual increase of party and faction.

Ingratitude is among them a capital crime, as we read it to have been in some other countries: for they reason thus; that whoever makes ill returns to his benefactor, must needs be a common enemy to the rest of mankind, from whom he has received no obligation, and therefore such a man is not fit to live.

Their notions relating to the duties of parents and children differ extremely from ours. For, since the conjunction of male and female is founded upon the great law of nature, in order to propagate and continue the species, the Lilliputians will needs have it, that men and women are joined together, like other animals, by the motives of concupiscence; and that their tenderness towards their young proceeds from the like natural principle: for which reason they will never allow that a child is under any obligation to his father for begetting him, or to his mother for bringing him into the world; which, considering the miseries of human life, was neither a benefit in itself, nor intended so by his parents, whose thoughts, in their love encounters, were otherwise employed. Upon these, and the like reasonings, their opinion is, that parents are the last of all others to be trusted with the education of their own children; and therefore they have in every town public nurseries, where all parents, except cottagers and labourers, are obliged to send their infants of both sexes to be reared and educated, when they come to the age of twenty moons, at which time they are supposed to have some rudiments of docility. These schools are of several kinds, suited to different qualities, and both sexes. They have certain professors well skilled in preparing children for such a condition of life as befits the rank of their parents, and their own capacities, as well as inclinations. I shall first say something of the male nurseries, and then of the female.

The nurseries for males of noble or eminent birth, are provided with grave and learned professors, and their several deputies. The clothes and food of the children are plain and simple. They are bred up in the principles of honour, justice, courage, modesty, clemency, religion, and love of their country; they are always employed in some business, except in the times of eating and sleeping, which are very short, and two hours for diversions consisting of bodily exercises. They are dressed by men till four years of age, and then are obliged to dress themselves, although their quality be ever so great; and the women attendant, who are aged proportionably to ours at fifty, perform only the most menial offices. They are never suffered to converse with servants, but go together in smaller or greater numbers to take their diversions, and always in the presence of a professor, or one of his deputies; whereby they avoid those early bad impressions of folly and vice, to which our children are subject. Their parents are suffered to see them only twice a year; the visit is to last but an hour; they are allowed to kiss the child at meeting and parting; but a professor, who always stands by on those occasions, will not suffer them to whisper, or use any fondling expressions, or bring any presents of toys, sweetmeats, and the like.

The pension from each family for the education and entertainment of a child, upon failure of due payment, is levied by the emperor's officers.

The nurseries for children of ordinary gentlemen, merchants, traders, and handicrafts, are managed proportionably after the same manner; only those designed for trades are put out apprentices at eleven years old, whereas those of persons of quality continue in their exercises till fifteen, which answers to twenty-one with us: but the confinement is gradually lessened for the last three years.

In the female nurseries, the young girls of quality are

educated much like the males, only they are dressed by orderly servants of their own sex; but always in the presence of a professor or deputy, till they come to dress themselves, which is at five years old. And if it be found that these nurses ever presume to entertain the girls with frightful or foolish stories, or the common follies practised by chambermaids among us, they are publicly whipped thrice about the city, imprisoned for a year, and banished for life to the most desolate part of the country. Thus the young ladies are as much ashamed of being cowards and fools as the men, and despise all personal ornaments, beyond decency and cleanliness: neither did I perceive any difference in their education made by their difference of sex, only that the exercises of the females were not altogether so robust; and that some rules were given them relating to domestic life, and a smaller compass of learning was enjoined them: for their maxim is, that among peoples of quality, a wife should be always a reasonable and agreeable companion, because she cannot always be young. When the girls are twelve years old, which among them is the marriageable age, their parents or guardians take them home, with great expressions of gratitude to the professors, and seldom without tears of the young lady and her companions.

In the nurseries of females of the meaner sort, the children are instructed in all kinds of works proper for their sex, and their several degrees: those intended for apprentices are dismissed at seven years old, the rest are kept to eleven.

The meaner families who have children at these nurseries, are obliged, besides their annual pension, which is as low as possible, to return to the steward of the nursery a small monthly share of their gettings, to be a portion for the child; and therefore all parents are limited in their expenses by the law. For the Lilliputians think nothing can be more unjust, than for people, in subservience to their own appetites, to bring children into the world, and leave the burthen of supporting them on the public. As to persons of quality, they give security to appropriate a certain sum for each child, suitable to their condition; and these funds are always managed with good husbandry and the most exact justice.

The cottagers and labourers keep their children at home, their business being only to till and cultivate the earth, and therefore their education is of little consequence to the public: but the old and diseased among them, are supported by hospitals; for begging is a trade unknown in this empire.

And here it may, perhaps, divert the curious reader, to give some account of my domestics, and my manner of living in this country, during a residence of nine months, and thirteen days. Having a head mechanically turned, and being likewise forced by necessity, I had made for myself a table and chair convenient enough, out of the largest trees in the royal park. Two hundred sempstresses were employed to make me shirts, and linen for my bed and table, all of the strongest and coarsest kind they could get; which, however, they were forced to quilt together in several folds, for the thickest was some degrees finer than lawn. Their linen is usually three inches wide, and three feet make a piece. The sempstresses took my measure as I lay on the ground, one standing at my neck, and another at my mid-leg, with a strong cord extended, that each held by the end, while a third measured the length of the cord with a rule of an inch long. Then they measured my right thumb, and desired no more; for by a mathematical computation, that twice round the thumb is once round the wrist, and so on to the neck and the waist, and by the help of my old shirt, which I displayed on the ground before them for a pattern, they fitted me exactly.

Three hundred tailors were employed in the same manner to make me clothes; but they had another contrivance for taking my measure. I kneeled down, and they raised a ladder from the ground to my neck; upon this ladder one of them mounted, and let fall a plumb-line from my collar to the floor, which just answered the length of my coat: but my waist and arms I measured myself. When my clothes were finished, which was done in my house (for the largest of theirs would not have been able to hold them), they looked like the patch-work made by the ladies in England, only that mine were all of a colour.

I had three hundred cooks to dress my victuals, in little convenient huts built about my house, where they and their families lived, and prepared me two dishes a-piece. I took up twenty waiters in my hand, and placed them on the table: a hundred more attended below on the ground, some with dishes of meat, and some with barrels of wine and other liquors slung on their shoulders; all which the waiters above drew up, as I wanted, in a very ingenious manner, by certain cords, as we draw the bucket up a well in Europe. A dish of their meat was a good mouthful, and a barrel of their liquor a reasonable draught. Their mutton yields to ours, but their beef is excellent. I have had a sirloin so large, that I have been forced to make three bites of it; but this is rare. My servants were astonished to see me eat it, bones and all, as in our country we do the leg of a lark. Their geese and turkeys I usually ate at a mouthful, and I confess they far exceed ours. Of their smaller fowl I could take up twenty or thirty at the end of my knife.

One day his imperial Majesty, being informed of my way of living, desired that himself and his royal consort, with the young princes of the blood of both sexes, might have the happiness, as he was pleased to call it, of dining with me. They came accordingly, and I placed them in chairs of state, upon my table, just over against me, with their guards about them. Flimnap, the lord high treasurer, attended there likewise with his white staff; and I observed he often looked on me with a sour countenance, which I would not seem to regard, but ate more than usual, in honour to my dear country, as well as to fill the court with admiration. I have some private reasons to believe, that this visit from his Majesty gave Flimnap an opportunity of doing me ill offices to his master. That minister had always been my secret enemy, though he outwardly caressed me more than was usual to the moroseness of his nature. He represented to the emperor the low condition of his treasury; that he was forced to take up money at a great discount; that exchequer bills would not circulate under nine per cent. below par; that I had cost his Majesty above a million and a half of sprugs (their greatest gold coin, about the bigness of a spangle) and, upon the whole, that it would be advisable in the emperor to take the first fair occasion of dismissing me.

I am here obliged to vindicate the reputation of an excellent lady, who was an innocent sufferer upon my account. The treasurer took a fancy to be jealous of his wife, from the malice of some evil tongues, who informed him that her Grace had taken a violent affection for my person; and the court scandal ran for some time, that she once came privately to my lodging. This I solemnly declare to be a most infamous falsehood, without any grounds, further than that her Grace was pleased to treat me with all innocent marks of freedom and friendship.

I own she came often to my house, but always publicly, nor ever without three more in the coach, who were usually her sister and young daughter, and some particular acquaintance; but this was common to many other ladies of the court. And I still appeal to my servants round, whether they at any time saw a coach at my door, without knowing what persons were in it. On those occasions, when a servant had given me notice, my custom was to go immediately to the door, and, after paying my respects, to take up the coach and two horses very carefully in my hands (for, if there were six horses, the postillion always unharnessed four,) and place them on a table, where I had fixed a movable rim quite round, of five inches high, to prevent accidents. And I have often had four coaches and horses at once on my table, full of company, while I sat in my chair, leaning my face towards them; and when I was engaged with one set, the coachmen would gently drive the others round my table. I have passed many an afternoon very agreeably in these conversations. But I defy the treasurer, or his two informers (I will name them, and let them make the best of it) Clustril and Drunlo, to prove that any person ever came to me incognito, except the secretary Reldresal, who was sent by express command of his imperial Majesty, as I have before related.

I should not have dwelt so long upon this particular, if it had not been a point wherein the reputation of a great lady is so nearly concerned, to say nothing of my own; though I then had the honour to be a *nardac*, which the treasurer himself is not; for all the world knows, that he is only a *glumglum*, a title inferior by one degree, as that of a marquis is to a duke in England; yet I allow he preceded me in right of his post. These false informations, which I afterwards came to the knowledge of by an accident not proper to mention, made the treasurer show his lady for some time an ill countenance, and me a worse; and although he was at last undeceived and reconciled to her, yet I lost all credit with him, and found my interest decline very fast with the emperor himself, who was, indeed, too much governed by that favourite.

CHAPTER VII

The author, being informed of a design to accuse him of high-treason, makes his escape to Blefuscu. His reception there.

Before I proceed to give an account of my leaving this kingdom, it may be proper to inform the reader of a private intrigue which had been for two months forming against me.

I had been hitherto, all my life, a stranger to courts, for which I was unqualified by the meanness of my condition. I had indeed heard and read enough of the dispositions of great princes and ministers, but never expected to have found such terrible effects of them, in so remote a country, governed, as I thought, by very different maxims from those in Europe.

When I was just preparing to pay my attendance on the emperor of Blefuscu, a considerable person at court (to whom I had been very serviceable, at a time when he lay under the highest displeasure of his imperial Majesty) came to my house very privately at night, in a close chair, and, without sending his name, desired admittance. The chairmen were dismissed; I put the chair, with his lordship in it, into my coat-pocket: and, giving orders to a trusty servant, to say I was indisposed and gone to sleep, I fastened the door of my house, placed the chair on the table, according to my usual custom, and sat down by it. After the common salutations were over, observing his lordship's countenance full of concern, and inquiring into the reason, he desired I would hear him with patience, in a matter that highly concerned my honour and my life. His speech was to the following effect, for I took notes of it as soon as he left me:

"You are to know," said he, that several committees of council have been lately called, in the most private manner, on your account; and it is but two days since his Majesty came to a full resolution.

"You are very sensible that Skyresh Bolgolam (*galbet*, or high-admiral) has been your mortal enemy, almost ever since your arrival. His original reasons I know not; but his hatred is increased since your great success against Blefuscu, by which his glory as admiral is much obscured. This lord, in conjunction with Flimnap the high-treasurer, whose enmity against you is notorious on account of his lady, Limtoc the general, Lalcon the chamberlain, and Balmuff the grand justiciary, have prepared articles of impeachment against you, for treason and other capital crimes."

This preface made me so impatient, being conscious of my own merits and innocence, that I was going to interrupt him; when he entreated me to be silent, and thus proceeded,-

Out of gratitude for the favours you have done me, I procured information of the whole proceedings, and a copy of the articles; wherein I venture my head for your service.

'*Articles of Impeachment against* QUINBUS FLESTRIN, (*the* MAN MOUNTAIN).

"ARTICLE I

"That the said Quinbus Flestrin, having brought the imperial fleet of Blefuscu into the royal port, and being afterwards commanded by his imperial Majesty to seize all the other ships of the said empire of Blefuscu, and reduce that empire to a province, to be governed by a viceroy from hence, and to destroy and put to death, not only all the Big-endian exiles, but likewise all the people of that empire who would not immediately forsake the Big-endian heresy, he, the said Flestrin, like a false traitor against his most auspicious, serene, imperial Majesty, did petition to be excused from the said service, upon pretence of unwillingness to force the consciences, or destroy the liberties and lives of an innocent people.

"Article II

"That, whereas certain ambassadors arrived from the Court of Blefuscu, to sue for peace in his Majesty's court, he, the said Flestrin, did, like a false traitor, aid, abet, comfort, and divert, the said ambassadors, although he knew them to be servants to a prince who was lately an open enemy to his imperial Majesty, and in an open war against his said Majesty .

"Article III

"That the said Quinbus Flestrin, contrary to the duty of a faithful subject, is now preparing to make a voyage to the court and empire of Blefuscu, for which he has received only verbal license from his imperial Majesty; and, under colour of the said license, does falsely and traitorously intend to take the said voyage, and thereby to aid, comfort, and abet the emperor of Blefuscu, so lately an enemy, and in open war with his imperial Majesty aforesaid.'

"There are some other articles; but these are the most important, of which I have read you an abstract.

"In the several debates upon this impeachment, it must be confessed that his Majesty gave many marks of his great lenity; often urging the services you had done him, and endeavouring to extenuate your crimes. The treasurer and admiral insisted that you should be put to the most painful and ignominious death, by setting fire to your house at night, and the general was to attend with twenty thousand men, armed with poisoned arrows, to shoot you on the face and hands. Some of your servants were to have private orders to strew a poisonous juice on your shirts and sheets, which would soon make you tear your own flesh, and die in the utmost torture. The general came into the same opinion; so that for a long time there was a majority against you; but his Majesty resolving, if possible, to spare your life, at last brought off the chamberlain.

"Upon this incident, Reldresal, principal secretary for private affairs, who always approved himself your true friend, was commanded by the emperor to deliver his opinion, which he accordingly did; and therein justified the good thoughts you have of him. He allowed your crimes to be great, but that still there was room for mercy, the most commendable virtue in a prince, and for which his Majesty was so justly celebrated. He said, the friendship between you and him was so well known to the world, that perhaps the most honourable board might think him partial; however, in obedience to the command he had received, he would freely offer his sentiments.

"That if his Majesty, in consideration of your services, and pursuant to his own merciful disposition, would please to spare your life, and only give orders to put out both your eyes, he humbly conceived, that by this expedient justice might in some measure be satisfied, and all the world would applaud the lenity of the emperor, as well as the fair and generous proceedings of those who have the honour to be his counsellors. That the loss of your eyes would be no impediment to your bodily strength, by which you might still be useful to his Majesty; that blindness is an addition to courage, by concealing dangers from us; that the fear you had for your eyes, was the greatest difficulty in bringing over the enemy's fleet, and it would be sufficient for you to see by the eyes of the ministers, since the greatest princes do no more.

"This proposal was received with the utmost disapprobation by the whole board. Bolgolam, the admiral, could not preserve his temper, but, rising up in fury, said, he wondered how the secretary durst presume to give his opinion for preserving the life of a traitor; that the services you had performed were, by all true reasons of state, the great aggravation of your crimes; that you, who were able to extinguish the fire by discharge of urine in her Majesty's apartment (which he mentioned with horror), might, at another time, raise an inundation by the same means, to drown the whole palace; and the same strength which enabled you to bring over the enemy's fleet, might serve, upon the first discontent, to carry it back; that he had good reasons to think you were a Big-endian in your heart; and, as treason begins in the heart, before it appears in overt-acts, so he accused you as a traitor on that account, and therefore insisted you should be put to death.

"The treasurer was of the same opinion: he showed to what straits his Majesty's revenue was reduced, by the charge of maintaining you, which would soon grow insupportable; that the secretary's expedient of putting out your eyes, was so far from being a remedy against this evil, that it would probably increase it, as is manifest from the common practice of blinding some kind of fowls, after which they fed the faster, and grew sooner fat; that his sacred Majesty and the council, who are your judges, were, in their own consciences, fully convinced of your guilt, which was a sufficient argument to condemn you to death, without the formal proofs required by the strict letter of the law.

"But his imperial Majesty, fully determined against capital punishment, was graciously pleased to say, that since the council thought the loss of your eyes too easy a censure, some other way may be inflicted hereafter. And your friend the secretary, humbly desiring to be heard again, in answer to what the treasurer had objected, concerning the great charge his Majesty was at in maintaining you, said, that his Excellency, who had the sole disposal of the emperor's revenue, might easily provide against that evil, by gradually lessening your establishment; by which, for want of sufficient for you would grow weak and faint, and lose your appetite, and consequently, decay, and consume in a few months; neither would the stench of your carcass be then so dangerous, when it should become more than half diminished; and immediately upon your death five or six thousand of his Majesty's subjects might, in two or three days, cut your flesh from your bones, take it away by cart-loads, and bury it in distant parts, to prevent infection, leaving the skeleton as a monument of admiration to posterity.

"Thus, by the great friendship of the secretary, the whole affair was compromised. It was strictly enjoined, that the project of starving you by degrees should be kept a secret; but the sentence of putting out your eyes was entered on the books; none dissenting, except Bolgolam the admiral, who, being a creature of the empress, was perpetually instigated by her Majesty to insist upon your death.

"In three days your friend the secretary will be directed to come to your house, and read before you the articles of impeachment; and then to signify the great lenity and favour of his Majesty and council, whereby you are only condemned to the loss of your eyes, which his Majesty does not question you will gratefully and humbly submit to; and twenty of his Majesty's surgeons will attend, in order to see the operation well performed, by discharging very sharp-pointed arrows into the balls of your eyes, as you lie on the ground.

"I leave to your prudence what measures you will take; and to avoid suspicion, I must immediately return in as private a manner as I came.

His lordship did so; and I remained alone, under many doubts and perplexities of mind.

It was a custom introduced by this prince and his ministry (very different, as I have been assured, from the practice of former times,) that after the court had decreed any cruel execution, either to gratify the monarch's resentment, or the malice of a favourite, the emperor always made a speech to his whole council, expressing his great lenity and tenderness, as qualities known and confessed by all the world. This speech was immediately published throughout the kingdom; nor did any thing terrify the people so much as those encomiums on his Majesty's mercy; because it was observed, that the more these praises were enlarged and insisted on, the more inhuman was the punishment, and the sufferer more innocent.

Yet, as to myself, I must confess, having never been designed for a courtier, either by my birth or education, I was so ill a judge of things, that I could not discover the lenity and favour of this sentence, but conceived it (perhaps erroneously) rather to be rigorous than gentle. I sometimes thought of standing my trial, for, although I could not deny the facts alleged in the several articles, yet I hoped they would admit of some extenuation. But having in my life perused many state-trials, which I ever observed to terminate as the judges thought fit to direct, I durst not rely on so dangerous a decision, in so critical a juncture, and against such powerful enemies.

Once I was strongly bent upon resistance, for, while I had liberty the whole strength of that empire could hardly subdue me, and I might easily with stones pelt the metropolis to pieces; but I soon rejected that project with horror, by remembering the oath I had made to the emperor, the favours I received from him, and the high title of *nardac* he conferred upon me. Neither had I so soon learned the gratitude of courtiers, to persuade myself, that his Majesty's present seventies acquitted me of all past obligations.

At last, I fixed upon a resolution, for which it is probable I may incur some censure, and not unjustly; for I confess I owe the preserving of mine eyes, and consequently my liberty, to my own great rashness and want of experience; because, if I had then known the nature of princes and ministers, which I have since observed in many other courts, and their methods of treating criminals less obnoxious than myself, I should, with great alacrity and readiness, have submitted to so easy a punishment.

But hurried on by the precipitancy of youth, and having his imperial Majesty's license to pay my attendance upon the emperor of Blefuscu, I took this opportunity, before the three days were elapsed, to send a letter to my friend the secretary, signifying my resolution of setting out that morning for Blefuscu, pursuant to the leave I had got; and, without waiting for an answer, I went to that side of the island where our fleet lay. I seized a large man of war, tied a cable to the prow, and, lifting up the anchors, I stripped myself, put my clothes (together with my coverlet, which I carried under my arm) into the vessel, and, drawing it after me, between wading and swimming arrived at the royal port of Blefuscu, where the people had long expected me: they lent me two guides to direct me to the capital city, which is of the same name. I held them in my hands, till I came within two hundred yards of the gate, and desired them to signify my arrival to one of the secretaries, and let him know, I there waited his Majesty's command. I had an answer in about an hour, that his Majesty, attended by the royal family, and great officers of the court, was coming out to receive me. I advanced a hundred yards. The emperor and his train alighted from their horses, the empress and ladies from their coaches, and I did not perceive they were in any fright or concern. I lay on the ground to kiss his Majesty's and the empress's hands. I told his Majesty, that I was come according to my promise, and with the license of the emperor my master, to have the honour of seeing so mighty a monarch, and to offer him any service in my power, consistent with my duty to my own prince; not mentioning a word of my disgrace, because I had hitherto no regular information of it, and might suppose myself wholly ignorant of any such design; neither could I reasonably conceive that the emperor would discover the secret, while I was out of his power; wherein, however, it soon appeared I was deceived.

I shall not trouble the reader with the particular account of my reception at this court, which was suitable to the generosity of so great a prince; nor of the difficulties I was in for want of a house and bed, being forced to lie on the ground, wrapped up in my coverlet.

CHAPTER VIII

The author, by a lucky accident, finds means to leave Blefuscu; and, after some difficulties, returns safe to his native country.

Three days after my arrival, walking out of curiosity to the north-east coast of the island, I observed, about half a league off in the sea, somewhat that looked like a boat overturned. I pulled off my shoes and stockings, and, wailing two or three hundred yards, I found the object to approach nearer by force of the tide; and then plainly saw it to be a real boat, which I supposed might by some tempest have been driven from a ship. Whereupon, I returned immediately towards the city, and desired his imperial Majesty to lend me twenty of the tallest vessels he had left, after the loss of his fleet, and three thousand seamen, under the command of his vice-admiral. This fleet sailed round, while I went back the shortest way to the coast, where I first discovered the boat. I found the tide had driven it still nearer. The seamen were all provided with cordage, which I had beforehand twisted to a sufficient strength. When the ships came up, I stripped myself, and waded till I came within a hundred yards off the boat, after which I was forced to swim till I got up to it. The seamen threw me the end of the cord, which I fastened to a hole in the fore-part of the boat, and the other end to a man of war.

But I found all my labour to little purpose; for, being out of my depth, I was not able to work. In this necessity I was forced to swim behind, and push the boat forward, as often as I could, with one of my hands; and the tide favouring me,

I advanced so far that I could just hold up my chin and feel the ground. I rested two or three minutes, and then gave the boat another shove, and so on, till the sea was no higher than my arm-pits; and now, the most laborious part being over, I took out my other cables, which were stowed in one of the ships, and fastened them first to the boat, and then to nine of the vessels which attended me; the wind being favourable, the seamen towed, and I shoved, until we arrived within forty yards of the shore; and, waiting till the tide was out, I got dry to the boat, and by the assistance of two thousand men, with ropes and engines, I made a shift to turn it on its bottom, and found it was but little damaged.

I shall not trouble the reader with the difficulties I was under, by the help of certain paddles, which cost me ten days making, to get my boat to the royal port of Blefuscu, where a mighty concourse of people appeared upon my arrival, full of wonder at the sight of so prodigious a vessel. I told the emperor that my good fortune had thrown this boat in my way, to carry me to some place whence I might return into my native country; and begged his Majesty's orders for getting materials to fit it up, together with his license to depart; which, after some kind expostulations, he was pleased to grant.

I did very much wonder, in all this time, not to have heard of any express relating to me from our emperor to the court of Blefuscu. But I was afterward given privately to understand, that his imperial Majesty, never imagining I had the least notice of his designs, believed I was only gone to Blefuscu in performance of my promise, according to the license he had given me, which was well known at our court, and would return in a few days, when the ceremony was ended. But he was at last in pain at my long absence; and after consulting with the treasurer and the rest of that cabal, a person of quality was dispatched with the copy of the articles against me.

This envoy had instructions to represent to the monarch of Blefuscu, the great lenity of his master, who was content to punish me no farther than with the loss of mine eyes; that I had fled from justice; and if I did not return in two hours, I should be deprived of my title of *nardac*, and declared a traitor. The envoy further added, that in order to maintain the peace and amity between both empires, his master expected that his brother of Blefuscu would give orders to have me sent back to Lilliput, bound hand and foot, to be punished as a traitor.

The emperor of Blefuscu, having taken three days to consult, returned an answer consisting of many civilities and excuses. He said, that as for sending me bound, his brother knew it was impossible; that, although I had deprived him of his fleet, yet he owed great obligations to me for many good offices I had done him in making the peace. That, however, both their majesties would soon be made easy; for I had found a prodigious vessel on the shore, able to carry me on the sea, which he had given orders to fit up, with my own assistance and direction; and he hoped, in a few weeks, both empires would be freed from so insupportable an incumbrance.

With this answer the envoy returned to Lilliput; and the monarch of Blefuscu related to me all that had passed; offering me at the same time (but under the strictest confidence) his gracious protection, if I would continue in his service; wherein, although I believed him sincere, yet I resolved never more to put any confidence in princes or ministers, where I could possibly avoid it; and therefore, with all due acknowledgments for his favourable intentions, I humbly begged to be excused. I told him, that since fortune, whether good or evil, had thrown a vessel in my way, I was resolved to venture myself on the ocean, rather than be an occasion of difference between two such mighty monarchs. Neither did I find the emperor at all displeased; and I discovered, by a certain accident, that he was very glad of my resolution, and so were most of his ministers.

These considerations moved me to hasten my departure somewhat sooner than I intended; to which the court, impatient to have me gone, very readily contributed. Five hundred workmen were employed to make two sails to my boat, according to my directions, by quilting thirteen folds of their strongest linen together. I was at the pains of making ropes and cables, by twisting ten, twenty, or thirty of the thickest and strongest of theirs. A great stone that I happened to find, after a long search, by the sea-shore, served me for an anchor. I had the tallow of three hundred cows, for greasing my boat, and other uses. I was at incredible pains in cutting down some of the largest timber-trees, for oars and masts, wherein I was, however, much assisted by his Majesty's ship-carpenters, who helped me in smoothing them, after I had done the rough work.

In about a month, when all was prepared, I sent to receive his Majesty's commands, and to take my leave. The emperor and royal family came out of the palace; I lay down on my face to kiss his hand, which he very graciously gave me: so did the empress and young princes of the blood. His Majesty presented me with fifty purses of two hundred *sprugs* a-piece, together with his picture at full length, which I put immediately into one of my gloves, to keep it from being hurt. The ceremonies at my departure were too many to trouble the reader with at this time.

I stored the boat with the carcases of a hundred oxen, and three hundred sheep, with bread and drink proportionable, and as much meat ready dressed as four hundred cooks could provide. I took with me six cows and two bulls alive, with as many ewes and rams, intending to carry them into my own country, and propagate the breed. And to feed them on board,

I had a good bundle of hay, and a bag of corn. I would gladly have taken a dozen of the natives, but this was a thing the emperor would by no means permit; and, besides a diligent search into my pockets, his Majesty engaged my honour not to carry away any of his subjects, although with their own consent and desire.

Having thus prepared all things as well as I was able, I set sail on the twenty-fourth day of September 1701, at six in the morning; and when I had gone about four-leagues to the northward, the wind being at south-east, at six in the evening I descried a small island, about half a league to the north-west. I advanced forward, and cast anchor on the lee-side of the island, which seemed to be uninhabited. I then took some refreshment, and went to my rest. I slept well, and as I conjectured at least six hours, for I found the day broke in two hours after I awaked. It was a clear night. I ate my breakfast before the sun was up; and heaving anchor, the wind being favourable, I steered the same course that I had done the day before, wherein I was directed by my pocket compass. My intention was to reach, if possible, one of those islands which I had reason to believe lay to the north-east of Van Diemen's Land.

I discovered nothing all that day; but upon the next, about three in the afternoon, when I had by my computation made twenty-four leagues from Blefuscu, I descried a sail steering to the south-east; my course was due east. I hailed her, but could get no answer; yet I found I gained upon her, for the wind slackened. I made all the sail I could, and in half an hour she spied me, then hung out her ancient, and discharged a gun.

It is not easy to express the joy I was in, upon the unexpected hope of once more seeing my beloved country, and the dear pledges I left in it. The ship slackened her sails, and I came up with her between five and six in the evening, September 26th; but my heart leaped within me to see her English colours. I put my cows and sheep into my coat-pockets, and got on board with all my little cargo of provisions.

The vessel was an English merchantman, returning from Japan by the North and South seas; the captain, Mr. John Biddel, of Deptford, a very civil man, and an excellent sailor. We were now in the latitude of 30 degrees south; there were about fifty men in the ship; and here I met an old comrade of mine, one Peter Williams, who gave me a good character to the captain. This gentleman treated me with kindness, and desired I would let him know what place I came from last, and whither I was bound; which I did in a few words, but he thought I was raving, and that the dangers I underwent had disturbed my head; whereupon I took my black cattle and sheep out of my pocket, which, after great astonishment, clearly convinced him of my veracity. I then showed him the gold given me by the emperor of Blefuscu, together with his Majesty's picture at full length, and some other rarities of that country. I gave him two purses of two hundreds *sprugs* each, and promised, when we arrived in England, to make him a present of a cow and a sheep big with young.

I shall not trouble the reader with a particular account of this voyage, which was very prosperous for the most part. We arrived in the Downs on the 13th of April, 1702. I had only one misfortune, that the rats on board carried away one of my sheep; I found her bones in a hole, picked clean from the flesh. The rest of my cattle I got safe ashore, and set them a-grazing in a bowling-green at Greenwich, where the fineness of the grass made them feed very heartily, though I had always feared the contrary: neither could I possibly have preserved them in so long a voyage, if the captain had not allowed me some of his best biscuit, which, rubbed to powder, and mingled with water, was their constant food. The short time I continued in England, I made a considerable profit by showing my cattle to many persons of quality and others: and before I began my second voyage, I sold them for six hundred pounds. Since my last return I find the breed is considerably increased, especially the sheep, which I hope will prove much to the advantage of the woollen manufacture, by the fineness of the fleeces.

I stayed but two months with my wife and family, for my insatiable desire of seeing foreign countries, would suffer me to continue no longer. I left fifteen hundred pounds with my wife, and fixed her in a good house at Redriff. My remaining stock I carried with me, part in money and part in goods, in hopes to improve my fortunes. My eldest uncle John had left me an estate in land, near Epping, of about thirty pounds a-year; and I had a long lease of the Black Bull in Fetter-Lane, which yielded me as much more; so that I was not in any danger of leaving my family upon the parish. My son Johnny, named so after his uncle, was at the grammar-school, and a towardly child. My daughter Betty (who is now well married, and has children) was then at her needle-work. I took leave of my wife, and boy and girl, with tears on both sides, and went on board the Adventure, a merchant ship of three hundred tons, bound for Surat, captain John Nicholas, of Liverpool, commander. But my account of this voyage must be referred to the Second Part of my Travels.

PART II

A Voyage to Brobdingnag

CHAPTER I

A great storm described; the long boat sent to fetch water; the author goes with it to discover the country. He is left on shore, is seized by one of the natives, and carried to a farmer's house. His reception, with several accidents that happened there. A description of the inhabitants.

Having been condemned, by nature and fortune, to active and restless life, in two months after my return, I again left my native country, and took shipping in the Downs, on the 20th day of June, 1702, in the Adventure, Captain John Nicholas, a Cornish man, commander, bound for Surat.

We had a very prosperous gale, till we arrived at the Cape of Good Hope, where we landed for fresh water; but discovering a leak, we unshipped our goods and wintered there; for the captain falling sick of an ague, we could not leave the Cape till the end of March. We then set sail, and had a good voyage till we passed the Straits of Madagascar; but having got northward of that island, and to about five degrees south latitude, the winds, which in those seas are observed to blow a constant equal gale between the north and west, from the beginning of December to the beginning of May, on the 19th of April began to blow with much greater violence, and more westerly than usual, continuing so for twenty days together: during which time, we were driven a little to the east of the Molucca Islands, and about three degrees northward of the line, as our captain found by an observation he took the 2nd of May, at which time the wind ceased, and it was a perfect calm, whereat I was not a little rejoiced. But he, being a man well experienced in the navigation of those seas, bid us all prepare against a storm, which accordingly happened the day following: for the southern wind, called the southern monsoon, began to set in.

Finding it was likely to overblow, we took in our sprit-sail, and stood by to hand the fore-sail; but making foul weather, we looked the guns were all fast, and handed the mizen. The ship lay very broad off, so we thought it better spooning before the sea, than trying or hulling. We reefed the fore-sail and set him, and hauled aft the fore-sheet; the helm was hard a-weather. The ship wore bravely. We belayed the fore down-haul; but the sail was split, and we hauled down the yard, and got the sail into the ship, and unbound all the things clear of it.

It was a very fierce storm; the sea broke strange and dangerous. We hauled off upon the laniard of the whip-staff, and helped the man at the helm. We would not get down our topmast, but let all stand, because she scudded before the sea very well, and we knew that the top-mast being aloft, the ship was the wholesomer, and made better way through the sea, seeing we had sea-room.

When the storm was over, we set fore-sail and main-sail, and brought the ship to. Then we set the mizen, main-top-sail, and the fore-top-sail. Our course was east-north-east, the wind was at south-west. We got the starboard tacks aboard, we cast off our weather-braces and lifts; we set in the lee-braces, and hauled forward by the weather-bowlings, and hauled them tight, and belayed them, and hauled over the mizen tack to windward, and kept her full and by as near as she would lie.

During this storm, which was followed by a strong wind west-south-west, we were carried, by my computation, about five hundred leagues to the east, so that the oldest sailor on board could not tell in what part of the world we were. Our provisions held out well, our ship was staunch, and our crew all in good health; but we lay in the utmost distress for water.

We thought it best to hold on the same course, rather than turn more northerly, which might have brought us to the north-west part of Great Tartary, and into the Frozen Sea.

On the 16th day of June, 1703, a boy on the top-mast discovered land. On the 17th, we came in full view of a great island, or continent (for we knew not whether;) on the south side whereof was a small neck of land jutting out into the sea, and a creek too shallow to hold a ship of above one hundred tons. We cast anchor within a league of this creek, and our captain sent a dozen of his men well armed in the long-boat, with vessels for water, if any could be found. I desired his leave to go with them, that I might see the country, and make what discoveries I could.

When we came to land we saw no river or spring, nor any sign of inhabitants. Our men therefore wandered on the shore to find out some fresh water near the sea, and I walked alone about a mile on the other side, where I observed the country all barren and rocky. I now began to be weary, and seeing nothing to entertain my curiosity, I returned gently down towards the creek; and the sea being full in my view, I saw our men already got into the boat, and rowing for life to the ship. I was going to holla after them, although it had been to little purpose, when I observed a huge creature walking after them in the sea, as fast as he could: he waded not much deeper than his knees, and took prodigious strides: but our men had the start of him half a league, and, the sea thereabouts being full of sharp-pointed rocks, the monster was not able to overtake the boat. This I was afterwards told, for I durst not stay to see the issue of the adventure; but ran as fast as I could the way I first went, and then climbed up a steep hill, which gave me some prospect of the country. I found it fully cultivated; but that which first surprised me was the length of the grass, which, in those grounds that seemed to be kept for hay, was about twenty feet high.

I fell into a high road, for so I took it to be, though it served to the inhabitants only as a foot-path through a field of barley. Here I walked on for some time, but could see little on either side, it being now near harvest, and the corn rising at least forty feet.

I was an hour walking to the end of this field, which was fenced in with a hedge of at least one hundred and twenty feet high, and the trees so lofty that I could make no computation of their altitude. There was a stile to pass from this field into the next. It had four steps, and a stone to cross over when you came to the uppermost. It was impossible for me to climb this stile, because every step was six-feet high, and the upper stone about twenty. I was endeavouring to find some gap in the hedge, when I discovered one of the inhabitants in the next field, advancing towards the stile, of the same size with him whom I saw in the sea pursuing our boat. He appeared as tall as an ordinary spire steeple, and took about ten yards at every stride, as near as I could guess. I was struck with the utmost fear and astonishment, and ran to hide myself in the corn, whence I saw him at the top of the stile looking back into the next field on the right hand, and heard him call in a voice many degrees louder than a speaking-trumpet: but the noise was so high in the air, that at first I certainly thought it was thunder.

Whereupon seven monsters, like himself, came towards him with reaping-hooks in their hands, each hook about the largeness of six scythes. These people were not so well clad as the first, whose servants or labourers they seemed to be; for, upon some words he spoke, they went to reap the corn in the field where I lay. I kept from them at as great a distance as I could, but was forced to move with extreme difficulty, for the stalks of the corn were sometimes not above a foot distant, so that I could hardly squeeze my body betwixt them.

However, I made a shift to go forward, till I came to a part of the field where the corn had been laid by the rain and wind. Here it was impossible for me to advance a step; for the stalks were so interwoven, that I could not creep through, and the beards of the fallen ears so strong and pointed, that they pierced through my clothes into my flesh. At the same time I heard the reapers not a hundred yards behind me. Being quite dispirited with toil, and wholly overcome by grief and dispair, I lay down between two ridges, and heartily wished I might there end my days. I bemoaned my desolate widow and fatherless children. I lamented my own folly and wilfulness, in attempting a second voyage, against the advice of all my friends and relations.

In this terrible agitation of mind, I could not forbear thinking of Lilliput, whose inhabitants looked upon me as the greatest prodigy that ever appeared in the world; where I was able to draw an imperial fleet in my hand, and perform those other actions, which will be recorded for ever in the chronicles of that empire, while posterity shall hardly believe them, although attested by millions. I reflected what a mortification it must prove to me, to appear as inconsiderable in this nation, as one single Lilliputian would be among us. But this I conceived was to be the least of my misfortunes; for, as human creatures are observed to be more savage and cruel in proportion to their bulk, what could I expect but to be a morsel in the mouth of the first among these enormous barbarians that should happen to seize me?

Undoubtedly philosophers are in the right, when they tell us that nothing is great or little otherwise than by comparison. It might have pleased fortune, to have let the Lilliputians find some nation, where the people were as diminutive with respect to them, as they were to me. And who knows but that even this prodigious race of mortals might be equally overmatched in some distant part of the world, whereof we have yet no discovery.

Scared and confounded as I was, I could not forbear going on with these reflections, when one of the reapers, approaching within ten yards of the ridge where I lay, made me apprehend that with the next step I should be squashed to death under his foot, or cut in two with his reaping-hook. And therefore, when he was again about to move, I screamed as loud as fear could make me: whereupon the huge creature trod short, and, looking round about under him for some time, at last espied me as I lay on the ground.

He considered awhile, with the caution of one who endeavours to lay hold on a small dangerous animal in such a manner that it shall not be able either to scratch or bite him, as I myself have sometimes done with a weasel in England.

At length he ventured to take me behind, by the middle, between his fore-finger and thumb, and brought me within three yards of his eyes, that he might behold my shape more perfectly. I guessed his meaning, and my good fortune gave me so much presence of mind, that I resolved not to struggle in the least as he held me in the air above sixty feet from the ground, although he grievously pinched my sides, for fear I should slip through his fingers. All I ventured was to raise mine eyes towards the sun, and place my hands together in a supplicating posture, and to speak some words in a humble melancholy tone, suitable to the condition I then was in: for I apprehended every moment that he would dash me against the ground, as we usually do any little hateful animal, which we have a mind to destroy. But my good star would have it, that he appeared pleased with my voice and gestures, and began to look upon me as a curiosity, much wondering to hear me pronounce articulate words, although he could not understand them.

In the meantime I was not able to forbear groaning and shedding tears, and turning my head towards my sides; letting him know, as well as I could, how cruelly I was hurt by the pressure of his thumb and finger. He seemed to apprehend my meaning; for, lifting up the lappet of his coat, he put me gently into it, and immediately ran along with me to his master, who was a substantial farmer, and the same person I had first seen in the field.

The farmer having (as I suppose by their talk) received such an account of me as his servant could give him, took a piece of a small straw, about the size of a walking-staff, and therewith lifted up the lappets of my coat; which it seems he thought to be some kind of covering that nature had given me. He blew my hairs aside to take a better view of my face. He called his hinds about him, and asked them, as I afterwards learned, whether they had ever seen in the fields any little creature that resembled me. He then placed me softly on the ground upon all fours, but I got immediately up, and walked slowly backward and forward, to let those people see I had no intent to run away.

They all sat down in a circle about me, the better to observe my motions. I pulled off my hat, and made a low bow towards the farmer. I fell on my knees, and lifted up my hands and eyes, and spoke several words as loud as I could: I took a purse of gold out of my pocket, and humbly presented it to him. He received it on the palm of his hand, then applied it close to his eye to see what it was, and afterwards turned it several times with the point of a pin (which he took out of his sleeve,) but could make nothing of it. Whereupon I made a sign that he should place his hand on the ground.

I then took the purse, and, opening it, poured all the gold into his palm. There were six Spanish pieces of four pistoles each, beside twenty or thirty smaller coins. I saw him wet the tip of his little finger upon his tongue, and take up one of my largest pieces, and then another; but he seemed to be wholly ignorant what they were. He made me a sign to put them again into my purse, and the purse again into my pocket, which, after offering it to him several times, I thought it best to do.

The farmer, by this time, was convinced I must be a rational creature. He spoke often to me; but the sound of his voice pierced my ears like that of a water-mill, yet his words were articulate enough. I answered as loud as I could in several languages, and he often laid his ear within two yards of me: but all in vain, for we were wholly unintelligible to each other. He then sent his servants to their work, and taking his handkerchief out of his pocket, he doubled and spread it on his left hand, which he placed flat on the ground with the palm upward, making me a sign to step into it, as I could easily do, for it was not above a foot in thickness. I thought it my part to obey, and, for fear of falling, laid myself at full length upon the handkerchief, with the remainder of which he lapped me up to the head for further security, and in this manner carried me home to his house. There he called his wife, and showed me to her; but she screamed and ran back, as women in England do at the sight of a toad or a spider. However, when she had a while seen my behaviour, and how well I observed the signs her husband made, she was soon reconciled, and by degrees grew extremely tender of me.

It was about twelve at noon, and a servant brought in dinner. It was only one substantial dish of meat (fit for the plain condition of a husbandman,) in a dish of about four-and-twenty feet diameter. The company were, the farmer and his wife, three children, and an old grandmother. When they were sat down, the farmer placed me at some distance from him on the table, which was thirty feet high from the floor. I was in a terrible fright, and kept as far as I could from the edge, for fear of falling. The wife minced a bit of meat, then crumbled some bread on a trencher, and placed it before me.

I made her a low bow, took out my knife and fork, and fell to eat, which gave them exceeding delight. The mistress sent her maid for a small dram cup, which held about two gallons, and filled it with drink; I took up the vessel with much difficulty in both hands, and in a most respectful manner drank to her ladyship's health, expressing the words as loud as I could in English, which made the company laugh so heartily, that I was almost deafened with the noise. This liquor tasted like a small cider, and was not unpleasant.

Then the master made me a sign to come to his trencher side; but as I walked on the table, being in great surprise all the time, as the indulgent reader will easily conceive and excuse, I happened to stumble against a crust, and fell flat on my face, but received no hurt. I got up immediately, and observing the good people to be in much concern, I took my hat (which I held under my arm out of good manners,) and waving it over my head, made three huzzas, to show I had got no mischief by my fall.

But advancing forward towards my master (as I shall henceforth call him,) his youngest son, who sat next to him, an arch boy of about ten years old, took me up by the legs, and held me so high in the air, that I trembled every limb: but his father snatched me from him, and at the same time gave him such a box on the left ear, as would have felled an European troop of horse to the earth, ordering him to be taken from the table. But being afraid the boy might owe me a spite, and well remembering how mischievous all children among us naturally are to sparrows, rabbits, young kittens, and puppy dogs, I fell on my knees, and pointing to the boy, made my master to understand, as well as I could, that I desired his son might be pardoned. The father complied, and the lad took his seat again, whereupon I went to him, and kissed his hand, which my master took, and made him stroke me gently with it.

In the midst of dinner, my mistress's favourite cat leaped into her lap. I heard a noise behind me like that of a dozen stocking-weavers at work; and turning my head, I found it proceeded from the purring of that animal, who seemed to be three times larger than an ox, as I computed by the view of her head, and one of her paws, while her mistress was feeding and stroking her. The fierceness of this creature's countenance altogether discomposed me; though I stood at the farther end of the table, above fifty feet off; and although my mistress held her fast, for fear she might give a spring, and seize me in her talons.

But it happened there was no danger, for the cat took not the least notice of me when my master placed me within three yards of her. And as I have been always told, and found true by experience in my travels, that flying or discovering fear before a fierce animal, is a certain way to make it pursue or attack you, so I resolved, in this dangerous juncture, to show no manner of concern. I walked with intrepidity five or six times before the very head of the cat, and came within half a yard of her; whereupon she drew herself back, as if she were more afraid of me.

I had less apprehension concerning the dogs, whereof three or four came into the room, as it is usual in farmers' houses; one of which was a mastiff, equal in bulk to four elephants, and another a greyhound, somewhat taller than the mastiff, but not so large.

When dinner was almost done, the nurse came in with a child of a year old in her arms, who immediately spied me, and began a squall that you might have heard from London-Bridge to Chelsea, after the usual oratory of infants, to get me for a plaything. The mother, out of pure indulgence, took me up, and put me towards the child, who presently seized me by the middle, and got my head into his mouth, where I roared so loud that the urchin was frighted, and let me drop, and I should infallibly have broke my neck, if the mother had not held her apron under me. The nurse, to quiet her babe, made use of a rattle which was a kind of hollow vessel filled with great stones, and fastened by a cable to the child's waist: but all in vain; so that she was forced to apply the last remedy by giving it suck. I must confess no object ever disgusted me so much as the sight of her monstrous breast, which I cannot tell what to compare with, so as to give the curious reader an idea of its bulk, shape, and colour. It stood prominent six feet, and could not be less than sixteen in circumference. The nipple was about half the bigness of my head, and the hue both of that and the dug, so varied with spots, pimples, and freckles, that nothing could appear more nauseous: for I had a near sight of her, she sitting down, the more conveniently to give suck, and I standing on the table. This made me reflect upon the fair skins of our English ladies, who appear so beautiful to us, only because they are of our own size, and their defects not to be seen but through a magnifying glass; where we find by experiment that the smoothest and whitest skins look rough, and coarse, and ill-coloured.

I remember when I was at Lilliput, the complexion of those diminutive people appeared to me the fairest in the world; and talking upon this subject with a person of learning there, who was an intimate friend of mine, he said that my face appeared much fairer and smoother when he looked on me from the ground, than it did upon a nearer view, when I took him up in my hand, and brought him close, which he confessed was at first a very shocking sight. He said, he could discover great holes in my skin; that the stumps of my beard were ten times stronger than the bristles of a boar, and my complexion made up of several colours altogether disagreeable: although I must beg leave to say for myself, that

I am as fair as most of my sex and country, and very little sunburnt by all my travels. On the other side, discoursing of the ladies in that emperor's court, he used to tell me, one had freckles; another too wide a mouth; a third too large a nose; nothing of which I was able to distinguish. I confess this reflection was obvious enough; which, however, I could not forbear, lest the reader might think those vast creatures were actually deformed: for I must do them the justice to say, they are a comely race of people.

When dinner was done, my master went out to his labourers, and, as I could discover by his voice and gesture, gave his wife strict charge to take care of me. I was very much tired, and disposed to sleep, which my mistress perceiving, she put me on her own bed, and covered me with a clean white handkerchief, but larger and coarser than the mainsail of a man-of-war.

I slept about two hours, and dreamt I was at home with my wife and children, which aggravated my sorrows when I awaked, and found myself alone in a vast room, between two and three hundred feet wide, and above two hundred high, lying in a bed twenty yards wide. My mistress was gone about her household affairs, and had locked me in. The bed was eight yards from the floor.

While I was under these circumstances, two rats crept up the curtains, and ran smelling backwards and forwards on the bed. One of them came up almost to my face, whereupon I rose in a fright, and drew out my hanger to defend myself. These horrible animals had the boldness to attack me on both sides, and one of them held his fore-feet at my collar; but I had the good fortune to rip up his belly before he could do me any mischief. He fell down at my feet; and the other, seeing the fate of his comrade, made his escape, but not without one good wound on the back, which I gave him as he fled, and made the blood run trickling from him.

After this exploit, I walked gently to and fro on the bed, to recover my breath and loss of spirits. These creatures were of the size of a large mastiff, but infinitely more nimble and fierce; so that if I had taken off my belt before I went to sleep, I must have infallibly been torn to pieces and devoured. I measured the tail of the dead rat, and found it to be two yards long, wanting an inch; but it went against my stomach to drag the carcass off the bed, where it lay still bleeding; I observed it had yet some life, but with a strong slash across the neck, I thoroughly despatched it.

Soon after my mistress came into the room, who seeing me all bloody, ran and took me up in her hand. I pointed to the dead rat, smiling, and making other signs to show I was not hurt; whereat she was extremely rejoiced, calling the maid to take up the dead rat with a pair of tongs, and throw it out of the window. Then she set me on a table, where I showed her my hanger all bloody, and wiping it on the lappet of my coat, returned it to the scabbard.

I hope the gentle reader will excuse me for dwelling on these and the like particulars, which, however insignificant they may appear to groveling vulgar minds, yet will certainly help a philosopher to enlarge his thoughts and imagination, and apply them to the benefit of public as well as private life, which was my sole design in presenting this and other accounts of my travels to the world; wherein I have been chiefly studious of truth, without affecting any ornaments of learning or of style. But the whole scene of this voyage made so strong an impression on my mind, and is so deeply fixed in my memory, that, in committing it to paper I did not omit one material circumstance: however, upon a strict review, I blotted out several passages. Of less moment which were in my first copy, for fear of being censured as tedious and trifling, whereof travellers are often, perhaps not without justice, accused.

CHAPTER II

A description of the farmer's daughter. The author carried to a market-town, and then to the metropolis. The particulars of his journey.

My mistress had a daughter of nine years old, a child of towardly parts for her age, very dexterous at her needle, and skilful in dressing her baby. Her mother and she contrived to fit up the baby's cradle for me against night: the cradle was put into a small drawer of a cabinet, and the drawer placed upon a hanging shelf for fear of the rats. This was my bed all the time I staid with those people, though made more convenient by degrees, as I began to learn their language and make my wants known. This young girl was so handy, that after I had once or twice pulled off my clothes before her, she was able to dress and undress me, though I never gave her that trouble when she would let me do either myself. She made me seven shirts, and some other linen, of as fine cloth as could be got, which indeed was coarser than sackcloth; and these she constantly washed for me with her own hands.

She was likewise my school-mistress, to teach me the language: when I pointed to any thing, she told me the name of it in her own tongue, so that in a few days I was able to call for whatever I had a mind to. She was very good-natured, and not above forty feet high, being little for her age. She gave me the name of Grildrig, which the family took up, and afterwards the whole kingdom. The word imports what the Latins call Nanunculus, the Italians Homunceletino, and the English Mannikin. To her I chiefly owe my preservation in that country: we never parted while I was there; I called her my Glumdalclitch, or little nurse; and should be guilty of great ingratitude, if I omitted this honourable mention of her care and affection towards me, which I heartily wish it lay in my power to requite as she deserves, instead of being the innocent, but unhappy instrument of her disgrace, as I have too much reason to fear.

It now began to be known and talked of in the neighbourhood, that my master had found a strange animal in the field, about the bigness of a *splacnuck*, but exactly shaped in every part like a human creature; which it likewise imitated in all its actions; seemed to speak in a little language of its own, had already learned several words of theirs, went erect upon two legs, was tame and gentle, would come when it was called, do whatever it was bid, had the finest limbs in the world, and a complexion fairer than a nobleman's daughter of three years old. Another farmer, who lived hard by, and was a particular friend of my master, came on a visit on purpose to inquire into the truth of this story. I was immediately produced, and placed upon a table, where I walked as I was commanded, drew my hanger, put it up again, made my reverence to my master's guest, asked him in his own language how he did, and told him he was welcome, just as my little nurse had instructed me.

This man, who was old and dim-sighted, put on his spectacles to behold me better; at which I could not forbear laughing very heartily, for his eyes appeared like the full moon shining into a chamber at two windows. Our people, who discovered the cause of my mirth, bore me company in laughing, at which the old fellow was fool enough to be angry and out of countenance. He had the character of a great miser; and, to my misfortune, he well deserved it, by the cursed advice he gave my master, to show me as a sight upon a market-day in the next town, which was half an hour's riding, about two-and-twenty miles from our house.

I guessed there was some mischief when I observed my master and his friend whispering together, sometimes pointing at me; and my fears made me fancy that I overheard and understood some of their words. But the next morning Glumdalclitch, my little nurse, told me the whole matter, which she had cunningly picked out from her mother. The poor girl laid me on her bosom, and fell a weeping with shame and grief. She apprehended some mischief would happen to me from rude vulgar folks, who might squeeze me to death, or break one of my limbs by taking me in their hands. She had also observed how modest I was in my nature, how nicely I regarded my honour, and what an indignity I should conceive it, to be exposed for money as a public spectacle, to the meanest of the people. She said, her papa and mamma had promised that Grildrig should be hers; but now she found they meant to serve her as they did last year, when they pretended to give her a lamb, and yet, as soon as it was fat, sold it to a butcher.

For my own part, I may truly affirm, that I was less concerned than my nurse. I had a strong hope, which never left me, that I should one day recover my liberty: and as to the ignominy of being carried about for a monster, I considered myself to be a perfect stranger in the country, and that such a misfortune could never be charged upon me as a reproach, if ever I should return to England, since the king of Great Britain himself, in my condition, must have undergone the same distress.

My master, pursuant to the advice of his friend, carried me in a box the next market-day to the neighbouring town, and took along with him his little daughter, my nurse, upon a pillion behind him. The box was close on every side, with a little door for me to go in and out, and a few gimlet holes to let in air. The girl had been so careful as to put the quilt of her baby's bed into it, for me to lie down on. However, I was terribly shaken and discomposed in this journey, though it was but of half an hour: for the horse went about forty feet at every step and trotted so high, that the agitation was equal to the rising and falling of a ship in a great storm, but much more frequent. Our journey was somewhat farther than from London to St. Albans.

My master alighted at an inn which he used to frequent; and after consulting awhile with the inn-keeper, and making some necessary preparations, he hired the *grultrud*, or crier, to give notice through the town of a strange creature to be seen at the sign of the Green Eagle, not so big as a *splacnuck* (an animal in that country very finely shaped, about six feet long,) and in every part of the body resembling a human creature, could speak several words, and perform a hundred diverting tricks.

I was placed upon a table in the largest room of the inn, which might be near three hundred feet square. My little nurse stood on a low stool close to the table, to take care of me, and direct what I should do. My master, to avoid a crowd, would suffer only thirty people at a time to see me. I walked about on the table as the girl commanded; she asked me questions, as far as she knew my understanding of the language reached, and I answered them as loud as I could. I turned about several times to the company, paid my humble respects, said they were welcome, and used some other speeches I had been taught. I took up a thimble filled with liquor, which Glumdalclitch had given me for a cup, and drank their health, I drew out my hanger, and flourished with it after the manner of fencers in England. My nurse gave me a part of a straw, which I exercised as a pike, having learnt the art in my youth.

I was that day shown to twelve sets of company, and as often forced to act over again the same fopperies, till I was half dead with weariness and vexation; for those who had seen me made such wonderful reports, that the people were ready to break down the doors to come in.

My master, for his own interest, would not suffer any one to touch me except my nurse; and to prevent danger, benches were set round the table at such a distance as to put me out of every body's reach. However, an unlucky school-boy aimed a hazel nut directly at my head, which very narrowly missed me; otherwise it came with so much violence, that it would have infallibly knocked out my brains, for it was almost as large as a small pumpkin, but I had the satisfaction to see the young rogue well beaten, and turned out of the room.

My master gave public notice that he would show me again the next market-day; and in the meantime he prepared a convenient vehicle for me, which he had reason enough to do; for I was so tired with my first journey, and with entertaining company for eight hours together, that I could hardly stand upon my legs, or speak a word. It was at least three days before I recovered my strength; and that I might have no rest at home, all the neighbouring gentlemen from a hundred miles round, hearing of my fame, came to see me at my master's own house. There could not be fewer than thirty persons with their wives and children (for the country is very populous;) and my master demanded the rate of a full room whenever he showed me at home, although it were only to a single family; so that for some time I had but little ease every day of the week (except Wednesday, which is their Sabbath,) although I were not carried to the town.

My master, finding how profitable I was likely to be, resolved to carry me to the most considerable cities of the kingdom. Having therefore provided himself with all things necessary for a long journey, and settled his affairs at home, he took leave of his wife, and upon the 17th of August, 1703, about two months after my arrival, we set out for the metropolis, situate near the middle of that empire, and about three thousand miles distance from our house. My master made his daughter Glumdalclitch ride behind him. She carried me on her lap, in a box tied about her waist. The girl had lined it on all sides with the softest cloth she could get, well quilted underneath, furnished it with her baby's bed, provided me with linen and other necessaries, and made everything as convenient as she could. We had no other company but a boy of the house, who rode after us with the luggage.

My master's design was to show me in all the towns by the way, and to step out of the road for fifty or a hundred miles, to any village, or person of quality's house, where he might expect custom. We made easy journeys, of not above seven or eight score miles a-day; for Glumdalclitch, on purpose to spare me, complained she was tired with the trotting of the horse. She often took me out of my box, at my own desire, to give me air, and show me the country, but always held me fast by a leading-string.

We passed over five or six rivers, many degrees broader and deeper than the Nile or the Ganges: and there was hardly a rivulet so small as the Thames at London-bridge. We were ten weeks in our journey, and I was shown in eighteen large towns, besides many villages, and private families.

On the 26th day of October we arrived at the metropolis, called in their language *Lorbrulgrud*, or Pride of the Universe. My master took a lodging in the principal street of the city, not far from the royal palace, and put out bills in the usual form, containing an exact description of my person and parts. He hired a large room between three and four hundred feet wide. He provided a table sixty feet in diameter, upon which I was to act my part, and pallisadoed it round three feet from the edge, and as many high, to prevent my falling over. I was shown ten times a-day, to the wonder and satisfaction of all people. I could now speak the language tolerably well, and perfectly understood every word, that was spoken to me. Besides, I had learnt their alphabet, and could make a shift to explain a sentence here and there; for Glumdalclitch had been my instructor while we were at home, and at leisure hours during our journey. She carried a little book in her pocket, not much larger than a Sanson's Atlas; it was a common treatise for the use of young girls, giving a short account of their religion: out of this she taught me my letters, and interpreted the words.

CHAPTER III

The author sent for to court. The queen buys him of his master the farmer, and presents him to the king. He disputes with his Majesty's great scholars. An apartment at court provided for the author. He is in high favour with the queen. He stands up for the honour of his own country. His quarrels with the queen's dwarf.

The frequent labours I underwent every day, made, in a few weeks, a very considerable change in my health: the more my master got by me, the more insatiable he grew. I had quite lost my stomach, and was almost reduced to a skeleton. The farmer observed it, and concluding I must soon die, resolved to make as good a hand of me as he could.

While he was thus reasoning and resolving with himself, a *slardral*, or gentleman-usher, came from court, commanding my master to carry me immediately thither for the diversion of the queen and her ladies. Some of the latter had already been to see me, and reported strange things of my beauty, behaviour, and good sense. Her Majesty, and those who attended her, were beyond measure delighted with my demeanour. I fell on my knees, and begged the honour of kissing her imperial foot; but this gracious princess held out her little finger towards me, after I was set on the table, which I embraced in both my arms, and put the tip of it with the utmost respect to my lip. She made me some general questions about my country and my travels, which I answered as distinctly, and in as few words as I could. She asked, whether I could be content to live at court? I bowed down to the board of the table, and humbly answered that I was my master's slave: but, if I were at my own disposal, I should be proud to devote my life to her Majesty's service. She then asked my master, whether he was willing to sell me at a good price? He, who apprehended I could not live a month, was ready enough to part with me, and demanded a thousand pieces of gold, which were ordered him on the spot, each piece being about the bigness of eight hundred moidores; but allowing for the proportion of all things between that country and Europe, and the high price of gold among them, was hardly so great a sum as a thousand guineas would be in England.

I then said to the queen, since I was now her Majesty's most humble creature and vassal, I must beg the favour, that Glumdalclitch, who had always tended me with so much care and kindness, and understood to do it so well, might be admitted into her service, and continue to be my nurse and instructor.

Her Majesty agreed to my petition, and easily got the farmer's consent, who was glad enough to have his daughter preferred at court, and the poor girl herself was not able to hide her joy. My late master withdrew, bidding me farewell, and saying he had left me in a good service; to which I replied not a word, only making him a slight bow.

The queen observed my coldness; and, when the farmer was gone out of the apartment, asked me the reason. I made bold to tell her Majesty, that I owed no other obligation to my late master, than his not dashing out the brains of a poor harmless creature, found by chance in his fields: which obligation was amply recompensed, by the gain he had made in showing me through half the kingdom, and the price he had now sold me for. That the life I had since led was laborious enough to kill an animal of ten times my strength. That my health was much impaired, by the continual drudgery of entertaining the rabble every hour of the day; and that, if my master had not thought my life in danger, her Majesty would not have got so cheap a bargain. But as I was out of all fear of being ill-treated under the protection of so great and good an empress, the ornament of nature, the darling of the world, the delight of her subjects, the phoenix of the creation, so I hoped my late master's apprehensions would appear to be groundless; for I already found my spirits revive, by the influence of her most august presence.

This was the sum of my speech, delivered with great improprieties and hesitation. The latter part was altogether framed in the style peculiar to that people, whereof I learned some phrases from Glumdalclitch, while she was carrying me to court.

The queen, giving great allowance for my defectiveness in speaking, was, however, surprised at so much wit and good sense in so diminutive an animal. She took me in her own hand, and carried me to the king, who was then retired to his cabinet. His Majesty, a prince of much gravity and austere countenance, not well observing my shape at first view, asked the queen after a cold manner how long it was since she grew fond of a *splacnuck*? for such it seems he took me to be, as I lay upon my breast in her Majesty's right hand. But this princess, who has an infinite deal of wit and humour, set me gently on my feet upon the scrutoire, and commanded me to give his Majesty an account of myself, which I did in a very few words: and Glumdalclitch who attended at the cabinet door, and could not endure I should be out of her sight, being admitted, confirmed all that had passed from my arrival at her father's house.

The king, although he be as learned a person as any in his dominions, had been educated in the study of philosophy, and particularly mathematics; yet when he observed my shape exactly, and saw me walk erect, before I began to speak, conceived I might be a piece of clock-work (which is in that country arrived to a very great perfection) contrived by some ingenious artist. But when he heard my voice, and found what I delivered to be regular and rational, he could not conceal his astonishment.

He was by no means satisfied with the relation I gave him of the manner I came into his kingdom, but thought it a story concerted between Glumdalclitch and her father, who had taught me a set of words to make me sell at a better price. Upon this imagination, he put several other questions to me, and still received rational answers: no otherwise defective than by a foreign accent, and an imperfect knowledge in the language, with some rustic phrases which I had learned at the farmer's house, and did not suit the polite style of a court.

His Majesty sent for three great scholars, who were then in their weekly waiting, according to the custom in that country. These gentlemen, after they had a while examined my shape with much nicety, were of different opinions concerning me. They all agreed that I could not be produced according to the regular laws of nature, because I was not framed with a capacity of preserving my life, either by swiftness, or climbing of trees, or digging holes in the earth. They observed by my teeth, which they viewed with great exactness, that I was a carnivorous animal; yet most quadrupeds being an overmatch for me, and field mice, with some others, too nimble, they could not imagine how I should be able to support myself, unless I fed upon snails and other insects, which they offered, by many learned arguments, to evince that I could not possibly do. One of these virtuosi seemed to think that I might be an embryo, or abortive birth. But this opinion was rejected by the other two, who observed my limbs to be perfect and finished; and that I had lived several years, as it was manifest from my beard, the stumps whereof they plainly discovered through a magnifying glass. They would not allow me to be a dwarf, because my littleness was beyond all degrees of comparison; for the queen's favourite dwarf, the smallest ever known in that kingdom, was near thirty feet high. After much debate, they concluded unanimously, that I was only *relplum scalcath*, which is interpreted literally *lusus naturoe*; a determination exactly agreeable to the modern philosophy of Europe, whose professors, disdaining the old evasion of occult causes, whereby the followers of Aristotle endeavoured in vain to disguise their ignorance, have invented this wonderful solution of all difficulties, to the unspeakable advancement of human knowledge.

After this decisive conclusion, I entreated to be heard a word or two. I applied myself to the king, and assured his Majesty that I came from a country which abounded with several millions of both sexes, and of my own stature; where the animals, trees, and houses, were all in proportion, and where, by consequence, I might be as able to defend myself, and to find sustenance, as any of his Majesty's subjects could do here; which I took for a full answer to those gentlemen's arguments. To this they only replied with a smile of contempt, saying, that the farmer had instructed me very well in my lesson.

The king, who had a much better understanding, dismissing his learned men, sent for the farmer, who by good fortune was not yet gone out of town. Having therefore first examined him privately, and then confronted him with me and the young girl, his Majesty began to think that what we told him might possibly be true. He desired the queen to order that a particular care should be taken of me; and was of opinion that Glumdalclitch should still continue in her office of tending me, because he observed we had a great affection for each other. A convenient apartment was provided for her at court: she had a sort of governess appointed to take care of her education, a maid to dress her, and two other servants for menial offices; but the care of me was wholly appropriated to herself.

The queen commanded her own cabinet-maker to contrive a box, that might serve me for a bedchamber, after the model that Glumdalclitch and I should agree upon. This man was a most ingenious artist, and according to my direction, in three weeks finished for me a wooden chamber of sixteen feet square, and twelve high, with sash-windows, a door, and two closets, like a London bed-chamber. The board, that made the ceiling, was to be lifted up and down by two hinges, to put in a bed ready furnished by her Majesty's upholsterer, which Glumdalclitch took out every day to air, made it with her own hands, and letting it down at night, locked up the roof over me.

A nice workman, who was famous for little curiosities, undertook to make me two chairs, with backs and frames, of a substance not unlike ivory, and two tables, with a cabinet to put my things in. The room was quilted on all sides, as well as the floor and the ceiling, to prevent any accident from the carelessness of those who carried me, and to break the force of a jolt, when I went in a coach. I desired a lock for my door, to prevent rats and mice from coming in. The smith, after several attempts, made the smallest that ever was seen among them, for I have known a larger at the gate of a gentleman's house in England. I made a shift to keep the key in a pocket of my own, fearing Glumdalclitch might lose it.

The queen likewise ordered the thinnest silks that could be gotten, to make me clothes, not much thicker than an English blanket, very cumbersome till I was accustomed to them. They were after the fashion of the kingdom, partly resembling the Persian, and partly the Chinese, and are a very grave and decent habit.

The queen became so fond of my company, that she could not dine without me. I had a table placed upon the same at which her Majesty ate, just at her left elbow, and a chair to sit on. Glumdalclitch stood on a stool on the floor near my table, to assist and take care of me. I had an entire set of silver dishes and plates, and other necessaries, which, in proportion to those of the queen, were not much bigger than what I have seen in a London toy-shop for the furniture of a baby-house: these my little nurse kept in her pocket in a silver box, and gave me at meals as I wanted them, always cleaning them herself.

No person dined with the queen but the two princesses royal, the eldest sixteen years old, and the younger at that time thirteen and a month. Her Majesty used to put a bit of meat upon one of my dishes, out of which I carved for myself, and her diversion was to see me eat in miniature: for the queen (who had indeed but a weak stomach) took up, at one mouthful, as much as a dozen English farmers could eat at a meal, which to me was for some time a very nauseous sight. She would craunch the wing of a lark, bones and all, between her teeth, although it were nine times as large as that of a full-grown turkey; and put a bit of bread into her mouth as big as two twelve-penny loaves. She drank out of a golden cup, above a hogshead at a draught. Her knives were twice as long as a scythe, set straight upon the handle. The spoons, forks, and other instruments, were all in the same proportion. I remember when Glumdalclitch carried me, out of curiosity, to see some of the tables at court, where ten or a dozen of those enormous knives and forks were lifted up together, I thought I had never till then beheld so terrible a sight.

It is the custom, that every Wednesday (which, as I have observed, is their Sabbath) the king and queen, with the royal issue of both sexes, dine together in the apartment of his Majesty, to whom I was now become a great favourite; and at these times, my little chair and table were placed at his left hand, before one of the salt-cellars. This prince took a pleasure in conversing with me, inquiring into the manners, religion, laws, government, and learning of Europe; wherein I gave him the best account I was able. His apprehension was so clear, and his judgment so exact, that he made very wise reflections and observations upon all I said.

But I confess, that, after I had been a little too copious in talking of my own beloved country, of our trade and wars by sea and land, of our schisms in religion, and parties in the state; the prejudices of his education prevailed so far, that he could not forbear taking me up in his right hand, and stroking me gently with the other, after a hearty fit of laughing, asked me, whether I was a Whig or Tory.

Then turning to his first minister, who waited behind him with a white staff, near as tall as the mainmast of the *Royal Sovereign*, he observed how contemptible a thing was human grandeur, which could be mimicked by such diminutive insects as I: and yet, says he, I dare engage these creatures have their titles and distinctions of honour; they contrive little nests and burrows, that they call houses and cities; they make a figure in dress and equipage; they love, they fight, they dispute, they cheat, they betray! And thus he continued on, while my colour came and went several times, with indignation, to hear our noble country, the mistress of arts and arms, the scourge of France, the arbitress of Europe, the seat of virtue, piety, honour, and truth, the pride and envy of the world, so contemptuously treated.

But as I was not in a condition to resent injuries, so upon mature thoughts I began to doubt whether I was injured or no. For, after having been accustomed several months to the sight and converse of this people, and observed every object upon which I cast mine eyes to be of proportionable magnitude, the horror I had at first conceived from their bulk and aspect was so far worn off, that if I had then beheld a company of English lords and ladies in their finery and birth-day clothes, acting their several parts in the most courtly manner of strutting, and bowing, and prating, to say the truth, I should have been strongly tempted to laugh as much at them as the king and his grandees did at me.

Neither, indeed, could I forbear smiling at myself, when the queen used to place me upon her hand towards a looking-glass, by which both our persons appeared before me in full view together; and there could be nothing more ridiculous than the comparison; so that I really began to imagine myself dwindled many degrees below my usual size.

Nothing angered and mortified me so much as the queen's dwarf; who being of the lowest stature that was ever in that country (for I verily think he was not full thirty feet high), became so insolent at seeing a creature so much beneath him, that he would always affect to swagger and look big as he passed by me in the queen's antechamber, while I was standing on some table talking with the lords or ladies of the court, and he seldom failed of a smart word or two upon my littleness; against which I could only revenge myself by calling him brother, challenging him to wrestle, and such repartees as are usually in the mouths of court pages.

One day, at dinner, this malicious little cub was so nettled with something I had said to him, that, raising himself upon the frame of her Majesty's chair, he took me up by the middle, as I was sitting down, not thinking any harm, and let me drop into a large silver bowl of cream, and then ran away as fast as he could. I fell over head and ears, and, if I had not been a good swimmer, it might have gone very hard with me; for Glumdalclitch in that instant happened to be at the other end of the room, and the queen was in such a fright, that she wanted presence of mind to assist me. But my little nurse ran to my relief, and took me out, after I had swallowed above a quart of cream. I was put to bed:

however, I received no other damage than the loss of a suit of clothes, which was utterly spoiled.

The dwarf was soundly whipt, and as a farther punishment, forced to drink up the bowl of cream into which he had thrown me: neither was he ever restored to favour; for soon after the queen bestowed him on a lady of high quality, so that I saw him no more, to my very great satisfaction; for I could not tell to what extremities such a malicious urchin might have carried his resentment.

He had before served me a scurvy trick, which set the queen a-laughing, although at the same time she was heartily vexed, and would have immediately cashiered him, if I had not been so generous as to intercede. Her Majesty had taken a marrow-bone upon her plate, and, after knocking out the marrow, placed the bone again in the dish erect, as it stood before; the dwarf, watching his opportunity, while Glumdalclitch was gone to the side-board, mounted the stool that she stood on to take care of me at meals, took me up in both hands, and squeezing my legs together, wedged them into the marrow bone above my waist, where I stuck for some time, and made a very ridiculous figure.

I believe it was near a minute before any one knew what was become of me; for I thought it below me to cry out. But, as princes seldom get their meat hot, my legs were not scalded, only my stockings and breeches in a sad condition. The dwarf, at my entreaty, had no other punishment than a sound whipping.

I was frequently rallied by the queen upon account of my fearfulness; and she used to ask me whether the people of my country were as great cowards as myself? The occasion was this: the kingdom is much pestered with flies in summer; and these odious insects, each of them as big as a Dunstable lark, hardly gave me any rest while I sat at dinner, with their continual humming and buzzing about mine ears. They would sometimes alight upon my victuals, and leave their loathsome excrement, or spawn behind, which to me was very visible, though not to the natives of that country, whose large optics were not so acute as mine, in viewing smaller objects. Sometimes they would fix upon my nose, or forehead, where they stung me to the quick, smelling very offensively; and I could easily trace that viscous matter, which, our naturalists tell us, enables those creatures to walk with their feet upwards upon a ceiling.

I had much ado to defend myself against these detestable animals, and could not forbear starting when they came on my face. It was the common practice of the dwarf, to catch a number of these insects in his hand, as schoolboys do among us, and let them out suddenly under my nose, on purpose to frighten me, and divert the queen. My remedy was to cut them in pieces with my knife, as they flew in the air, wherein my dexterity was much admired.

I remember, one morning, when Glumdalclitch had set me in a box upon a window, as she usually did in fair days to give me air (for I durst not venture to let the box be hung on a nail out of the window, as we do with cages in England), after I had lifted up one of my sashes, and sat down at my table to eat a piece of sweet cake for my breakfast, above twenty wasps, allured by the smell, came flying into the room, humming louder than the drones of as many bagpipes.

Some of them seized my cake, and carried it piecemeal away; others flew about my head and face, confounding me with the noise, and putting me in the utmost terror of their stings. However, I had the courage to rise and draw my hanger, and attack them in the air. I dispatched four of them, but the rest got away, and I presently shut my window. These insects were as large as partridges: I took out their stings, found them an inch and a half long, and as sharp as needles. I carefully preserved them all; and having since shown them, with some other curiosities, in several parts of Europe, upon my return to England I gave three of them to Gresham College, and kept the fourth for myself.

CHAPTER IV

The country described. A proposal for correcting modern maps. The king's palace; and some account of the metropolis. The author's way of travelling. The chief temple described.

I now intend to give the reader a short description of this country, as far as I travelled in it, which was not above two thousand miles round Lorbrulgrud, the metropolis. For the queen, whom I always attended, never went farther when she accompanied the king in his progresses, and there staid till his Majesty returned from viewing his frontiers. The whole extent of this prince's dominions reaches about six thousand miles in length, and from three to five in breadth: whence I cannot but conclude, that our geographers of Europe are in a great error, by supposing nothing but sea between Japan and California; for it was ever my opinion, that there must be a balance of earth to counterpoise the great continent of Tartary; and therefore they ought to correct their maps and charts, by joining this vast tract of land to the north-west parts of America, wherein I shall be ready to lend them my assistance.

The kingdom is a peninsula, terminated to the north-east by a ridge of mountains thirty miles high, which are altogether impassable, by reason of the volcanoes upon the tops: neither do the most learned know what sort of mortals inhabit beyond those mountains, or whether they be inhabited at all. On the three other sides, it is bounded by the ocean. There is not one seaport in the whole kingdom: and those parts of the coasts into which the rivers issue, are so full of pointed rocks, and the sea generally so rough, that there is no venturing with the smallest of their boats; so that these people are wholly excluded from any commerce with the rest of the world. But the large rivers are full of vessels, and abound with excellent fish; for they seldom get any from the sea, because the sea fish are of the same size with those in Europe, and consequently not worth catching; whereby it is manifest, that nature, in the production of plants and animals of so extraordinary a bulk, is wholly confined to this continent, of which I leave the reasons to be determined by philosophers. However, now and then they take a whale that happens to be dashed against the rocks, which the common people feed on heartily. These whales I have known so large, that a man could hardly carry one upon his shoulders; and sometimes, for curiosity, they are brought in hampers to Lorbrulgrud; I saw one of them in a dish at the king's table, which passed for a rarity, but I did not observe he was fond of it; for I think, indeed, the bigness disgusted him, although I have seen one somewhat larger in Greenland.

The country is well inhabited, for it contains fifty-one cities, near a hundred walled towns, and a great number of villages. To satisfy my curious reader, it may be sufficient to describe Lorbrulgrud. This city stands upon almost two equal parts, on each side the river that passes through. It contains above eighty thousand houses, and about six hundred thousand inhabitants. It is in length three *glomglungs* (which make about fifty-four English miles,) and two and a half in breadth; as I measured it myself in the royal map made by the king's order, which was laid on the ground on purpose for me, and extended a hundred feet: I paced the diameter and circumference several times barefoot, and, computing by the scale, measured it pretty exactly.

The king's palace is no regular edifice, but a heap of buildings, about seven miles round: the chief rooms are generally two hundred and forty feet high, and broad and long in proportion. A coach was allowed to Glumdalclitch and me, wherein her governess frequently took her out to see the town, or go among the shops; and I was always of the party, carried in my box; although the girl, at my own desire, would often take me out, and hold me in her hand, that I might more conveniently view the houses and the people, as we passed along the streets. I reckoned our coach to be about a square of Westminster-hall, but not altogether so high: however, I cannot be very exact.

One day the governess ordered our coachman to stop at several shops, where the beggars, watching their opportunity, crowded to the sides of the coach, and gave me the most horrible spectacle that ever a European eye beheld. There was a woman with a cancer in her breast, swelled to a monstrous size, full of holes, in two or three of which I could have easily crept, and covered my whole body. There was a fellow with a wen in his neck, larger than five wool-packs; and another, with a couple of wooden legs, each about twenty feet high. But the most hateful sight of all, was the lice crawling on their clothes.

Besides the large box in which I was usually carried, the queen ordered a smaller one to be made for me, of about twelve feet square, and ten high, for the convenience of travelling; because the other was somewhat too large for Glumdalclitch's lap, and cumbersome in the coach; it was made by the same artist, whom I directed in the whole contrivance. This travelling-closet was an exact square, with a window in the middle of three of the squares, and each window was latticed with iron wire on the outside, to prevent accidents in long journeys.

On the fourth side, which had no window, two strong staples were fixed, through which the person that carried me, when I had a mind to be on horseback, put a leathern belt, and buckled it about his waist. This was always the office of some grave trusty servant, in whom I could confide, whether I attended the king and queen in their progresses, or were disposed to see the gardens, or pay a visit to some great lady or minister of state in the court, when Glumdalclitch happened to be out of order; for I soon began to be known and esteemed among the greatest officers, I suppose more upon account of their majesties' favour, than any merit of my own. In journeys, when I was weary of the coach, a servant on horseback would buckle on my box, and place it upon a cushion before him; and there I had a full prospect of the country on three sides, from my three windows.

I had in this closet, a field-bed and a hammock, hung from the ceiling, two chairs and a table, neatly screwed to the floor, to prevent being tossed about by the agitation of the horse or the coach. And having been long used to sea-voyages, those motions, although sometimes very violent, did not much discompose me.

Whenever I had a mind to see the town, it was always in my travelling-closet; which Glumdalclitch held in her lap in a kind of open sedan, after the fashion of the country, borne by four men, and attended by two others in the queen's livery. The people, who had often heard of me, were very curious to crowd about the sedan, and the girl was complaisant enough to make the bearers stop, and to take me in her hand, that I might be more conveniently seen.

I was very desirous to see the chief temple, and particularly the tower belonging to it, which is reckoned the highest in the kingdom. Accordingly one day my nurse carried me thither, but I may truly say I came back disappointed; for the height is not above three thousand feet, reckoning from the ground to the highest pinnacle top; which, allowing for the difference between the size of those people and us in Europe, is no great matter for admiration, nor at all equal in proportion (if I rightly remember) to Salisbury Steeple.

But, not to detract from a nation, to which, during my life, I shall acknowledge myself extremely obliged, it must be allowed, that whatever this famous tower wants in height, is amply made up in beauty and strength: for the walls are near a hundred feet thick, built of hewn stone, whereof each is about forty feet square, and adorned on all sides with statues of gods and emperors, cut in marble, larger than the life, placed in their several niches. I measured a little finger which had fallen down from one of these statues, and lay unperceived among some rubbish, and found it exactly four feet and an inch in length. Glumdalclitch wrapped it up in her handkerchief, and carried it home in her pocket, to keep among other trinkets, of which the girl was very fond, as children at her age usually are.

The king's kitchen is indeed a noble building, vaulted at top, and about six hundred feet high. The great oven is not so wide, by ten paces, as the cupola at St. Paul's: for I measured the latter on purpose, after my return. But if I should describe the kitchen grate, the prodigious pots and kettles, the joints of meat turning on the spits, with many other particulars, perhaps I should be hardly believed; at least a severe critic would be apt to think I enlarged a little, as travellers are often suspected to do. To avoid which censure I fear I have run too much into the other extreme; and that if this treatise should happen to be translated into the language of Brobdingnag (which is the general name of that kingdom,) and transmitted thither, the king and his people would have reason to complain that I had done them an injury, by a false and diminutive representation.

His Majesty seldom keeps above six hundred horses in his stables: they are generally from fifty-four to sixty feet high. But, when he goes abroad on solemn days, he is attended, for state, by a military guard of five hundred horse, which, indeed, I thought was the most splendid sight that could be ever beheld, till I saw part of his army in battalia, whereof I shall find another occasion to speak.

CHAPTER V

Several adventurers that happened to the author. The execution of a criminal. The author shows his skill in navigation.

I should have lived happy enough in that country, if my littleness had not exposed me to several ridiculous and troublesome accidents; some of which I shall venture to relate. Glumdalclitch often carried me into the gardens of the court in my smaller box, and would sometimes take me out of it, and hold me in her hand, or set me down to walk.

I remember, before the dwarf left the queen, he followed us one day into those gardens, and my nurse having set me down, he and I being close together, near some dwarf apple trees, I must needs show my wit, by a silly allusion between him and the trees, which happens to hold in their language as it does in ours. Whereupon, the malicious rogue, watching his opportunity, when I was walking under one of them, shook it directly over my head, by which a dozen apples, each of them near as large as a Bristol barrel, came tumbling about my ears; one of them hit me on the back as I chanced to stoop, and knocked me down flat on my face; but I received no other hurt, and the dwarf was pardoned at my desire, because I had given the provocation.

Another day, Glumdalclitch left me on a smooth grass-plot to divert myself, while she walked at some distance with her governess. In the meantime, there suddenly fell such a violent shower of hail, that I was immediately by the force of it, struck to the ground: and when I was down, the hailstones gave me such cruel bangs all over the body, as if I had been pelted with tennis-balls; however, I made a shift to creep on all fours, and shelter myself, by lying flat on my face, on the lee-side of a border of lemon-thyme, but so bruised from head to foot, that I could not go abroad in ten days. Neither is this at all to be wondered at, because nature, in that country, observing the same proportion through all her operations, a hailstone is near eighteen hundred times as large as one in Europe; which I can assert upon experience, having been so curious as to weigh and measure them.

But a more dangerous accident happened to me in the same garden, when my little nurse, believing she had put me in a secure place (which I often entreated her to do, that I might enjoy my own thoughts,) and having left my box at home, to avoid the trouble of carrying it, went to another part of the garden with her governess and some ladies of her acquaintance. While she was absent, and out of hearing, a small white spaniel that belonged to one of the chief gardeners, having got by accident into the garden, happened to range near the place where I lay: the dog, following the scent, came directly up, and taking me in his mouth, ran straight to his master wagging his tail, and set me gently on the ground. By good fortune he had been so well taught, that I was carried between his teeth without the least hurt, or even tearing my clothes.

But the poor gardener, who knew me well, and had a great kindness for me, was in a terrible fright: he gently took me up in both his hands, and asked me how I did? but I was so amazed and out of breath, that I could not speak a word. In a few minutes I came to myself, and he carried me safe to my little nurse, who, by this time, had returned to the place where she left me, and was in cruel agonies when I did not appear, nor answer when she called. She severely reprimanded the gardener on account of his dog. But the thing was hushed up, and never known at court, for the girl was afraid of the queen's anger; and truly, as to myself, I thought it would not be for my reputation, that such a story should go about.

This accident absolutely determined Glumdalclitch never to trust me abroad for the future out of her sight. I had been long afraid of this resolution, and therefore concealed from her some little unlucky adventures, that happened in those times when I was left by myself. Once a kite, hovering over the garden, made a stoop at me, and if I had not resolutely drawn my hanger, and run under a thick espalier, he would have certainly carried me away in his talons. Another time, walking to the top of a fresh mole-hill, I fell to my neck in the hole, through which that animal had cast up the earth, and coined some lie, not worth remembering, to excuse myself for spoiling my clothes. I likewise broke my right shin against the shell of a snail, which I happened to stumble over, as I was walking alone and thinking on poor England.

I cannot tell whether I were more pleased or mortified to observe, in those solitary walks, that the smaller birds did not appear to be at all afraid of me, but would hop about within a yard's distance, looking for worms and other food, with as much indifference and security as if no creature at all were near them. I remember, a thrush had the confidence to snatch out of my hand, with his bill, a of cake that Glumdalclitch had just given me for my breakfast. When I attempted to catch any of these birds, they would boldly turn against me, endeavouring to peck my fingers, which I durst not venture within their reach; and then they would hop back unconcerned, to hunt for worms or snails, as they did before.

But one day, I took a thick cudgel, and threw it with all my strength so luckily, at a linnet, that I knocked him down, and seizing him by the neck with both my hands, ran with him in triumph to my nurse. However, the bird, who had only been stunned, recovering himself gave me so many boxes with his wings, on both sides of my head and body, though I held him at arm's-length, and was out of the reach of his claws, that I was twenty times thinking to let him go. But I was soon relieved by one of our servants, who wrung off the bird's neck, and I had him next day for dinner, by the queen's command. This linnet, as near as I can remember, seemed to be somewhat larger than an English swan.

One day, a young gentleman, who was nephew to my nurse's governess, came and pressed them both to see an execution. It was of a man, who had murdered one of that gentleman's intimate acquaintance. Glumdalclitch was prevailed on to be of the company, very much against her inclination, for she was naturally tender-hearted: and, as for myself, although I abhorred such kind of spectacles, yet my curiosity tempted me to see something that I thought must be extraordinary.

The malefactor was fixed in a chair upon a scaffold erected for that purpose, and his head cut off at one blow, with a sword of about forty feet long. The veins and arteries spouted up such a prodigious quantity of blood, and so high in the air, that the great *jet d'eau* at Versailles was not equal to it for the time it lasted: and the head, when it fell on the scaffold floor, gave such a bounce as made me start, although I was at least half an English mile distant.

The queen, who often used to hear me talk of my sea-voyages, and took all occasions to divert me when I was melancholy, asked me whether I understood how to handle a sail or an oar, and whether a little exercise of rowing might not be convenient for my health? I answered, that I understood both very well: for although my proper employment had been to be surgeon or doctor to the ship, yet often, upon a pinch, I was forced to work like a common mariner. But I could not see how this could be done in their country, where the smallest wherry was equal to a first-rate man of war among us; and such a boat as I could manage would never live in any of their rivers. Her Majesty said, if I would contrive a boat, her own joiner should make it, and she would provide a place for me to sail in.

The fellow was an ingenious workman, and by my instructions, in ten days, finished a pleasure-boat with all its tackling, able conveniently to hold eight Europeans. When it was finished, the queen was so delighted, that she ran with it in her lap to the king, who ordered it to be put into a cistern full of water, with me in it, by way of trial, where I could not manage my two sculls, or little oars, for want of room. But the queen had before contrived another project. She ordered the joiner to make a wooden trough of three hundred feet long, fifty broad, and eight deep; which, being well pitched, to prevent leaking, was placed on the floor, along the wall, in an outer room of the palace. It had a cock near the bottom to let out the water, when it began to grow stale; and two servants could easily fill it in half an hour.

Here I often used to row for my own diversion, as well as that of the queen and her ladies, who thought themselves well entertained with my skill and agility. Sometimes I would put up my sail, and then my business was only to steer, while the ladies gave me a gale with their fans; and, when they were weary, some of their pages would blow my sail forward with their breath, while I showed my art by steering starboard or larboard as I pleased. When I had done, Glumdalclitch always carried back my boat into her closet, and hung it on a nail to dry.

In this exercise I once met an accident, which had like to have cost me my life; for, one of the pages having put my boat into the trough, the governess who attended Glumdalclitch very officiously lifted me up, to place me in the boat: but I happened to slip through her fingers, and should infallibly have fallen down forty feet upon the floor, if, by the luckiest chance in the world, I had not been stopped by a corking-pin that stuck in the good gentlewoman's stomacher; the head of the pin passing between my shirt and the waistband of my breeches, and thus I was held by the middle in the air, till Glumdalclitch ran to my relief.

Another time, one of the servants, whose office it was to fill my trough every third day with fresh water, was so careless as to let a huge frog (not perceiving it) slip out of his pail. The frog lay concealed till I was put into my boat, but then, seeing a resting-place, climbed up, and made it lean so much on one side, that I was forced to balance it with all my weight on the other, to prevent overturning. When the frog was got in, it hopped at once half the length of the boat, and then over my head, backward and forward, daubing my face and clothes with its odious slime. The largeness of its features made it appear the most deformed animal that can be conceived. However, I desired Glumdalclitch to let me deal with it alone. I banged it a good while with one of my sculls, and at last forced it to leap out of the boat.

But the greatest danger I ever underwent in that kingdom, was from a monkey, who belonged to one of the clerks of the kitchen. Glumdalclitch had locked me up in her closet, while she went somewhere upon business, or a visit. The weather being very warm, the closet-window was left open, as well as the windows and the door of my bigger box, in which I usually lived, because of its largeness and conveniency.

As I sat quietly meditating at my table, I heard something bounce in at the closet-window, and skip about from one side to the other: whereat, although I was much alarmed, yet I ventured to look out, but not stirring from my seat; and then I saw this frolicsome animal frisking and leaping up and down, till at last he came to my box, which he seemed to view with great pleasure and curiosity, peeping in at the door and every window. I retreated to the farther corner of my room; or box; but the monkey looking in at every side, put me in such a fright, that I wanted presence of mind to conceal myself under the bed, as I might easily have done.

After some time spent in peeping, grinning, and chattering, he at last espied me; and reaching one of his paws in at the door, as a cat does when she plays with a mouse, although I often shifted place to avoid him, he at length seized the lappet of my coat (which being made of that country silk, was very thick and strong), and dragged me out. He took me up in his right fore-foot and held me as a nurse does a child she is going to suckle, just as I have seen the same sort of creature do with a kitten in Europe; and when I offered to struggle he squeezed me so hard, that I thought it more prudent to submit. I have good reason to believe, that he took me for a young one of his own species, by his often stroking my face very gently with his other paw.

In these diversions he was interrupted by a noise at the closet door, as if somebody were opening it: whereupon he suddenly leaped up to the window at which he had come in, and thence upon the leads and gutters, walking upon three legs, and holding me in the fourth, till he clambered up to a roof that was next to ours. I heard Glumdalclitch give a shriek at the moment he was carrying me out. The poor girl was almost distracted: that quarter of the palace was all in an uproar; the servants ran for ladders; the monkey was seen by hundreds in the court, sitting upon the ridge of a building, holding me like a baby in one of his forepaws, and feeding me with the other, by cramming into my mouth some victuals he had squeezed out of the bag on one side of his chaps, and patting me when I would not eat; whereat many of the rabble below could not forbear laughing; neither do I think they justly ought to be blamed, for, without question, the sight was ridiculous enough to every body but myself. Some of the people threw up stones, hoping to drive the monkey down; but this was strictly forbidden, or else, very probably, my brains had been dashed out.

The ladders were now applied, and mounted by several men; which the monkey observing, and finding himself almost encompassed, not being able to make speed enough with his three legs, let me drop on a ridge tile, and made his escape. Here I sat for some time, five hundred yards from the ground, expecting every moment to be blown down by the wind, or to fall by my own giddiness, and come tumbling over and over from the ridge to the eaves; but an honest lad, one of my nurse's footmen, climbed up, and putting me into his breeches pocket, brought me down safe.

I was almost choked with the filthy stuff the monkey had crammed down my throat: but my dear little nurse picked it out of my mouth with a small needle, and then I fell a-vomiting, which gave me great relief. Yet I was so weak and bruised in the sides with the squeezes given me by this odious animal, that I was forced to keep my bed a fortnight. The king, queen, and all the court, sent every day to inquire after my health; and her Majesty made me several visits during my sickness. The monkey was killed, and an order made, that no such animal should be kept about the palace.

When I attended the king after my recovery, to return him thanks for his favours, he was pleased to rally me a good deal upon this adventure. He asked me, what my thoughts and speculations were, while I lay in the monkey's paw; how I liked the victuals he gave me; his manner of feeding; and whether the fresh air on the roof had sharpened my stomach. He desired to know, what I would have done upon such an occasion in my own country. I told his Majesty, that in Europe we had no monkeys, except such as were brought for curiosity from other places, and so small, that I could deal with a dozen of them together, if they presumed to attack me.

As for that monstrous animal with whom I was so lately engaged (it was indeed as large as an elephant), if my fears had suffered me to think so far as to make use of my hanger, (looking fiercely, and clapping my hand on the hilt, as I spoke) when he poked his paw into my chamber, perhaps I should have given him such a wound, as would have made him glad to withdraw it with more haste than he put it in. This I delivered in a firm tone, like a person who was jealous lest his courage should be called in question.

However, my speech produced nothing else beside a laud laughter, which all the respect due to his Majesty from those about him could not make them contain. This made me reflect, how vain an attempt it is for a man to endeavour to do himself honour among those who are out of all degree of equality or comparison with him. And yet I have seen the moral of my own behaviour very frequent in England since my return; where a little contemptible varlet, without the least title to birth, person, wit, or common-sense, shall presume to look with importance, and put himself upon a foot with the greatest persons of the kingdom.

I was every day furnishing the court with some ridiculous story: and Glumdalclitch, although she loved me to excess, yet was arch enough to inform the queen, whenever I committed any folly that she thought would be diverting to her Majesty.

The girl, who had been out of order, was carried by her governess to take the air about an hour's distance, or thirty miles from town. They alighted out of the coach near a small foot-path in a field, and Glumdalclitch setting down my travelling box, I went out of it to walk. There was a cow-dung in the path, and I must need try my activity by attempting to leap over it. I took a run, but unfortunately jumped short, and found myself just in the middle up to my knees. I waded through with some difficulty, and one of the footmen wiped me as clean as he could with his handkerchief, for I was filthily bemired; and my nurse confined me to my box, till we returned home; where the queen was soon informed of what had passed, and the footmen spread it about the court: so that all the mirth for some days was at my expense.

CHAPTER VI

Several contrivances of the author to please the king and queen. He shows his skill in music. The king inquires into the state of England, which the author relates to him. The king's observations thereon.

I used to attend the king's levee once or twice a week, and had often seen him under the barber's hand, which indeed was at first very terrible to behold; for the razor was almost twice as long as an ordinary scythe. His Majesty, according to the custom of the country, was only shaved twice a-week. I once prevailed on the barber to give me some of the suds or lather, out of which I picked forty or fifty of the strongest stumps of hair. I then took a piece of fine wood, and cut it like the back of a comb, making several holes in it at equal distances with as small a needle as I could get from Glumdalclitch. I fixed in the stumps so artificially, scraping and sloping them with my knife toward the points, that I made a very tolerable comb; which was a seasonable supply, my own being so much broken in the teeth, that it was almost useless: neither did I know any artist in that country so nice and exact, as would undertake to make me another.

And this puts me in mind of an amusement, wherein I spent many of my leisure hours. I desired the queen's woman to save for me the combings of her Majesty's hair, whereof in time I got a good quantity; and consulting with my friend the cabinet-maker, who had received general orders to do little jobs for me, I directed him to make two chair-frames, no larger than those I had in my box, and to bore little holes with a fine awl, round those parts where I designed the backs and seats; through these holes I wove the strongest hairs I could pick out, just after the manner of cane chairs in England.

When they were finished, I made a present of them to her Majesty; who kept them in her cabinet, and used to show them for curiosities, as indeed they were the wonder of every one that beheld them.

The queen would have me sit upon one of these chairs, but I absolutely refused to obey her, protesting I would rather die than place a dishonourable part of my body on those precious hairs, that once adorned her Majesty's head. Of these hairs (as I had always a mechanical genius) I likewise made a neat little purse, about five feet long, with her Majesty's name deciphered in gold letters, which I gave to Glumdalclitch, by the queen's consent. To say the truth, it was more for show than use, being not of strength to bear the weight of the larger coins, and therefore she kept nothing in it but some little toys that girls are fond of.

The king, who delighted in music, had frequent concerts at court, to which I was sometimes carried, and set in my box on a table to hear them: but the noise was so great that I could hardly distinguish the tunes. I am confident that all the drums and trumpets of a royal army, beating and sounding together just at your ears, could not equal it. My practice was to have my box removed from the place where the performers sat, as far as I could, then to shut the doors and windows of it, and draw the window curtains; after which I found their music not disagreeable.

I had learned in my youth to play a little upon the spinet. Glumdalclitch kept one in her chamber, and a master attended twice a-week to teach her: I called it a spinet, because it somewhat resembled that instrument, and was played upon in the same manner. A fancy came into my head, that I would entertain the king and queen with an English tune upon this instrument. But this appeared extremely difficult: for the spinet was near sixty feet long, each key being almost a foot wide, so that with my arms extended I could not reach to above five keys, and to press them down required a good smart stroke with my fist, which would be too great a labour, and to no purpose.

The method I contrived was this: I prepared two round sticks, about the bigness of common cudgels; they were thicker at one end than the other, and I covered the thicker ends with pieces of a mouse's skin, that by rapping on them I might neither damage the tops of the keys nor interrupt the sound. Before the spinet a bench was placed, about four feet below the keys, and I was put upon the bench. I ran sideling upon it, that way and this, as fast as I could, banging the proper keys with my two sticks, and made a shift to play a jig, to the great satisfaction of both their majesties; but it was the most violent exercise I ever underwent; and yet I could not strike above sixteen keys, nor consequently play the bass and treble together, as other artists do; which was a great disadvantage to my performance.

The king, who, as I before observed, was a prince of excellent understanding, would frequently order that I should be brought in my box, and set upon the table in his closet: he would then command me to bring one of my chairs out of the box, and sit down within three yards distance upon the top of the cabinet, which brought me almost to a level with his face. In this manner I had several conversations with him. I one day took the freedom to tell his Majesty, that the contempt he discovered towards Europe, and the rest of the world, did not seem answerable to those excellent qualities of mind that he was master of; that reason did not extend itself with the bulk of the body; on the contrary, we observed in our country, that the tallest persons were usually the least provided with it; that among other animals, bees and ants had the reputation of more industry, art, and sagacity, than many of the larger kinds; and that, as inconsiderable as he took me to be, I hoped I might live to do his Majesty some signal service. The king heard me with attention, and began to conceive a much better opinion of me than he had ever before. He desired I would give him as exact an account of the government of England as I possibly could; because, as fond as princes commonly are of their own customs (for so he conjectured of other monarchs, by my former discourses), he should be glad to hear of any thing that might deserve imitation.

Imagine with thyself, courteous reader, how often I then wished for the tongue of Demosthenes or Cicero, that might have enabled me to celebrate the praise of my own dear native country in a style equal to its merits and felicity.

I began my discourse by informing his Majesty, that our dominions consisted of two islands, which composed three mighty kingdoms, under one sovereign, beside our plantations in America. I dwelt long upon the fertility of our soil, and the temperature of our climate. I then spoke at large upon the constitution of an English parliament; partly made up of an illustrious body called the House of Peers; persons of the noblest blood, and of the most ancient and ample patrimonies.

I described that extraordinary care always taken of their education in arts and arms, to qualify them for being counsellors both to the king and kingdom; to have a share in the legislature; to be members of the highest court of judicature, whence there can be no appeal; and to be champions always ready for the defence of their prince and country, by their valour, conduct, and fidelity. That these were the ornament and bulwark of the kingdom, worthy followers of their most renowned ancestors, whose honour had been the reward of their virtue, from which their posterity were never once known to degenerate. To these were joined several holy persons, as part of that assembly, under the title of bishops, whose peculiar business is to take care of religion, and of those who instruct the people therein. These were searched and sought out through the whole nation, by the prince and his wisest counsellors, among such of the priesthood as were most deservedly distinguished by the sanctity of their lives, and the depth of their erudition; who were indeed the spiritual fathers of the clergy and the people.

That the other part of the parliament consisted of an assembly called the House of Commons, who were all principal gentlemen, *freely* picked and culled out by the people themselves, for their great abilities and love of their country, to represent the wisdom of the whole nation. And that these two bodies made up the most august assembly in Europe; to whom, in conjunction with the prince, the whole legislature is committed.

I then descended to the courts of justice; over which the judges, those venerable sages and interpreters of the law, presided, for determining the disputed rights and properties of men, as well as for the punishment of vice and protection of innocence. I mentioned the prudent management of our treasury; the valour and achievements of our forces, by sea and land. I computed the number of our people, by reckoning how many millions there might be of each religious sect, or political party among us. I did not omit even our sports and pastimes, or any other particular which I thought might redound to the honour of my country. And I finished all with a brief historical account of affairs and events in England for about a hundred years past.

This conversation was not ended under five audiences, each of several hours; and the king heard the whole with great attention, frequently taking notes of what I spoke, as well as memorandums of what questions he intended to ask me.

When I had put an end to these long discources, his Majesty, in a sixth audience, consulting his notes, proposed many doubts, queries, and objections, upon every article. He asked, What methods were used to cultivate the minds and bodies of our young nobility, and in what kind of business they commonly spent the first and teachable parts of their lives? What course was taken to supply that assembly, when any noble family became extinct? What qualifications were necessary in those who are to be created new lords: whether the humour of the prince, a sum of money to a court lady, or a design of strengthening a party opposite to the public interest, ever happened to be the motive in those advancements? What share of knowledge these lords had in the laws of their country, and how they came by it, so as to enable them to decide the properties of their fellow-subjects in the last resort? Whether they were always so free from avarice, partialities, or want, that a bribe, or some other sinister view, could have no place among them? Whether those holy lords I spoke of were always promoted to that rank upon account of their knowledge in religious matters, and the sanctity of their lives; had never been compliers with the times, while they were common priests; or slavish prostitute chaplains to some nobleman, whose opinions they continued servilely to follow, after they were admitted into that assembly.

He then desired to know What arts were practised in electing those whom I called commoners: whether a stranger, with a strong purse, might not influence the vulgar voters to choose him before their own landlord, or the most considerable gentleman in the neighbourhood? How it came to pass, that people were so violently bent upon getting into this assembly, which I allowed to be a great trouble and expense, often to the ruin of their families, without any salary or pension? because this appeared such an exalted strain of virtue and public spirit, that his Majesty seemed to doubt it might possibly not be always sincere: And he desired to know, Whether such zealous gentlemen could have any views of refunding themselves for the charges and trouble they were at by sacrificing the public good to the designs of a weak and vicious prince, in conjunction with a corrupted ministry. He multiplied his questions, and sifted me thoroughly upon every part of this head, proposing numberless inquiries and objections, which I think it not prudent or convenient to repeat.

Upon what I said in relation to our courts of justice, his Majesty desired to be satisfied in several points: and this I was the better able to do, having been formerly almost ruined by a long suit in chancery, which was decreed for me with costs. He asked, What time was usually spent in determining between right and wrong, and what degree of expense? Whether advocates and orators had liberty to plead in causes manifestly known to be unjust, vexatious, or oppressive? Whether party, in religion or politics, were observed to be of any weight in the scale of justice? Whether those pleading orators were persons educated in the general knowledge of equity, or only in provincial, national, and other local customs? Whether they or their judges had any part in penning those laws, which they assumed the liberty of interpreting, and glossing upon at their pleasure? Whether they had ever, at different times, pleaded for and against the same cause, and cited precedents to prove contrary opinions? Whether they were a rich or a poor corporation? Whether they received any pecuniary reward for pleading, or delivering their opinions? And particularly, whether they were ever admitted as members in the lower senate?

He fell next upon the management of our treasury; and said, he thought my memory had failed me, because I computed our taxes at about five or six millions a-year, and when I came to mention the issues, he found they sometimes amounted to more than double; for the notes he had taken were very particular in this point, because he hoped, as he told me, that the knowledge of our conduct might be useful to him, and he could not be deceived in his calculations. But, if what I told him were true, he was still at a loss how a kingdom could run out of its estate, like a private person. He asked me, who were our creditors, and where we found money to pay them. He wondered to hear me talk of such chargeable and expensive wars; that certainly we must be a quarrelsome people, or live among very bad neighbours, and that our generals must needs be richer than our kings. He asked, what business we had out of our own islands, unless upon the score of trade, or treaty, or to defend the coasts with our fleet? Above all, he was amazed to hear me talk of a mercenary standing army, in the midst of peace, and among a free people.

He said, if we were governed by our own consent, in the persons of our representatives, he could not imagine of whom we were afraid, or against whom we were to fight; and would hear my opinion, whether a private man's house might not be better defended by himself, his children, and family, than by half-a-dozen rascals, picked up at a venture in the streets for small wages, who might get a hundred times more by cutting their throats.

He laughed at my odd kind of arithmetic, as he was pleased to call it, in reckoning the numbers of our people, by a computation drawn from the several sects among us, in religion and politics. He said, he knew no reason why those, who entertain opinions prejudicial to the public, should be obliged to change, or should not be obliged to conceal them. And as it was tyranny in any government to require the first, so it was weakness not to enforce the second: for a man may be allowed to keep poisons in his closet, but not to vend them about for cordials.

He observed that among the diversions of our nobility and gentry, I had mentioned gaming: he desired to know at what age this entertainment was usually taken up, and when it was laid down; how much of their time it employed; whether it ever went so high as to affect their fortunes; whether mean, vicious people, by their dexterity in that art, might not arrive at great riches, and sometimes keep our very nobles in dependence, as well as habituate them to vile companions, wholly take them from the improvement of their minds, and force them, by the losses they received, to learn and practise that infamous dexterity upon others.

He was perfectly astonished with the historical account gave him of our affairs during the last century; protesting it was only a heap of conspiracies, rebellions, murders, massacres, revolutions, banishments, the very worst effects that avarice, faction, hypocrisy, perfidiousness, cruelty, rage, madness, hatred, envy, lust, malice, and ambition, could produce.

His Majesty, in another audience, was at the pains to recapitulate the sum of all I had spoken; compared the questions he made with the answers I had given; then taking me into his hands, and stroking me gently, delivered himself in these words, which I shall never forget, nor the manner he spoke them in: My little friend Grildrig, you have made a most admirable panegyric upon your country; you have clearly proved, that ignorance, idleness, and vice, are the proper ingredients for qualifying a legislator; that laws are best explained, interpreted, and applied, by those whose interest and abilities lie in perverting, confounding, and eluding them. I observe among you some lines of an institution, which, in its original, might have been tolerable, but these half erased, and the rest wholly blurred and blotted by corruptions. It does not appear, from all you have said, how any one perfection is required toward the procurement of any one station among you; much less, that men are ennobled on account of their virtue; that priests are advanced for their piety or learning; soldiers, for their conduct or valour; judges, for their integrity; senators, for the love of their country; or counsellors for their wisdom.

"As for yourself, continued the king, who have spent the greatest part of your life in travelling, I am well disposed to hope you may hitherto have escaped many vices of your country. But by what I have gathered from your own relation, and the answers I have with much pains wrung and extorted from you, I cannot but conclude the bulk of your natives to be the most pernicious race of little odious vermin that nature ever suffered to crawl upon the surface of the earth."

CHAPTER VII

The author's love of his country. He makes a proposal of much advantage to the king, which is rejected. The king's great ignorance in politics. The learning of that country very imperfect and confined. The laws, and military affairs, and parties in the state.

Nothing but an extreme love of truth could have hindered me from concealing this part of my story. It was in vain to discover my resentments, which were always turned into ridicule; and I was forced to rest with patience, while my noble and beloved country was so injuriously treated. I am as heartily sorry as any of my readers can possibly be, that such an occasion was given: but this prince happened to be so curious and inquisitive upon every particular, that it could not consist either with gratitude or good manners, to refuse giving him what satisfaction I was able.

Yet thus much I may be allowed to say in my own vindication, that I artfully eluded many of his questions, and gave to every point a more favourable turn, by many degrees, than the strictness of truth would allow. For I have always borne that laudable partiality to my own country, which Dionysius Halicarnassensis, with so much justice, recommends to an historian: I would hide the frailties and deformities of my political mother, and place her virtues and beauties in the most advantageous light. This was my sincere endeavour in those many discourses I had with that monarch, although it unfortunately failed of success.

But great allowances should be given to a king, who lives wholly secluded from the rest of the world, and must therefore be altogether unacquainted with the manners and customs that most prevail in other nations: the want of which knowledge will ever produce many prejudices, and a certain narrowness of thinking, from which we, and the politer countries of Europe, are wholly exempted. And it would be hard indeed, if so remote a prince's notions of virtue and vice were to be offered as a standard for all mankind.

To confirm what I have now said, and further to show the miserable effects of a confined education, I shall here insert a passage, which will hardly obtain belief. In hopes to ingratiate myself further into his Majesty's favour, I told him of an invention, discovered between three and four hundred years ago, to make a certain powder, into a heap of which, the smallest spark of fire falling, would kindle the whole in a moment, although it were as big as a mountain, and make it all fly up in the air together, with a noise and agitation greater than thunder.

That a proper quantity of this powder rammed into a hollow tube of brass or iron, according to its bigness, would drive a ball of iron or lead, with such violence and speed, as nothing was able to sustain its force. That the largest balls thus discharged, would not only destroy whole ranks of an army at once, but batter the strongest walls to the ground, sink down ships, with a thousand men in each, to the bottom of the sea, and when linked together by a chain, would cut through masts and rigging, divide hundreds of bodies in the middle, and lay all waste before them. That we often put this powder into large hollow balls of iron, and discharged them by an engine into some city we were besieging, which would rip up the pavements, tear the houses to pieces, burst and throw splinters on every side, dashing out the brains of all who came near.

That I knew the ingredients very well, which were cheap and common; I understood the manner of compounding them, and could direct his workmen how to make those tubes, of a size proportionable to all other things in his Majesty's kingdom, and the largest need not be above a hundred feet long; twenty or thirty of which tubes, charged with the proper quantity of powder and balls, would batter down the walls of the strongest town in his dominions in a few hours, or destroy the whole metropolis, if ever it should pretend to dispute his absolute commands. This I humbly offered to his Majesty, as a small tribute of acknowledgment, in turn for so many marks that I had received, of his royal favour and protection.

The king was struck with horror at the description I had given of those terrible engines, and the proposal I had made. He was amazed, how so impotent and grovelling an insect as I (these were his expressions) could entertain such inhuman ideas, and in so familiar a manner, as to appear wholly unmoved at all the scenes of blood and desolation which I had painted as the common effects of those destructive machines; whereof, he said, some evil genius, enemy to mankind, must have been the first contriver. As for himself, he protested, that although few things delighted him so much as new discoveries in art or in nature, yet he would rather lose half his kingdom, than be privy to such a secret; which he commanded me, as I valued any life, never to mention any more.

A strange effect of narrow principles and views! that a prince possessed of every quality which procures veneration, love, and esteem; of strong parts, great wisdom, and profound learning, endowed with admirable talents, and almost adored by his subjects, should, from a nice, unnecessary scruple, whereof in Europe we can have no conception, let slip an opportunity put into his hands that would have made him absolute master of the lives, the liberties, and the fortunes of his people.

Neither do I say this, with the least intention to detract from the many virtues of that excellent king, whose character, I am sensible, will, on this account, be very much lessened in the opinion of an English reader: but I take this defect among them to have risen from their ignorance, by not having hitherto reduced politics into a science, as the more acute wits of Europe have done. For, I remember very well, in a discourse one day with the king, when I happened to say, there were several thousand books among us written upon the art of government, it gave him (directly contrary to my intention) a very mean opinion of our understandings. He professed both to abominate and despise all mystery, refinement, and intrigue, either in a prince or a minister.

He could not tell what I meant by secrets of state, where an enemy, or some rival nation, were not in the case. He confined the knowledge of governing within very narrow bounds, to common sense and reason, to justice and lenity, to the speedy determination of civil and criminal causes; with some other obvious topics, which are not worth considering. And he gave it for his opinion, that whoever could make two ears of corn, or two blades of grass, to grow upon a spot of ground where only one grew before, would deserve better of mankind, and do more essential service to his country, than the whole race of politicians put together.

The learning of this people is very defective, consisting only in morality, history, poetry, and mathematics, wherein they must be allowed to excel. But the last of these is wholly applied to what may be useful in life, to the improvement of agriculture, and all mechanical arts; so that among us, it would be little esteemed. And as to ideas, entities, abstractions, and transcendentals, I could never drive the least conception into their heads.

No law in that country must exceed in words the number of

letters in their alphabet, which consists only of two and twenty. But indeed few of them extend even to that length. They are expressed in the most plain and simple terms, wherein those people are not mercurial enough to discover above one interpretation: and to write a comment upon any law, is a capital crime. As to the decision of civil causes, or proceedings against criminals, their precedents are so few, that they have little reason to boast of any extraordinary skill in either.

They have had the art of printing, as well as the Chinese, time out of mind: but their libraries are not very large; for that of the king, which is reckoned the largest, does not amount to above a thousand volumes, placed in a gallery of twelve hundred feet long, whence I had liberty to borrow what books I pleased. The queen's joiner had contrived in one of Glumdalclitch's rooms, a kind of wooden machine five-and-twenty feet high, formed like a standing ladder; the steps were each fifty feet long. It was indeed a moveable pair of stairs, the lowest end placed at ten feet distance from the wall of the chamber.

The book I had a mind to read, was put up leaning against the wall: I first mounted to the upper step of the ladder, and turning my face towards the book, began at the top of the page, and so walking to the right and left about eight or ten paces, according to the length of the lines, till I had gotten a little below the level of mine eyes, and then descending gradually till I came to the bottom: after which I mounted again, and began the other page in the same manner, and so turned over the leaf, which I could easily do with both my hands, for it was as thick and stiff as a pasteboard, and in the largest folios not above eighteen or twenty feet long.

Their style is clear, masculine, and smooth, but not florid; for they avoid nothing more than multiplying unnecessary words, or using various expressions. I have perused many of their books, especially those in history and morality. Among the rest, I was much diverted with a little old treatise, which always lay in Glumdalclitch's bed chamber, and belonged to her governess, a grave elderly gentlewoman, who dealt in writings of morality and devotion. The book treats of the weakness of human kind, and is in little esteem, except among the women and the vulgar.

However, I was curious to see what an author of that country could say upon such a subject. This writer went through all the usual topics of European moralists, showing how diminutive, contemptible, and helpless an animal was man in his own nature; how unable to defend himself from inclemencies of the air, or the fury of wild beasts: how much he was excelled by one creature in strength, by another in speed, by a third in foresight, by a fourth in industry. He added, that nature was degenerated in these latter declining ages of the world, and could now produce only small abortive births, in comparison of those in ancient times. He said it was very reasonable to think, not only that the species of men were originally much larger, but also that there must have been giants in former ages; which, as it is asserted by history and tradition, so it has been confirmed by huge bones and skulls, casually dug up in several parts of the kingdom, far exceeding the common dwindled race of men in our days.

He argued, that the very laws of nature absolutely required we should have been made, in the beginning of a size more large and robust; not so liable to destruction from every little accident, of a tile falling from a house, or a stone cast from the hand of a boy, or being drowned in a little brook. From this way of reasoning, the author drew several moral applications, useful in the conduct of life, but needless here to repeat. For my own part, I could not avoid reflecting how universally this talent was spread, of drawing lectures in morality, or indeed rather matter of discontent and repining, from the quarrels we raise with nature. And I believe, upon a strict inquiry, those quarrels might be shown as ill-grounded among us as they are among that people.

As to their military affairs, they boast that the king's army consists of a hundred and seventy-six thousand foot, and thirty-two thousand horse: if that may be called an army, which is made up of tradesmen in the several cities, and farmers in the country, whose commanders are only the nobility and gentry, without pay or reward. They are indeed perfect enough in their exercises, and under very good discipline, wherein I saw no great merit; for how should it be otherwise, where every farmer is under the command of his own landlord, and every citizen under that of the principal men in his own city, chosen after the manner of Venice, by ballot!

I have often seen the militia of Lorbrulgrud drawn out to exercise, in a great field near the city of twenty miles square. They were in all not above twenty-five thousand foot, and six thousand horse; but it was impossible for me to compute their number, considering the space of ground they took up. A cavalier, mounted on a large steed, might be about ninety feet high. I have seen this whole body of horse, upon a word of command, draw their swords at once, and brandish them in the air. Imagination can figure nothing so grand, so surprising, and so astonishing! it looked as if ten thousand flashes of lightning were darting at the same time from every quarter of the sky.

I was curious to know how this prince, to whose dominions there is no access from any other country, came to think of armies, or to teach his people the practice of military discipline. But I was soon informed, both by conversation and reading their histories; for, in the course of many ages, they have been troubled with the same disease to which the whole race of mankind is subject; the nobility often contending for power, the people for liberty, and the king for absolute dominion. All which, however happily tempered by the laws of that kingdom, have been sometimes violated by each of the three parties, and have more than once occasioned civil wars; the last whereof was happily put an end to by this prince's grand-father, in a general composition; and the militia, then settled with common consent, has been ever since kept in the strictest duty.

CHAPTER VIII

The king and queen make a progress to the frontiers. The author attends them. The manner in which he leaves the country very particularly related. He returns to England.

I had always a strong impulse that I should some time recover my liberty, though it was impossible to conjecture by what means, or to form any project with the least hope of succeeding. The ship in which I sailed, was the first ever known to be driven within sight of that coast, and the king had given strict orders, that if at any time another appeared, it should be taken ashore, and with all its crew and passengers brought in a tumbril to Lorbrulgrud. He was strongly bent to get me a woman of my own size, by whom I might propagate the breed: but I think I should rather have died than undergone the disgrace of leaving a posterity to be kept in cages, like tame canary-birds, and perhaps, in time, sold about the kingdom, to persons of quality, for curiosities. I was indeed treated with much kindness: I was the favourite of a great king and queen, and the delight of the whole court; but it was upon such a foot as ill became the dignity of humankind. I could never forget those domestic pledges I had left behind me. I wanted to be among people, with whom I could converse upon even terms, and walk about the streets and fields without being afraid of being trod to death like a frog or a young puppy. But my deliverance came sooner than I expected, and in a manner not very common; the whole story and circumstances of which I shall faithfully relate.

I had now been two years in this country; and about the beginning of the third, Glumdalclitch and I attended the king and queen, in a progress to the south coast of the kingdom. I was carried, as usual, in my travelling-box, which as I have already described, was a very convenient closet, of twelve feet wide. And I had ordered a hammock to be fixed, by silken ropes from the four corners at the top, to break the jolts, when a servant carried me before him on horseback, as I sometimes desired; and would often sleep in my hammock, while we were upon the road. On the roof of my closet, not directly over the middle of the hammock, I ordered the joiner to cut out a hole of a foot square, to give me air in hot weather, as I slept; which hole I shut at pleasure with a board that drew backward and forward through a groove.

When we came to our journey's end, the king thought proper to pass a few days at a palace he has near Flanflasnic, a city within eighteen English miles of the seaside. Glumdalclitch and I were much fatigued: I had gotten a small cold, but the poor girl was so ill as to be confined to her chamber. I longed to see the ocean, which must be the only scene of my escape, if ever it should happen. I pretended to be worse than I really was, and desired leave to take the fresh air of the sea, with a page, whom I was very fond of, and who had sometimes been trusted with me.

I shall never forget with what unwillingness Glumdalclitch consented, nor the strict charge she gave the page to be careful of me, bursting at the same time into a flood of tears, as if she had some forboding of what was to happen. The boy took me out in my box, about half an hours walk from the palace, towards the rocks on the sea-shore. I ordered him to set me down, and lifting up one of my sashes, cast many a wistful melancholy look towards the sea. I found myself not very well, and told the page that I had a mind to take a nap in my hammock, which I hoped would do me good. I got in, and the boy shut the window close down, to keep out the cold.

I soon fell asleep, and all I can conjecture is, while I slept, the page, thinking no danger could happen, went among the rocks to look for birds' eggs, having before observed him from my window searching about, and picking up one or two in the clefts. Be that as it will, I found myself suddenly awaked with a violent pull upon the ring, which was fastened at the top of my box for the conveniency of carriage. I felt my box raised very high in the air, and then borne forward with prodigious speed. The first jolt had like to have shaken me out of my hammock, but afterward the motion was easy enough. I called out several times, as loud as I could raise my voice, but all to no purpose. I looked towards my windows, and could see nothing but the clouds and sky.

I heard a noise just over my head, like the clapping of wings, and then began to perceive the woful condition I was in; that some eagle had got the ring of my box in his beak, with an intent to let it fall on a rock, like a tortoise in a shell, and then pick out my body, and devour it: for the sagacity and smell of this bird enables him to discover his quarry at a great distance, though better concealed than I could be within a two-inch board.

In a little time, I observed the noise and flutter of wings to increase very fast, and my box was tossed up and down, like a sign in a windy day. I heard several bangs or buffets, as I thought given to the eagle (for such I am certain it must have been that held the ring of my box in his beak), and then, all on a sudden, felt myself falling perpendicularly down, for above a minute, but with such incredible swiftness, that I almost lost my breath. My fall was stopped by a terrible squash, that sounded louder to my ears than the cataract of Niagara; after which, I was quite in the dark for another minute, and then my box began to rise so high, that I could see light from the tops of the windows. I now perceived I was fallen into the sea.

My box, by the weight of my body, the goods that were in, and the broad plates of iron fixed for strength at the four corners of the top and bottom, floated about five feet deep in water. I did then, and do now suppose, that the eagle which flew away with my box was pursued by two or three others, and forced to let me drop, while he defended himself against the rest, who hoped to share in the prey. The plates of iron fastened at the bottom of the box (for those were the strongest) preserved the balance while it fell, and hindered it from being broken on the surface of the water. Every joint of it was well grooved; and the door did not move on hinges, but up and down like a sash, which kept my closet so tight that very little water came in. I got with much difficulty out of my hammock, having first ventured to draw back the slip-board on the roof already mentioned, contrived on purpose to let in air, for want of which I found myself almost stifled.

How often did I then wish myself with my dear Glumdalclitch, from whom one single hour had so far divided me! And I may say with truth, that in the midst of my own misfortunes I could not forbear lamenting my poor nurse, the grief she would suffer for my loss, the displeasure of the queen, and the ruin of her fortune. Perhaps many travellers have not been under greater difficulties and distress than I was at this juncture, expecting every moment to see my box dashed to pieces, or at least overset by the first violent blast, or rising wave. A breach in one single pane of glass would have been immediate death: nor could any thing have preserved the windows, but the strong lattice wires placed on the outside, against accidents in travelling.

I saw the water ooze in at several crannies, although the leaks were not considerable, and I endeavoured to stop them as well as I could. I was not able to lift up the roof of my closet, which otherwise I certainly should have done, and sat on the top of it; where I might at least preserve myself some hours longer, than by being shut up (as I may call it) in the hold. Or if I escaped these dangers for a day or two, what could I expect but a miserable death of cold and hunger? I was four hours under these circumstances, expecting, and indeed wishing, every moment to be my last.

I have already told the reader that there were two strong staples fixed upon that side of my box which had no window, and into which the servant, who used to carry me on horseback, would put a leathern belt, and buckle it about his waist. Being in this disconsolate state, I heard, or at least thought I heard, some kind of grating noise on that side of my box where the staples were fixed; and soon after I began to fancy that the box was pulled or towed along the sea; for I now and then felt a sort of tugging, which made the waves rise near the tops of my windows, leaving me almost in the dark. This gave me some faint hopes of relief, although I was not able to imagine how it could be brought about.

I ventured to unscrew one of my chairs, which were always fastened to the floor; and having made a hard shift to screw it down again, directly under the slipping-board that I had lately opened, I mounted on the chair, and putting my mouth as near as I could to the hole, I called for help in a loud voice, and in all the languages I understood. I then fastened my handkerchief to a stick I usually carried, and thrusting it up the hole, waved it several times in the air, that if any boat or ship were near, the seamen might conjecture some unhappy mortal to be shut up in the box.

I found no effect from all I could do, but plainly perceived my closet to be moved along; and in the space of an hour, or better, that side of the box where the staples were, and had no windows, struck against something that was hard. I apprehended it to be a rock, and found myself tossed more than ever. I plainly heard a noise upon the cover of my closet, like that of a cable, and the grating of it as it passed through the ring. I then found myself hoisted up, by degrees, at least three feet higher than I was before. Whereupon I again thrust up my stick and handkerchief, calling for help till I was almost hoarse. In return to which, I heard a great shout repeated three times, giving me such transports of joy as are not to be conceived but by those who feel them.

I now heard a trampling over my head, and somebody calling through the hole with a loud voice, in the English tongue, If there be any body below, let them speak. I answered, I was an Englishman, drawn by ill fortune into the greatest calamity that ever any creature underwent, and begged, by all that was moving, to be delivered out of the dungeon I was in. The voice replied, I was safe, for my box was fastened to their ship; and the carpenter should immediately come and saw a hole in the cover, large enough to pull me out. I answered, that was needless, and would take up too much time; for there was no more to be done, but let one of the crew put his finger into the ring, and take the box out of the sea into the ship, and so into the captain's cabin.

Some of them, upon hearing me talk so wildly, thought I was mad: others laughed; for indeed it never came into my head, that I was now got among people of my own stature and strength. The carpenter came, and in a few minutes sawed a passage about four feet square, then let down a small ladder, upon which I mounted, and thence was taken into the ship in a very weak condition.

The sailors were all in amazement, and asked me a thousand questions, which I had no inclination to answer. I was equally confounded at the sight of so many pigmies, for such I took them to be, after having so long accustomed mine eyes to the monstrous objects I had left. But the captain, Mr. Thomas Wilcocks, an honest worthy Shropshire man, observing I was ready to faint, took me into his cabin, gave me a cordial to comfort me, and made me turn in upon his own bed, advising me to take a little rest, of which I had great need.

Before I went to sleep, I gave him to understand that I had some valuable furniture in my box, too good to be lost: a fine hammock, a handsome field-bed, two chairs, a table, and a cabinet; that my closet was hung on all sides, or rather quilted, with silk and cotton; that if he would let one of the crew bring my closet into his cabin, I would open it there before him, and show him my goods. The captain, hearing me utter these absurdities, concluded I was raving; however (I suppose to pacify me) he promised to give order as I desired, and going upon deck, sent some of his men down into my closet, whence (as I afterwards found) they drew up all my goods, and stripped off the quilting; but the chairs, cabinet, and bedstead, being screwed to the floor, were much damaged by the ignorance of the seamen, who tore them up by force.

Then they knocked off some of the boards for the use of the ship, and when they had got all they had a mind for, let the hull drop into the sea, which by reason of many breaches made in the bottom and sides, sunk to rights. And, indeed, I was glad not to have been a spectator of the havoc they made, because I am confident it would have sensibly touched me, by bringing former passages into my mind, which I would rather have forgot.

I slept some hours, but perpetually disturbed with dreams of the place I had left, and the dangers I had escaped. However, upon waking, I found myself much recovered. It was now about eight o'clock at night, and the captain ordered supper immediately, thinking I had already fasted too long. He entertained me with great kindness, observing me not to look wildly, or talk inconsistently: and, when we were left alone, desired I would give him a relation of my travels, and by what accident I came to be set adrift, in that monstrous wooden chest.

He said that about twelve o'clock at noon, as he was looking through his glass, he spied it at a distance, and thought it was a sail, which he had a mind to make, being not much out of his course, in hopes of buying some biscuit, his own beginning to fall short. That upon coming nearer, and finding his error, he sent out his long-boat to discover what it was; that his men came back in a fright, swearing they had seen a swimming house. That he laughed at their folly, and went himself in the boat, ordering his men to take a strong cable along with them. That the weather being calm, he rowed round me several times, observed my windows and wire lattices that defended them. That he discovered two staples upon one side, which was all of boards, without any passage for light. He then commanded his men to row up to that side, and fastening a cable to one of the staples, ordered them to tow my chest, as they called it, toward the ship.

When it was there, he gave directions to fasten another cable to the ring fixed in the cover, and to raise up my chest with pulleys, which all the sailors were not able to do above two or three feet. He said, they saw my stick and handkerchief thrust out of the hole, and concluded that some unhappy man must be shut up in the cavity. I asked, whether he or the crew had seen any prodigious birds in the air, about the time he first discovered me. To which he answered, that discoursing this matter with the sailors while I was asleep, one of them said, he had observed three eagles flying towards the north, but remarked nothing of their being larger than the usual size: which I suppose must be imputed to the great height they were at; and he could not guess the reason of my question.

I then asked the captain, how far he reckoned we might be from land? He said, by the best computation he could make, we were at least a hundred leagues. I assured him, that he must be mistaken by almost half, for I had not left the country whence I came above two hours before I dropped into the sea. Whereupon he began again to think that my brain was disturbed, of which he gave me a hint, and advised me to go to bed in a cabin he had provided. I assured him, I was well refreshed with his good entertainment and company, and as much in my senses as ever I was in my life.

He then grew serious, and desired to ask me freely whether I were not troubled in my mind by the consciousness of some enormous crime, for which I was punished, at the command of some prince, by exposing me in that chest; as great criminals, in other countries, have been forced to sea in a leaky vessel, without provisions: for although he should be sorry to have taken so ill a man into his ship, yet he would engage his word to set me safe ashore, in the first port where we arrived. He added, that his suspicions were much increased by some very absurd speeches I had delivered at first to his sailors, and afterwards to himself, in relation to my closet or chest, as well as by my odd looks and behaviour while I was at supper.

I begged his patience to hear me tell my story, which I faithfully did, from the last time I left England, to the moment he first discovered me. And, as truth always forces its way into rational minds, so this honest worthy gentleman, who had some tincture of learning, and very good sense, was immediately convinced of my candour and veracity. But further to confirm all I had said, I entreated him to give order that my cabinet should be brought, of which I had the key in my pocket (for he had already informed me how the seamen disposed of my closet).

I opened it in his own presence, and showed him the small collection of rarities I made in the country from which I had been so strangely delivered. There was the comb I had contrived out of the stumps of the king's beard, and another of the same materials, but fixed into a paring of her Majesty's thumb-nail, which served for the back. There was a collection of needles and pins, from a foot to half a yard long; four wasp stings, like joiner's tacks; some combings of the queen's hair; a gold ring, which one day she made me a present of, in a most obliging manner, taking it from her little finger, and throwing it over my head like a collar. I desired the captain would please to accept this ring in return for his civilities; which he absolutely refused. I showed him a corn that I had cut off with my own hand, from a maid of honour's toe; it was about the bigness of Kentish pippin, and grown so hard, that when I returned England, I got it hollowed into a cup, and set in silver. Lastly, I desired him to see the breeches I had then on, which were made of a mouse's skin.

I could force nothing on him but a footman's tooth, which I observed him to examine with great curiosity, and found he had a fancy for it. He received it with abundance of thanks, more than such a trifle could deserve. It was drawn by an unskilful surgeon, in a mistake, from one of Glumdalclitch's men, who was afflicted with the tooth-ache, but it was as sound as any in his head. I got it cleaned, and put it into my cabinet. It was about a foot long, and four inches in diameter.

The captain was very well satisfied with this plain relation I had given him, and said, he hoped, when we returned to England, I would oblige the world by putting it on paper, and making it public. My answer was, that I thought we were already overstocked with books of travels: that nothing could now pass which was not extraordinary; wherein I doubted some authors less consulted truth, than their own vanity, or interest, or the diversion of ignorant readers; that my story could contain little beside common events, without those ornamental descriptions of strange plants, trees, birds, and other animals; or of the barbarous customs and idolatry of savage people, with which most writers abound. However, I thanked him for his good opinion, and promised to take the matter into my thoughts.

He said he wondered at one thing very much, which was, to hear me speak so loud; asking me whether the king or queen of that country were thick of hearing, I told him, it was what I had been used to for above two years past, and that I admired as much at the voices of him and his men, who seemed to me only to whisper, and yet I could hear them well enough. But, when I spoke in that country, it was like a man talking in the streets, to another looking out from the top of a steeple, unless when I was placed on a table, or held in any person's hand.

I told him I had likewise observed another thing, that, when I first got into the ship, and the sailors stood all about me, I thought they were the most little contemptible creatures I had ever beheld. For indeed, while I was in that prince's country, I could never endure to look in a glass, after mine eyes had been accustomed to such prodigious objects, because the comparison gave me so despicable a conceit of myself. The captain said, that while we were at supper, he observed me to look at every thing with a sort of wonder, and that I often seemed hardly able to contain my laughter, which he knew not well how to take, but imputed it to some disorder in my brain.

I answered it was very true; and I wondered how I could forbear, when I saw his dishes of the size of a silver three-pence, a leg of pork hardly a mouthful, a cup not so big as a nut-shell; and so I went on, describing the rest of his household-stuff and provisions, after the same manner. For, although he queen had ordered a little equipage of all things necessary for me, while I was in her service, yet my ideas were wholly taken up with what I saw on every side of me, and I winked at my own littleness, as people do at their own faults.

The captain understood my raillery very well, and merrily replied with the old English proverb, that he doubted mine eyes were bigger than my belly, for he did not observe my stomach so good, although I had fasted all day; and, continuing in his mirth, protested he would have gladly given a hundred pounds, to have seen my closet in the eagle's bill, and afterwards in its fall from so great a height into the sea; which would certainly have been a most astonishing object, worthy to have the description of it transmitted to future ages: and the comparison of Phaëton was so obvious, that he could not forbear applying it, although I did not much admire the conceit.

The captain having been at Tonquin, was, in his return to England, driven north-eastward to the latitude of 44 degrees, and longitude of 143. But meeting a trade-wind two days after I came on board him, we sailed southward a long time, and coasting New Holland, kept our course west-south-west, and then south-south-west, till we doubled the Cape of Good Hope. Our voyage was very prosperous, but I shall not trouble the reader with a journal of it. The captain called in at one or two ports, and sent in his long-boat for provisions and fresh water; but I never went out of the ship till we came into the Downs, which was on the third day of June, 1706, about nine months after my escape.

I offered to leave my goods in security for payment of my freight: but the captain protested he would not receive one farthing. We took a kind leave of each other, and I made him promise he would come to see me at my house in Redriff. I hired a horse and guide for five shillings, which I borrowed of the captain.

As I was on the road, observing the littleness of the houses, the trees, the cattle, and the people, I began to think myself in Lilliput. I was afraid of trampling on every traveller I met, and often called aloud to have them stand out of the way, so that I had like to have gotten one or two broken heads for my impertinence.

When I came to my own house, for which I was forced to inquire, one of the servants opening the door, I bent down to go in, (like a goose under a gate,) for fear of striking my head. My wife run out to embrace me, but I stooped lower than her knees, thinking she could otherwise never be able to reach my mouth. My daughter kneeled to ask my blessing, but I could not see her till she arose, having been so long used to stand with my head and eyes erect to above sixty feet; and then I went to take her up with one hand by the waist.

I looked down upon the servants, and one or two friends who were in the house, as if they had been pigmies and I a giant. I told my wife, she had been too thrifty, for I found she had starved herself and her daughter to nothing. In short, I behaved myself so unaccountably, that they were all of the captain's opinion when he first saw me, and concluded I had lost my wits. This I mention as an instance of the great power of habit and prejudice.

In a little time, I and my family and friends came to a right understanding: but my wife protested I should never go to sea any more; although my evil destiny so ordered, that she had not power to hinder me, as the reader may know hereafter. In the mean time, I here conclude the second part of my unfortunate voyages.

PART III

A Voyage to Laputa, Balnibarbi, Luggnagg, Glubbdubdrib and Japan

CHAPTER I

The author sets out on his third voyage. Is taken by pirates. The malice of a Dutchman. His arrival at an island. He is received into Laputa.

I had not been at home above ten days, when Captain William Robinson, a Cornish man, commander of the *Hope Well*, a stout ship of three hundred tons, came to my house. I had formerly been surgeon of another ship where he was master, and a fourth part owner, in a voyage to the Levant. He had always treated me more like a brother, than an inferior officer; and, hearing of my arrival, made me a visit, as I apprehended only out of friendship, for nothing passed more than what is usual after long absences. But repeating his visits often, expressing his joy to find I me in good health, asking, whether I were now settled for life? adding, that he intended a voyage to the East Indies in two months, at last he plainly invited me, though with some apologies, to be surgeon of the ship; that I should have another surgeon under me, beside our two mates; that my salary should be double to the usual pay; and that having experienced my knowledge in sea-affairs to be at least equal to his, he would enter into any engagement to follow my advice, as much as if I had shared in the command.

He said so many other obliging things, and I knew him to be so honest a man, that I could not reject this proposal; the thirst I had of seeing the world, notwithstanding my past misfortunes, continuing as violent as ever. The only difficulty that remained, was to persuade my wife, whose consent however I at last obtained, by the prospect of advantage she proposed to her children.

We set out the 5th day of August, 1706, and arrived at Fort St. George the 11th of April, 1707. We staid there three weeks to refresh our crew, many of whom were sick. From thence we went to Tonquin, where the captain resolved to continue some time, because many of the goods he intended to buy were not ready, nor could he expect to be dispatched in several months. Therefore, in hopes to defray some of the charges he must be at, he bought a sloop, loaded it with several sorts of goods, wherewith the Tonquinese usually trade to the neighbouring islands, and putting fourteen men on board, whereof three were of the country, he appointed me master of the sloop, and gave me power to traffic, while he transacted his affairs at Tonquin.

We had not sailed above three days, when a great storm arising, we were driven five days to the north-north-east, and then to the east: after which we had fair weather, but still with a pretty strong gale from the west. Upon the tenth day we were chased by two pirates, who soon overtook us; for my sloop was so deep laden, that she sailed very slow, neither were we in a condition to defend ourselves.

We were boarded about the same time by both the pirates, who entered furiously at the head of their men; but finding us all prostrate upon our faces (for so I gave order), they pinioned us with strong ropes, and setting guard upon us, went to search the sloop.

I observed among them a Dutchman, who seemed to be of some authority, though he was not commander of either ship. He knew us by our countenances to be Englishmen, and jabbering to us in his own language, swore we should be tied back to back and thrown into the sea. I spoken Dutch tolerably well; I told him who we were, and begged him, in consideration of our being Christians and Protestants, of neighbouring countries in strict alliance, that he would move the captains to take some pity on us. This inflamed his rage; he repeated his threatenings, and turning to his companions, spoke with great vehemence in the Japanese language, as I suppose, often using the word *Christianos*.

The largest of the two pirate ships was commanded by a Japanese captain, who spoke a little Dutch, but very imperfectly. He came up to me, and after several questions, which I answered in great humility, he said, we should not die. I made the captain a very low bow, and then, turning to the Dutchman, said, I was sorry to find more mercy in a heathen, than in a brother christian. But I had soon reason to repent those foolish words: for that malicious reprobate, having often endeavoured in vain to persuade both the captains that I might be thrown into the sea (which they would not yield to, after the promise made me that I should not die), however, prevailed so far, as to have a punishment inflicted on me, worse, in all human appearance, than death itself.

My men were sent by an equal division into both the pirate ships, and my sloop new manned. As to myself, it was determined that I should be set adrift in a small canoe, with paddles and a sail, and four days' provisions; which last, the Japanese captain was so kind to double out of his own stores, and would permit no man to search me. I got down into the canoe, while the Dutchman, standing upon the deck, loaded me with all the curses and injurious terms his language could afford.

About an hour before we saw the pirates I had taken an observation, and found we were in the latitude of 46 N. and longitude of 183. When I was at some distance from the pirates, I discovered, by my pocket-glass, several islands to the south-east. I set up my sail, the wind being fair, with a design to reach the nearest of those islands, which I made a shift to do, in about three hours. It was all rocky: however I got many birds' eggs; and, striking fire, I kindled some heath and dry sea-weed, by which I roasted my eggs. I ate no other supper, being resolved to spare my provisions as much as I could. I passed the night under the shelter of a rock, strewing some heath under me, and slept pretty well.

The next day I sailed to another island, and thence to a third and fourth, sometimes using my sail, and sometimes my paddles. But, not to trouble the reader with a particular account of my distresses, let it suffice, that on the fifth day I arrived at the last island in my sight, which lay south-south-east to the former.

This island was at a greater distance than I expected, and I did not reach it in less than five hours. I encompassed it almost round, before I could find a convenient place to land in; which was a small creek, about three times the wideness of my canoe. I found the island to be all rocky, only a little intermingled with tufts of grass, and sweet-smelling herbs. I took out my small provisions and after having refreshed myself, I secured the remainder in a cave, whereof there were great numbers; I gathered plenty of eggs upon the rocks, and got a quantity of dry sea-weed, and parched grass, which I designed to kindle the next day, and roast my eggs as well as I could, for I had about me my flint, steel, match, and burning-glass.

I lay all night in the cave where I had lodged my provisions. My bed was the same dry grass and sea-weed which I intended for fuel. I slept very little, for the disquiets of my mind prevailed over my weariness, and kept me awake. I considered how impossible it was to preserve my life in so desolate a place, and how miserable my end must be: yet found myself so listless and desponding, that I had not the heart to rise; and before I could get spirits enough to creep out of my cave, the day was far advanced. I walked awhile among the rocks: the sky was perfectly clear, and the sun so hot, that I was forced to turn my face from it: when all on a sudden it became obscure, as I thought, in a manner very different from what happens by the interposition of a cloud. I turned back, and perceived a vast opaque body between me and the sun moving forwards towards the island: it seemed to be about two miles high, and hid the sun six or seven minutes; but I did not observe the air to be much colder, or the sky more darkened, than if I had stood under the shade of a mountain.

As it approached nearer over the place where I was, it appeared to be a firm substance, the bottom flat, smooth, and shining very bright, from the reflection of the sea below. I stood upon a height about two hundred yards from the shore, and saw this vast body descending almost to a parallel with me, at less than an English mile distance. I took out my pocket perspective, and could plainly discover numbers of people moving up and down the sides of it, which appeared to be sloping; but what those people where doing I was not able to distinguish.

The natural love of life gave me some inward motion of joy, and I was ready to entertain a hope that this adventure might, some way or other, help to deliver me from the desolate place and condition I was in. But at the same time the reader can hardly conceive my astonishment, to behold an island in the air, inhabited by men, who were able (as it should seem) to raise or sink, or put it into progressive motion, as they pleased. But not being at that time in a disposition to philosophise upon this phenomenon, I rather chose to observe what course the island would take, because it seemed for awhile to stand still. Yet soon after, it advanced nearer, and I could see the sides of it encompassed with several gradations of galleries, and stairs, at certain intervals, to descend from one to the other.

In the lowest gallery, I beheld some people fishing with long angling rods, and others looking on. I waved my cap (for my hat was long since worn out) and my handkerchief toward the island; and upon its nearer approach, I called and shouted with the utmost strength of my voice; and then looking circumspectly, I beheld a crowd gather to that side which was most in my view. I found by their pointing towards me and to each other, that they plainly discovered me, although they made no return to my shouting. But I could see four or five men running in great haste, up the stairs, to the top of the island, who then disappeared. I happened rightly to conjecture, that these were sent for orders to some person in authority upon this occasion.

The number of people increased, and, in less than half all hour, the island was moved and raised in such a manner, that the lowest gallery appeared in a parallel of less then a hundred yards distance from the height where I stood. I then put myself in the most supplicating posture, and spoke in the humblest accent, but received no answer. Those who stood nearest over against me, seemed to be persons of distinction, as I supposed by their habit. They conferred earnestly with each other, looking often upon me. At length one of them called out in a clear, polite, smooth dialect, not unlike in sound to the Italian: and therefore I returned an answer in that language, hoping at least that the cadence might be more agreeable to his ears. Although neither of us understood the other, yet my meaning was easily known, for the people saw the distress I was in.

They made signs for me to come down from the rock, and go towards the shore, which I accordingly did; and the flying island being raised to a convenient height, the verge directly over me, a chain was let down from the lowest gallery, with a seat fastened to the bottom, to which I fixed myself, and was drawn up by pulleys.

CHAPTER II

The humours and dispositions of the Laputians described. An account of their learning. Of the king and his court. The author's reception there. The inhabitants subject to fear and disquietudes. An account of the women.

At my alighting, I was surrounded with a crowd of people, but those who stood nearest seemed to be of better quality. They beheld me with all the marks and circumstances of wonder; neither indeed was I much in their debt, having never till then seen a race of mortals so singular in their shapes, habits, and countenances. Their heads were all reclined, either to the right, or the left; one of their eyes turned inward, and the other directly up to the zenith. Their outward garments were adorned with the figures of suns, moons, and stars; interwoven with those of fiddles, flutes, harps, trumpets, guitars, harpsichords, and many other instruments of music, unknown to us in Europe. I observed, here and there, many in the habit of servants, with a blown bladder, fastened like a flail to the end of a stick, which they carried in their hands. In each bladder was a small quantity of dried peas, or little pebbles, as I was afterwards informed. With these bladders, they now and then flapped the mouths and ears of those who stood near them, of which practice I could not then conceive the meaning. It seems the minds of these people are so taken up with intense speculations, that they neither can speak, nor attend to the discourses of others, without being roused by some external taction upon the organs of speech and hearing; for which reason, those persons who are able to afford it always keep a flapper (the original is *climenole*) in their family, as one of their domestics; nor ever walk abroad, or make visits, without him. And the business of this officer is, when two, three, or more persons are in company, gently to strike with his bladder the mouth of him who is to speak, and the right ear of him or them to whom the speaker addresses himself. This flapper is likewise employed diligently to attend his master in his walks, and upon occasion to give him a soft flap on his eyes; because he is always so wrapped up in cogitation, that he is in manifest danger of falling down every precipice, and bouncing his head against every post; and in the streets, of justling others, or being justled himself into the kennel.

It was necessary to give the reader this information, without which he would be at the same loss with me to understand the proceedings of these people, as they conducted me up the stairs to the top of the island, and from thence to the royal palace. While we were ascending, they forgot several times what they were about, and left me to myself, till their memories were again roused by their flappers; for they appeared altogether unmoved by the sight of my foreign habit and countenance, and by the shouts of the vulgar, whose thoughts and minds were more disengaged.

At last we entered the palace, and proceeded into the chamber of presence, where I saw the king seated on his throne, attended on each side by persons of prime quality. Before the throne, was a large table filled with globes and spheres, and mathematical instruments of all kinds. His Majesty took not the least notice of us, although our entrance was not without sufficient noise, by the concourse of all persons belonging to the court. But he was then deep in a problem; and we attended at least an hour, before he could solve it.

There stood by him, on each side, a young page with flaps

in their hands, and when they saw he was at leisure, one of them gently struck his mouth, and the other his right ear; at which he startled like one awaked on the sudden, and looking towards me and the company I was in, recollected the occasion of our coming, whereof he had been informed before. He spoke some words, whereupon immediately a young man with a flap came up to my side, and flapped me gently on the right ear; but I made signs, as well as I could, that I had no occasion for such an instrument; which, as I afterwards found, gave his Majesty, and the whole court, a very mean opinion of my understanding.

The king, as far as I could conjecture, asked me several questions, and I addressed myself to him in all the languages I had. When it was found I could neither understand nor be understood, I was conducted by his order to an apartment in his palace (this prince being distinguished above all his predecessors for his hospitality to strangers), where two servants were appointed to attend me. My dinner was brought, and four persons of quality, whom I remembered to have seen very near the king's person, did me the honour to dine with me.

We had two courses, of three dishes each. In the first course, there was a shoulder of mutton cut into an equilateral triangle, a piece of beef into a rhomboides, and a pudding into a cycloid. The second course was two ducks trussed up in the form of fiddles; sausages and puddings resembling flutes and hautboys, and a breast of veal in the shape of a harp. The servants cut our bread into cones, cylinders, parallelograms, and several other mathematical figures.

While we were at dinner, I made bold to ask the names of several things in their language, and those noble persons, by the assistance of their flappers, delighted to give me answers, hoping to raise my admiration of their great abilities if I could be brought to converse with them. I was soon able to call for bread and drink, or whatever else I wanted.

After dinner my company withdrew, and a person was sent to me by the king's order, attended by a flapper. He brought with him pen, ink, and paper, and three or four books, giving me to understand by signs, that he was sent to teach me the language. We sat together four hours, in which time I wrote down a great number of words in columns, with the translations over against them; I likewise made a shift to learn several short sentences; for my tutor would order one of my servants to fetch something, to turn about, to make a bow, to sit, or to stand, or walk, and the like. Then I took down the sentence in writing.

He showed me also, in one of his books, the figures of the sun, moon, and stars, the zodiac, the tropics, and polar circles, together with the denominations of many plains and solids. He gave me the names and descriptions of all the musical instruments, and the general terms of art in playing on each of them. After he had left me, I placed all my words, with their interpretations, in alphabetical order. And thus, in a few days, by the help of a very faithful memory, I got some insight into their language.

The word, which I interpret the flying or floating island, is in the original, *Laputa*, whereof I could never learn the true etymology. *Lap*, in the old obsolete language, signifies high; and *untuh*, a governor; from which they say, by corruption, was derived *Laputa*, from *Lapuntuh*. But I do not approve of this derivation, which seems to be a little strained. I ventured to offer to the learned among them a conjecture of my own, that Laputa was *quasi lap outed*; *lap*, signifying properly, the dancing of the sunbeams in the sea, and *outed*, a wing; which, however, I shall not obtrude, but submit to the judicious reader.

Those to whom the king had entrusted me, observing how ill I was clad, ordered a tailor to come next morning, and take measure for a suit of clothes. This operator did his office after a different manner from those of his trade in Europe. He first took my altitude by a quadrant, and then, with a rule and compasses, described the dimensions and outlines of my whole body, all which he entered upon paper; and in six days brought my clothes very ill made, and quite out of shape, by happening to mistake a figure in the calculation. But my comfort was, that I observed such accidents very frequent, and little regarded.

During my confinement for want of clothes, and by an indisposition that held me some days longer, I much enlarged my dictionary; and when I went next to court, was able to understand many things the king spoke, and to return him some kind of answers. His Majesty had given orders, that the island should move north-east and by east, to the vertical point over Lagado, the metropolis of the whole kingdom below, upon the firm earth. It was about ninety leagues distant, and our voyage lasted four days and a half. I was not in the least sensible of the progressive motion made in the air by the island.

On the second morning, about eleven o'clock, the king himself in person, attended by his nobility, courtiers, and officers, having prepared all their musical instruments, played on them for three hours without intermission, so that I was quite stunned with the noise; neither could I possibly guess the meaning, till my tutor informed me. He said that, the people of their island had their ears adapted to hear the music of the spheres, which always played at certain periods, and the court was now prepared to bear their part, in whatever instrument they most excelled.

In our journey towards Lagado, the capital city, his Majesty ordered that the island should stop over certain towns and villages, from whence he might receive the petitions of his subjects. And to this purpose, several packthreads were let down, with small weights at the bottom. On these packthreads the people strung their petitions, which mounted up directly, like the scraps of paper fastened by school boys at the end of the string that holds their kite. Sometimes we received wine and victuals from below, which were drawn up by pulleys.

The knowledge I had in mathematics, gave me great assistance in acquiring their phraseology, which depended much upon that science, and music; and in the latter I was not unskilled. Their ideas are perpetually conversant in lines and figures. If they would, for example, praise the beauty of a woman, or any other animal, they describe it by rhombs, circles, parallelograms, ellipses, and other geometrical terms, or by words of art drawn from music, needless here to repeat. I observed in the king's kitchen all sorts of mathematical and musical instruments, after the figures of which they cut up the joints that were served to his Majesty's table.

Their houses are very ill built, the walls bevil, without one right angle in any apartment; and this defect arises from the contempt they bear to practical geometry, which they despise as vulgar and mechanic; those instructions they give being too refined for the intellects of their workmen, which occasions perpetual mistakes. And although they are dexterous enough upon a piece of paper, in the management of the rule, the pencil, and the divider, yet in the common actions and behaviour of life, I have not seen a more clumsy, awkward, and unhandy people, nor so slow and perplexed in their conceptions upon all other subjects, except those of mathematics and music. They are very bad reasoners, and vehemently given to opposition, unless when they happen to be of the right opinion, which is seldom their case. Imagination, fancy, and invention, they are wholly strangers to, nor have any words in their language, by which those ideas can be expressed; the whole compass of their thoughts and mind being shut up within the two forementioned sciences.

Most of them, and especially those who deal in the astronomical part, have great faith in judicial astrology, although they are ashamed to own it publicly. But what I chiefly admired, and thought altogether unaccountable, was the strong disposition I observed in them towards news and politics, perpetually inquiring into public affairs, giving their judgments in matters of state, and passionately disputing every inch of a party opinion.

I have indeed observed the same disposition among most of the mathematicians I have known in Europe, although I could never discover the least analogy between the two sciences; unless those people suppose, that because the smallest circle has as many degrees as the largest, therefore the regulation and management of the world require no more abilities than the handling and turning of a globe; but I rather take this quality to spring from a very common infirmity of human nature, inclining us to be most curious and conceited in matters where we have least concern, and for which we are least adapted by study or nature.

These people are under continual disquietudes, never enjoying a minutes peace of mind; and their disturbances proceed from causes which very little affect the rest of mortals. Their apprehensions arise from several changes they dread in the celestial bodies: for instance, that the earth, by the continual approaches of the sun towards it, must, in course of time, be absorbed, or swallowed up; that the face of the sun, will, by degrees, be encrusted with its own effluvia, and give no more light to the world; that the earth very narrowly escaped a brush from the tail of the last comet, which would have infallibly reduced it to ashes; and that the next, which they have calculated for one-and-thirty years hence, will probably destroy us.

If in its perihelion, it should approach within a certain degree of the sun (as by their calculations they have reason to dread) it will receive a degree of heat ten thousand times more intense than that of red hot glowing iron, and in its absence from the sun, carry a blazing tail ten hundred thousand and fourteen miles long, through which, if the earth should pass at the distance of one hundred thousand miles from the nucleus, or main body of the comet, it must in its passage be set on fire, and reduced to ashes: that the sun, daily spending its rays without any nutriment to supply them, will at last be wholly consumed and annihilated; which must be attended with the destruction of this earth, and of all the planets that receive their light from it.

They are so perpetually alarmed with the apprehensions of these, and the like impending dangers, that they can neither sleep quietly in their beds, nor have any relish for the common pleasures and amusements of life. When they meet an acquaintance in the morning, the first question is about the sun's health, how he looked at his setting and rising, and what hopes they have to avoid the stroke of the approaching comet. This conversation they are apt to run into with the same temper that boys discover in delighting to hear terrible stories of spirits and hobgoblins, which they greedily listen to, and dare not go to bed for fear.

The women of the island have abundance of vivacity: they, contemn their husbands, and are exceedingly fond of strangers, whereof there is always a considerable number from the continent below, attending at court, either upon affairs of the several towns and corporations, or their own particular occasions, but are much despised, because they want the same endowments. Among these the ladies choose their gallants: but the vexation is, that they act with too much ease and security; for the husband is always so rapt in speculation, that the mistress and lover may proceed to the greatest familiarities before his face, if he be but provided with paper and implements, and without his flapper at his side.

The wives and daughters lament their confinement to the island, although I think it the most delicious spot of ground in the world; and although they live here in the greatest plenty and magnificence, and are allowed to do whatever they please, they long to see the world, and take the diversions of the metropolis, which they are not allowed to do without a particular license from the king; and this is not easy to be obtained, because the people of quality have found, by frequent experience, how hard it is to persuade their women to return from below.

This may perhaps pass with the reader rather for an European or English story, than for one of a country so remote. But he may please to consider, that the caprices of womankind are not limited by any climate or nation, and that they are much more uniform, than can be easily imagined.

In about a month's time, I had made a tolerable proficiency in their language, and was able to answer most of the king's questions, when I had the honour to attend him. His Majesty discovered not the least curiosity to inquire into the laws, government, history, religion, or manners of the countries where I had been; but confined his questions to the state of mathematics, and received the account I gave him with great contempt and indifference, though often roused by his flapper on each side.

CHAPTER III

A phenomenon solved by modern philosophy and astronomy. The Laputians' great improvements in the latter. The king's method of suppressing insurrections.

I desired leave of this prince to see the curiosities of the island, which he was graciously pleased to grant, and ordered my tutor to attend me. I chiefly wanted to know, to what cause, in art or in nature, it owed its several motions, whereof I will now give a philosophical account to the reader.

The flying or floating island is exactly circular, its diameter 7837 yards, or about four miles and a half, and consequently contains ten thousand acres. It is three hundred yards thick. The bottom, or under surface, which appears to those who view it below, is one even regular plate of adamant, shooting up to the height of about two hundred yards. Above it lie the several minerals in their usual order, and over all is a coat of rich mould, ten or twelve feet deep.

The declivity of the upper surface, from the circumference to the centre, is the natural cause why all the dews and rains, which fall upon the island, are conveyed in small rivulets toward the middle, where they are emptied into four large basins, each of about half a mile in circuit, and two hundred yards distant from the centre. From these basins the water is continually exhaled by the sun in the daytime, which effectually prevents their overflowing. Besides, as it is in the power of the monarch to raise the island above the region of clouds and vapours, he can prevent the falling of dews and rain whenever he pleases. For the highest clouds cannot rise above two miles, as naturalists agree, at least they were never known to do so in that country.

At the centre of the island there is a chasm about fifty yards in diameter, whence the astronomers descend into a large dome, which is therefore called *flandona gagnole*, or the astronomer's cave, situated at the depth of a hundred yards beneath the upper surface of the adamant. In this cave are twenty lamps continually burning, which, from the reflection of the adamant, cast a strong light into every part. The place is stored with great variety of sextants, quadrants, telescopes, astrolabes, and other astronomical instruments.

But the greatest curiosity, upon which the fate of the island depends, is a loadstone of a prodigious size, in shape resembling a weaver's shuttle. It is in length six yards, and in the thickest part at least three yards over. This magnet is sustained by a very strong axle of adamant passing through its middle, upon which it plays, and is poised so exactly that the weakest hand can turn it. It is hooped round with a hollow cylinder of adamant, four feet yards in diameter, placed horizontally, and supported by eight adamantine feet, each six yards high. In the middle of the concave side, there is a groove twelve inches deep, in which the extremities of the axle are lodged, and turned round as there is occasion.

The stone cannot be removed from its place by any force, because the hoop and its feet are one continued piece with that body of adamant which constitutes the bottom of the island.

By means of this loadstone, the island is made to rise and fall, and move from one place to another. For, with respect to that part of the earth over which the monarch presides, the stone is endued at one of its sides with an attractive power, and at the other with a repulsive. Upon placing the magnet erect, with its attracting end towards the earth, the island descends; but when the repelling extremity points downwards, the island mounts directly upwards. When the position of the stone is oblique, the motion of the island is so too: for in this magnet, the forces always act in lines parallel to its direction.

By this oblique motion, the island is conveyed to different parts of the monarch's dominions. To explain the manner of its progress, let *A B* represent a line drawn across the dominions of Balnibarbi, let the line *c d* represent the loadstone, of which let *d* be the repelling end, and *c* the attracting end, the island being over *C*: let the stone be placed in position *c d*, with its repelling end downwards; then the island will be driven upwards obliquely towards *D*. When it is arrived at *D*, let the stone be turned upon its axle, till its attracting end points towards *E*, and then the island will be carried obliquely towards *E*; where, if the stone be again turned upon its axle till it stands in the position *EF*, with its repelling point downwards, the island will rise obliquely towards *F*, where, by directing the attracting end towards *G*, the island may be carried to *G*, and from *G* to *H*, by turning the stone, so as to make its repelling extremity to point directly downward.

Thus, by changing the situation of the stone, as often as there is occasion, the island is made to rise and fall by turns in an oblique direction, and by those alternate risings and fallings (the obliquity being not considerable) is conveyed from one part of the dominions to the other.

But it must be observed, that this island cannot move beyond the extent of the dominions below, nor can it rise above the height of four miles. For which the astronomers (who have written large systems concerning the stone) assign the following reason: that the magnetic virtue does not extend beyond the distance of four miles, and that the mineral, which acts upon the stone in the bowels of the earth, and in the sea about six leagues distant from the shore, is not diffused through the whole globe, but terminated with the limits of the king's dominions; and it was easy, from the great advantage of such a superior situation, for a prince to bring under his obedience whatever country lay within the attraction of that magnet.

When the stone is put parallel to the plane of the horizon, the island stands still; for in that case the extremities of it, being at equal distance from the earth, act with equal force, the one in drawing downwards, the other in pushing upwards, and consequently no motion can ensue.

This loadstone is under the care of certain astronomers, who, from time to time, give it such positions as the monarch directs. They spend the greatest part of their lives in observing the celestial bodies, which they do by the assistance of glasses, far excelling ours in goodness. For, although their largest telescopes do not exceed three feet, they magnify much more than those of a hundred with us, and show the stars with greater clearness. This advantage has enabled them to extend their discoveries much further than our astronomers in Europe; for they have made a catalogue of ten thousand fixed stars, whereas the largest of ours do not contain above one third part of that number. They have likewise discovered two lesser stars, or satellites, which revolve about Mars; whereof the innermost is distant from the centre of the primary planet exactly three of his diameters, and the outermost, five; the former revolves in the space of ten hours, and the latter in twenty-one and a half; so that the squares of their periodical times are very near in the same proportion with the cubes of their distance from the centre of Mars; which evidently shows them to be governed by the same law of gravitation that influences the other heavenly bodies.

They have observed ninety-three different comets, and settled their periods with great exactness. If this be true (and they affirm it with great confidence) it is much to be wished, that their observations were made public, whereby the theory of comets, which at present is very lame and defective, might be brought to the same perfection with other arts of astronomy.

The king would be the most absolute prince in the universe, if he could but prevail on a ministry to join with him; but these having their estates below on the continent, and considering that the office of a favourite has a very uncertain tenure, would never consent to the enslaving of their country.

If any town should engage in rebellion or mutiny, fall into violent factions, or refuse to pay the usual tribute, the king has two methods of reducing them to obedience. The first and the mildest course is, by keeping the island hovering over such a town, and the lands about it, whereby he can deprive them of the benefit of the sun and the rain, and consequently afflict the inhabitants with dearth and diseases: and if the crime deserve it, they are at the same time pelted from above with great stones, against which they have no defence but by creeping into cellars or caves, while the roofs of their houses are beaten to pieces.

But if they still continue obstinate, or offer to raise insurrections, he proceeds to the last remedy, by letting the island drop directly upon their heads, which makes a universal destruction both of houses and men. However, this is an extremity to which the prince is seldom driven, neither indeed is he willing to put it in execution; nor dare his ministers advise him to an action, which, as it would render them odious to the people, so it would be a great damage to their own estates, which all lie below; for the island is the king's demesne.

But there is still indeed a more weighty reason, why the kings of this country have been always averse from executing so terrible an action, unless upon the utmost necessity. For, if the town intended to be destroyed should have in it any tall rocks, as it generally falls out in the larger cities, a situation probably chosen at first with a view to prevent such a catastrophe; or if it abound in high spires, or pillars of stone, a sudden fall might endanger the bottom or under surface of the island, which, although it consist, as I have said, of one entire adamant, two hundred yards thick, might happen to crack by too great a shock, or burst by approaching too near the fires from the houses below, as the backs, both of iron and stone, will often do in our chimneys.

Of all this the people are well apprised, and understand how far to carry their obstinacy, where their liberty or property is concerned. And the king, when he is highest provoked, and most determined to press a city to rubbish, orders the island to descend with great gentleness, out of a pretence of tenderness to his people, but, indeed, for fear of breaking the adamantine bottom; in which case, it is the opinion of all their philosophers, that the loadstone could no longer hold it up, and the whole mass would fall to the ground.

By a fundamental law of this realm, neither the king, nor either of his two eldest sons, are permitted to leave the island; nor the queen, till she is past child-bearing.

CHAPTER IV

The author leaves Laputa; is conveyed to Balnibarbi; arrives at the metropolis. A description of the metropolis, and the country adjoining. The author hospitably received by a great lord. His conversation with that lord.

Although I cannot say that I was ill treated in this island, yet I must confess I thought myself too much neglected, not without some degree of contempt; for neither prince nor people appeared to be curious in any part of knowledge, except mathematics and music, wherein I was far their inferior, and upon that account very little regarded.

On the other side, after having seen all the curiosities of the island, I was very desirous to leave it, being heartily weary of those people. They were indeed excellent in two sciences for which I have great esteem, and wherein I am not unversed; but, at the same time, so abstracted and involved in speculation, that I never met with such disagreeable companions. I conversed only with women, tradesmen, flappers, and court-pages, during two months of my abode there; by which, at last, I rendered myself extremely contemptible; yet these were the only people from whom I could ever receive a reasonable answer.

I had obtained, by hard study, a good degree of knowledge in their language: I was weary of being confined to an island where I received so little countenance, and resolved to leave it with the first opportunity.

There was a great lord at court, nearly related to the king, and for that reason alone used with respect. He was universally reckoned the most ignorant and stupid person among them. He had performed many eminent services for the crown, had great natural and acquired parts, adorned with integrity and honour; but so ill an ear for music, that his detractors reported, he had been often known to beat time in the wrong place; neither could his tutors, without extreme difficulty, teach him to demonstrate the most easy proposition in the mathematics.

He was pleased to show me many marks of favour, often did me the honour of a visit, desired to be informed in the affairs of Europe, the laws and customs, the manners and learning of the several countries where I had travelled. He listened to me with great attention, and made very wise observations on all I spoke. He had two flappers attending him for state, but never made use of them, except at court and in visits of ceremony, and would always command them to withdraw, when we were alone together.

I entreated this illustrious person, to intercede in my behalf with his Majesty, for leave to depart; which he accordingly did, as he was pleased to tell me, with regret: for indeed he had made me several offers very advantageous, which, however, I refused, with expressions of the highest acknowledgment.

On the 16th of February I took leave of his Majesty and the court. The king made me a present to the value of about two hundred pounds English, and my protector, his kinsman, as much more, together with a letter of recommendation to a friend of his in Lagado, the metropolis. The island being then hovering over a mountain about two miles from it, I was let down from the lowest gallery, in the same manner as I had been taken up.

The continent, as far as it is subject to the monarch of the flying island, passes under the general name of *Balnibarbi*; and the metropolis, as I said before, is called *Lagado*. I felt some little satisfaction in finding myself on firm ground. I walked to the city without any concern, being clad like one of the natives, and sufficiently instructed to converse with them. I soon found out the person's house to whom I was recommended, presented my letter from his friend the grandee in the island, and was received with much kindness. This great lord, whose name was Munodi, ordered me an apartment in his own house, where I continued during my stay, and was entertained in a most hospitable manner.

The next morning after my arrival, he took me in his chariot to see the town, which is about half the bigness of London; but the houses very strangely built, and most of them out of repair. The people in the streets walked fast, looked wild, their eyes fixed, and were generally in rags. We passed through one of the town gates, and went about three miles into the country, where I saw many labourers working with several sorts of tools in the ground, but was not able to conjecture what they were about: neither did observe any expectation either of corn or grass, although the soil appeared to be excellent. I could not forbear admiring at these odd appearances, both in town and country; and I made bold to desire my conductor, that he would be pleased to explain to me, what could be meant by so many busy heads, hands, and faces, both in the streets and the fields, because I did not discover any good effects they produced; but, on the contrary, I never knew a soil so unhappily cultivated, houses so ill contrived and so ruinous, or a people whose countenances and habit expressed so much misery and want.

This lord Munodi was a person of the first rank, and had been some years governor of Lagado; but, by a cabal of ministers, was discharged for insufficiency. However, the king treated him with tenderness, as a well-meaning man, but of a low contemptible understanding.

When I gave that free censure of the country and its inhabitants, he made no further answer than by telling me, that

I had not been long enough among them to form a judgment; and that the different nations of the world had different customs; with other common topics to the same purpose. But, when we returned to his palace, he asked me how I liked the building, what absurdities I observed, and what quarrel I had with the dress or looks of his domestics? This he might safely do; because every thing about him was magnificent, regular, and polite. I answered, that his Excellency's prudence, quality, and fortune, had exempted him from those defects, which folly and beggary had produced in others. He said, if I would go with him to his country-house, about twenty miles distant, where his estate lay, there would be more leisure for this kind of conversation. I told his Excellency that I was entirely at his disposal; and accordingly we set out next morning.

During our journey he made me observe the several methods used by farmers in managing their lands, which to me were wholly unaccountable; for, except in some very few places, I could not discover one ear of corn or blade of grass. But, in three hours travelling, the scene was wholly altered; we came into a most beautiful country; farmers' houses, at small distances, neatly built; the fields enclosed, containing vineyards, corn-grounds, and meadows. Neither do I remember to have seen a more delightful prospect. His Excellency observed my countenance to clear up; he told me, with a sigh, that there his estate began, and would continue the same, till we should come to his house: that his countrymen ridiculed and despised him, for managing his affairs no better, and for setting so ill an example to the kingdom; which, however, was followed by very few, such as were old, and wilful, and weak like himself.

We came at length to the house, which was indeed a noble structure, built according to the best rules of ancient architecture. The fountains, gardens, walks, avenues, and groves, were all disposed with exact judgment and taste. I gave due praises to every thing I saw, whereof his Excellency took not the least notice till after supper; when, there being no third companion, he told me with a very melancholy air that he doubted he must throw down his houses in town and country, to rebuild them after the present mode; destroy all his plantations, and cast others into such a form as modern usage required, and give the same directions to all his tenants, unless he would submit to incur the censure of pride, singularity, affectation, ignorance, caprice, and perhaps increase his Majesty's displeasure; that the admiration I appeared to be under would cease or diminish, when he had informed me of some particulars which, probably, I never heard of at court, the people there being too much taken up in their own speculations, to have regard to what passed here below.

The sum of his discourse was to this effect: That about forty years ago, certain persons went up to Laputa, either upon business or diversion, and, after five months continuance, came back with a very little smattering in mathematics, but full of volatile spirits acquired in that airy region: that these persons, upon their return, began to dislike the management of every thing below, and fell into schemes of putting all arts, sciences, languages, and mechanics, upon a new foot. To this end, they procured a royal patent for erecting an academy of projectors in Lagado; and the humour prevailed so strongly among the people, that there is not a town of any consequence in the kingdom without such an academy. In these colleges the professors contrive new rules and methods of agriculture and building, and new instruments, and tools for all trades and manufactures; whereby, as they undertake, one man shall do the work of ten; a palace may be built in a week, of materials so durable as to last for ever without repairing. All the fruits of the earth shall come to maturity at whatever season we think fit to choose, and increase a hundred fold more than they do at present; with innumerable other happy proposals.

The only inconvenience is, that none of these projects are yet brought to perfection; and in the mean time, the whole country lies miserably waste, the houses in ruins, and the people without food or clothes. By all which, instead of being discouraged, they are fifty times more violently bent upon prosecuting their schemes, driven equally on by hope and despair: that as for himself, being not of an enterprising spirit, he was content to go on in the old forms, to live in the houses his ancestors had built, and act as they did, in every part of life, without innovation: that some few other persons of quality and gentry had done the same, but were looked on with an eye of contempt and ill-will, as enemies to art, ignorant, and ill common-wealth's men, preferring their own ease and sloth before the general improvement of their country.

His lordship added that he would not, by any further particulars, prevent the pleasure I should certainly take in viewing the grand academy, whither he was resolved I should go. He only desired me to observe a ruined building, upon the side of a mountain about three miles distant, of which he gave me this account: That he had a very convenient mill within half a mile of his house, turned by a current from a large river, and sufficient for his own family, as well as a great number of his tenants.

About seven years ago, a club of those projectors came to him with proposals to destroy this mill, and build another on the side of that mountain, on the long ridge whereof a long canal must be cut, for a repository of water, to be conveyed up by pipes and engines to supply the mill, because the wind and air upon a height agitated the water, and thereby made it fitter for motion, and because the water, descending down a declivity, would turn the mill with half the current of a river whose course is more upon a level. He said, that being then not very well with the court, and pressed by many of his friends, he complied with the proposal; and after employing a hundred men for two years, the work miscarried, the projectors went off, laying the blame entirely upon him, railing at him ever since, and putting others upon the same experiment, with equal assurance of success, as well as equal disappointment.

In a few days we came back to town; and his Excellency, considering the bad character he had in the academy, would not go with me himself, but recommended me to a friend of his, to bear me company thither. My lord was pleased to represent me as a great admirer of projects, and a person of much curiosity and easy belief; which, indeed, was not without truth; for I had myself been a sort of projector in my younger days.

CHAPTER V

The author permitted to see the grand academy of Lagado. The academy largely described. The arts wherein the professors employ themselves.

This academy is not an entire single building, but a continuation of several houses on both sides of a street, which growing waste, was purchased and applied to that use.

I was received very kindly by the warden, and went for many days to the academy. Every room has in it one or more projectors; and I believe I could not be in fewer than five hundred rooms.

The first man I saw was of a meagre aspect, with sooty hands and face, his hair and beard long, ragged, and singed in several places. His clothes, shirt, and skin, were all of the same colour. He has been eight years upon a project for extracting sunbeams out of cucumbers, which were to be put in phials hermetically sealed, and let out to warm the air in raw inclement summers. He told me, he did not doubt, that, in eight years more, he should be able to supply the governor's gardens with sunshine, at a reasonable rate: but he complained that his stock was low, and entreated me to give him something as an encouragement to ingenuity, especially since this had been a very dear season for cucumbers. I made him a small present, for my lord had furnished me with money on purpose, because he knew their practice of begging from all who go to see them.

I saw another at work to calcine ice into gunpowder; who likewise showed me a treatise he had written concerning the malleability of fire, which he intended to publish.

There was a most ingenious architect, who had contrived a new method for building houses, by beginning at the roof, and working downward to the foundation; which he justified to me, by the like practice of those two prudent insects, the bee and the spider.

There was a man born blind, who had several apprentices in his own condition: their employment was to mix colours for painters, which their master taught them to distinguish by feeling and smelling. It was indeed my misfortune to find them at that time not very perfect in their lessons, and the professor himself happened to be generally mistaken. This artist is much encouraged and esteemed by the whole fraternity.

In another apartment I was highly pleased with a projector who had found a device of ploughing the ground with hogs, to save the charges of ploughs, cattle, and labour. The method is this: in an acre of ground you bury, at six inches distance and eight deep, a quantity of acorns, dates, chestnuts, and other mast or vegetables, whereof these animals are fondest; then you drive six hundred or more of them into the field, where, in a few days, they will root up the whole ground in search of their food, and make it fit for sowing, at the same time manuring it with their dung: it is true, upon experiment, they found the charge and trouble very great, and they had little or no crop. However it is not doubted, that this invention may be capable of great improvement.

I went into another room, where the walls and ceiling were all hung round with cobwebs, except a narrow passage for the artist to go in and out. At my entrance, he called aloud to me, not to disturb his webs. He lamented the fatal mistake the world had been so long in, of using silkworms, while we had such plenty of domestic insects who infinitely excelled the former, because they understood how to weave, as well as spin. And he proposed further, that by employing spiders, the charge of dyeing silks should be wholly saved; whereof I was fully convinced, when he showed me a vast number of flies most beautifully coloured, wherewith he fed his spiders, assuring us that the webs would take a tincture from them; and as he had them of all hues, he hoped to fit everybody's fancy, as soon as he could find proper food for the flies, of certain gums, oils, and other glutinous matter, to give a strength and consistence to the threads.

There was an astronomer, who had undertaken to place a sun-dial upon the great weathercock on the town-house, by adjusting the annual and diurnal motions of the earth and sun, so as to answer and coincide with all accidental turnings of the wind.

I visited many other apartments, but shall not trouble my reader with all the curiosities I observed, being studious of brevity.

I had hitherto seen only one side of the academy, the other being appropriated to the advancers of speculative learning, of whom I shall say something, when I have mentioned one illustrious person more, who is called among them the universal artist. He told us he had been thirty years employing his thoughts for the improvement of human life. He had two large rooms full of wonderful curiosities, and fifty men at work. Some were condensing air into a dry tangible substance, by extracting the nitre, and letting the aqueous or fluid particles percolate; others softening marble, for pillows and pin-cushions; others petrifying the hoofs of a living horse, to preserve them from foundering.

The artist himself was at that time busy upon two great designs; the first, to sow land with chaff, wherein he affirmed the true seminal virtue to be contained, as he demonstrated by several experiments, which I was not skilful enough to comprehend. The other was, by a certain composition of gums, minerals, and vegetables, outwardly applied, to prevent the growth of wool upon two young lambs; and he hoped, in a reasonable time to propagate the breed of naked sheep, all over the kingdom.

We crossed a walk to the other part of the academy, where, as I have already said, the projectors in speculative learning resided.

The first professor I saw, was in a very large room, with forty pupils about him. After salutation, observing me to look earnestly upon a frame, which took up the greatest part of both the length and breadth of the room, he said, Perhaps I might wonder to see him employed in a project for improving speculative knowledge, by practical and mechanical operations. But the world would soon be sensible of its usefulness; and he flattered himself, that a more noble, exalted thought never sprang in any other man's head. Every one knew how laborious the usual method is of attaining to arts and sciences; whereas, by his contrivance, the most ignorant person, at a reasonable charge, and with a little bodily labour, might write books in philosophy, poetry, politics, laws, mathematics, and theology, without the least assistance from genius or study.

He then led me to the frame, about the sides, whereof all his pupils stood in ranks. It was twenty feet square, placed in the middle of the room. The superfices was composed of several bits of wood, about the bigness of a die, but some larger than others. They were all linked together by slender wires. These bits of wood were covered, on every square, with paper pasted on them; and on these papers were written all the words of their language, in their several moods, tenses, and declensions; but without any order. The professor then desired me to observe; for he was going to set his engine at work. The pupils, at his command, took each of them hold of an iron handle, whereof there were forty fixed round the edges of the frame; and giving them a sudden turn, the whole disposition of the words was entirely changed.

He then commanded six-and-thirty of the lads, to read the several lines softly, as they appeared upon the frame; and where they found three or four words together that might make part of a sentence, they dictated to the four remaining boys, who were scribes. This work was repeated three or four times, and at every turn, the engine was so contrived, that the words shifted into new places, as the square bits of wood moved upside down.

Six hours a day the young students were employed in this labour; and the professor showed me several volumes in large folio, already collected, of broken sentences, which he intended to piece together, and out of those rich materials, to give the world a complete body of all arts and sciences; which, however, might be still improved, and much expedited, if the public would raise a fund for making and employing five hundred such frames in Lagado, and oblige the managers to contribute in common their several collections.

He assured me that this invention had employed all his thoughts from his youth; that he had emptied the whole vocabulary into his frame, and made the strictest computation of the general proportion there is in books between the numbers of particles, nouns, and verbs, and other parts of speech.

I made my humblest acknowledgment to this illustrious person, for his great communicativeness; and promised, if ever I had the good fortune to return to my native country, that I would do him justice, as the sole inventor of this wonderful machine; the form and contrivance of which I desired leave to delineate on paper, as in the figure here annexed. I told him, although it were the custom of our learned in Europe to steal inventions from each other, who had thereby at least this advantage, that it became a controversy which was the right owner; yet I would take such caution, that he should have the honour entire, without a rival.

We next went to the school of languages, where three professors sat in consultation upon improving that of their own country.

The first project was, to shorten discourse, by cutting polysyllables into one, and leaving out verbs and participles, because, in reality, all things imaginable are but nouns.

The other project was, a scheme for entirely abolishing all words whatsoever; and this was urged as a great advantage in point of health, as well as brevity. For it is plain, that every word we speak is, in some degree, a diminution of our lunge by corrosion, and, consequently, contributes to the shortening of our lives. An expedient was therefore offered, that since words are only names for things, it would be more convenient for all men to carry about them such things as were necessary to express a particular business they are to discourse on. And this invention would certainly have taken place, to the great ease as well as health of the subject, if the women, in conjunction with the vulgar and illiterate, had not threatened to raise a rebellion unless they might be allowed the liberty to speak with their tongues, after the manner of their forefathers; such constant irreconcilable enemies to science are the common people.

However, many of the most learned and wise adhere to the new scheme of expressing themselves by things; which has only this inconvenience attending it, that if a man's business be very great, and of various kinds, he must be obliged, in proportion, to carry a greater bundle of things upon his back, unless he can afford one or two strong servants to attend him. I have often beheld two of those sages almost sinking under the weight of their packs, like pedlars among us, who, when they met in the street, would lay down their loads, open their sacks, and hold conversation for an hour together; then put up their implements, help each other to resume their burdens, and take their leave.

But for short conversations, a man may carry implements in his pockets, and under his arms, enough to supply him; and in his house, he cannot be at a loss. Therefore the room where company meet who practise this art, is full of all things, ready at hand, requisite to furnish matter for this kind of artificial converse.

Another great advantage proposed by this invention was, that it would serve as a universal language, to be understood in all civilised nations, whose goods and utensils are generally of the same kind, or nearly resembling, so that their uses might easily be comprehended. And thus ambassadors would be qualified to treat with foreign princes, or ministers of state, to whose tongues they were utter strangers.

I was at the mathematical school, where the master taught his pupils after a method scarce imaginable to us in Europe. The proposition, and demonstration, were fairly written on a thin wafer, with ink composed of a cephalic tincture. This, the student was to swallow upon a fasting stomach, and for three days following, eat nothing but bread and water. As the wafer digested, the tincture mounted to his brain, bearing the proposition along with it. But the success has not hitherto been answerable, partly by some error in the *quantum* or composition, and partly by the perverseness of lads, to whom this bolus is so nauseous, that they generally steal aside, and discharge it upwards, before it can operate; neither have they been yet persuaded to use so long an abstinence, as the prescription requires.

CHAPTER VI

A further account of the academy. The author proposes some improvements, which are honourably received.

In the school of political projectors, I was but ill entertained; the professors appearing, in my judgment, wholly out of their senses, which is a scene that never fails to make me melancholy. These unhappy people were proposing schemes for persuading monarchs to choose favourites upon the score of their wisdom, capacity, and virtue; of teaching ministers to consult the public good; of rewarding merit, great abilities, eminent services; of instructing princes to know their true interest, by placing it on the same foundation with that of their people; of choosing for employments persons qualified to exercise them, with many other wild, impossible chimeras, that never entered before into the heart of man to conceive; and confirmed in me the old observation, that there is nothing so extravagant and irrational, which some philosophers have not maintained for truth.

But, however, I shall so far do justice to this part of the Academy, as to acknowledge that all of them were not so visionary. There was a most ingenious doctor, who seemed to be perfectly versed in the whole nature and system of government. This illustrious person had very usefully employed his studies, in finding out effectual remedies for all diseases and corruptions to which the several kinds of public administration are subject, by the vices or infirmities of those who govern, as well as by the licentiousness of those who are to obey.

For instance: whereas all writers and reasoners have agreed, that there is a strict universal resemblance between the natural and the political body; can there be any thing more evident, than that the health of both must be preserved, and the diseases cured, by the same prescriptions? It is allowed, that senates and great councils are often troubled with redundant, ebullient, and other peccant humours; with many diseases of the head, and more of the heart; with strong convulsions, with grievous contractions of the nerves and sinews in both hands, but especially the right; with spleen, flatus, vertigos, and deliriums; with scrofulous tumours, full of fetid purulent matter; with sour frothy ructations: with canine appetites, and crudeness of digestion, besides many others, needless to mention.

This doctor therefore proposed, that upon the meeting of the senate, certain physicians should attend it the three first days of their sitting, and at the close of each day's debate feel the pulses of every senator; after which, having maturely considered and consulted upon the nature of the several maladies, and the methods of cure, they should on the fourth day return to the senate house, attended by their apothecaries stored with proper medicines; and before the members sat, administer to each of them lenitives, aperitives, abstersives, corrosives, restringents, palliatives, laxatives, cephalalgics, icterics, apophlegmatics, acoustics, as their several cases required; and, according as these medicines should operate, repeat, alter, or omit them, at the next meeting.

This project could not be of any great expense to the public; and might in my poor opinion, be of much use for the despatch of business, in those countries where senates have any share in the legislative power; beget unanimity, shorten debates, open a few mouths which are now closed, and close many more which are now open; curb the petulancy of the young, and correct the positiveness of the old; rouse the stupid, and damp the pert.

Again: because it is a general complaint, that the favourites of princes are troubled with short and weak memories; the same doctor proposed, that whoever attended a first minister, after having told his business, with the utmost brevity and in the plainest words, should, at his departure, give the said minister a tweak by the nose, or a kick in the belly, or tread on his corns, or lug him thrice by both ears, or run a pin into his breech; or pinch his arm black and blue, to prevent forgetfulness; and at every levee day, repeat the same operation, till the business were done, or absolutely refused.

He likewise directed, that every senator in the great council of a nation, after he had delivered his opinion, and argued in the defence of it, should be obliged to give his vote directly contrary; because if that were done, the result would infallibly terminate in the good of the public.

When parties in a state are violent, he offered a wonderful contrivance to reconcile them. The method is this: You take a hundred leaders of each party; you dispose them into couples of such whose heads are nearest of a size; then let two nice operators saw off the occiput of each couple at the same time, in such a manner that the brain may be equally divided. Let the occiputs, thus cut off, be interchanged, applying each to the head of his opposite party-man. It seems indeed to be a work that requires some exactness, but the professor assured us, that if it were dexterously performed, the cure would be infallible.

For he argued thus: that the two half brains being left to debate the matter between themselves within the space of one skull, would soon come to a good understanding, and produce that moderation, as well as regularity of thinking, so much to be wished for in the heads of those, who imagine they come into the world only to watch and govern its motion: and as to the difference of brains, in quantity or quality, among those who are directors in faction, the doctor assured us, from his own knowledge, that it was a perfect trifle.

I heard a very warm debate between two professors, about the most commodious and effectual ways and means of raising money, without grieving the subject. The first affirmed, the justest method would be, to lay a certain tax upon vices and folly; and the sum fixed upon every man to be rated, after the fairest manner, by a jury of his neighbours. The second was of an opinion directly contrary; to tax those qualities of body and mind, for which men chiefly value themselves; the rate to be more or less, according to the degrees of excelling; the decision whereof should be left entirely to their own breast.

The highest tax was upon men who are the greatest favourites of the other sex, and the assessments, according to the number and nature of the favours they have received; for which, they are allowed to be their own vouchers. Wit, valour, and politeness, were likewise proposed to be largely taxed, and collected in the same manner, by every person's giving his own word for the quantum of what he possessed. But as to honour, justice, wisdom, and learning, they should not be taxed at all; because they are qualifications of so singular a kind, that no man will either allow them in his neighbour or value them in himself.

The women were proposed to be taxed according to their beauty and skill in dressing, wherein they had the same privilege with the men, to be determined by their own judgment. But constancy, chastity, good sense, and good nature, were not rated, because they would not bear the charge of collecting.

To keep senators in the interest of the crown, it was proposed that the members should raffle for employment; every man first taking an oath, and giving security, that he would vote for the court, whether he won or not; after which, the losers had, in their turn, the liberty of raffling upon the next vacancy. Thus, hope and expectation would be kept alive; none would complain of broken promises, but impute their disappointments wholly to fortune, whose shoulders are broader and stronger than those of a ministry.

Another professor showed me a large paper of instructions for discovering plots and conspiracies against the government. He advised great statesmen to examine into the diet of all suspected persons; their times of eating; upon which side they lay in bed; with which hand they wipe their posteriors; take a strict view of their excrements, and, from the colour, the odour, the taste, the consistence, the crudeness or maturity of digestion, form a judgment of their thoughts and designs; because men are never so serious, thoughtful, and intent, as when they are at stool, which he found by frequent experiment; for, in such conjunctures, when he used, merely as a trial, to consider which was the best way of murdering the king, his ordure would have a tincture of green; but quite different, when he thought only of raising an insurrection, or burning the metropolis.

The whole discourse was written with great acuteness, containing many observations, both curious and useful for politicians; but, as I conceived, not altogether complete. This I ventured to tell the author, and offered, if he pleased, to supply him with some additions. He received my proposition with more compliance than is usual among writers, especially those of the projecting species, professing he would be glad to receive further information.

I told him, that in the kingdom of Tribnia,[3] by the natives called Langdon, where I had sojourned some time in my travels, the bulk of the people consist in a manner wholly of discoverers, witnesses, informers, accusers, prosecutors, evidences, swearers, together with their several subservient and subaltern instruments, all under the colours, the conduct, and the pay of ministers of state, and their deputies. The plots, in that kingdom, are usually the workmanship of those persons who desire to raise their own characters of profound politicians; to restore new vigour to a crazy administration; to stifle or divert general discontents; to fill their coffers with forfeitures; and raise, or sink the opinion of public credit, as either shall best answer their private advantage.

It is first agreed and settled among them, what suspected persons shall be accused of a plot; then, effectual care is taken to secure all their letters and papers, and put the owners in chains. These papers are delivered to a set of artists, very dexterous in finding out the mysterious meanings of words, syllables, and letters: for instance, they can discover a close stool, to signify a privy council; a flock of geese, a senate; a lame dog, an invader; the plague, a standing army; a buzzard, a prime minister; the gout, a high priest; a gibbet, a secretary of state; a chamber pot, a committee of grandees; a sieve, a court lady; a broom, a revolution; a mouse-trap, an employment; a bottomless pit, a treasury; a sink, a court; a cap and bells, a favourite; a broken reed, a court of justice; an empty tun, a general; a running sore, the administration.[5]

Where this method fails, they have two others more effectual, which the learned among them call acrostics and anagrams. First, they can decipher all initial letters into political meanings. Thus *N*, shall signify a plot; *B*, a regiment of horse; *L*, a fleet at sea; or, secondly, by transposing the letters of the alphabet in any suspected paper, they can lay open the deepest designs of a discontented party. So, for example, if I should say, in a letter to a friend, 'Our brother Tom has just got the piles,' a skilful decipherer would discover, that the same letters which compose that sentence, may be analysed into the following words: Resist, a plot is brought home, the tour. And this is the anagrammatic method.

The professor made me great acknowledgments for communicating these observations, and promised to make honourable mention of me in his treatise.

I saw nothing in this country that could invite me to a longer continuance, and began to think of returning home to England.

CHAPTER VII

The author leaves Lagado: arrives at Maldonada. No ship ready. He takes a short voyage to Glubbdubdrib. His reception by the governor.

The continent, of which this kingdom is apart, extends itself, as I have reason to believe, eastward, to that unknown tract of America westward of California; and north, to the Pacific Ocean, which is not above a hundred and fifty miles from Lagado; where there is a good port, and much commerce with the great island of Luggnagg, situated to the north-west about 29 degrees north latitude, and 140 longitude. This island of Luggnagg stands south-eastward of Japan, about a hundred leagues distant. There is a strict alliance between the Japanese emperor and the king of Luggnagg; which affords frequent opportunities of sailing from one island to the other. I determined therefore to direct my course this way, in order to my return to Europe. I hired two mules, with a guide, to show me the way, and carry my small baggage. I took leave of my noble protector, who had shown me so much favour, and made me a generous present at my departure.

My journey was without any accident or adventure worth relating. When I arrived at the port of Maldonada (for so it is called) there was no ship in the harbour bound for Luggnagg, nor likely to be in some time. The town is about as large as Portsmouth. I soon fell into some acquaintance, and was very hospitably received. A gentleman of distinction said to me, that since the ships bound for Luggnagg could not be ready in less than a month, it might be no disagreeable amusement for me to take a trip to the little island of Glubbdubdrib, about five leagues off to the south-west. He offered himself and a friend to accompany me, and that I should be provided with a small convenient bark for the voyage.

Glubbdubdrib, as nearly as I can interpret the word, signifies the island of sorcerers or magicians. It is about one third as large as the Isle of Wight, and extremely fruitful: it is governed by the head of a certain tribe, who are all magicians. This tribe marries only among each other, and the eldest in succession is prince or governor. He has a noble palace, and a park of about three thousand acres, surrounded by a wall of hewn stone twenty feet high. In this park are several small enclosures for cattle, corn, and gardening.

The governor and his family are served and attended by domestics of a kind somewhat unusual. By his skill in necromancy he has a power of calling whom he pleases from the dead, and commanding their service for twenty-four hours, but no longer; nor can he call the same persons up again in less than three months, except upon very extraordinary occasions.

When we arrived at the island, which was about eleven in the morning, one of the gentlemen who accompanied me went to the governor, and desired admittance for a stranger, who came on purpose to have the honour of attending on his highness. This was immediately granted, and we all three entered the gate of the palace between two rows of guards, armed and dressed after a very antic manner, and with something in their countenances that made my flesh creep with a horror I cannot express. We passed through several apartments, between servants of the same sort, ranked on each side as before, till we came to the chamber of presence; where, after three profound obeisances, and a few general questions, we were permitted to sit on three stools, near the lowest step of his highness's throne.

He understood the language of Balnibarbi, although it was

different from that of this island. He desired me to give him some account of my travels; and, to let me see that I should be treated without ceremony, he dismissed all his attendants with a turn of his finger; at which, to my great astonishment, they vanished in an instant, like visions in a dream when we awake on a sudden. I could not recover myself in some time, till the governor assured me, that I should receive no hurt: and observing my two companions to be under no concern, who had been often entertained in the same manner, I began to take courage, and related to his highness a short history of my several adventures; yet not without some hesitation, and frequently looking behind me to the place where I had seen those domestic spectres.

I had the honour to dine with the governor, where a new set of ghosts served up the meat, and waited at table. I now observed myself to be less terrified than I had been in the morning. I stayed till sunset, but humbly desired his highness to excuse me for not accepting his invitation of lodging in the palace. My two friends and I lay at a private house in the town adjoining, which is the capital of this little island; and the next morning we returned to pay our duty to the governor, as he was pleased to command us.

After this manner we continued in the island for ten days, most part of every day with the governor, and at night in our lodging. I soon grew so familiarized to the sight of spirits, that after the third or fourth time they gave me no emotion at all: or, if I had any apprehensions left, my curiosity prevailed over them. For his highness the governor ordered me to call up whatever persons I would choose to name, and in whatever numbers, among all the dead from the beginning of the world to the present time, and command them to answer any questions I should think fit to ask; with this condition, that my questions must be confined within the compass of the times they lived in. And one thing I might depend upon, that they would certainly tell me the truth, for lying was a talent of no use in the lower world.

I made my humble acknowledgments to his highness for so great a favour. We were in a chamber, from whence there was a fair prospect into the park. And because my first inclination was to be entertained with scenes of pomp and magnificence, I desired to see Alexander the Great at the head of his army, just after the battle of Arbela: which, upon a motion of the governor's finger, immediately appeared in a large field, under the window where we stood. Alexander was called up into the room: it was with great difficulty that I understood his Greek, and had but little of my own. He assured me upon his honour that he was not poisoned, but died of a bad fever by excessive drinking.

Next, I saw Hannibal passing the Alps, who told me he had not a drop of vinegar in his camp.

I saw Caesar and Pompey at the head of their troops, just ready to engage. I saw the former, in his last great triumph. I desired that the senate of Rome might appear before me, in one large chamber, and an assembly of somewhat a later age in counterview, in another. The first seemed to be an assembly of heroes and demigods; the other, a knot of pedlars, pick-pockets, highwayman, and bullies.

The governor, at my request, gave the sign for Caesar and Brutus to advance towards us. I was struck with a profound veneration at the sight of Brutus, and could easily discover the most consummate virtue, the greatest intrepidity and firmness of mind, the truest love of his country, and general benevolence for mankind, in every lineament of his countenance. I observed, with much pleasure, that these two persons were in good intelligence with each other; and Caesar freely confessed to me, that the greatest actions of his own life were not equal, by many degrees, to the glory of taking it away. I had the honour to have much conversation with Brutus, and was told that his ancestor Junius, Socrates, Epaminondas, Cato the younger, Sir Thomas More, and himself were perpetually together: a sextum-virate, to which all the ages of the world cannot add a seventh.

It would be tedious to trouble the reader with relating what vast numbers of illustrious persons were called up to gratify that insatiable desire I had to see the world in every period of antiquity placed before me. I chiefly fed mine eyes with beholding the destroyers of tyrants and usurpers, and the restorers of liberty to oppressed and injured nations. But it is impossible to express the satisfaction I received in my own mind, after such a manner as to make it a suitable entertainment to the reader.

CHAPTER VIII

A further account of Glubbdubdrib. Ancient and modern history corrected.

Having a desire to see those ancients who were most renowned for wit and learning, I set apart one day on purpose. I proposed that Homer and Aristotle might appear at the head of all their commentators; but these were so numerous, that some hundreds were forced to attend in the court, and outward rooms of the palace. I knew, and could distinguish those two heroes, at first sight, not only from the crowd, but from each other. Homer was the taller and comelier person of the two, walked very erect for one of his age, and his eyes were the most quick and piercing I ever beheld. Aristotle stooped much, and made use of a staff. His visage was meagre, his hair lank and thin, and his voice hollow.

I soon discovered that both of them were perfect strangers to the rest of the company, and had never seen or heard of them before; and I had a whisper from a ghost who shall be nameless, that these commentators always kept in the most distant quarters from their principals, in the lower world, through a consciousness of shame and guilt, because they had so horribly misrepresented the meaning of those authors to posterity.

I introduced Didymus and Eustathius to Homer, and prevailed on him to treat them better than perhaps they deserved, for he soon found they wanted a genius to enter into the spirit of a poet. But Aristotle was out of all patience with the account I gave him of Scotus and Ramus, as I presented them to him; and he asked them, whether the rest of the tribe were as great dunces as themselves.

I then desired the governor to call up Descartes and Gassendi, with whom I prevailed to explain their systems to Aristotle. This great philosopher freely acknowledged his own mistakes in natural philosophy, because he proceeded in many things upon conjecture, as all men must do; and he found that Gassendi, who had made the doctrine of Epicurus as palatable as he could, and the vortices of Descartes, were equally to be exploded. He predicted the same fate to *attraction*, whereof the present learned are such zealous asserters. He said, that new systems of nature were but new fashions, which would vary in every age; and even those, who pretend to demonstrate them from mathematical principles, would flourish but a short period of time, and be out of vogue when that was determined.

I spent five days in conversing with many others of the ancient learned. I saw most of the first Roman emperors. I prevailed on the governor to call up Heliogabalus's cooks to dress us a dinner, but they could not show us much of their skill, for want of materials. A helot of Agesilaus made us a dish of Spartan broth, but I was not able to get down a second spoonful.

The two gentlemen, who conducted me to the island, were pressed by their private affairs to return in three days, which I employed in seeing some of the modern dead, who had made the greatest figure, for two or three hundred years past, in our own and other countries of Europe; and having been always a great admirer of old illustrious families, I desired the governor would call up a dozen or two of kings, with their ancestors in order for eight or nine generations. But my disappointment was grievous and unexpected. For, instead of a long train with royal diadems, I saw in one family two fiddlers, three spruce courtiers, and an Italian prelate. In another, a barber, an abbot, and two cardinals. I have too great a veneration for crowned heads, to dwell any longer on so nice a subject. But as to counts, marquises, dukes, earls, and the like, I was not so scrupulous.

And I confess, it was not without some pleasure, that I found myself able to trace the particular features, by which certain families are distinguished, up to their originals. I could plainly discover whence one family derives a long chin; why a second has abounded with knaves for two generations, and fools for two more; why a third happened to be crack-brained, and a fourth to be sharpers; whence it came, what Polydore Virgil says of a certain great house, *Nec vir fortis, nec foemina casta*; how cruelty, falsehood, and cowardice, grew to be characteristics by which certain families are distinguished as much as by their coats of arms.

I was chiefly disgusted with modern history. For having strictly examined all the persons of greatest name in the courts of princes, for a hundred years past, I found how the world had been misled by prostitute writers, to ascribe the greatest exploits in war, to cowards; the wisest counsel, to fools; sincerity, to flatterers; Roman virtue, to betrayers of their country; piety, to atheists; chastity, to sodomites; truth, to informers: how many innocent and excellent persons had been condemned to death or banishment by the practising of great ministers upon the corruption of judges, and the malice of factions: how many villains had been exalted to the highest places of trust, power, dignity, and profit: how great a share in the motions and events of courts, councils, and senates might be challenged by bawds, whores, pimps, parasites, and buffoons. How low an opinion I had of human wisdom and integrity, when I was truly informed of the springs and motives of great enterprises and revolutions in the world, and of the contemptible accidents to which they owed their success.

Here I discovered the roguery and ignorance of those who pretend to write anecdotes, or secret history; who send so many kings to their graves with a cup of poison; will repeat the discourse between a prince and chief minister, where no witness was by; unlock the thoughts and cabinets of ambassadors and secretaries of state; and have the perpetual misfortune to be mistaken.

Here I discovered the true causes of many great events that have surprised the world; how a whore can govern the back-stairs, the back-stairs a council, and the council a senate. A general confessed, in my presence, that he got a victory purely by the force of cowardice and ill conduct; and an admiral, that, for want of proper intelligence, he beat the enemy, to whom he intended to betray the fleet. Three kings protested to me, that in their whole reigns they never did once prefer any person of merit, unless by mistake, or treachery of some minister in whom they confided; neither would they do it if they were to live again: and they showed, with great strength of reason, that the royal throne could not be supported without corruption, because that positive, confident, restiff temper, which virtue infused into a man, was a perpetual clog to public business.

I had the curiosity to inquire in a particular manner, by what methods great numbers had procured to themselves high titles of honour, and prodigious estates; and I confined my inquiry to a very modern period: however, without grating upon present times, because I would be sure to give no offence even to foreigners (for I hope the reader need not be told, that I do not in the least intend my own country, in what I say upon this occasion,) a great number of persons concerned were called up; and, upon a very slight examination, discovered such a scene of infamy, that I cannot reflect upon it without some seriousness.

Perjury, oppression, subornation, fraud, pandarism, and

the like infirmities, were among the most excusable arts they had to mention; and for these I gave, as it was reasonable, great allowance. But when some confessed they owed their greatness and wealth to sodomy, or incest; others, to the prostituting of their own wives and daughters; others, to the betraying of their country or their prince; some, to poisoning; more to the perverting of justice, in order to destroy the innocent, I hope I may be pardoned, if these discoveries inclined me a little to abate of that profound veneration, which I am naturally apt to pay to persons of high rank, who ought to be treated with the utmost respect due to their sublime dignity, by us their inferiors.

I had often read of some great services done to princes and states, and desired to see the persons by whom those services were performed. Upon inquiry I was told, that their names were to be found on no record, except a few of them, whom history has represented as the vilest of rogues and traitors. As to the rest, I had never once heard of them. They all appeared with dejected looks, and in the meanest habit; most of them telling me, they died in poverty and disgrace, and the rest on a scaffold or a gibbet.

Among others, there was one person, whose case appeared a little singular. He had a youth about eighteen years old standing by his side. He told me, he had for many years been commander of a ship; and in the sea fight at Actium had the good fortune to break through the enemy's great line of battle, sink three of their capital ships, and take a fourth, which was the sole cause of Antony's flight, and of the victory that ensued; that the youth standing by him, his only son, was killed in the action.

He added, that upon the confidence of some merit, the war being at an end, he went to Rome, and solicited at the court of Augustus to be preferred to a greater ship, whose commander had been killed; but, without any regard to his pretensions, it was given to a boy who had never seen the sea, the son of Libertina, who waited on one of the emperor's mistresses. Returning back to his own vessel, he was charged with neglect of duty, and the ship given to a favourite page of Publicola, the vice-admiral; whereupon he retired to a poor farm at a great distance from Rome, and there ended his life. I was so curious to know the truth of this story, that I desired Agrippa might be called, who was admiral in that fight. He appeared, and confirmed the whole account: but with much more advantage to the captain, whose modesty had extenuated or concealed a great part of his merit.

I was surprised to find corruption grown so high and so quick in that empire, by the force of luxury so lately introduced; which made me less wonder at many parallel cases in other countries, where vices of all kinds have reigned so much longer, and where the whole praise, as well as pillage, has been engrossed by the chief commander, who perhaps had the least title to either.

As every person called up made exactly the same appearance he had done in the world, it gave me melancholy reflections to observe how much the race of human kind was degenerated among us within these hundred years past.

I descended so low, as to desire some English yeoman of the old stamp might be summoned to appear; once so famous for the simplicity of their manners, diet, and dress; for justice in their dealings; for their true spirit of liberty; for their valour, and love of their country. Neither could I be wholly unmoved, after comparing the living with the dead, when I considered how all these pure native virtues were prostituted for a piece of money by their grand-children; who, in selling their votes and managing at elections, have acquired every vice and corruption that can possibly be learned in a court.

CHAPTER IX

The author returns to Maldonada. Sails to the kingdom of Luggnagg. The author confined. He is sent for to court. The manner of his admittance. The king's great lenity to his subjects.

The day of our departure being come, I took leave of his highness, the Governor of Glubbdubdrib, and returned with my two companions to Maldonada, where, after a fortnight's waiting, a ship was ready to sail for Luggnagg. The two gentlemen, and some others, were so generous and kind as to furnish me with provisions, and see me on board. I was a month in this voyage. We had one violent storm, and were under a necessity of steering westward to get into the trade wind, which holds for above sixty leagues. On the 21st of April, 1708, we sailed into the river of Clumegnig, which is a seaport town, at the south-east point of Luggnagg. We cast anchor within a league of the town, and made a signal for a pilot. Two of them came on board in less than half an hour, by whom we were guided between certain shoals and rocks, which are very dangerous in the passage, to a large basin, where a fleet may ride in safety within a cable's length of the town-wall.

Some of our sailors, whether out of treachery or inadvertence, had informed the pilots that I was a stranger, and great traveller; whereof these gave notice to a custom-house officer, by whom I was examined very strictly upon my landing. This officer spoke to me in the language of Balnibarbi, which, by the force of much commerce, is generally understood in that town, especially by seamen and those employed in the customs. I gave him a short account of some particulars, and made my story as plausible and consistent as I could; but I thought it necessary to disguise my country, and call myself a Hollander; because my intentions were for Japan, and I knew the Dutch were the only Europeans permitted to enter into that kingdom.

I therefore told the officer, that having been shipwrecked on the coast of Balnibarbi, and cast on a rock, I was received up into Laputa, or the flying island (of which he had often heard), and was now endeavouring to get to Japan, whence I might find a convenience of returning to my own country. The officer said, I must be confined till he could receive orders from court, for which he would write immediately, and hoped to receive an answer in a fortnight. I was carried to a convenient lodging with a sentry placed at the door; however, I had the liberty of a large garden, and was treated with humanity enough, being maintained all the time at the king's charge. I was invited by several persons, chiefly out of curiosity, because it was reported that I came from countries very remote, of which they had never heard.

I hired a young man, who came in the same ship, to be an interpreter; he was a native of Luggnagg, but had lived some years at Maldonada, and was a perfect master of both languages. By his assistance, I was able to hold a conversation with those who came to visit me; but this consisted only of their questions, and my answers.

The despatch came from court about the time we expected. It contained a warrant for conducting me and my retinue to Traldragdubh, Trildrogdrib for it is pronounced both ways as near as I can remember, by a party of ten horse. All my retinue was that poor lad for an interpreter, whom I persuaded into my service, and, at my humble request, we had each of us a mule to ride on. A messenger was despatched half a day's journey before us, to give the king notice of my approach, and to desire, that his Majesty would please to appoint a day and hour, when it would by his gracious pleasure that I might have the honour to lick the dust before his footstool.

This is the court style, and I found it to be more than matter of form: for, upon my admittance two days after my arrival, I was commanded to crawl upon my belly, and lick the floor as I advanced; but, on account of my being a stranger, care was taken to have it made so clean, that the dust was not offensive. However, this was a peculiar grace, not allowed to any but persons of the highest rank, when they desire an admittance. Nay, sometimes the floor is strewed with dust on purpose, when the person to be admitted happens to have powerful enemies at court; and I have seen a great lord with his mouth so crammed, that when he had crept to the proper distance from the throne; he was not able to speak a word. Neither is there any remedy; because it is capital for those, who receive an audience to spit or wipe their mouths in his Majesty's presence.

There is indeed another custom, which I cannot altogether approve of: when the king has a mind to put any of his nobles to death in a gentle indulgent manner, he commands the floor to be strewed with a certain brown powder of a deadly composition, which being licked up, infallibly kills him in twenty-four hours. But in justice to this prince's great clemency, and the care he has of his subjects' lives (wherein it were much to be wished that the Monarchs of Europe would imitate him), it must be mentioned for his honour, that strict orders are given to have the infected parts of the floor well washed after every such execution, which, if his domestics neglect, they are in danger of incurring his royal displeasure.

I myself heard him give directions, that one of his pages should be whipped, whose turn it was to give notice about washing the floor after an execution, but maliciously had omitted it; by which neglect a young lord of great hopes, coming to an audience, was unfortunately poisoned, although the king at that time had no design against his life. But this good prince was so gracious as to forgive the poor page his whipping, upon promise that he would do so no more, without special orders.

To return from this digression. When I had crept within four yards of the throne, I raised myself gently upon my knees, and then striking my forehead seven times against the ground, I pronounced the following words, as they had been taught me the night before, *Ickpling gloffthrobb squut serumm blhiop mlashnalt zwin tnodbalkuffh slhiophad gurdlubh asht.* This is the compliment, established by the laws of the land, for all persons admitted to the king's presence. It may be rendered into English thus: May your celestial Majesty outlive the sun, eleven moons and a half.

To this the king returned some answer, which, although I could not understand, yet I replied as I had been directed: *Fluft drin yalerick dwuldom prastrad mirpush*, which properly signifies, My tongue is in the mouth of my friend; and by this expression was meant, that I desired leave to bring my interpreter; whereupon the young man already mentioned was accordingly introduced, by whose intervention I answered as many questions as his Majesty could put in above an hour. I spoke in the Balnibarbian tongue, and my interpreter delivered my meaning in that of Luggnagg.

The king was much delighted with my company, and ordered his *bliffmarklub*, or high-chamberlain, to appoint a lodging in the court for me and my interpreter; with a daily allowance for my table, and a large purse of gold for my common expenses.

I staid three months in this country, out of perfect obedience to his Majesty; who was pleased highly to favour me, and made me very honourable offers. But I thought it more consistent with prudence and justice to pass the remainder of my days with my wife and family.

CHAPTER X

The Luggnaggians commended. A particular description of the Struldbrugs, with many conversations between the author and some eminent persons upon that subject.

The Luggnaggians are a polite and generous people; and although they are not without some share of that pride which is peculiar to all Eastern countries, yet they show themselves courteous to strangers, especially such who are countenanced by the court. I had many acquaintance, and among persons of the best fashion; and being always attended by my interpreter, the conversation we had was not disagreeable.

One day, in much good company, I was asked by a person of quality, whether I had seen any of their struldbrugs, or immortals? I said, I had not; and desired he would explain to me what he meant by such an appellation, applied to a mortal creature. He told me that sometimes, though very rarely, a child happened to be born in a family, with a red circular spot in the forehead, directly over the left eyebrow, which was an infallible mark that it should never die. The spot, as he described it, was about the compass of a silver threepence, but in the course of time grew larger, and changed its colour; for at twelve years old it became green, so continued till five and twenty, then turned to a deep blue: at five and forty it grew coal black, and as large as an English shilling; but never admitted any further alteration.

He said, these births were so rare, that he did not believe there could be above eleven hundred struldbrugs, of both sexes, in the whole kingdom; of which he computed about fifty in the metropolis, and, among the rest, a young girl born; about three years ago: that these productions were not peculiar to any family, but a mere effect of chance; and the children of the struldbrugs themselves were equally mortal with the rest of the people.

I freely own myself to have been struck with inexpressible delight, upon hearing this account: and the person who gave it me happening to understand the Balnibarbian language, which I spoke very well, I could not forbear breaking out into expressions, perhaps a little too extravagant. I cried out, as in a rapture, Happy nation, where every child hath at least a chance for being immortal! Happy people, who enjoy so many living examples of ancient virtue, and have masters ready to instruct them in the wisdom of all former ages! but happiest, beyond all comparison, are those excellent struldbrugs, who, being born exempt from that universal calamity of human nature, have their minds free and disengaged, without the weight and depression of spirits caused by the continual apprehensions of death!

I discovered my admiration that I had not observed any of these illustrious persons at court; the black spot on the forehead being so remarkable a distinction, that I could not have easily overlooked it: and it was impossible that his Majesty, a most judicious prince, should not provide himself with a good number of such wise and able counsellors. Yet perhaps the virtue of those reverend sages was too strict for the corrupt and libertine manners of a court: and we often find by experience, that young men are too opinionated and volatile to be guided by the sober dictates of their seniors.

However, since the king was pleased to allow me access to his royal person, I was resolved, upon the very first occasion, to deliver my opinion to him on this matter freely and at large, by the help of my interpreter; and whether he would please to take my advice or not, yet in one thing I was determined, that his Majesty having frequently offered me an establishment in this country, I would, with great thankfulness, accept the favour, and pass my life here in the conversation of those superior beings the struldbrugs, if they would please to admit me.

The gentleman to whom I addressed my discourse, because (as I have already observed) he spoke the language of Balnibarbi, said to me, with a sort of a smile which usually arises from pity to the ignorant, that he was glad of any occasion to keep me among them, and desired my permission to explain to the company what I had spoke. He did so, and they talked together for some time in their own language, whereof I understood not a syllable, neither could I observe by their countenances, what impression my discourse had made on them. After a short silence, the same person told me, that his friends and mine (so he thought fit to express himself) were very much pleased with the judicious remarks I had made on the great happiness and advantages of immortal life, and they were desirous to know, in a particular manner, what scheme of living I should have formed to myself, if it had fallen to my lot to have been born a *struldbrug*.

I answered, it was easy to be eloquent on so copious and delightful a subject, especially to me, who had been often apt to amuse myself with visions of what I should do, if I were a king, a general, or a great lord: and upon this very case, I had frequently run over the whole system how I should employ myself, and pass the time, if I were sure to live for ever.

That, if it had been my good fortune to come into the world a *struldbrug*, as soon as I could discover my own happiness, by understanding the difference between life and death, I would first resolve, by all arts and methods, whatsoever, to procure myself riches. In the pursuit of which, by thrift and management, I might reasonably expect, in about two hundred years, to be the wealthiest man in the kingdom. In the second place, I would, from my earliest youth, apply myself to the study of arts and sciences, by which I should arrive in time to excel all others in learning. Lastly, I would carefully record every action and event of consequence, that happened in the public, impartially draw the characters of the several successions of princes and great ministers of state, with my own observations on every point. I would exactly set down the several changes in customs, language, fashions of dress, diet, and diversions. By all which acquirements, I should be a living treasure of knowledge and wisdom, and certainly become the oracle of the nation.

I would never marry after threescore, but live in a hospitable manner, yet still on the saving side. I would entertain myself in forming and directing the minds of hopeful young men, by convincing them, from my own remembrance, experience, and observation, fortified by numerous examples, of the usefulness of virtue in public and private life. But my choice and constant companions should be a set of my own immortal brotherhood; among whom, I would elect a dozen from the most ancient, down to my own contemporaries.

Where any of these wanted fortunes, I would provide them with convenient lodges round my own estate, and have some of them always at my table; only mingling a few of the most valuable among you mortals, whom length of time would harden me to lose with little or no reluctance, and treat your posterity after the same manner; just as a man diverts himself with the annual succession of pinks and tulips in his garden, without regretting the loss of those which withered the preceding year.

These struldbrugs and I would mutually communicate our observations and memorials, through the course of time; remark the several gradations by which corruption steals into the world, and oppose it in every step, by giving perpetual warning and instruction to mankind; which, added to the strong influence of our own example, would probably prevent that continual degeneracy of human nature so justly complained of in all ages.

Add to this, the pleasure of seeing the various revolutions of states and empires; the changes in the lower and upper world; ancient cities in ruins, and obscure villages become the seats of kings; famous rivers lessening into shallow brooks; the ocean leaving one coast dry, and overwhelming another; the discovery of many countries yet unknown; barbarity overrunning the politest nations, and the most barbarous become civilized. I should then see the discovery of the longitude, the perpetual motion, the universal medicine, and many other great inventions, brought to the utmost perfection.

What wonderful discoveries should we make in astronomy, by outliving and confirming our own predictions; by observing the progress and return of comets, with the changes of motion in the sun, moon, and stars.

I enlarged upon many other topics, which the natural desire of endless life, and sublunary happiness, could easily furnish me with. When I had ended, and the sum of my discourse had been interpreted, as before, to the rest of the company, there was a good deal of talk among them in the language of the country, not without some laughter at my expense. At last, the same gentleman who had been my interpreter, said, he was desired by the rest to set me right in a few mistakes, which I had fallen into through the common imbecility of human nature, and upon that allowance was less answerable for them.

This breed of struldbrugs was peculiar to their country, for there were no such people either in Balnibarbi or Japan, where he had the honour to be ambassador from his Majesty, and found the natives in both those kingdoms very hard to believe that the fact was possible: and it appeared from my astonishment when he first mentioned the matter to me, that I received it as a thing wholly new, and scarcely to be credited. That in the two kingdoms above mentioned, where, during his residence, he had conversed very much, he observed long life to be the universal desire and wish of mankind. That whoever had one foot in the grave was sure to hold back the other as strongly as he could. That the oldest had still hopes of living one day longer, and looked on death as the greatest evil, from which nature always prompted him to retreat. Only in this island of Luggnagg the appetite for living was not so eager, from the continual example of the struldbrugs before their eyes.

That the system of living contrived by me, was unreasonable and unjust; because it supposed a perpetuity of youth, health, and vigour, which no man could be so foolish to hope, however extravagant he may be in his wishes. That the question therefore was not, whether a man would choose to be always in the prime of youth, attended with prosperity and health; but how he would pass a perpetual life under all the usual disadvantages which old age brings along with it. For although few men will avow their desires of being immortal, upon such hard conditions, yet in the two kingdoms before mentioned, of Balnibarbi and Japan, he observed that every man desired to put off death some time longer, let it approach ever so late: and he rarely heard of any man who died willingly, except he were incited by the extremity of grief or torture. And he appealed to me, whether in those countries I had travelled, as well as my own, I had not observed the same general disposition.

After this preface, he gave me a particular account of the struldbrugs among them. He said, they commonly acted like mortals till about thirty years old; after which, by degrees, they grew melancholy and dejected, increasing in both till they came to fourscore. This he learned from their own confession: for otherwise, there not being above two or three of that species born in an age, they were too few to form a general observation by. When they came to fourscore years, which is reckoned the extremity of living in this country, they had not only all the follies and infirmities of other old men, but many more which arose from the dreadful prospect of never dying. They were not only opinionative, peevish, covetous, morose, vain, talkative, but incapable of friendship, and dead to all natural affection, which never descended below their grandchildren. Envy and impotent desires are their prevailing passions. But those objects against which their envy seems principally directed, are the vices of the younger sort and the deaths of the old. By reflecting on the former, they find themselves cut off from all possibility of pleasure; and whenever they see a funeral, they lament and repine that others have gone to a harbour of rest to which they themselves never can hope to arrive.

They have no remembrance of anything but what they learned and observed in their youth and middle-age, and even that is very imperfect; and for the truth or particulars of any fact, it is safer to depend on common tradition, than upon their best recollections. The least miserable among them appear to be those who turn to dotage, and entirely lose their memories; these meet with more pity and assistance, because they want many bad qualities which abound in others.

If a struldbrug happen to marry one of his own kind, the marriage is dissolved of course, by the courtesy of the kingdom, as soon as the younger of the two comes to be fourscore; for the law thinks it a reasonable indulgence, that those who are condemned, without any fault of their own, to a perpetual continuance in the world, should not have their misery doubled by the load of a wife.

As soon as they have completed the term of eighty years, they are looked on as dead in law; their heirs immediately succeed to their estates; only a small pittance is reserved for their support; and the poor ones are maintained at the public charge. After that period, they are held incapable of any employment of trust or profit; they cannot purchase lands, or take leases; neither are they allowed to be witnesses in any cause, either civil or criminal, not even for the decision of meers and bounds.

At ninety, they lose their teeth and hair; they have at that age no distinction of taste, but eat and drink whatever they can get, without relish or appetite. The diseases they were subject to still continue, without increasing or diminishing. In talking, they forget the common appellation of things, and the names of persons, even of those who are their nearest friends and relations. For the same reason, they never can amuse themselves with reading, because their memory will not serve to carry them from the beginning of a sentence to the end; and by this defect, they are deprived of the only entertainment whereof they might otherwise be capable.

The language of this country being always upon the flux, the struldbrugs of one age do not understand those of another; neither are they able, after two hundred years, to hold any conversation (farther than by a few general words) with their neighbours the mortals; and thus they lie under the disadvantage of living like foreigners in their own country.

This was the account given me of the struldbrugs, as near as I can remember. I afterwards saw five or six of different ages, the youngest not above two hundred years old, who were brought to me at several times by some of my friends; but although they were told, that I was a great traveller, and had seen all the world, they had not the least curiosity to ask me a question; only desired I would give them *slumskudask*, or a token of remembrance; which is a modest way of begging, to avoid the law, that strictly forbids it, because they are provided for by the public, although indeed with a very scanty allowance.

They are despised and hated by all sorts of people. When one of them is born, it is reckoned ominous, and their birth is recorded very particularly so that you may know their age by consulting the register, which, however, has not been kept above a thousand years past, or at least has been destroyed by time or public disturbances. But the usual way of computing how old they are, is by asking them what kings or great persons they can remember, and then consulting history; for infallibly the last prince in their mind did not begin his reign after they were fourscore years old.

They were the most mortifying sight I ever beheld; and the women more horrible than the men. Besides the usual deformities in extreme old age, they acquired an additional ghastliness, in proportion to their number of years, which is not to be described; and among half a dozen, I soon distinguished which was the eldest, although there was not above a century or two between them.

The reader will easily believe, that from what I had hear and seen, my keen appetite for perpetuity of life was much abated. I grew heartily ashamed of the pleasing visions I had formed; and thought no tyrant could invent a death into which I would not run with pleasure, from such a life. The king heard of all that had passed between me and my friends upon this occasion, and rallied me very pleasantly; wishing I could send a couple of struldbrugs to my own country, to arm our people against the fear of death; but this, it seems, is forbidden by the fundamental laws of the kingdom, or else I should have been well content with the trouble and expense of transporting them.

I could not but agree, that the laws of this kingdom relative to the struldbrugs were founded upon the strongest reasons, and such as any other country would be under the necessity of enacting, in the like circumstances. Otherwise, as avarice is the necessary consequence of old age, those immortals would in time become proprietors of the whole nation, and engross the civil power, which, for want of abilities to manage, must end in the ruin of the public.

CHAPTER XI

The author leaves Luggnagg, and sails to Japan. From thence he returns in a Dutch ship to Amsterdam, and from Amsterdam to England.

I thought this account of the struldbrugs might be some entertainment to the reader, because it seems to be a little out of the common way; at least I do not remember to have met the like in any book of travels that has come to my hands: and if I am deceived, my excuse must be, that it is necessary for travellers who describe the same country, very often to agree in dwelling on the same particulars, without deserving the censure of having borrowed or transcribed from those who wrote before them.

There is indeed a perpetual commerce between this kingdom and the great empire of Japan; and it is very probable, that the Japanese authors may have given some account of the struldbrugs; but my stay in Japan was so short, and I was so entirely a stranger to the language, that I was not qualified to make any inquiries. But I hope the Dutch, upon this notice, will be curious and able enough to supply my defects.

His Majesty having often pressed me to accept some employment in his court, and finding me absolutely determined to return to my native country, was pleased to give me his license to depart; and honoured me with a letter of recommendation, under his own hand, to the Emperor of Japan. He likewise presented me with four hundred and forty-four large pieces of gold (this nation delighting in even numbers), and a red diamond, which I sold in England for eleven hundred pounds.

On the 6th of May, 1709, I took a solemn leave of his Majesty, and all my friends. This prince was so gracious as to order a guard to conduct me to Glanguenstald, which is a royal port to the south-west part of the island. In six days I found a vessel ready to carry me to Japan, and spent fifteen days in the voyage. We landed at a small port-town called Xamoschi, situated on the south-east part of Japan; the town lies on the western point, where there is a narrow strait leading northward into along arm of the sea, upon the north-west part of which, Yedo, the metropolis, stands.

At landing, I showed the custom-house officers my letter from the king of Luggnagg to his imperial Majesty . They knew the seal perfectly well; it was as broad as the palm of my hand. The impression was, *A* king lifting up a lame beggar from the earth. The magistrates of the town, hearing of my letter, received me as a public minister. They provided me with carriages and servants, and bore my charges to Yedo; where I was admitted to an audience, and delivered my letter, which was opened with great ceremony, and explained to the Emperor by an interpreter, who then gave me notice, by his Majesty's order, that I should signify my request, and, whatever it were, it should be granted, for the sake of his royal brother of Luggnagg.

This interpreter was a person employed to transact affairs with the Hollanders. He soon conjectured, by my countenance, that I was a European, and therefore repeated his Majesty's commands in Low Dutch, which he spoke perfectly well. I answered, as I had before determined, that I was a Dutch merchant, shipwrecked in a very remote country, whence I had travelled by sea and land to Luggnagg, and then took shipping for Japan; where I knew my countrymen often traded, and with some of these I hoped to get an opportunity of returning into Europe: I therefore most humbly entreated his royal favour, to give order that I should be conducted in safety to Nangasac. To this I added another petition, that for the sake of my patron the king of Luggnagg, his Majesty would condescend to excuse my performing the ceremony imposed on my countrymen, of trampling upon the crucifix: because I had been thrown into his kingdom by my misfortunes, without any intention of trading.

When this latter petition was interpreted to the Emperor, he seemed a little surprised; and said, he believed I was the first of my countrymen who ever made any scruple in this point; and that he began to doubt, whether I was a real Hollander, or not; but rather suspected I must be a Christian. However, for the reasons I had offered, but chiefly to gratify the king of Luggnagg by an uncommon mark of his favour, he would comply with the singularity of my humour; but the affair must be managed with dexterity, and his officers should be commanded to let me pass, as it were by forgetfulness. For he assured me, that if the secret should be discovered by my countrymen the Dutch, they would cut my throat in the voyage. I returned my thanks, by the interpreter, for so unusual a favour; and some troops being at that time on their march to Nangasac, the commanding officer had orders to convey me safe thither, with particular instructions about the business of the crucifix.

On the 9th day of June, 1709, I arrived at Nangasac, after a very long and troublesome journey. I soon fell into the company of some Dutch sailors belonging to the Amboyna, of Amsterdam, a stout ship of 450 tons. I had lived long in Holland, pursuing my studies at Leyden, and I spoke Dutch well. The seamen soon knew whence I came last: they were curious to inquire into my voyages and course of life. I made up a story as short and probable as I could, but concealed the greatest part. I knew many persons in Holland. I was able to invent names for my parents, whom I pretended to be obscure people in the province of Gelderland. I would have given the captain (one Theodorus Vangrult) what he pleased to ask for my voyage to Holland; but understanding I was a surgeon, he was contented to take half the usual rate, on condition that I would serve him in the way of my calling.

Before we took shipping, I was often asked by some of the crew, whether I had performed the ceremony above mentioned? I evaded the question by general answers; that I had satisfied the Emperor and court in all particulars. However, a malicious rogue of a skipper went to an officer, and pointing to me, told him, I had not yet trampled on the crucifix; but the other, who had received instructions to let me pass, gave the rascal twenty strokes on the shoulders with a bamboo; after which I was no more troubled with such questions.

Nothing happened worth mentioning in this voyage. We sailed with a fair wind to the Cape of Good Hope, where we staid only to take in fresh water. On the 10th of April, 1710, we arrived safe at Amsterdam, having lost only three men by sickness in the voyage, and a fourth, who fell from the foremast into the sea, not far from the coast of Guinea. From Amsterdam I soon after set sail for England, in a small vessel belonging to that city.

On the 16th of April we put in at the Downs. I landed next morning, and saw once more my native country, after an absence of five years and six months complete. I went straight to Redriff, where I arrived the same day at two in the afternoon, and found my wife and family in good health.

PART IV

A Voyage to the Country of the Houyhnhnms

CHAPTER I

The author sets out as captain of a ship. His men conspire against him, confine him a long time to his cabin, and set him on shore in an unknown land. He travels up into the country. The Yahoos, a strange sort of animal, described. The author meets two Houyhnhnms.

I continued at home with my wife and children about five months, in a very happy condition, if I could have learned the lesson of knowing when I was well. I left my poor wife big with child, and accepted an advantageous offer made me to be captain of the Adventurer, a stout merchantman of 350 tons: for I understood navigation well, and being grown weary of a surgeon's employment at sea, which, however, I could exercise upon occasion, I took a skilful young man of that calling, one Robert Purefoy, into my ship.

We set sail from Portsmouth upon the 7th day of September, 1710; on the 14th we met with Captain Pocock, of Bristol, at Teneriffe, who was going to the bay of Campechy to cut logwood. On the 16th, he was parted from us by a storm; I heard since my return, that his ship foundered, and none escaped but one cabin boy. He was an honest man, and a good sailor, but a little too positive in his own opinions, which was the cause of his destruction, as it has been with several others; for if he had followed my advice, he might have been safe at home with his family at this time, as well as myself.

I had several men who died in my ship of calentures, so that I was forced to get recruits out of Barbadoes and the Leeward Islands, where I touched, by the direction of the merchants who employed me; which I had soon too much cause to repent: for I found afterwards, that most of them had been buccaneers. I had fifty hands onboard; and my orders were, that I should trade with the Indians in the South-Sea, and make what discoveries I could. These rogues, whom I had picked up, debauched my other men, and they all formed a conspiracy to seize the ship, and secure me; which they did one morning, rushing into my cabin, and binding me hand and foot, threatening to throw me overboard, if I offered to stir. I told them, I was their prisoner, and would submit. This they made me swear to do, and then they unbound me, only fastening one of my legs with a chain, near my bed, and placed a sentry at my door with his piece charged, who was commanded to shoot me dead if I attempted my liberty.

They sent me own victuals and drink, and took the government of the ship to themselves. Their design was to turn pirates and, plunder the Spaniards, which they could not do till they got more men. But first they resolved to sell the goods the ship, and then go to Madagascar for recruits, several among them having died since my confinement. They sailed many weeks, and traded with the Indians; but I knew not what course they took, being kept a close prisoner in my cabin, and expecting nothing less than to be murdered, as they often threatened me.

Upon the 9th day of May, 1711, one James Welch came down to my cabin, and said, he had orders from the captain to set me ashore. I expostulated with him, but in vain; neither would he so much as tell me who their new captain was. They forced me into the long-boat, letting me put on my best suit of clothes, which were as good as new, and take a small bundle of linen, but no arms, except my hanger; and they were so civil as not to search my pockets, into which I conveyed what money I had, with some other little necessaries.

They rowed about a league, and then set me down on a strand. I desired them to tell me what country it was. They all swore, they knew no more than myself; but said, that the captain (as they called him) was resolved, after they had sold the lading, to get rid of me in the first place where they could discover land. They pushed off immediately, advising me to make haste for fear of being overtaken by the tide, and so bade me farewell.

In this desolate condition I advanced forward, and soon got upon firm ground, where I sat down on a bank to rest myself, and consider what I had best do. When I was a little refreshed, I went up into the country, resolving to deliver myself to the first savages I should meet, and purchase my life from them by some bracelets, glass rings, and other toys, which sailors usually provide themselves with in those voyages, and whereof I had some about me. The land was divided by long rows of trees, not regularly planted, but naturally growing; there was great plenty of grass, and several fields of oats.

I walked very circumspectly, for fear of being surprised, or suddenly shot with an arrow from behind, or on either side. I fell into a beaten road, where I saw many tracts of human feet, and some of cows, but most of horses. At last I beheld several animals in a field, and one or two of the same kind sitting in trees. Their shape was very singular and deformed, which a little discomposed me, so that I lay down behind a thicket to observe them better. Some of them coming forward near the place where I lay, gave me an opportunity of distinctly marking their form.

Their heads and breasts were covered with a thick hair, some frizzled, and others lank; they had beards like goats, and a long ridge of hair down their backs, and the fore parts of their legs and feet; but the rest of their bodies was bare, so that I might see their skins, which were of a brown buff colour.

They had no tails, nor any hair at all on their buttocks, except about the anus, which, I presume, nature had placed there to defend them as they sat on the ground, for this posture they used, as well as lying down, and often stood on their hind feet. They climbed high trees as nimbly as a squirrel, for they had strong extended claws before and behind, terminating in sharp points, and hooked. They would often spring, and bound, and leap, with prodigious agility. The females were not so large as the males; they had long lank hair on their heads, but none on their faces, nor any thing more than a sort of down on the rest of their bodies, except about the anus and pudenda. The dugs hung between their fore feet, and often reached almost to the ground as they walked. The hair of both sexes was of several colours, brown, red, black, and yellow. Upon the whole, I never beheld, in all my travels, so disagreeable an animal, or one against which I naturally conceived so strong an antipathy. So that, thinking I had seen enough, full of contempt and aversion, I got up, and pursued the beaten road, hoping it might direct me to the cabin of some Indian.

I had not got far, when I met one of these creatures full in my way, and coming up directly to me. The ugly monster, when he saw me, distorted several ways, every feature of his visage, and stared, as at an object he had never seen before; then approaching nearer, lifted up his fore-paw, whether out of curiosity or mischief I could not tell; but I drew my hanger, and gave him a good blow with the flat side of it, for I durst not strike with the edge, fearing the inhabitants might be provoked against me, if they should come to know that I had killed or maimed any of their cattle. When the beast felt the smart, he drew back, and roared so loud, that a herd of at least forty came flocking about me from the next field, howling and making odious faces; but I ran to the body of a tree, and leaning my back against it, kept them off by waving my hanger.

In the midst of this distress, I observed them all to run away on a sudden as fast as they could; at which I ventured to leave the tree and pursue the road, wondering what it was that could put them into this fright. But looking on my left hand, I saw a horse walking softly in the field; which my persecutors having sooner discovered, was the cause of their flight. The horse started a little, when he came near me, but soon recovering himself, looked full in my face with manifest tokens of wonder; he viewed my hands and feet, walking round me several times. I would have pursued my journey, but he placed himself directly in the way, yet looking with a very mild aspect, never offering the least violence.

We stood gazing at each other for some time; at last I took the boldness to reach my hand towards his neck with a design to stroke it, using the common style and whistle of jockeys, when they are going to handle a strange horse. But this animal seemed to receive my civilities with disdain, shook his head, and bent his brows, softly raising up his right fore-foot to remove my hand. Then he neighed three or four times, but in so different a cadence, that I almost began to think he was speaking to himself, in some language of his own.

While he and I were thus employed, another horse came up; who applying himself to the first in a very formal manner, they gently struck each other's right hoof before, neighing several times by turns, and varying the sound, which seemed to be almost articulate. They went some paces off, as if it were to confer together, walking side by side, backward and forward, like persons deliberating upon some affair of weight, but often turning their eyes towards me, as it were to watch that I might not escape. I was amazed to see such actions and behaviour in brute beasts; and concluded with myself, that if the inhabitants of this country were endued with a proportionable degree of reason, they must needs be the wisest people upon earth.

This thought gave me so much comfort, that I resolved to go forward, until I could discover some house or village, or meet with any of the natives, leaving the two horses to discourse together as they pleased. But the first, who was a dapple gray, observing me to steal off, neighed after me in so expressive a tone, that I fancied myself to understand what he meant; whereupon I turned back, and came near to him to expect his farther commands: but concealing my fear as much as I could, for I began to be in some pain how this adventure might terminate; and the reader will easily believe I did not much like my present situation.

The two horses came up close to me, looking with great earnestness upon my face and hands. The gray steed rubbed my hat all round with his right fore-hoof, and discomposed it so much that I was forced to adjust it better by taking it off and settling it again; whereat, both he and his companion (who was a brown bay) appeared to be much surprised: the latter felt the lappet of my coat, and finding it to hang loose about me, they both looked with new signs of wonder. He stroked my right hand, seeming to admire the softness and colour; but he squeezed it so hard between his hoof and his pastern, that I was forced to roar; after which they both touched me with all possible tenderness. They were under great perplexity about my shoes and stockings, which they felt very often, neighing to each other, and using various gestures, not unlike those of a philosopher, when he would attempt to solve some new and difficult phenomenon.

Upon the whole, the behaviour of these animals was so orderly and rational, so acute and judicious, that I at last concluded they must needs be magicians, who had thus metamorphosed themselves upon some design, and seeing a stranger in the way, resolved to divert themselves with him; or, perhaps, were really amazed at the sight of a man so very different in habit, feature, and complexion, from those who might probably live in so remote a climate.

Upon the strength of this reasoning, I ventured to address them in the following manner: Gentlemen, if you be conjurers, as I have good cause to believe, you can understand my language; therefore I make bold to let your worships know that I am a poor distressed Englishman, driven by his misfortunes upon your coast; and I entreat one of you to let me ride upon his back, as if he were a real horse, to some house or village where I can be relieved. In return of which favour, I will make you a present of this knife and bracelet (taking them out of my pocket).

The two creatures stood silent while I spoke, seeming to listen with great attention, and when I had ended, they neighed frequently towards each other, as if they were engaged in serious conversation. I plainly observed that their language expressed the passions very well, and the words might, with little pains, be resolved into an alphabet more easily than the Chinese.

I could frequently distinguish the word Yahoo, which was repeated by each of them several times: and although it was impossible for me to conjecture what it meant, yet while the two horses were busy in conversation, I endeavoured to practise this word upon my tongue; and as soon as they were silent, I boldly pronounced Yahoo in a loud voice, imitating at the same time, as near as I could, the neighing of a horse; at which they were both visibly surprised; and the gray repeated the same word twice, as if he meant to teach me the right accent; wherein I spoke after him as well as I could, and found myself perceivably to improve every time, though very far from any degree of perfection. Then the bay tried me with a second word, much harder to be pronounced; but reducing it to the English orthography, may be spelt thus, Houyhnhnm. I did not succeed in this so well as in the former; but after two or three farther trials, I had better fortune; and they both appeared amazed at my capacity.

After some further discourse, which I then conjectured might relate to me, the two friends took their leaves, with the same compliment of striking each other's hoof; and the gray made me signs that I should walk before him; wherein I thought it prudent to comply, till I could find a better director. When I offered to slacken my pace, he would cry *Hhuun Hhuun*: I guessed his meaning, and gave him to understand, as well as I could, that I was weary, and not able to walk faster; upon which he would stand awhile to let me rest.

CHAPTER II

The author conducted by a Houyhnhnm to his house. The house described. The author's reception. The food of the Houyhnhnms. The author in distress for want of meat. Is at last relieved. His manner of feeding in this country.

Having travelled about three miles, we came to a long kind of building, made of timber stuck in the ground, and wattled across; the roof was low and covered with straw. I now began to be a little comforted; and took out some toys, which travellers usually carry for presents to the savage Indians of America, and other parts, in hopes the people of the house would be thereby encouraged to receive me kindly. The horse made me a sign to go in first; it was a large room with a smooth clay floor, and a rack and manger, extending the whole length on one side.

There were three nags and two mares, not eating, but some of them sitting down upon their hams, which I very much wondered at; but wondered more to see the rest employed in domestic business; these seemed but ordinary cattle. However, this confirmed my first opinion, that a people who could so far civilise brute animals, must needs excel in wisdom all the nations of the world. The gray came in just after, and thereby prevented any ill treatment which the others might have given me. He neighed to them several times in a style of authority, and received answers.

Beyond this room there were three others, reaching the length of the house, to which you passed through three doors, opposite to each other, in the manner of a vista.

We went through the second room towards the third. Here the gray walked in first, beckoning me to attend: I waited in the second room, and got ready my presents for the master and mistress of the house; they were two knives, three bracelets of false pearls, a small looking-glass, and a bead necklace. The horse neighed three or four times, and I waited to hear some answers in a human voice, but I heard no other returns than in the same dialect, only one or two a little shriller than his. I began to think that this house must belong to some person of great note among them, because there appeared so much ceremony before I could gain admittance.

But that a man of quality should be served all by horses, was beyond my comprehension. I feared my brain was disturbed by my sufferings and misfortunes. I roused myself, and looked about me in the room where I was left alone: this was furnished like the first, only after a more elegant manner. I rubbed my eyes often, but the same objects still occurred. I pinched my arms and sides to awake myself, hoping I might be in a dream. I then absolutely concluded, that all these appearances could be nothing else but necromancy and magic. But I had no time to pursue these reflections; for the gray horse came to the door, and made me a sign to follow him into the third room where I saw a very comely mare, together with a colt and foal, sitting on their haunches upon mats of straw, not unartfully made, and perfectly neat and clean.

The mare soon after my entrance rose from her mat, and coming up close, after having nicely observed my hands and face, gave me a most contemptuous look; and turning to the horse, I heard the word Yahoo often repeated betwixt them; the meaning of which word I could not then comprehend, although it was the first I had learned to pronounce. But I was soon better informed, to my everlasting mortification; for the horse, beckoning to me with his head, and repeating the

Hhuun, Hhuun, as he did upon the road, which I understood was to attend him, led me out into a kind of court, where was another building, at some distance from the house.

Here we entered, and I saw three of those detestable creatures, which I first met after my landing, feeding upon roots, and the flesh of some animals, which I afterwards found to be that of asses and dogs, and now and then a cow, dead by accident or disease. They were all tied by the neck with strong withes fastened to a beam; they held their food between the claws of their fore feet, and tore it with their teeth.

The master horse ordered a sorrel nag, one of his servants, to untie the largest of these animals, and take him into the yard. The beast and I were brought close together, and by our countenances diligently compared both by master and servant, who thereupon repeated several times the word Yahoo. My horror and astonishment are not to be described, when I observed in this abominable animal, a perfect human figure: the face of it indeed was flat and broad, the nose depressed, the lips large, and the mouth wide; but these differences are common to all savage nations, where the lineaments of the countenance are distorted, by the natives suffering their infants to lie grovelling on the earth, or by carrying them on their backs, nuzzling with their face against the mothers' shoulders. The fore-feet of the Yahoo differed from my hands in nothing else but the length of the nails, the coarseness and brownness of the palms, and the hairiness on the backs. There was the same resemblance between our feet, with the same differences; which I knew very well, though the horses did not, because of my shoes and stockings; the same in every part of our bodies except as to hairiness and colour, which I have already described.

The great difficulty that seemed to stick with the two horses, was to see the rest of my body so very different from that of a

Yahoo, for which I was obliged to my clothes, whereof they had no conception. The sorrel nag offered me a root, which he held (after their manner, as we shall describe in its proper place) between his hoof and pastern; I took it in my hand, and, having smelt it, returned it to him again as civilly as I could. He brought out of the Yahoos' kennel a piece of ass's flesh; but it smelt so offensively that I turned from it with loathing: he then threw it to the Yahoo, by whom it was greedily devoured. He afterwards showed me a wisp of hay, and a fetlock full of oats; but I shook my head, to signify that neither of these were food for me.

Indeed I now apprehended that I must absolutely starve, if I did not get to some of my own species; for as to those filthy Yahoos, although there were few greater lovers of mankind at that time than myself, yet I confess I never saw any sensitive being so detestable on all accounts; and the more I came near them the more hateful they grew, while I stayed in that country. This the master horse observed by my behaviour, and therefore sent the Yahoo back to his kennel. He then put his fore-hoof to his mouth, at which I was much surprised, although he did it with ease, and with a motion that appeared perfectly natural, and made other signs, to know what I would eat; but I could not return him such an answer as he was able to apprehend; and if he had understood me, I did not see how it was possible to contrive any way for finding myself nourishment.

While we were thus engaged, I observed a cow passing by, whereupon I pointed to her, and expressed a desire to go and milk her. This had its effect; for he led me back into the house, and ordered a mare-servant to open a room, where a good store of milk lay in earthen and wooden vessels, after a very orderly and cleanly manner. She gave me a large bowlful, of which I drank very heartily, and found myself well refreshed.

About noon, I saw coming towards the house a kind of vehicle drawn like a sledge by four Yahoos. There was in it an old steed, who seemed to be of quality; he alighted with his hind-feet forward, having by accident got a hurt in his left fore-foot. He came to dine with our horse, who received him with great civility. They dined in the best room, and had oats boiled in milk for the second course, which the old horse ate warm, but the rest cold. Their mangers were placed circular in the middle of the room, and divided into several partitions, round which they sat on their haunches, upon bosses of straw.

In the middle was a large rack, with angles answering to every partition of the manger; so that each horse and mare ate their own hay, and their own mash of oats and milk, with much decency and regularity. The behaviour of the young colt and foal appeared very modest, and that of the master and mistress extremely cheerful and complaisant to their guest. The gray ordered me to stand by him; and much discourse passed between him and his friend concerning me, as I found by the stranger's often looking on me, and the frequent repetition of the word Yahoo.

I happened to wear my gloves, which the master gray observing, seemed perplexed, discovering signs of wonder what I had done to my fore-feet. He put his hoof three or four times to them, as if he would signify, that I should reduce them to their former shape, which I presently did, pulling off both my gloves, and putting them into my pocket. This occasioned farther talk; and I saw the company was pleased with my behaviour, whereof I soon found the good effects. I was ordered to speak the few words I understood; and while they were at dinner, the master taught me the names for oats, milk, fire, water, and some others, which I could readily pronounce after him, having from my youth a great facility in learning languages.

When dinner was done, the master horse took me aside, and by signs and words made me understand the concern he was in that I had nothing to eat. Oats in their tongue are called *hlunnh*. This word I pronounced two or three times; for although I had refused them at first, yet, upon second thoughts, I considered that I could contrive to make of them a kind of bread, which might be sufficient, with milk, to keep me alive, till I could make my escape to some other country, and to creatures of my own species. The horse immediately ordered a white mare servant of his family to bring me a good quantity of oats in a sort of wooden tray. These I heated before the fire, as well as I could, and rubbed them till the husks came off, which I made a shift to winnow from the grain. I ground and beat them between two stones; then took water, and made them into a paste or cake, which I toasted at the fire and eat warm with milk. It was at first a very insipid diet, though common enough in many parts of Europe, but grew tolerable by time; and having been often reduced to hard fare in my life, this was not the first experiment I had made how easily nature is satisfied.

And I cannot but observe, that I never had one hours sickness while I stayed in this island. It is true, I sometimes made a shift to catch a rabbit, or bird, by springs made of Yahoo's hairs; and I often gathered wholesome herbs, which I boiled, and ate as salads with my bread; and now and then, for a rarity, I made a little butter, and drank the whey. I was at first at a great loss for salt, but custom soon reconciled me to the want of it; and I am confident that the frequent use of salt among us is an effect of luxury, and was first introduced only as a provocative to drink, except where it is necessary for preserving flesh in long voyages, or in places remote from great markets; for we observe no animal to be fond of it but man, and as to myself, when I left this country, it was a great while before I could endure the taste of it in anything that I ate.

This is enough to say upon the subject of my diet, wherewith other travellers fill their books, as if the readers were personally concerned whether we fare well or ill. However, it was necessary to mention this matter, lest the world should think it impossible that I could find sustenance for three years in such a country, and among such inhabitants.

When it grew towards evening, the master horse ordered a place for me to lodge in; it was but six yards from the house and separated from the stable of the Yahoos. Here I got some straw, and covering myself with my own clothes, slept very sound. But I was in a short time better accommodated, as the reader shall know hereafter, when I come to treat more particularly about my way of living.

CHAPTER III

The author studies to learn the language. The Houyhnhnm, his master, assists in teaching him. The language described. Several Houyhnhnms of quality come out of curiosity to see the author. He gives his master a short account of his voyage.

My principal endeavour was to learn the language, which my master (for so I shall henceforth call him), and his children, and every servant of his house, were desirous to teach me; for they looked upon it as a prodigy, that a brute animal should discover such marks of a rational creature. I pointed to every thing, and inquired the name of it, which I wrote down in my journal-book when I was alone, and corrected my bad accent by desiring those of the family to pronounce it often. In this employment, a sorrel nag, one of the under-servants, was very ready to assist me.

In speaking, they pronounced through the nose and throat, and their language approaches nearest to the High-Dutch, or German, of any I know in Europe; but is much more graceful and significant. The emperor Charles V. made almost the same observation, when he said that if he were to speak to his horse, it should be in High-Dutch.

The curiosity and impatience of my master were so great, that he spent many hours of his leisure to instruct me. He was convinced (as he afterwards told me) that I must be a Yahoo; but my teachableness, civility, and cleanliness, astonished him; which were qualities altogether opposite to those animals. He was most perplexed about my clothes, reasoning sometimes with himself, whether they were a part of my body: for I never pulled them off till the family were asleep, and got them on before they waked in the morning. My master was eager to learn whence I came; how I acquired those appearances of reason, which I discovered in all my actions; and to know my story from my own mouth, which he hoped he should soon do by the great proficiency I made in learning and pronouncing their words and sentences. To help my memory, I formed all I learned into the English alphabet, and writ the words down, with the translations. This last, after some time, I ventured to do in my master's presence. It cost me much trouble to explain to him what I was doing; for the inhabitants have not the least idea of books or literature.

In about ten weeks time, I was able to understand most of his questions; and in three months, could give him some tolerable answers. He was extremely curious to know from what part of the country I came, and how I was taught to imitate a rational creature; because the Yahoos (whom he saw I exactly resembled in my head, hands, and face, that were only visible), with some appearance of cunning, and the strongest disposition to mischief, were observed to be the most unteachable of all brutes.

I answered that I came over the sea, from a far place, with many others of my own kind, in a great hollow vessel made of the bodies of trees: that my companions forced me to land on this coast, and then left me to shift for myself. It was with some difficulty, and by the help of many signs, that I brought him to understand me. He replied, that I must needs be mistaken, or that I said the thing which was not; for they have no word in their language to express lying or falsehood. He knew it was impossible that there could be a country beyond the sea, or that a parcel of brutes could move a wooden vessel whither they pleased upon water. He was sure no Houyhnhnm alive could make such a vessel, nor would trust Yahoos to manage it.

The word Houyhnhnm, in their tongue, signifies a horse, and, in its etymology, the perfection of nature. I told my master, that I was at a loss for expression, but would improve as fast as I could; and hoped, in a short time, I should be able to tell him wonders. He was pleased to direct his own mare, his colt, and foal, and the servants of the family, to take all opportunities of instructing me; and every day, for two or three hours, he was at the same pains himself. Several horses and mares of quality in the neighbourhood came often to our house, upon the report spread of a wonderful Yahoo, that could speak like a Houyhnhnm, and seemed, in his words and actions, to discover some glimmerings of reason. These delighted to converse with me: they put many questions, and received such answers as I was able to return. By all these advantages I made so great a progress, that, in five months from my arrival I understood whatever was spoken, and could express myself tolerably well.

The Houyhnhnm*s*, who came to visit my master out of a design of seeing and talking with me, could hardly believe me to be a right Yahoo, because my body had a different covering from others of my kind. They were astonished to observe me without the usual hair or skin, except on my head, face, and hands; but I discovered that secret to my master upon an accident which happened about a fortnight before.

I have already told the reader, that every night, when the family were gone to bed, it was my custom to strip, and cover myself with my clothes. It happened, one morning early, that my master sent for me by the sorrel nag, who was his valet. When he came I was fast asleep, my clothes fallen off on one side, and my shirt above my waist. I awaked at the noise he made, and observed him to deliver his message in some disorder; after which he went to my master, and in a great fright gave him a very confused account of what he had seen. This I presently discovered, for, going as soon as I was dressed to pay my attendance upon his honour, he asked me the meaning of what his servant had reported: that I was not the same thing when I slept, as I appeared to be at other times.

I had hitherto concealed the secret of my dress, in order to distinguish myself, as much as possible, from that cursed race of Yahoos; but now I found it in vain to do so any longer. Besides, I considered that my clothes and shoes would soon wear out, which already were in a declining condition, and must be supplied by some contrivance from the hides of Yahoos, or other brutes; whereby the whole secret would be known. I therefore told my master, that in the country whence I came, those of my kind always covered their bodies with the hairs of certain animals prepared by art, as well for decency as to avoid the inclemencies of air, both hot and cold; of which, as to my own person, I would give him immediate conviction, if he pleased to command me. Whereupon I first unbuttoned my coat, and pulled it off. I did the same with my waistcoat. I drew off my shoes, stockings, and breeches.

My master observed the whole performance with great signs of curiosity and admiration. He took up all my clothes in his pastern, one piece after another, and examined them diligently; he then stroked my body very gently, and looked round me several times; after which, he said, it was plain I must be a perfect Yahoo; but that I differed very much from the rest of my species in the softness, whiteness, and smoothness of my skin; my want of hair in several parts of my body; the shape and shortness of my claws behind and before; and my affectation of walking continually on my two hinder feet. He desired to see no more; and gave me leave to put on my clothes again, for I was shuddering with cold.

I expressed my uneasiness at his giving me so often the appellation of Yahoo, an odious animal, for which I had so utter a hatred and contempt: I begged he would forbear applying that word to me, and make the same order in his family and among his friends whom he suffered to see me. I requested likewise, that the secret of my having a false covering to my body, might be known to none but himself, at least as long as my present clothing should last; for as to what the sorrel nag, his valet, had observed, his honour might command him to conceal it.

All this my master very graciously consented to; and thus the secret was kept till my clothes began to wear out, which I was forced to supply by several contrivances that shall hereafter be mentioned. In the meantime, he desired I would go on with my utmost diligence to learn their language, because he was more astonished at my capacity for speech and reason, than at the figure of my body, whether it were covered or not; adding, that he waited with some impatience to hear the wonders which I promised to tell him.

From thenceforward he doubled the pains he had been at to instruct me: he brought me into all company, and made them treat me with civility; because, as he told them, privately, this would put me into good humour, and make me more diverting.

Every day, when I waited on him, beside the trouble he was at in teaching, he would ask me several questions concerning myself, which I answered as well as I could, and by these means he had already received some general ideas, though very imperfect. It would be tedious to relate the several steps by which I advanced to a more regular conversation; but the first account I gave of myself in any order and length was to this purpose:

That I came from a very far country, as I already had attempted to tell him, with about fifty more of my own species;

that we travelled upon the seas in a great hollow vessel made of wood, and larger than his Honour's house. I described the ship to him in the best terms I could, and explained, by the help of my handkerchief displayed, how it was driven forward by the wind. That upon a quarrel among us, I was set on shore on this coast, where I walked forward, without knowing whither, till he delivered me from the persecution of those execrable Yahoos.

He asked me, who made the ship, and how it was possible that the Houyhnhnms of my country would leave it to the management of brutes? My answer was, that I durst proceed no further in my relation, unless he would give me his word and honour that he would not be offended, and then I would tell him the wonders I had so often promised. He agreed; and I went on by assuring him, that the ship was made by creatures like myself; who, in all the countries I had travelled, as well as in my own, were the only governing rational animals; and that upon my arrival hither, I was as much astonished to see the Houyhnhnms act like rational beings, as he, or his friends, could be, in finding some marks of reason in a creature he was pleased to call a Yahoo; to which I owned my resemblance in every part, but could not account for their degenerate and brutal nature.

I said farther, that if good fortune ever restored me to my native country, to relate my travels hither, as I resolved to do, everybody would believe, that I said the thing that was not, that I invented the story out of my own head; and (with all possible respect to himself, his family, and friends, and under his promise of not being offended) our countrymen would hardly think it probable that a Houyhnhnm should be the presiding creature of a nation, and a Yahoo the brute.

CHAPTER IV

The Houyhnhnm's notion of truth and falsehood. The author's discourse disapproved by his master. The author gives a more particular account of himself, and the accidents of his voyage.

My master heard me with great appearances of uneasiness in his countenance; because doubting, or not believing, are so little known in this country, that the inhabitants cannot tell how to behave themselves under such circumstances. And I remember, in frequent discourses with my master concerning the nature of manhood in other parts of the world, having occasion to talk of lying and false representation, it was with much difficulty that he comprehended what I meant, although he had otherwise a most acute judgment.

For he argued thus: that the use of speech was to make us understand one another, and to receive information of facts; now, if any one said the thing which was not, these ends were defeated, because I cannot properly be said to understand him; and I am so far from receiving information, that he leaves me worse than in ignorance; for I am led to believe a thing black, when it is white, and short, when it is long. And these were all the notions he had concerning that faculty of lying, so perfectly well understood, and so universally practised, among human creatures.

To return from this digression. When I asserted that the Yahoos were the only governing animals in my country, which my master said was altogether past his conception, he desired to know, whether we had Houyhnhnm*s* among us, and what was their employment? I told him, we had great numbers; that in summer they grazed in the fields, and in winter were kept in houses with hay and oats, where Yahoo servants were employed to rub their skins smooth, comb their manes, pick their feet, serve them with food, and make their beds.

I understand you well, said my master: it is now very plain, from all you have spoken, that whatever share of reason the Yahoos pretend to, the Houyhnhnm*s* are your masters; I heartily wish our Yahoos would be so tractable.

I begged his Honour would please to excuse me from proceeding any further, because I was very certain that the account he expected from me would be highly displeasing. But he insisted in commanding me to let him know the best and the worst. I told him he should be obeyed.

I owned that the Houyhnhnm*s* among us, whom we called horses, were the most generous and comely animals we had; that they excelled in strength and swiftness; and when they belonged to persons of quality, were employed in travelling, racing, or drawing chariots; they were treated with much kindness and care, till they fell into diseases, or became foundered in the feet; but then they were sold, and used to all kind of drudgery till they died; after which their skins were stripped, and sold for what they were worth, and their bodies left to be devoured by dogs and birds of prey. But the common race of horses had not so good fortune, being kept by farmers and carriers, and other mean people, who put them to greater labour, and fed them worse. I described, as well as I could, our way of riding; the shape and use of a bridle, a saddle, a spur, and a whip; of harness and wheels. I added, that we fastened plates of a certain hard substance, called iron, at the bottom of their feet, to preserve their hoofs from being broken by the stony ways, on which we often travelled.

My master, after some expressions of great indignation, wondered how we dared to venture upon a Houyhnhnm's back; for he was sure, that the weakest servant in his house would be able to shake off the strongest Yahoo; or by lying down and rolling on his back, squeeze the brute to death. I answered that our horses were trained up, from three or four years old, to the several uses we intended them for; that if any of them proved intolerably vicious, they were employed for carriages; that they were severely beaten, while they were young, for any mischievous tricks; that the males, designed for the common use of riding or draught, were generally castrated about two years after their birth, to take down their spirits, and make them more tame and gentle; that they were indeed sensible of rewards and punishments; but his honour would please to consider, that they had not the least tincture of reason, any more than the Yahoos in this country.

It put me to the pains of many circumlocutions, to give my master a right idea of what I spoke; for their language does not abound in variety of words, because their wants and passions are fewer than among us. But it is impossible to express his noble resentment at our savage treatment of the Houyhnhnm race; particularly after I had explained the manner and use of castrating horses among us, to hinder them from propagating their kind, and to render them more servile. He said, if it were possible there could be any country where Yahoos alone were endued with reason, they certainly must be the governing animal; because reason in time will always prevail against brutal strength. But, considering the frame of our bodies, and especially of mine, he thought no creature of equal bulk was so ill-contrived for employing that reason in the common offices of life; whereupon he desired to know whether those among whom I lived resembled me, or the Yahoos of his country.

I assured him, that I was as well shaped as most of my age; but the younger, and the females, were much more soft and tender, and the skins of the latter generally as white as milk.

He said, I differed indeed from other Yahoos, being much more cleanly, and not altogether so deformed; but, in point of real advantage, he thought I differed for the worse: that my nails were of no use either to my fore or hinder feet; as to my fore feet, he could not properly call them by that name, for he never observed me to walk upon them; that they were too soft to bear the ground; that I generally went with them uncovered; neither was the covering I sometimes wore on them of the same shape, or so strong as that on my feet behind: that I could not walk with any security, for if either of my hinder feet slipped, I must inevitably fail.

He then began to find fault with other parts of my body: the flatness of my face, the prominence of my nose, mine eyes placed directly in front, so that I could not look on either side without turning my head: that I was not able to feed myself, without lifting one of my fore-feet to my mouth: and therefore nature had placed those joints to answer that necessity. He knew not what could be the use of those several clefts and divisions in my feet behind; that these were too soft to bear the hardness and sharpness of stones, without a covering made from the skin of some other brute; that my whole body wanted a fence against heat and cold, which I was forced to put on and off every day, with tediousness and trouble.

Lastly, that he observed every animal in this country naturally to abhor the Yahoos, whom the weaker avoided, and the stronger drove from them. So that, supposing us to have the gift of reason, he could not see how it were possible to cure that natural antipathy, which every creature discovered against us; nor consequently how we could tame and render them serviceable. However, he would, as he said, debate the matter no farther, because he was more desirous to know my own story, the country where I was born, and the several actions and events of my life, before I came hither.

I assured him how extremely desirous I was that he should be satisfied on every point; but I doubted much, whether it would be possible for me to explain myself on several subjects, whereof his honour could have no conception; because I saw nothing in his country to which I could resemble them; that, however, I would do my best, and strive to express myself by similitudes, humbly desiring his assistance when I wanted proper words; which he was pleased to promise me.

I said my birth was of honest parents, in an island called England; which was remote from his country, as many days' journey as the strongest of his honour's servants could travel in the annual course of the sun; that I was bred a surgeon, whose trade it is to cure wounds and hurts in the body, gotten by accident or violence; that my country was governed by a female man, whom we called queen; that I left it to get riches, whereby I might maintain myself and family, when I should return; that, in my last voyage, I was commander of the ship, and had about fifty Yahoos under me, many of which died at sea, and I was forced to supply them by others picked out from several nations; that our ship was twice in danger of being sunk, the first time by a great storm, and the second by striking against a rock.

Here my master interposed, by asking me, how I could persuade strangers, out of different countries, to venture with me, after the losses I had sustained, and the hazards I had run? I said, they were fellows of desperate fortunes, forced to fly from the places of their birth on account of their poverty or their crimes. Some were undone by lawsuits; others spent all they had in drinking, whoring, and gaming; others fled for treason; many for murder, theft, poisoning, robbery, perjury, forgery, coining false money, for committing rapes, or sodomy; for flying from their colours, or deserting to the enemy; and most of them had broken prison; none of these durst return to their native countries, for fear of being hanged, or of starving in a jail; and therefore they were under the necessity of seeking a livelihood in other places.

During this discourse, my master was pleased to interrupt me several times. I had made use of many circumlocutions in describing to him the nature of the several crimes for which most of our crew had been forced to fly their country. This labour took up several days' conversation, before he was able to comprehend me. He was wholly at a loss to know what could be the use or necessity of practising those vices. To clear up which, I endeavoured to give some ideas of the desire of power and riches; of the terrible effects of lust, intemperance, malice, and envy.

All this I was forced to define and describe by putting cases and making suppositions. After which, like one whose imagination was struck with something never seen or heard of before, he would lift up his eyes with amazement and indignation. Power, government, war, law, punishment, and a thousand other things, had no terms wherein that language could express them, which made the difficulty almost insuperable, to give my master any conception of what I meant. But being of an excellent understanding, much improved by contemplation and converse, he at last arrived at a competent knowledge of what human nature, in our parts of the world, is capable to perform, and desired I would give him some particular account of that land which we call Europe, but especially of my own country.

CHAPTER V

The author at his master's command, informs him of the state of England. The causes of war among the princes of Europe. The author begins to explain the English constitution.

The reader may please to observe, that the following extract of many conversations I had with my master, contains a summary of the most material points which were discoursed at several times for above two years; his honour often desiring fuller satisfaction, as I farther improved in the Houyhnhnm tongue. I laid before him, as well as I could, the whole state of Europe; I discoursed of trade and manufactures, of arts and sciences; and the answers I gave to all the questions he made, as they arose upon several subjects, were a fund of conversation not to be exhausted.

But I shall here only set down the substance of what passed between us concerning my own country, reducing it in order as well as I can, without any regard to time or other circumstances, while I strictly adhere to truth. My only concern is, that I shall hardly be able to do justice to my master's arguments and expressions, which must needs suffer by my want of capacity, as well as by a translation into our barbarous English.

In obedience, therefore, to his honour's commands, I related to him the Revolution under the Prince of Orange; the long war with France, entered into by the said prince, and renewed by his successor, the present queen, wherein the greatest powers of Christendom were engaged, and which still continued: I computed, at his request, that about a million of

Yahoos might have been killed in the whole progress of it; and perhaps a hundred or more cities taken, and five times as many ships burnt or sunk.

He asked me, what were the usual causes or motives that made one country go to war with another.

I answered they were innumerable; but I should only mention a few of the chief. Sometimes the ambition of princes, who never think they have land or people enough to govern; sometimes the corruption of ministers, who engage their master in a war, in order to stifle or divert the clamour of the subjects against their evil administration. Difference in opinions has cost many millions of lives: for instance, whether flesh be bread, or bread be flesh; whether the juice of a certain berry be blood or wine; whether whistling be a vice or a virtue; whether it be better to kiss a post, or throw it into the fire; what is the best colour for a coat, whether black, white, red, or gray; and whether it should be long or short, narrow or wide, dirty or clean; with many more. Neither are any wars so furious and bloody, or of so long a continuance, as those occasioned by difference in opinion, especially if it be in things indifferent.

Sometimes the quarrel between two princes is to decide which of them shall dispossess a third of his dominions, where neither of them pretend to any right. Sometimes one prince quarrels with another for fear the other should quarrel with him. Sometimes a war is entered upon, because the enemy is too strong; and sometimes, because he is too weak. Sometimes our neighbours want the things which we have, or have the things which we want, and we both fight, till they take ours, or give us theirs. It is a very justifiable cause of a war, to invade a country after the people have been wasted by famine, destroyed by pestilence, or embroiled by factions among themselves.

It is justifiable to enter into war against our nearest ally, when one of his towns lies convenient for us, or a territory of land, that would render our dominions round and complete.

If a prince sends forces into a nation, where the people are poor and ignorant, he may lawfully put half of them to death, and make slaves of the rest, in order to civilize and reduce them from their barbarous way of living. It is a very kingly, honourable, and frequent practice, when one prince desires the assistance of another, to secure him against an invasion, that the assistant, when he has driven out the invader, should seize on the dominions himself, and kill, imprison, or banish, the prince he came to relieve.

Alliance by blood, or marriage, is a frequent cause of war between princes; and the nearer the kindred is, the greater their disposition to quarrel; poor nations are hungry, and rich nations are proud; and pride and hunger will ever be at variance.

For these reasons, the trade of a soldier is held the most honourable of all others; because a soldier is a Yahoo hired to kill, in cold blood, as many of his own species, who have never offended him, as possibly he can.

There is likewise a kind of beggarly princes in Europe, not able to make war by themselves, who hire out their troops to richer nations, for so much a day to each man; of which they keep three-fourths to themselves, and it is the best part of their maintenance: such are those in many northern parts of Europe.

What you have told me, said my master, upon the subject of war, does indeed discover most admirably the effects of that reason you pretend to: however, it is happy that the shame is greater than the danger; and that nature has left you utterly incapable of doing much mischief.

For your mouths lying flat with your faces, you can hardly bite each other to any purpose, unless by consent. Then as to the claws upon your feet before and behind, they are so short and tender, that one of our Yahoos would drive a dozen of yours before him. And therefore, in recounting the numbers of those who have been killed in battle, I cannot but think you have said the thing which is not.

I could not forbear shaking my head, and smiling a little at his ignorance. And being no stranger to the art of war, I gave him a description of cannons, culverins, muskets, carabines, pistols, bullets, powder, swords, bayonets, battles, sieges, retreats, attacks, undermines, countermines, bombardments, sea fights, ships sunk with a thousand men, twenty thousand killed on each side, dying groans, limbs flying in the air, smoke, noise, confusion, trampling to death under horses' feet, flight, pursuit, victory; fields strewed with carcases, left for food to dogs and wolves and birds of prey; plundering, stripping, ravishing, burning, and destroying. And to set forth the valour of my own dear countrymen, I assured him, that I had seen them blow up a hundred enemies at once in a siege, and as many in a ship, and beheld the dead bodies drop down in pieces from the clouds, to the great diversion of the spectators.

I was going on to more particulars, when my master commanded me silence. He said, whoever understood the nature of Yahoos, might easily believe it possible for so vile an animal to be capable of every action I had named, if their strength and cunning equalled their malice. But as my discourse had increased his abhorrence of the whole species, so he found it gave him a disturbance in his mind to which he was wholly a stranger before.

He thought his ears, being used to such abominable words, might, by degrees, admit them with less detestation: that although he hated the Yahoos of this country, yet he no more blamed them for their odious qualities, than he did a *gnnayh* (a bird of prey) for its cruelty, or a sharp stone for cutting his hoof. But when a creature pretending to reason could be capable of such enormities, he dreaded lest the corruption of that faculty might be worse than brutality itself. He seemed therefore confident, that, instead of reason we were only possessed of some quality fitted to increase our natural vices; as the reflection from a troubled stream returns the image of an ill shapen body, not only larger but more distorted.

He added, that he had heard too much upon the subject of war, both in this and some former discourses. There was another point, which a little perplexed him at present. I had informed him, that some of our crew left their country on account of being ruined by law; that I had already explained the meaning of the word; but he was at a loss how it should come to pass, that the law, which was intended for every man's preservation, should be any man's ruin. Therefore he desired to be further satisfied what I meant by law, and the dispensers thereof, according to the present practice in my own country; because he thought nature and reason were sufficient guides for a reasonable animal, as we pretended to be, in showing us what he ought to do, and what to avoid.

I assured his Honour, that the law was a science in which I had not much conversed, further than by employing advocates, in vain, upon some injustices that had been done me: however, I would give him all the satisfaction I was able.

I said there was a society of men among us, bred up from their youth in the art of proving, by words multiplied for the purpose, that white is black, and black is white, according as they are paid. To this society all the rest of the people are slaves. For example, if my neighbour has a mind to my cow, he has a lawyer to prove that he ought to have my cow from me. I must then hire another to defend my right, it being against all rules of law that any man should be allowed to speak for himself. Now, in this case, I, who am the right owner, lie under two great disadvantages: first, my lawyer, being practised almost from his cradle in defending falsehood, is quite out of his element when he would be an advocate for justice, which is an unnatural office he always attempts with great awkwardness, if not with ill-will.

The second disadvantage is, that my lawyer must proceed with great caution, or else he will be reprimanded by the judges, and abhorred by his brethren, as one that would lessen the practice of the law. And therefore I have but two methods to preserve my cow. The first is, to gain over my adversary's lawyer with a double fee, who will then betray his client by insinuating that he hath justice on his side. The second way is for my lawyer to make my cause appear as unjust as he can, by allowing the cow to belong to my adversary: and this, if it be skilfully done, will certainly bespeak the favour of the bench.

Now your Honour is to know, that these judges are persons appointed to decide all controversies of property, as well as for the trial of criminals, and picked out from the most dexterous lawyers, who are grown old or lazy; and having been biassed all their lives against truth and equity, lie under such a fatal necessity of favouring fraud, perjury, and oppression, that I have known some of them refuse a large bribe from the side where justice lay, rather than injure the faculty, by doing any thing unbecoming their nature or their office.

"It is a maxim among these lawyers that whatever has been done before, may legally be done again: and therefore they take special care to record all the decisions formerly made against common justice, and the general reason of mankind. These, under the name of precedents, they produce as authorities to justify the most iniquitous opinions; and the judges never fail of directing accordingly.

"In pleading, they studiously avoid entering into the merits of the cause; but are loud, violent, and tedious, in dwelling upon all circumstances which are not to the purpose. For instance, in the case already mentioned; they never desire to know what claim or title my adversary has to my cow; but whether the said cow were red or black; her horns long or short; whether the field I graze her in be round or square; whether she was milked at home or abroad; what diseases she is subject to, and the like; after which they consult precedents, adjourn the cause from time to time, and in ten, twenty, or thirty years, come to an issue.

"It is likewise to be observed, that this society has a peculiar cant and jargon of their own, that no other mortal can understand, and wherein all their laws are written, which they take special care to multiply; whereby they have wholly confounded the very essence of truth and falsehood, of right and wrong; so that it will take thirty years to decide, whether the field left me by my ancestors for six generations belongs to me, or to a stranger three hundred miles off.

"In the trial of persons accused for crimes against the state, the method is much more short and commendable: the judge first sends to sound the disposition of those in power, after which he can easily hang or save a criminal, strictly preserving all due forms of law.

Here my master interposing, said, it was a pity, that creatures endowed with such prodigious abilities of mind, as these lawyers, by the description I gave of them, must certainly be, were not rather encouraged to be instructors of others in wisdom and knowledge. In answer to which I assured his honour, that in all points out of their own trade, they were usually the most ignorant and stupid generation among us, the most despicable in common conversation, avowed enemies to all knowledge and learning, and equally disposed to pervert the general reason of mankind in every other subject of discourse as in that of their own profession.

CHAPTER VI

A continuation of the state of England under Queen Anne. The character of a first minister of state in European courts.

My master was yet wholly at a loss to understand what motives could incite this race of lawyers to perplex, disquiet, and weary themselves, and engage in a confederacy of injustice, merely for the sake of injuring their fellow-animals; neither could he comprehend what I meant in saying, they did it for hire. Whereupon I was at much pains to describe to him the use of money, the materials it was made of, and the value of the metals; that when a Yahoo had got a great store of this precious substance, he was able to purchase whatever he had a mind to; the finest clothing, the noblest houses, great tracts of land, the most costly meats and drinks, and have his choice of the most beautiful females.

Therefore since money alone was able to perform all these feats, our Yahoos thought they could never have enough of it to spend, or to save, as they found themselves inclined, from their natural bent either to profusion or avarice; that the rich man enjoyed the fruit of the poor man's labour, and the latter were a thousand to one in proportion to the former; that the bulk of our people were forced to live miserably, by labouring every day for small wages, to make a few live plentifully.

I enlarged myself much on these, and many other particulars to the same purpose; but his honour was still to seek; for he went upon a supposition, that all animals had a title to their share in the productions of the earth, and especially those who presided over the rest. Therefore he desired I would let him know, what these costly meats were, and how any of us happened to want them? Whereupon I enumerated as many sorts as came into my head, with the various methods of dressing them, which could not be done without sending vessels by sea to every part of the world, as well for liquors to drink as for sauces and innumerable other conveniences. I assured him that this whole globe of earth must be at least three times gone round before one of our better female Yahoos could get her breakfast, or a cup to put it in.

He said that must needs be a miserable country which cannot furnish food for its own inhabitants. But what he chiefly wondered at was, how such vast tracts of ground as I described should be wholly without fresh water, and the people put to the necessity of sending over the sea for drink. I replied that England (the dear place of my nativity) was computed to produce three times the quantity of food more than its inhabitants are able to consume, as well as liquors extracted from grain, or pressed out of the fruit of certain trees, which made excellent drink, and the same proportion in every other convenience of life. But, in order to feed the luxury and intemperance of the males, and the vanity of the females, we sent away the greatest part of our necessary things to other countries, whence, in return, we brought the materials of diseases, folly, and vice, to spend among ourselves. Hence it follows of necessity, that vast numbers of our people are compelled to seek their livelihood by begging, robbing, stealing, cheating, pimping, flattering, suborning, forswearing, forging, gaming, lying, fawning, hectoring, voting, scribbling, star-gazing, poisoning, whoring, canting, libelling, freethinking, and the like occupations: every one of which terms I was at much pains to make him understand.

That wine was not imported among us from foreign countries to supply the want of water or other drinks, but because it was a sort of liquid which made us merry by putting us out of our senses, diverted all melancholy thoughts, begat wild extravagant imaginations in the brain, raised our hopes and banished our fears, suspended every office of reason for a time, and deprived us of the use of our limbs, till we fell into a profound sleep; although it must be confessed, that we always awaked sick and dispirited; and that the use of this liquor filled us with diseases which made our lives uncomfortable and short.

But beside all this, the bulk of our people supported themselves by furnishing the necessities or conveniences of life to the rich and to each other. For instance, when I am at home, and dressed as I ought to be, I carry on my body the workmanship of a hundred tradesmen; the building and furniture of my house employ as many more, and five times the number to adorn my wife.

I was going on to tell him of another sort of people, who get their livelihood by attending the sick, having, upon some occasions, informed his honour that many of my crew had died of diseases. But here it was with the utmost difficulty that I brought him to apprehend what I meant. He could easily conceive, that a Houyhnhnm, grew weak and heavy a few days before his death, or by some accident might hurt a limb; but that nature, who works all things to perfection, should suffer any pains to breed in our bodies, he thought impossible, and desired to know the reason of so unaccountable an evil.

I told him we fed on a thousand things which operated contrary to each other; that we ate when we were not hungry, and drank without the provocation of thirst; that we sat whole nights drinking strong liquors, without eating a bit, which disposed us to sloth, inflamed our bodies, and precipitated or prevented digestion; that prostitute femaleYahoos acquired a certain malady, which bred rottenness in the bones of those who fell into their embraces; that this, and many other diseases, were propagated from father to son; so that great numbers came into the world with complicated maladies upon them; that it would be endless to give him a catalogue of all diseases incident to human bodies, for they would not be fewer than five or six hundred, spread over every limb and joint in short, every part, external and intestine, having diseases appropriated to itself. To remedy which, there was a sort of people bred up among us in the profession, or pretence, of curing the sick. And because I had some skill in the faculty, I would, in gratitude to his honour, let him know the whole mystery and method by which they proceed.

Their fundamental is, that all diseases arise from repletion; whence they conclude, that a great evacuation of the body is necessary, either through the natural passage or upwards at the mouth. Their next business is from herbs, minerals, gums, oils, shells, salts, juices, sea-weed, excrements, barks of trees, serpents, toads, frogs, spiders, dead men's flesh and bones, birds, beasts, and fishes, to form a composition, for smell and taste, the most abominable, nauseous, and detestable, they can possibly contrive, which the stomach immediately rejects with loathing, and this they call a vomit; or else, from the same storehouse, with some other poisonous additions, they command us to take in at the orifice above or below (just as the physician then happens to be disposed) a medicine equally annoying and disgustful to the bowels; which, relaxing the belly, drives down all before it; and this they call a purge.

But besides real diseases, we are subject to many that are only imaginary, for which the physicians have invented imaginary cures; these have their several names, and so have the drugs that are proper for them; and with these our female Yahoos are always infested.

One great Excellency in this tribe, is their skill at prognostics, wherein they seldom fail; their predictions in real diseases, when they rise to any degree of malignity, generally portending death, which is always in their power, when recovery is not: and therefore, upon any unexpected signs of amendment, after they have pronounced their sentence, rather than be accused as false prophets, they know how to approve their sagacity to the world, by a seasonable dose.

They are likewise of special use to husbands and wives who are grown weary of their mates; to eldest sons, to great ministers of state, and often to princes.

I had formerly, upon occasion, discoursed with my master upon the nature of government in general, and particularly of our own excellent constitution, deservedly the wonder and envy of the whole world. But having here accidentally mentioned a minister of state, he commanded me, some time after, to inform him, what species ofYahoo I particularly meant by that appellation.

I told him that a first or chief minister of state, who was the person I intended to describe, was the creature wholly exempt from joy and grief, love and hatred, pity and anger; at least, makes use of no other passions, but a violent desire of wealth, power, and titles; that he applies his words to all uses, except to the indication of his mind; that he never tells a truth but with an intent that you should take it for a lie; nor a lie, but with a design that you should take it for a truth; that those he speaks worst of behind their backs are in the surest way of preferment; and whenever he begins to praise you to others, or to yourself, you are from that day forlorn. The worst mark you can receive is a promise, especially when it is confirmed with an oath; after which, every wise man retires, and gives over all hopes.

There are three methods, by which a man may rise to be chief minister. The first is, by knowing how, with prudence, to dispose of a wife, a daughter, or a sister; the second, by betraying or undermining his predecessor; and the third is, by a furious zeal, in public assemblies, against the corruption's of the court. But a wise prince would rather choose to employ those who practise the last of these methods; because such zealots prove always the most obsequious and subservient to the will and passions of their master.

That these ministers, having all employments at their disposal, preserve themselves in power, by bribing the majority of a senate or great council; and at last, by an expedient, called an act of indemnity (whereof I described the nature to him), they secure themselves from after-reckonings, and retire from the public laden with the spoils of the nation.

The palace of a chief minister is a seminary to breed up others in his own trade: the pages, lackeys, and porters, by imitating their master, become ministers of state in their several districts, and learn to excel in the three principal ingredients, of insolence, lying, and bribery. Accordingly, they have a subaltern court paid to them by persons of the best rank; and sometimes by the force of dexterity and impudence, arrive, through several gradations, to be successors to their lord.

One day, in discourse, my master, having heard me mention the nobility of my country, was pleased to make me a compliment which I could not pretend to deserve: that he was sure I must have been born of some noble family, because I far exceeded in shape, colour, and cleanliness, all the Yahoos of his nation, although I seemed to fail in strength and agility, which must be imputed to my different way of living from those other brutes; and besides I was not only endowed with the faculty of speech, but likewise with some rudiments of reason, to a degree that, with all his acquaintance, I passed for a prodigy.

He made me observe that among the Houyhnhnms, the white, the sorrel, and the iron-gray, were not so exactly shaped as the bay, the dapple-gray, and the black; nor born with equal talents of mind, or a capacity to improve them; and therefore continued always in the condition of servants, without ever aspiring to match out of their own race, which in that country would be reckoned monstrous and unnatural.

I made his Honour my most humble acknowledgments for the good opinion he was pleased to conceive of me, but assured him at the same time, that my birth was of the lower sort, having been born of plain honest parents, who were just able to give me a tolerable education; that nobility, among us, was altogether a different thing from the idea he had of it; that our young noblemen are bred from their childhood in idleness and luxury; that, as soon as years will permit, they consume their vigour, and contract odious diseases among lewd females; and when their fortunes are almost ruined, they marry some woman of mean birth, disagreeable person, and unsound constitution (merely for the sake of money), whom they hate and despise. That the productions of such marriages are generally scrofulous, rickety, or deformed children; by which means the family seldom continues above three generations, unless the wife takes care to provide a healthy father, among her neighbours or domestics, in order to improve and continue the breed. That a weak diseased body, a meagre countenance, and sallow complexion, are the true marks of noble blood; and a healthy robust appearance is so disgraceful in a man of quality, that the world concludes his real father to have been a groom or a coachman. The imperfections of his mind run parallel with those of his body, being a composition of spleen, dullness, ignorance, caprice, sensuality, and pride.

Without the consent of this illustrious body, no law can be enacted, repealed, or altered: and these nobles have likewise the decision of all our possessions, without appeal.

CHAPTER VII

The author's great love of his native country. His master's observations upon the constitution and administration of England, as described by the author, with parallel cases and comparisons. His master's observations upon human nature.

The reader may be disposed to wonder how I could prevail on myself to give so free a representation of my own species, among a race of mortals who are already too apt to conceive the vilest opinion of humankind, from that entire congruity between me and their Yahoos. But I must freely confess, that the many virtues of those excellent quadrupeds, placed in opposite view to human corruptions, had so far opened my eyes and enlarged my understanding, that I began to view the actions and passions of man in a very different light, and to think the honour of my own kind not worth managing; which, besides, it was impossible for me to do, before a person of so acute a judgment as my master, who daily convinced me of a thousand faults in myself, whereof I had not the least perception before, and which, with us, would never be numbered even among human infirmities. I had likewise learned, from his example, an utter detestation of all falsehood or disguise; and truth appeared so amiable to me, that I determined upon sacrificing every thing to it.

Let me deal so candidly with the reader as to confess that there was yet a much stronger motive for the freedom I took in my representation of things. I had not yet been a year in this country before I contracted such a love and veneration for the inhabitants, that I entered on a firm resolution never to return to humankind, but to pass the rest of my life among these admirable Houyhnhnms, in the contemplation and practice of every virtue, where I could have no example or incitement to vice. But it was decreed by fortune, my perpetual enemy, that so great a felicity should not fall to my share. However, it is now some comfort to reflect, that in what I said of my countrymen, I extenuated their faults as much as I durst before so strict an examiner; and upon every article gave as favourable a turn as the matter would bear. For, indeed, who is there alive that will not be swayed by his bias and partiality to the place of his birth?

I have related the substance of several conversations I had with my master during the greatest part of the time I had the honour to be in his service; but have, indeed, for brevity sake, omitted much more than is here set down.

When I had answered all his questions, and his curiosity seemed to be fully satisfied, he sent for me one morning early, and commanded me to sit down at some distance (an honour which he had never before conferred upon me). He said, he had been very seriously considering my whole story, as far as it related both to myself and my country; that he looked upon us as a sort of animals, to whose share, by what accident he could not conjecture, some small pittance of reason had fallen, whereof we made no other use, than by its assistance, to aggravate our natural corruptions, and to acquire new ones, which nature had not given us; that we disarmed ourselves of the few abilities she had bestowed; had been very successful in multiplying our original wants, and seemed to spend our whole lives in vain endeavours to supply them by our own inventions.

That, as to myself, it was manifest I had neither the strength nor agility of a common Yahoo; that I walked infirmly on my hinder feet; had found out a contrivance to make my claws of no use or defence, and to remove the hair from my chin, which was intended as a shelter from the sun and the weather: lastly, that I could neither run with speed, nor climb trees like my brethren (as he called them) the Yahoos in his country.

That our institutions of government and law were plainly owing to our gross defects in reason, and by consequence in virtue; because reason alone is sufficient to govern a rational creature; which was, therefore, a character we had no pretence to challenge, even from the account I had given of my own people; although he manifestly perceived, that, in order to favour them, I had concealed many particulars, and often said the thing which was not.

He was the more confirmed in this opinion, because, he observed, that as I agreed in every feature of my body with other Yahoos, except where it was to my real disadvantage in point of strength, speed, and activity, the shortness of my claws, and some other particulars where nature had no part; so from the representation I had given him of our lives, our manners, and our actions, he found as near a resemblance in the disposition of our minds.

He said the Yahoos were known to hate one another, more than they did any different species of animals; and the reason usually assigned was, the odiousness of their own shapes, which all could see in the rest, but not in themselves. He had therefore begun to think it not unwise in us to cover our bodies, and by that invention conceal many of our deformities from each other, which would else be hardly supportable. But he now found he had been mistaken, and that the dissensions of those brutes in his country were owing to the same cause with ours, as I had described them. "For if" said he, "you throw among five Yahoos as much food as would be sufficient for fifty, they will, instead of eating peaceably, fall together by the ears, each single one impatient to have all to itself;" and therefore a servant was usually employed to stand by while they were feeding abroad, and those kept at home were tied at a distance from each other: that if a cow died of age or accident, before a Houyhnhnm could secure it for his own Yahoos, those in the neighbourhood would come in herds to seize it, and then would ensue such a battle as I had described, with terrible wounds made by their claws on both sides, although they seldom were able to kill one another, for want of such convenient instruments of death as we had invented. At other times, the like battles have been fought between the Yahoos of several neighbourhoods, without any visible cause; those of one district watching all opportunities to surprise the next, before they are prepared. But if they find their project has miscarried, they return home, and, for want of enemies, engage in what I call a civil war among themselves.

That in some fields of his country there are certain shining stones of several colours, whereof the Yahoos are violently fond: and when part of these stones is fixed in the earth, as it sometimes happens, they will dig with their claws for whole days to get them out; then carry them away, and hide them by heaps in their kennels; but still looking round with great caution, for fear their comrades should find out their treasure.

My master said, he could never discover the reason of this unnatural appetite, or how these stones could be of any use to a Yahoo; but now he believed it might proceed from the same principle of avarice which I had ascribed to mankind. That he had once, by way of experiment, privately removed a heap of these stones from the place where one of his Yahoos had buried it; whereupon the sordid animal, missing his treasure, by his loud lamenting brought the whole herd to the place, there miserably howled, then fell to biting and tearing the rest, began to pine away, would neither eat, nor sleep, nor work, till he ordered a servant privately to convey the stones into the same hole, and hide them as before; which, when his Yahoo had found, he presently recovered his spirits and good humour, but took good care to remove them to a better hiding place, and has ever since been a very serviceable brute.

My master further assured me, which I also observed myself, that in the fields where the shining stones abound, the fiercest and most frequent battles are fought, occasioned by perpetual inroads of the neighbouring Yahoos.

He said it was common, when two Yahoos discovered such a stone in a field, and were contending which of them should be the proprietor, a third would take the advantage, and carry it away from them both; which my master would needs contend to have some kind of resemblance with our suits at law; wherein I thought it for our credit not to undeceive him; since the decision he mentioned was much more equitable than many decrees among us; because the plaintiff and defendant there lost nothing beside the stone they contended for: whereas our courts of equity would never have dismissed the cause, while either of them had any thing left.

My master, continuing his discourse, said, there was nothing that rendered the Yahoos more odious, than their undistinguishing appetite to devour every thing that came in their way, whether herbs, roots, berries, the corrupted flesh of animals, or all mingled together: and it was peculiar in their temper, that they were fonder of what they could get by rapine or stealth, at a greater distance, than much better food provided for them at home. If their prey held out, they would eat till they were ready to burst; after which, nature had pointed out to them a certain root that gave them a general evacuation.

There was also another kind of root, very juicy, but somewhat rare and difficult to be found, which the Yahoos sought for with much eagerness, and would suck it with great delight; it produced in them the same effects that wine has upon us. It would make them sometimes hug, and sometimes tear one another; they would howl, and grin, and chatter, and reel, and tumble, and then fall asleep in the mud.

I did, indeed observe that the Yahoos were the only animals in this country subject to any diseases; which, however, were much fewer than horses have among us, and contracted, not by any ill-treatment they meet with, but by the nastiness and greediness of that sordid brute. Neither has their language any more than a general appellation for those maladies, which is borrowed from the name of the beast, and called *hnea*-Yahoo, or Yahoo*'s* evil.

As to learning, government, arts, manufactures, and the like, my master confessed, he could find little or no resemblance between the Yahoos of that country and those in ours; for he only meant to observe what parity there was in our natures.

He had heard, indeed, some curious Houyhnhnm*s* observe, that in most herds there was a sort of ruling Yahoo (as among us there is generally some leading or principal stag in a park), who was always more deformed in body, and mischievous in disposition, than any of the rest; that this leader had usually a favourite as like himself as he could get. This favourite is hated by the whole herd, and therefore, to protect himself, keeps always near the person of his leader. He usually continues in office till a worse can be found; but the very moment he is discarded, his successor, at the head of all theYahoos in that district, young and old, male and female, come in a body, and discharge their excrements upon him from head to foot. But how far this might be applicable to our courts, and favourites, and ministers of state, my master said I could best determine.

I durst make no return to this malicious insinuation, which debased human understanding below the sagacity of a common hound, who has judgment enough to distinguish and follow the cry of the ablest dog in the pack, without being ever mistaken.

Another thing he wondered at in the Yahoos, was their strange disposition to nastiness and dirt; whereas there appears to be a natural love of cleanliness in all other animals. As to the two former accusations, I was glad to let them pass without any reply, because I had not a word to offer upon them in defence of my species, which otherwise I certainly had done from my own inclinations. But I could have easily vindicated humankind from the imputation of singularity upon the last article, if there had been any swine in that country (as unluckily for me there were not), which, although it may be a sweeter quadruped than a Yahoo, cannot, I humbly conceive, in justice, pretend to more cleanliness; and so his honour himself must have owned, if he had seen their filthy way of feeding, and their custom of wallowing and sleeping in the mud.

My master likewise mentioned another quality which his servants had discovered in several Yahoos, and to him was wholly unaccountable. He said, a fancy would sometimes take a Yahoo to retire into a corner, to lie down, and howl, and groan, and spurn away all that came near him, although he were young and fat, wanted neither food nor water, nor did the servant imagine what could possibly ail him. And the only remedy they found was, to set him to hard work, after which he would infallibly come to himself. To this I was silent out of partiality to my own kind; yet here I could plainly discover the true seeds of spleen, which only seizes on the lazy, the luxurious, and the rich; who, if they were forced to undergo the same regimen, I would undertake for the cure.

CHAPTER VIII

The author relates several particulars of the Yahoos. The great virtues of the Houyhnhnm*s*. The education and exercise of their youth. Their general assembly.

As I ought to have understood human nature much better than I supposed it possible for my master to do, so it was easy to apply the character he gave of the Yahoos to myself and my countrymen; and I believed I could yet make further discoveries, from my own observation. I therefore often begged his honour to let me go among the herds of Yahoos in the neighbourhood; to which he always very graciously consented, being perfectly convinced that the hatred I bore these brutes would never suffer me to be corrupted by them; and his honour ordered one of his servants, a strong sorrel nag, very honest and good-natured, to be my guard; without whose protection I durst not undertake such adventures. For I have already told the reader how much I was pestered by these odious animals, upon my first arrival; and I afterwards failed very narrowly, three or four times, of falling into their clutches, when I happened to stray at any distance without my hanger. And I have reason to believe they had some imagination that I was of their own species, which I often assisted myself by stripping up my sleeves, and showing my naked arms and breasts in their sight, when my protector was with me. At which times they would approach as near as they durst, and imitate my actions after the manner of monkeys, but ever with great signs of hatred; as a tame jackdaw with cap and stockings is always persecuted by the wild ones, when he happens to be got among them.

They are prodigiously nimble from their infancy. However, I once caught a young male of three years old, and endeavoured, by all marks of tenderness, to make it quiet; but the little imp fell a squalling, and scratching, and biting with such violence, that I was forced to let it go; and it was high time, for a whole troop of old ones came about us at the noise, but finding the cub was safe (for away it ran), and my sorrel nag being by, they durst not venture near us. I observed the young animal's flesh to smell very rank, and the stink was somewhat between a weasel and a fox, but much more disagreeable.

By what I could discover, the Yahoos appear to be the most unteachable of all animals: their capacity never reaching higher than to draw or carry burdens. Yet I am of opinion, this defect arises chiefly from a perverse, restive disposition; for they are cunning, malicious, treacherous, and revengeful. They are strong and hardy, but of a cowardly spirit, and, by consequence, insolent, abject, and cruel. It is observed, that the red haired of both sexes are more libidinous and mischievous than the rest, whom yet they much exceed in strength and activity.

The Houyhnhnm*s* keep the Yahoos for present use in huts not far from the house; but the rest are sent abroad to certain fields, where they dig up roots, eat several kinds of herbs, and search about for carrion, or sometimes catch weasels and *luhimuhs* (a sort of wild rat), which they greedily devour. Nature has taught them to dig deep holes with their nails on the side of a rising ground, wherein they lie by themselves; only the kennels of the females are larger, sufficient to hold two or three cubs.

They swim from their infancy like frogs, and are able to continue long under water, where they often take fish, which the females carry home to their young.

Having lived three years in this country, the reader, I suppose, will expect that I should, like other travellers, give him some account of the manners and customs of its inhabitants, which it was indeed my principal study to learn.

As these noble Houyhnhnm*s* are endowed by nature with a general disposition to all virtues, and have no conceptions or ideas of what is evil in a rational creature, so their grand maxim is, to cultivate reason, and to be wholly governed by it. Neither is reason among them a point problematical, as with us, where men can argue with plausibility on both sides of the question, but strikes you with immediate conviction; as it must needs do, where it is not mingled, obscured, or discoloured, by passion and interest.

I remember it was with extreme difficulty that I could bring my master to understand the meaning of the word opinion, or how a point could be disputable; because reason taught us to affirm or deny only where we are certain; and beyond our knowledge we cannot do either. So that controversies, wranglings, disputes, and positiveness, in false or dubious propositions, are evils unknown among the Houyhnhnm*s*.

In the like manner, when I used to explain to him our several systems of natural philosophy, he would laugh, that a creature pretending to reason, should value itself upon the knowledge of other people's conjectures, and in things where that knowledge, if it were certain, could be of no use. Wherein he agreed entirely with the sentiments of Socrates, as Plato delivers them; which I mention as the highest honour I can do that prince of philosophers. I have often since reflected, what destruction such doctrine would make in the libraries of Europe; and how many paths of fame would be then shut up in the learned world.

Friendship and benevolence are the two principal virtues among the Houyhnhnm*s*; and these not confined to particular objects, but universal to the whole race; for a stranger from the remotest part is equally treated with the nearest neighbour, and wherever he goes, looks upon himself as at home. They preserve decency and civility in the highest degrees, but are altogether ignorant of ceremony. They have no fondness for their colts or foals, but the care they take in educating them proceeds entirely from the dictates of reason. And I observed my master to show the same affection to his neighbour's issue, that he had for his own. They will have it that nature teaches them to love the whole species, and it is reason only that makes a distinction of persons, where there is a superior degree of virtue.

In their marriages, they are exactly careful to choose such colours as will not make any disagreeable mixture in the breed. Strength is chiefly valued in the male, and comeliness in the female; not upon the account of love, but to preserve the race from degenerating; for where a female happens to excel in strength, a consort is chosen, with regard to comeliness.

Courtship, love, presents, jointures, settlements have no place in their thoughts, or terms whereby to express them in their language. The young couple meet, and are joined, merely because it is the determination of their parents and friends; it is what they see done every day, and they look upon it as one of the necessary actions of a reasonable being. But the violation of marriage, or any other unchastity, was never heard of; and the married pair pass their lives with the same friendship and mutual benevolence, that they bear to all others of the same species who come in their way, without jealousy, fondness, quarrelling, or discontent.

In educating the youth of both sexes, their method is admirable, and highly deserves our imitation. These are not suffered to taste a grain of oats, except upon certain days, till eighteen years old; nor milk, but very rarely; and in summer they graze two hours in the morning, and as many in the evening, which their parents likewise observe; but the servants are not allowed above half that time, and a great part of their grass is brought home, which they eat at the most convenient hours, when they can be best spared from work.

Temperance, industry, exercise, and cleanliness, are the lessons equally enjoined to the young ones of both sexes: and my master thought it monstrous in us, to give the females a different kind of education from the males, except in some articles of domestic management; whereby, as he truly observed, one half of our natives were good for nothing but bringing children into the world; and to trust the care of our children to such useless animals, he said, was yet a greater instance of brutality.

But the Houyhnhnm*s* train up their youth to strength, speed, and hardiness, by exercising them in running races up and down steep hills, and over hard stony grounds; and when they are all in a sweat, they are ordered to leap over head and ears into a pond or river. Four times a year the youth of a certain district meet to show their proficiency in running and leaping, and other feats of strength and agility; where the victor is rewarded with a song in his or her praise. On this festival, the servants drive a herd of Yahoos into the field, laden with hay, and oats, and milk, for a repast to the Houyhnhnm*s*; after which, these brutes are immediately driven back again, for fear of being noisome to the assembly.

Every fourth year, at the vernal equinox, there is a representative council of the whole nation, which meets in a plain about twenty miles from our house, and continues about five or six days. Here they inquire into the state and condition of the several districts; whether they abound or be deficient in hay or oats, or cows, or Yahoos.

And wherever there is any want (which is but seldom) it is immediately supplied by unanimous consent and contribution. Here likewise the regulation of children is settled: as for instance, if a Houyhnhnm has two males, he changes one of them with another that has two females; and when a child has been lost by any casualty, where the mother is past breeding, it is determined what family in the district shall breed another to supply the loss.

CHAPTER IX

A grand debate at the general assembly of the *Houyhnhnms*, and how it was determined. The learning of the *Houyhnhnms*. Their buildings. Their manner of burials. The defectiveness of their language.

One of these grand assemblies was held in my time, about three months before my departure, whither my master went as the representative of our district. In this council was resumed their old debate, and indeed the only debate that ever happened in their country; whereof my master, after his return, give me a very particular account.

The question to be debated was, whether the Yahoos should be exterminated from the face of the earth? One of the members for the affirmative offered several arguments of great strength and weight, alleging, that as the Yahoos were the most filthy, noisome, and deformed animals which nature ever produced, so they were the most restive and indocible, mischievous and malicious; they would privately suck the teats of the *Houyhnhnms'* cows, kill and devour their cats, trample down their oats and grass, if they were not continually watched, and commit a thousand other extravagancies.

He took notice of a general tradition, that Yahoos had not been always in their country; but that many ages ago, two of these brutes appeared together upon a mountain; whether produced by the heat of the sun upon corrupted mud and slime, or from the ooze and froth of the sea, was never known; that these Yahoos engendered, and their brood, in a short time, grew so numerous as to overrun and infest the whole nation; that the Houyhnhnm*s*, to get rid of this evil, made a general hunting, and at last enclosed the whole herd; and destroying the elder, every Houyhnhnm kept two young ones in a kennel, and brought them to such a degree of tameness, as an animal, so savage by nature, can be capable of acquiring, using them for draught and carriage.

That there seemed to be much truth in this tradition, and that those creatures could not be *yinhniamshy* (or aborigines of the land), because of the violent hatred the Houyhnhnm*s*, as well as all other animals, bore them, which, although their evil disposition sufficiently deserved, could never have arrived at so high a degree if they had been aborigines, or else they would have long since been rooted out; that the inhabitants, taking a fancy to use the service of the Yahoos, had, very imprudently, neglected to cultivate the breed of asses, which are a comely animal, easily kept, more tame and orderly, without any offensive smell, strong enough for labour, although they yield to the other in agility of body, and if their braying be no agreeable sound, it is far preferable to the horrible howlings of the Yahoos.

Several others declared their sentiments to the same purpose, when my master proposed an expedient to the assembly, whereof he had indeed borrowed the hint from me. He approved of the tradition mentioned by the honourable member who spoke before, and affirmed, that the two Yahoos said to be seen first among them, had been driven thither over the sea; that coming to land, and being forsaken by their companions, they retired to the mountains, and degenerating by degrees, became in process of time much more savage than those of their own species in the country whence these two originals came. The reason of this assertion was, that he had now in his possession a certain wonderful Yahoo (meaning myself) which most of them had heard of, and many of them had seen.

He then related to them how he first found me; that my body was all covered with an artificial composure of the skins and hairs of other animals; that I spoke in a language of my own, and had thoroughly learned theirs; that I had related to him the accidents which brought me thither; that when he saw me without my covering, I was an exact Yahoo in every part, only of a whiter colour, less hairy, and with shorter claws. He added, how I had endeavoured to persuade him, that in my own and other countries, the Yahoos acted as the governing, rational animal, and held the Houyhnhnm*s* in servitude; that he observed in me all the qualities of a Yahoo, only a little more civilized by some tincture of reason, which, however, was in a degree as far inferior to the Houyhnhnm race, as the Yahoos of their country were to me.

This was all my master thought fit to tell me, at that time, of what passed in the grand council. But he was pleased to conceal one particular, which related personally to myself, whereof I soon felt the unhappy effect, as the reader will know in its proper place, and whence I date all the succeeding misfortunes of my life.

The Houyhnhnms have no letters, and consequently their knowledge is all traditional. But there happening few events of any moment among a people so well united, naturally disposed to every virtue, wholly governed by reason, and cut off from all commerce with other nations, the historical part is easily preserved without burdening their memories.

I have already observed that they are subject to no diseases, and therefore can have no need of physicians. However, they have excellent medicines, composed of herbs, to cure accidental bruises and cuts in the pastern or frog of the foot, by sharp stones, as well as other maims and hurts in the several parts of the body.

They calculate the year by the revolution of the sun and moon, but use no subdivisions into weeks. They are well enough acquainted with the motions of those two luminaries, and understand the nature of eclipses; and this is the utmost progress of their astronomy.

In poetry, they must be allowed to excel all other mortals; wherein the justness of their similes, and the minuteness as well as exactness of their descriptions, are indeed inimitable. Their verses abound very much in both of these, and usually contain either some exalted notions of friendship and benevolence or the praises of those who were victors in races and other bodily exercises.

Their buildings, although very rude and simple, are not inconvenient, but well contrived to defend them from all injuries of cold and heat. They have a kind of tree, which at forty years old loosens in the root, and falls with the first storm: it grows very straight, and being pointed like stakes with a sharp stone (for the Houyhnhnm*s* know not the use of iron), they stick them erect in the ground, about ten inches asunder, and then weave in oat straw, or sometimes wattles, between them. The roof is made after the same manner, and so are the doors.

The Houyhnhnm*s* use the hollow part, between the pastern and the hoof of their fore-foot, as we do our hands, and this with greater dexterity than I could at first imagine. I have seen a white mare of our family thread a needle (which I lent her on purpose) with that joint. They milk their cows, reap their oats, and do all the work which requires hands, in the same manner.

They have a kind of hard flints, which, by grinding against other stones, they form into instruments, that serve instead of wedges, axes, and hammers. With tools made of these flints, they likewise cut their hay, and reap their oats, which there grow naturally in several fields; the Yahoos draw home the sheaves in carriages, and the servants tread them in certain covered huts to get out the grain, which is kept in stores. They make a rude kind of earthen and wooden vessels, and bake the former in the sun.

If they can avoid casualties, they die only of old age, and are buried in the obscurest places that can be found, their friends and relations expressing neither joy nor grief at their departure; nor does the dying person discover the least regret that he is leaving the world, any more than if he were upon returning home from a visit to one of his neighbours.

I remember my master having once made an appointment with a friend and his family to come to his house, upon some affair of importance: on the day fixed, the mistress and her two children came very late; she made two excuses, first for her husband, who, as she said, happened that very morning to *Ihnuwnh*. The word is strongly expressive in their language, but not easily rendered into English; it signifies, to retire to his first mother. Her excuse for not coming sooner, was, that her husband dying late in the morning, she was a good while consulting her servants about a convenient place where his body should be laid; and I observed, she behaved herself at our house as cheerfully as the rest. She died about three months after.

They live generally to seventy, or seventy-five years, very seldom to fourscore. Some weeks before their death, they feel a gradual decay; but without pain. During this time they are much visited by their friends, because they cannot go abroad with their usual ease and satisfaction. However, about ten days before their death, which they seldom fail in computing, they return the visits that have been made them by those who are nearest in the neighbourhood, being carried in a convenient sledge drawn byYahoos; which vehicle they use, not only upon this occasion, but when they grow old, upon long journeys, or when they are lamed by any accident: and therefore when the dying Houyhnhnm*s* return those visits, they take a solemn leave of their friends, as if they were going to some remote part of the country, where they designed to pass the rest of their lives.

I know not whether it may be worth observing, that the Houyhnhnms have no word in their language to express any thing that is evil, except what they borrow from the deformities or ill qualities of the Yahoos. Thus they denote the folly of a servant, an omission of a child, a stone that cuts their feet, a continuance of foul or unseasonable weather, and the like, by adding to each the epithet of Yahoo. For instance, *Hhnm Yahoo*; *Whnaholm Yahoo*, *Ynlhmndwihlma Yahoo*, and an ill-contrived house *Ynholmhnmrohlnw Yahoo*.

I could, with great pleasure, enlarge further upon the manners and virtues of this excellent people; but intending in a short time to publish a volume by itself, expressly upon that subject, I refer the reader thither; and, in the mean time, proceed to relate my own sad catastrophe.

CHAPTER X

The author's economy, and happy life, among the Houyhnhnms. His great improvement in virtue by conversing with them. Their conversations. The author has notice given him by his master, that he must depart from the country. He falls into a swoon for grief; but submits. He contrives and finishes a canoe by the help of a fellow-servant, and puts to sea at a venture.

I had settled my little economy to my own heart's content. My master had ordered a room to be made for me, after their manner, about six yards from the house: the sides and floors of which I plastered with clay, and covered with rush-mats of my own contriving. I had beaten hemp, which there grows wild, and made of it a sort of ticking; this I filled with the feathers of several birds I had taken with springes made of Yahoos' hairs, and were excellent food. I had worked two chairs with my knife, the sorrel nag helping me in the grosser and more laborious part.

When my clothes were worn to rags, I made myself others with the skins of rabbits, and of a certain beautiful animal, about the same size, called *Nnuhnoh*, the skin of which is covered with a fine down. Of these I also made very tolerable stockings. I soled my shoes with wood, which I cut from a tree, and fitted to the upper-leather; and when this was worn out, I supplied it with the skins of Yahoos dried in the sun. I often got honey out of hollow trees, which I mingled with water, or ate with my bread.

No man could more verify the truth of these two maxims,

That nature is very easily satisfied; and, That necessity is the mother of invention.

I enjoyed perfect health of body, and tranquillity of mind; I did not feel the treachery or inconstancy of a friend, nor the injuries of a secret or open enemy. I had no occasion of bribing, flattering, or pimping, to procure the favour of any great man, or of his minion; I wanted no fence against fraud or oppression: here was neither physician to destroy my body, nor lawyer to ruin my fortune; no informer to watch my words and actions, or forge accusations against me for hire: here were no gibers, censurers, backbiters, pickpockets, highwaymen, housebreakers, attorneys, bawds, buffoons, gamesters, politicians, wits, splenetics, tedious talkers, controvertists, ravishers, murderers, robbers, virtuosos; no leaders, or followers, of party and faction; no encouragers to vice, by seducement or examples; no dungeon, axes, gibbets, whipping-posts, or pillories; no cheating shopkeepers or mechanics; no pride, vanity, or affectation; no fops, bullies, drunkards, strolling whores, or poxes; no ranting, lewd, expensive wives; no stupid, proud pedants; no importunate, overbearing, quarrelsome, noisy, roaring, empty, conceited, swearing companions; no scoundrels raised from the dust upon the merit of their vices, or nobility thrown into it on account of their virtues; no lords, fiddlers, judges, or dancing-masters.

I had the favour of being admitted to several Houyhnhnms, who came to visit or dine with my master; where his honour graciously suffered me to wait in the room, and listen to their discourse. Both he and his company would often descend to ask me questions, and receive my answers. I had also sometimes the honour of attending my master in his visits to others. I never presumed to speak, except in answer to a question; and then I did it with inward regret, because it was a loss of so much time for improving myself; but I was infinitely delighted with the station of an humble auditor in such conversations, where nothing passed but what was useful, expressed in the fewest and most significant words; where, as I have already said, the greatest decency was observed, without the least degree of ceremony; where no person spoke without being pleased himself, and pleasing his companions; where there was no interruption, tediousness, heat, or difference of sentiments.

They have a notion, that when people are met together, a short silence does much improve conversation: this I found to be true; for during those little intermissions of talk, new ideas would arise in their minds, which very much enlivened the discourse. Their subjects are, generally on friendship and benevolence, on order and economy; sometimes upon the visible operations of nature, or ancient traditions; upon the bounds and limits of virtue; upon the unerring rules of reason, or upon some determinations to be taken at the next great assembly: and often upon the various excellences of poetry.

I may add, without vanity, that my presence often gave them sufficient matter for discourse, because it afforded my master an occasion of letting his friends into the history of me and my country, upon which they were all pleased to descant, in a manner not very advantageous to humankind: and for that reason I shall not repeat what they said; only I may be allowed to observe, that his honour, to my great admiration, appeared to understand the nature of Yahoos much better than myself. He went through all our vices and follies, and discovered many, which I had never mentioned to him, by only supposing what qualities a Yahoo of their country, with a small proportion of reason, might be capable of exerting; and concluded, with too much probability, how vile, as well as miserable, such a creature must be.

I freely confess, that all the little knowledge I have of any value, was acquired by the lectures I received from my master, and from hearing the discourses of him and his friends; to which I should be prouder to listen, than to dictate to the greatest and wisest assembly in Europe. I admired the strength, comeliness, and speed of the inhabitants; and such a constellation of virtues, in such amiable persons, produced in me the highest veneration. At first, indeed, I did not feel that natural awe, which theYahoos and all other animals bear toward them; but it grew upon me by decrees, much sooner than I imagined, and was mingled with a respectful love and gratitude, that they would condescend to distinguish me from the rest of my species.

When I thought of my family, my friends, my countrymen, or the human race in general, I considered them, as they really were, Yahoos in shape and disposition, perhaps a little more civilized, and qualified with the gift of speech; but making no other use of reason, than to improve and multiply those vices whereof their brethren in this country had only the share that nature allotted them. When I happened to behold the reflection of my own form in a lake or fountain, I turned away my face in horror and detestation of myself, and could better endure the sight of a common Yahoo than of my own person.

By conversing with the Houyhnhnms, and looking upon them with delight, I fell to imitate their gait and gesture, which is now grown into a habit; and my friends often tell me, in a blunt way, that I trot like a horse; which, however, I take for a great compliment. Neither shall I disown, that in speaking I am apt to fall into the voice and manner of the Houyhnhnms, and hear myself ridiculed on that account, without the least mortification.

In the midst of all this happiness, and when I looked upon myself to be fully settled for life, my master sent for me one morning a little earlier than his usual hour. I observed by his countenance that he was in some perplexity, and at a loss how to begin what he had to speak.

After a short silence, he told me, he did not know how I would take what he was going to say: that in the last general assembly, when the affair of the Yahoos was entered upon, the representatives had taken offence at his keeping a Yahoo (meaning myself) in his family, more like a Houyhnhnm than a brute animal; that he was known frequently to converse with me, as if he could receive some advantage or pleasure in my company; that such a practice was not agreeable to reason or nature, or a thing ever heard of before among them.

The assembly did therefore exhort him either to employ me like the rest of my species, or command me to swim back to the place whence I came: that the first of these expedients was utterly rejected by all the Houyhnhnm*s* who had ever seen me at his house or their own; for they alleged, that because I had some rudiments of reason, added to the natural pravity of those animals, it was to be feared I might be able to seduce them into the woody and mountainous parts of the country, and bring them in troops by night to destroy the Houyhnhnm*s'* cattle, as being naturally of the ravenous kind, and averse from labour.

My master added, that he was daily pressed by the Houyhnhnm*s* of the neighbourhood to have the assembly's exhortation executed, which he could not put off much longer. He doubted it would be impossible for me to swim to another country; and therefore wished I would contrive some sort of vehicle, resembling those I had described to him, that might carry me on the sea; in which work I should have the assistance of his own servants, as well as those of his neighbours. He concluded, that for his own part, he could have been content to keep me in his service as long as I lived; because he found I had cured myself of some bad habits and dispositions, by endeavouring, as far as my inferior nature was capable, to imitate the Houyhnhnm*s*.

I should here observe to the reader, that a decree of the general assembly in this country is expressed by the word *Hnhloayn*, which signifies an exhortation, as near as I can render it; for they have no conception how a rational creature can be compelled, but only advised, or exhorted; because no person can disobey reason, without giving up his claim to be a rational creature.

I was struck with the utmost grief and despair at my master's discourse; and being unable to support the agonies I was under, I fell into a swoon at his feet. When I came to myself, he told me that he concluded I had been dead; (for these people are subject to no such imbecilities of nature).

I answered in a faint voice, that death would have been too great a happiness; that although I could not blame the assembly's exhortation, or the urgency of his friends; yet, in my weak and corrupt judgment, I thought it might consist with reason to have been less rigorous; that I could not swim a league, and probably the nearest land to theirs might be distant above a hundred: that many materials, necessary for making a small vessel to carry me off, were wholly wanting in this country; which, however, I would attempt, in obedience and gratitude to his honour, although I concluded the thing to be impossible, and therefore looked on myself as already devoted to destruction.

That the certain prospect of an unnatural death was the least of my evils; for, supposing I should escape with life by some strange adventure, how could I think with temper of passing my days among Yahoos, and relapsing into my old corruptions, for want of examples to lead and keep me within the paths of virtue? that I knew too well upon what solid reasons all the determinations of the wise Houyhnhnm*s* were founded, not to be shaken by arguments of mine, a miserable Yahoo; and therefore, after presenting him with my humble thanks for the offer of his servants' assistance in making a vessel, and desiring a reasonable time for so difficult a work, I told him I would endeavour to preserve a wretched being; and if ever I returned to England, was not without hopes of being useful to my own species, by celebrating the praises of the renowned Houyhnhnms, and proposing their virtues to the imitation of mankind.

My master, in a few words, made me a very gracious reply; allowed me the space of two months to finish my boat; and ordered the sorrel nag, my fellow-servant (for so, at this distance, I may presume to call him), to follow my instruction; because I told my master, that his help would be sufficient, and I knew he had a tenderness for me.

In his company, my first business was to go to that part of the coast where my rebellious crew had ordered me to be set on shore. I got upon a height, and looking on every side into the sea; fancied I saw a small island toward the north-east. I took out my pocket glass, and could then clearly distinguish it above five leagues off, as I computed; but it appeared to the sorrel nag to be only a blue cloud: for as he had no conception of any country beside his own, so he could not be as expert in distinguishing remote objects at sea, as we who so much converse in that element.

After I had discovered this island, I considered no further; but resolved it should if possible, be the first place of my banishment, leaving the consequence to fortune.

I returned home, and consulting with the sorrel nag, we went into a copse at some distance, where I with my knife, and he with a sharp flint, fastened very artificially after their manner, to a wooden handle, cut down several oak wattles, about the thickness of a walking-staff, and some larger pieces.

But I shall not trouble the reader with a particular description of my own mechanics; let it suffice to say, that in six weeks time with the help of the sorrel nag, who performed the parts that required most labour, I finished a sort of Indian canoe, but much larger, covering it with the skins of Yahoos, well stitched together with hempen threads of my own making.

My sail was likewise composed of the skins of the same animal; but I made use of the youngest I could get, the older being too tough and thick; and I likewise provided myself with four paddles. I laid in a stock of boiled flesh, of rabbits and fowls, and took with me two vessels, one filled with milk and the other with water.

I tried my canoe in a large pond, near my master's house, and then corrected in it what was amiss; stopping all the chinks with Yahoos' tallow, till I found it staunch, and able to bear me and my freight; and, when it was as complete as I could possibly make it, I had it drawn on a carriage very gently by Yahoos to the sea-side, under the conduct of the sorrel nag and another servant.

When all was ready, and the day came for my departure, I took leave of my master and lady and the whole family, my eyes flowing with tears, and my heart quite sunk with grief. But his honour, out of curiosity, and, perhaps, (if I may speak without vanity,) partly out of kindness, was determined to see me in my canoe, and got several of his neighbouring friends to accompany him.

I was forced to wait above an hour for the tide; and then observing the wind very fortunately bearing toward the island to which I intended to steer my course, I took a second leave of my master: but as I was going to prostrate myself to kiss his hoof, he did me the honour to raise it gently to my mouth. I am not ignorant how much I have been censured for mentioning this last particular. Detractors are pleased to think it improbable, that so illustrious a person should descend to give so great a mark of distinction to a creature so inferior as I. Neither have I forgotten how apt some travellers are to boast of extraordinary favours they have received. But, if these censurers were better acquainted with the noble and courteous disposition of the Houyhnhnm*s*, they would soon change their opinion.

I paid my respects to the rest of the Houyhnhnm*s* in his honour's company; then getting into my canoe, I pushed off from shore.

CHAPTER XI

The author's dangerous voyage. He arrives at New Holland, hoping to settle there. Is wounded with an arrow by one of the natives. Is seized and carried by force into a Portuguese ship. The great civilities of the captain. The author arrives at England.

I began this desperate voyage on February 15, 1714–15, at nine o'clock in the morning. The wind was very favourable; however, I made use at first only of my paddles; but considering I should soon be weary, and that the wind might chop about, I ventured to set up my little sail; and thus, with the help of the tide, I went at the rate of a league and a half an hour, as near as I could guess. My master and his friends continued on the shore till I was almost out of sight; and I often heard the sorrel nag (who always loved me) crying out, *Hnuy illa nyha*, *majah Yahoo*, Take care of thyself, gentle Yahoo.

My design was, if possible, to discover some small island uninhabited, yet sufficient, by my labour, to furnish me with the necessaries of life, which I would have thought a greater happiness, than to be first minister in the politest court of Europe; so horrible was the idea I conceived of returning to live in the society, and under the government of Yahoos. For in such a solitude as I desired, I could at least enjoy my own thoughts, and reflect with delight on the virtues of those inimitable Houyhnhnms, without an opportunity of degenerating into the vices and corruptions of my own species.

The reader may remember what I related, when my crew conspired against me, and confined me to my cabin;

how I continued there several weeks without knowing what course we took; and when I was put ashore in the long-boat, how the sailors told me, with oaths, whether true or false, that they knew not in what part of the world we were. However, I did then believe us to be about 10 degrees southward of the Cape of Good Hope, or about 45 degrees southern latitude, as I gathered from some general words I overheard among them, being I supposed to the south-east in their intended voyage to Madagascar. And although this were little better than conjecture, yet I resolved to steer my course eastward, hoping to reach the south-west coast of New Holland, and perhaps some such island as I desired lying westward of it.

The wind was full west, and by six in the evening I computed I had gone eastward at least eighteen leagues; when I spied a very small island about half a league off, which I soon reached. It was nothing but a rock, with one creek naturally arched by the force of tempests. Here I put in my canoe, and climbing a part of the rock, I could plainly discover land to the east, extending from south to north.

I lay all night in my canoe; and repeating my voyage early in the morning, I arrived in seven hours to the south-east point of New Holland. This confirmed me in the opinion I have long entertained, that the maps and charts place this country at least three degrees more to the east than it really is; which thought I communicated many years ago to my worthy friend, Mr. Herman Moll, and gave him my reasons for it, although he has rather chosen to follow other authors.

I saw no inhabitants in the place where I landed, and being unarmed, I was afraid of venturing far into the country. I found some shellfish on the shore, and ate them raw, not daring to kindle a fire, for fear of being discovered by the natives. I continued three days feeding on oysters and limpets, to save my own provisions; and I fortunately found a brook of excellent water, which gave me great relief.

On the fourth day, venturing out early a little too far, I saw twenty or thirty natives upon a height not above five hundred yards from me. They were stark naked, men, women, and children, round a fire, as I could discover by the smoke. One of them spied me, and gave notice to the rest; five of them advanced toward me, leaving the women and children at the fire. I made what haste I could to the shore, and, getting into my canoe, shoved off: the savages, observing me retreat, ran after me: and before I could get far enough into the sea, discharged an arrow which wounded me deeply on the inside of my left knee: I shall carry the mark to my grave. I apprehended the arrow might be poisoned, and paddling out of the reach of their darts (being a calm day), I made a shift to suck the wound, and dress it as well as I could.

I was at a loss what to do, for I durst not return to the same landing-place, but stood to the north, and was forced to paddle, for the wind, though very gentle, was against me, blowing north-west. As I was looking about for a secure landing-place, I saw a sail to the north-north-east, which appearing every minute more visible, I was in some doubt whether I should wait for them or not; but at last my detestation of the Yahoo race prevailed: and turning my canoe, I sailed and paddled together to the south, and got into the same creek whence I set out in the morning, choosing rather to trust myself among these barbarians, than live with European Yahoos. I drew up my canoe as close as I could to the shore, and hid myself behind a stone by the little brook, which, as I have already said, was excellent water.

The ship came within half a league of this creek, and sent her long boat with vessels to take in fresh water (for the place, it seems, was very well known); but I did not observe it, till the boat was almost on shore; and it was too late to seek another hiding-place. The seamen at their landing observed my canoe, and rummaging it all over, easily conjectured that the owner could not be far off. Four of them, well armed, searched every cranny and lurking-hole, till at last they found me flat on my face behind the stone. They gazed awhile in admiration at my strange uncouth dress; my coat made of skins, my wooden-soled shoes, and my furred stockings; whence, however, they concluded, I was not a native of the place, who all go naked.

One of the seamen, in Portuguese, bid me rise, and asked who I was. I understood that language very well, and getting upon my feet, said, I was a poor Yahoo banished from the Houyhnhnms, and desired they would please to let me depart. They admired to hear me answer them in their own tongue, and saw by my complexion I must be a European; but were at a loss to know what I meant by Yahoos and Houyhnhnms; and at the same time fell a-laughing at my strange tone in speaking, which resembled the neighing of a horse. I trembled all the while betwixt fear and hatred. I again desired leave to depart, and was gently moving to my canoe; but they laid hold of me, desiring to know, what country I was of? whence I came? with many other questions. I told them I was born in England, whence I came about five years ago, and then their country and ours were at peace. I therefore hoped they would not treat me as an enemy, since I meant them no harm, but was a poor Yahoo seeking some desolate place where to pass the remainder of his unfortunate life.

When they began to talk, I thought I never heard or saw any thing more unnatural; for it appeared to me as monstrous as if a dog or a cow should speak in England, or aYahoo in Houyhnhnmland.

The honest Portuguese were equally amazed at my strange dress, and the odd manner of delivering my words, which, however, they understood very well. They spoke to me with great humanity, and said, they were sure the captain would carry me gratis to Lisbon, whence I might return to my own country; that two of the seamen would go back to the ship, inform the captain of what they had seen, and receive his orders; in the mean time, unless I would give my solemn oath not to fly, they would secure me by force. I thought it best to comply with their proposal. They were very curious to know my story, but I gave them very little satisfaction, and they all conjectured that my misfortunes had impaired my reason. In two hours the boat, which went laden with vessels of water, returned, with the captain's command to fetch me on board. I fell on my knees to preserve my liberty; but all was in vain; and the men, having tied me with cords, heaved me into the boat, whence I was taken into the ship, and thence into the captain's cabin.

His name was Pedro de Mendez; he was a very courteous and generous person. He entreated me to give some account of myself, and desired to know what I would eat or drink; said, I should be used as well as himself; and spoke so many obliging things, that I wondered to find such civilities from a Yahoo. However, I remained silent and sullen; I was ready to faint at the very smell of him and his men.

At last I desired something to eat out of my own canoe; but he ordered me a chicken, and some excellent wine, and then directed that I should be put to bed in a very clean cabin. I would not undress myself, but lay on the bed-clothes, and in half an hour stole out, when I thought the crew was at dinner, and getting to the side of the ship, was going to leap into the sea, and swim for my life, rather than continue among Yahoos. But one of the seamen prevented me, and having informed the captain, I was chained to my cabin.

After dinner, Don Pedro came to me, and desired to know

my reason for so desperate an attempt; assured me, he only meant to do me all the service he was able; and spoke so very movingly, that at last I descended to treat him like an animal which had some little portion of reason.

I gave him a very short relation of my voyage; of the conspiracy against me by my own men; of the country where they set me on shore, and of my five years residence there. All which he looked upon as if it were a dream or a vision; whereat I took great offence; for I had quite forgot the faculty of lying, so peculiar to Yahoos, in all countries where they preside, and, consequently, their disposition of suspecting truth in others of their own species.

I asked him, whether it were the custom in his country to say the thing which was not? I assured him, I had almost forgot what he meant by falsehood, and if I had lived a thousand years in Houyhnhnmland, I should never have heard a lie from the meanest servant; that I was altogether indifferent whether he believed me or not; but, however, in return for his favours, I would give so much allowance to the corruption of his nature, as to answer any objection he would please to make, and then he might easily discover the truth.

The captain, a wise man, after many endeavours to catch me tripping in some part of my story, at last began to have a better opinion of my veracity. But he added, that since I professed so inviolable an attachment to truth, I must give him my word and honour to bear him company in this voyage, without attempting any thing against my life; or else he would continue me a prisoner till we arrived at Lisbon. I gave him the promise he required; but at the same time protested, that I would suffer the greatest hardships, rather than return to live among Yahoos.

Our voyage passed without any considerable accident. In gratitude to the captain, I sometimes sat with him, at his earnest request, and strove to conceal my antipathy against human kind, although it often broke out; which he suffered to pass without observation. But the greatest part of the day I confined myself to my cabin, to avoid seeing any of the crew.

The captain had often entreated me to strip myself of my savage dress, and offered to lend me the best suit of clothes he had. This I would not be prevailed on to accept, abhorring to cover myself with any thing that had been on the back of a Yahoo. I only desired he would lend me two clean shirts, which, having been washed since he wore them, I believed would not so much defile me. These I changed every second day, and washed them myself.

We arrived at Lisbon, Nov. 5, 1715. At our landing, the captain forced me to cover myself with his cloak, to prevent the rabble from crowding about me. I was conveyed to his own house; and at my earnest request he led me up to the highest room backwards. I conjured him to conceal from all persons what I had told him of the Houyhnhnm*s*; because the least hint of such a story would not only draw numbers of people to see me, but probably put me in danger of being imprisoned, or burnt by the Inquisition.

The captain persuaded me to accept a suit of clothes newly made; but I would not suffer the tailor to take my measure; however, Don Pedro being almost of my size, they fitted me well enough. He accoutred me with other necessaries, all new, which I aired for twenty-four hours before I would use them.

The captain had no wife, nor above three servants, none of which were suffered to attend at meals; and his whole deportment was so obliging, added to very good human understanding, that I really began to tolerate his company. He gained so far upon me, that I ventured to look out of the back window. By degrees I was brought into another room, whence I peeped into the street, but drew my head back in a fright.

In a week's time he seduced me down to the door. I found my terror gradually lessened, but my hatred and contempt seemed to increase. I was at last bold enough to walk the street in his company, but kept my nose well stopped with rue, or sometimes with tobacco.

In ten days, Don Pedro, to whom I had given some account of my domestic affairs, put it upon me, as a matter of honour and conscience, that I ought to return to my native country, and live at home with my wife and children. He told me, there was an English ship in the port just ready to sail, and he would furnish me with all things necessary. It would be tedious to repeat his arguments, and my contradictions. He said it was altogether impossible to find such a solitary island as I desired to live in; but I might command in my own house, and pass my time in a manner as recluse as I pleased.

I complied at last, finding I could not do better. I left Lisbon the 24th day of November, in an English merchantman, but who was the master I never inquired. Don Pedro accompanied me to the ship, and lent me twenty pounds. He took kind leave of me, and embraced me at parting, which I bore as well as I could. During this last voyage I had no commerce with the master or any of his men; but, pretending I was sick, kept close in my cabin. On the fifth of December, 1715, we cast anchor in the Downs, about nine in the morning, and at three in the afternoon I got safe to my house at Rotherhith.

My wife and family received me with great surprise and joy, because they concluded me certainly dead; but I must freely confess the sight of them filled me only with hatred, disgust, and contempt; and the more, by reflecting on the near alliance I had to them. For although, since my unfortunate exile from the Houyhnhnm country, I had compelled myself to tolerate the sight of Yahoos, and to converse with Don Pedro de Mendez, yet my memory and imagination were perpetually filled with the virtues and ideas of those exalted Houyhnhnms.

As soon as I entered the house, my wife took me in her arms, and kissed me; at which, having not been used to the touch of that odious animal for so many years, I fell into a swoon for almost an hour. At the time I am writing, it is five years since my last return to England. During the first year, I could not endure my wife or children in my presence; the very smell of them was intolerable; much less could I suffer them to eat in the same room. To this hour they dare not presume to touch my bread, or drink out of the same cup, neither was I ever able to let one of them take me by the hand. The first money I laid out was to buy two young stone-horses, which I keep in a good stable; and next to them, the groom is my greatest favourite, for I feel my spirits revived by the smell he contracts in the stable. My horses understand me tolerably well; I converse with them at least four hours every day. They are strangers to bridle or saddle; they live in great amity with me and friendship to each other.

CHAPTER XII

The author's veracity. His design in publishing this work. His censure of those travellers who swerve from the truth. The author clears himself from any sinister ends in writing. An objection answered. The method of planting colonies. His native country commended. The right of the crown to those countries described by the author is justified. The difficulty of conquering them. The author takes his last leave of the reader; proposes his manner of living for the future; gives good advice, and concludeth.

Thus, gentle reader, I have given thee a faithful history of my travels for sixteen years and above seven months: wherein I have not been so studious of ornament as of truth. I could, perhaps, like others, have astonished thee with strange improbable tales; but I rather chose to relate plain matter of fact, in the simplest manner and style; because my principal design was to inform, and not to amuse thee.

It is easy for us who travel into remote countries, which are seldom visited by Englishmen or other Europeans, to form descriptions of wonderful animals both at sea and land. Whereas a traveller's chief aim should be to make men wiser and better, and to improve their minds by the bad, as well as good, example of what they deliver concerning foreign places.

I could heartily wish a law was enacted, that every traveller, before he were permitted to publish his voyages, should be obliged to make oath before the Lord High Chancellor, that all he intended to print was absolutely true to the best of his knowledge; for then the world would no longer be deceived, as it usually is, while some writers, to make their works pass the better upon the public, impose the grossest falsities on the unwary reader.

I have perused several books of travels with great delight in my younger days; but having since gone over most parts of the globe, and been able to contradict many fabulous accounts from my own observation, it has given me a great disgust against this part of reading, and some indignation to see the credulity of mankind so impudently abused. Therefore, since my acquaintance were pleased to think my poor endeavours might not be unacceptable to my country, I imposed on myself, as a maxim never to be swerved from, that I would strictly adhere to truth; neither indeed can I be ever under the least temptation to vary from it, while I retain in my mind the lectures and example of my noble master and the other illustrious Houyhnhnm*s* of whom I had so long the honour to be an humble hearer.

—Nec si miserum Fortuna Sinonem
Finxit, vanum etiam, mendacemque improba finget.

I know very well, how little reputation is to be got by writings which require neither genius nor learning, nor indeed any other talent, except a good memory, or an exact journal.

I know likewise, that writers of travels, like dictionary-makers, are sunk into oblivion by the weight and bulk of those who come last, and therefore lie uppermost. And it is highly probable, that such travellers, who shall hereafter visit the countries described in this work of mine, may, by detecting my errors (if there be any), and adding many new discoveries of their own, justle me out of vogue, and stand in my place, making the world forget that ever I was an author. This indeed would be too great a mortification, if I wrote for fame: but as my sole intention was the public good, I cannot be altogether disappointed. For who can read of the virtues I have mentioned in the glorious Houyhnhnms, without being ashamed of his own vices, when he considers himself as the reasoning, governing animal of his country?

I shall say nothing of those remote nations where Yahoos preside; among which the least corrupted are the Brobdingnagians, whose wise maxims in morality and government it would be our happiness to observe.

But I forbear descanting further, and rather leave the judicious reader to his own remarks and application.

I am not a little pleased that this work of mine can possibly meet with no censurers: for what objections can be made against a writer, who relates only plain facts, that happened in such distant countries, where we have not the least interest, with respect either to trade or negotiations?

I have carefully avoided every fault with which common writers of travels are often too justly charged. Besides, I meddle not the least with any party, but write without passion, prejudice, or ill-will against any man, or number of men, whatsoever. I write for the noblest end, to inform and instruct mankind; over whom I may, without breach of modesty, pretend to some superiority, from the advantages I received by conversing so long among the most accomplished Houyhnhnms. I write without any view to profit or praise. I never suffer a word to pass that may look like reflection, or possibly give the least offence, even to those who are most ready to take it. So that I hope I may with justice pronounce myself an author perfectly blameless; against whom the tribes of Answerers, Considerers, Observers, Reflectors, Detectors, Remarkers, will never be able to find matter for exercising their talents.

I confess, it was whispered to me, that I was bound in duty, as a subject of England, to have given in a memorial to a secretary of state at my first coming over; because, whatever lands are discovered by a subject belong to the crown. But I doubt whether our conquests in the countries I treat of would be as easy as those of Ferdinando Cortez over the naked Americans. The Lilliputians, I think, are hardly worth the charge of a fleet and army to reduce them; and I question whether it might be prudent or safe to attempt the Brobdingnagians; or whether an English army would be much at their ease with the Flying Island over their heads.

The Houyhnhnms indeed appear not to be so well prepared for war, a science to which they are perfect strangers, and especially against missive weapons. However, supposing myself to be a minister of state, I could never give my advice for invading them. Their prudence, unanimity, unacquaintedness with fear, and their love of their country, would amply supply all defects in the military art. Imagine twenty thousand of them breaking into the midst of an European army, confounding the ranks, overturning the carriages, battering the warriors' faces into mummy by terrible yerks from their hinder hoofs; for they would well deserve the character given to Augustus: *Recalcitrat undique tutus.*

But, instead of proposals for conquering that magnanimous nation, I rather wish they were in a capacity, or disposition, to send a sufficient number of their inhabitants for civilizing Europe, by teaching us the first principles of honour, justice, truth, temperance, public spirit, fortitude, chastity, friendship, benevolence, and fidelity. The names of all which virtues are still retained among us in most languages, and are to be met with in modern, as well as ancient authors; which I am able to assert from my own small reading.

But I had another reason, which made me less forward to enlarge his Majesty's dominions by my discoveries. To say the truth, I had conceived a few scruples with relation to the distributive justice of princes upon those occasions. For instance, a crew of pirates are driven by a storm they know not whither; at length a boy discovers land from the topmast; they go on shore to rob and plunder, they see a harmless people, are entertained with kindness; they give the country a new name; they take formal possession of it for their king; they set up a rotten plank, or a stone, for a memorial; they murder two or three dozen of the natives, bring away a couple more, by force, for a sample; return home, and get their pardon.

Here commences a new dominion acquired with a title by divine right. Ships are sent with the first opportunity; the natives driven out or destroyed; their princes tortured to discover their gold; a free license given to all acts of inhumanity and lust, the earth reeking with the blood of its inhabitants: and this execrable crew of butchers, employed in so pious an expedition, is a modern colony, sent to convert and civilize an idolatrous and barbarous people.

But this description, I confess, does by no means affect the British nation, who may be an example to the whole world for their wisdom, care, and justice in planting colonies; their liberal endowments for the advancement of religion and learning; their choice of devout and able pastors to propagate Christianity; their caution in stocking their provinces with people of sober lives and conversations from this the mother kingdom; their strict regard to the distribution of justice, in supplying the civil administration through all their colonies with officers of the greatest abilities, utter strangers to corruption; and, to crown all, by sending the most vigilant and virtuous governors, who have no other views than the happiness of the people over whom they preside, and the honour of the king their master.

But as those countries which I have described do not appear to have any desire of being conquered and enslaved, murdered or driven out by colonies, nor abound either in gold, silver, sugar, or tobacco, I did humbly conceive, they were by no means proper objects of our zeal, our valour, or our interest.

However, if those whom it more concerns think fit to be of another opinion, I am ready to depose, when I shall be lawfully called, that no European did ever visit those countries before me. I mean, if the inhabitants ought to be believed, unless a dispute may arise concerning the two Yahoos, said to have been seen many years ago upon a mountain in Houyhnhnmland.

But, as to the formality of taking possession in my sovereign's name, it never came once into my thoughts; and if it had, yet, as my affairs then stood, I should perhaps, in point of prudence and self-preservation, have put it off to a better opportunity.

Having thus answered the only objection that can ever be raised against me as a traveller, I here take a final leave of all my courteous readers, and return to enjoy my own speculations in my little garden at Redriff; to apply those excellent lessons of virtue which I learned among the Houyhnhnm*s*; to instruct the Yahoos of my own family, is far as I shall find them docible animals; to behold my figure often in a glass, and thus, if possible, habituate myself by time to tolerate the sight of a human creature; to lament the brutality to Houyhnhnm*s* in my own country, but always treat their persons with respect, for the sake of my noble master, his family, his friends, and the whole Houyhnhnm race, whom these of ours have the honour to resemble in all their lineaments, however their intellectuals came to degenerate.

I began last week to permit my wife to sit at dinner with me, at the farthest end of a long table; and to answer (but with the utmost brevity) the few questions I asked her. Yet, the smell of a Yahoo continuing very offensive, I always keep my nose well stopped with rue, lavender, or tobacco leaves. And, although it be hard for a man late in life to remove old habits, I am not altogether out of hopes, in some time, to suffer a neighbour Yahoo in my company, without the apprehensions I am yet under of his teeth or his claws.

My reconcilement to the Yahoo kind in general might not be so difficult, if they would be content with those vices and follies only which nature has entitled them to. I am not in the least provoked at the sight of a lawyer, a pickpocket, a colonel, a fool, a lord, a gamester, a politician, a whoremonger, a physician, an evidence, a suborner, an attorney, a traitor, or the like; this is all according to the due course of things: but when I behold a lump of deformity and diseases, both in body and mind, smitten with pride, it immediately breaks all the measures of my patience; neither shall I be ever able to comprehend how such an animal, and such a vice, could tally together.

The wise and virtuous Houyhnhnms, who abound in all excellences that can adorn a rational creature, have no name for this vice in their language, which has no terms to express any thing that is evil, except those whereby they describe the detestable qualities of their Yahoos, among which they were not able to distinguish this of pride, for want of thoroughly understanding human nature, as it shows itself in other countries where that animal presides. But I, who had more experience, could plainly observe some rudiments of it among the wild Yahoos.

But the Houyhnhnms, who live under the government of reason, are no more proud of the good qualities they possess, than I should be for not wanting a leg or an arm; which no man in his wits would boast of, although he must be miserable without them. I dwell the longer upon this subject from the desire I have to make the society of an English Yahoo by any means not insupportable; and therefore I here entreat those who have any tincture of this absurd vice, that they will not presume to come in my sight.